MASSACHUSETTS
AND THE
CIVIL WAR

MASSACHUSETTS AND THE CIVIL WAR

The Commonwealth and National Disunion

EDITED BY

Matthew Mason, Katheryn P. Viens,
and Conrad Edick Wright

University of Massachusetts Press
Amherst and Boston

IN ASSOCIATION WITH
Massachusetts Historical Society
Boston

Copyright © 2015 by University of Massachusetts Press
All rights reserved
Printed in the United States of America

ISBN 978-1-62534-150-1 (paperback); 149-5 (hardcover)

Designed by Sally Nichols
Set in Adobe Minion Pro
Printed and bound by Sheridan Books, Inc.

Library of Congress Cataloging-in-Publication Data

Massachusetts and the Civil War : the commonwealth and national disunion / edited by Matthew Mason, Conrad Edick Wright, and Katheryn P. Viens.
   pages cm
Includes bibliographical references and index.
ISBN 978-1-62534-150-1 (pbk. : alk. paper) — ISBN 978-1-62534-149-5 (hardcover : alk. paper) 1. Massachusetts—History—Civil War, 1861–1865. I. Mason, Matthew, 1968– II. Wright, Conrad Edick. III. Viens, Katheryn P., 1962–
E513.M53 2015
974.4′0—dc23
2015009308

British Library Cataloguing-in-Publication Data
A catalogue record for this book is available from the British Library.

CONTENTS

ACKNOWLEDGMENTS vii

INTRODUCTION
Unification and (Re-)Division
The Significance of Massachusetts in the Civil War Era
1

Part I
THE OPPOSITION TO SLAVERY

The Union of Abolitionists and Emancipationists
in Civil War–Era Massachusetts
JOHN STAUFFER
9

"Constitution or No Constitution, Law or No Law"
The Boston Vigilance Committees, 1841–1861
DEAN GRODZINS
47

"Today Abolitionist Is Merged in Citizen"
Radical Abolitionists and the Union War
PETER WIRZBICKI
74

The Rise and Fall of the Abolitionist Republic
RICHARD S. NEWMAN
103

Part II
THE WAR YEARS

The Politics of Unionism
Edward Everett, the Constitutional Union Party, and the Election of 1860
MATTHEW MASON
139

McClellan in the Hub
Boston's Financiers and the War for Emancipation
CAROL BUNDY
163

The Bonds of Print
Reading on Home Front and Battlefield
RONALD J. ZBORAY AND MARY SARACINO ZBORAY
195

Part III
RECONCILIATION

Mourning Charles Sumner
The Flag Resolution and the Complications of Civil War Memory
SARAH PURCELL
227

Reporting from the South
Massachusetts Teachers and Freedmen's Education
AMY F. MORSMAN
249

The Union of Gentlemen Restored
College-Educated Northern Veterans, Reconciliation, and Northern Honor
KANISORN WONGSRICHANALAI
275

ABOUT THE CONTRIBUTORS 299
INDEX 301

Acknowledgments

The sesquicentennial of the Civil War has afforded modern-day Americans an opportunity to revisit the most heart-wrenching and bloody of our nation's internal conflicts. In the early twenty-first century, when it sometimes seems that the United States is a nation divided, the Civil War offers a sobering lesson of the worst consequences of an inability to reason together.

A conference at the Massachusetts Historical Society April 4–6, 2013, provided an extended opportunity to consider the commonwealth's central place in the causes, course, and consequences of the war. The papers in this collection, first presented at that program, have been carefully revised for publication. We are grateful to everyone who played a role in that event. In addition to the scholars whose work appears in the volume we benefited from the participation of Millington Bergeson-Lockwood, Jim Downs, Crystal Feimster, Barbara Gannon, Martha Hodes, Drew R. McCoy, Kathryn Shively Meier, Margot Minardi, Megan Kate Nelson, Nina Silber, Manisha Sinha, Kathryn Tomasek, Conevery Bolton Valencius, Jordan Watkins, and Donald Yacovone. At the Massachusetts Historical Society, we also benefited from the full support of its president, Dennis A. Fiori, and from the efforts of many of the members of its staff, including William Beck, Christopher Coveney, Peter Drummey, Tammy Hamond, James P. Harrison III, Peter Hood, Carol Knauff, Nicole Leonard, Jennifer Smith, Daniel Sweeney, and Audrey Wolfe. We are also grateful for financial support from the Loring Family, the Lowell Institute, and an anonymous donor, which made possible the conference, and through it this collection of essays. At University of Massachusetts Press, our thanks go to its retired director, Bruce Wilcox, as well as to Clark Dougan, Carol Betsch, and Mary Bellino, and to two outside readers who commented profitably on the manuscript, Matthew Gallman and an anonymous referee.

MASSACHUSETTS
AND THE
CIVIL WAR

INTRODUCTION

Unification and (Re-)Division

*The Significance of Massachusetts
in the Civil War Era*

In February 1851, Senator William Archer of Virginia wrote to William Graham of North Carolina stressing the importance of some northern states' respective reactions to the Fugitive Slave Act. The only way to save the Union and the political fortunes of southern moderates was "to have strict enforcement of the Fugitive Bill, and especially in the State of Massachusetts," he argued, noting that "no Body cares for Vermont," but "not so New York and especially Massachusetts," where proceedings for and against enforcement of this law were what made national headlines and shaped national politics.[1] Archer's observation accords with one key premise of the present volume: that all states are not created equal, not at least when it comes to their influence on American history. The central themes around which these essays coalesce are the national significance of Massachusetts across the entire Civil War era, the ways in which the commonwealth reflected and even modeled the Union's precarious but real wartime unification, and the Bay State's postwar return to the schisms that had dominated before the war. Of all the northern states, only New York and, perhaps, Pennsylvania held comparable influence. Not an attempt to summarize the Civil War in Massachusetts or to report on every aspect of its contribution to the wartime Union (notably its military role), this collection focuses instead on what was distinctive or peculiar to the commonwealth's influence during the great crisis of national unity.

Bay Staters, the authors in this volume contend, wielded an influence over the fate of the nation in the Civil War era out of all proportion to the commonwealth's population and electoral weight in the Union. John Stauffer and Dean Grodzins posit that antislavery activists made Massachusetts as close to the headquarters of abolitionism as any one place could be said to be in this far-flung, fractious movement.[2] Essays by Matthew Mason and Carol Bundy remind us, however, both that Massachusetts was not synonymous with abolitionism and that Bay Staters figured unusually prominently in the Unionist and conservative circles of the North. The disproportionate impact of Massachusetts citizens becomes, perhaps, even clearer in the chapters treating the postwar years. Richard Newman's abolitionists, Carol Bundy's big-time investors, Amy Morsman's schoolteachers, and Kanisorn Wongsrichanalai's gentlemen of honor all contributed unusually influential voices to the national debate over the postwar southern social order and the reconstruction of the Union. The strength of their evidence makes it hard to dismiss this argument as merely special pleading from Massachusetts-centric historians, editors, and publishers. Taken together, the essays in this volume make a compelling case for the significance of the full range of players from Massachusetts—women and men, black and white, of all social classes—in the lead-up to the war and the development of the postwar order.

Ultimately, this collection as a whole argues that Massachusetts embodied and significantly helped broker the Union's wartime unity and postwar refragmentation. Attending to antebellum patterns of factionalism helps us to appreciate the work necessary to unite the North during the Civil War. The abolitionists' legendary internal discord is on full display in Grodzins's and Newman's essays. And an even fuller picture of the spectrum of northern opinion emerges when contrasting abolitionist positions on vital questions, such as the value of the Union and the nature of law and order, with those of the Unionist conservatives Mason and Bundy examine. Intersectional conflict still dominates the historiography of the Civil War era, but these essays challenge us to contemplate the extent to which the antebellum North was itself a house divided.[3]

The bulk of the essays describe how and on what grounds Massachusetts citizens modeled national consensus behind the war effort. Stauffer's contribution speaks powerfully to this point. In his narrative, specific organizations such as the Emancipation League made the push for freeing slaves a big-tent affair in the war years. Bundy likewise credits an organization, the Union Club, as well as Massachusetts governor John A. Andrew for his role as a broker of this alliance. Grodzins and Newman illustrate how and why notoriously factious abolitionists embraced this union: they had experience with coalition building, and this particular coalition fit nicely with their larger vision of achieving an abolitionist republic. As for the more conservative emancipationists, Mason's essay shows that politicians such as Abraham Lincoln had already honed their ability to appeal to more than hard-core supporters in pursuit of a larger league of similarly minded people. Taken together, these chapters help us understand how Bay Staters who had cheered on John Brown in late 1859 and those who had attended the Union meetings to protest Brown's actions could find common ground between 1861 and 1865.

Peter Wirzbicki's essay serves as a fulcrum for the big arguments unifying this collection. He provides a cogent analysis of the radical abolitionists' reasons for seeking union with Unionists. Such was their desire for harmony, he shows, that even the uncompromising Wendell Phillips was willing to admit that he had caricatured Unionists' motives as being "wholly choked with cotton-dust and cankered with gold." After the firing on Fort Sumter, the Unionist Everett likewise offered startling admissions of having been wrong. None were quite so direct or so public as during his landmark speech at the dedication of the national cemetery at Gettysburg, when he reflected that his fears of civil war "led me, perhaps too long, to tread in the path of hopeless compromise, in the fond endeavor to conciliate those who were predetermined not to be conciliated."[4] Furthermore, Wirzbicki's chapter adds emphasis to the importance of Massachusetts in this story by showing that ideas of New England generally, and the Bay State specifically, themselves provided key common ground between the likes of Phillips and Everett.

The authors of these essays, it should be added, provide an interpretation of Union unity that is nevertheless compatible with the considerable evidence of dissent in the North during the war. Governor Andrew's facilitation of unity, for instance, had real limits. In early 1861, when Caleb Cushing—who had aligned with Southern Rights Democrats and thus supported the Breckinridge ticket in 1860—wrote him seeking a position in either government or the army, the governor coolly rebuffed him. "Your frequently avowed opinions touching the ideas and sentiments of Massachusetts," Andrew wrote, as well as Cushing's coziness "with the leading secessionists of the Rebel States," prevented the governor from "finding you any place in the Council or the Camp. I am compelled sadly to declare that were I to accept your offer I should dishearten numerous good and loyal men, and tend to demoralize our military service."[5] This exchange foreshadowed how those hardcore dissenters who came to be called Copperheads would find no shelter under the big wartime tent, even when they sought it. The Copperheads may have been more easily marginalized in Massachusetts than in other northern states, but this was a difference in degree rather than kind.

Ronald and Mary Zboray's essay similarly emphasizes unity but should not be read as claiming unanimity for Massachusetts, let alone the North. They provide powerful evidence for the impact of the bonds of correspondence between soldiers and the home front. But correspondence did not necessarily, of course, facilitate harmonious exchanges of ideas. More specifically, Americans had known since at least the 1830s that the revolutionary developments in communication in the antebellum decades had not increased intersectional harmony.[6] That would also be the case during the war, given the sometimes severe political storms brewing around the Copperheads and other dissenters both on the home front and between the home front and soldiers. As the historian Steven Ramold has shown, frequent correspondence with civilians more often exacerbated than eased soldiers' exaggerated picture of the home front's failure to rally behind the cause.[7]

But as other essays in this collection demonstrate, the days of wartime consensus (fragile and limited though it was) seemed distant when that alliance once again fragmented after the war. Massachusetts women and men both represented and furthered that process, just as they had during the wartime merger. As Sarah Purcell shows in her essay, Charles Sumner certainly found out that he had overestimated postbellum northern unity when his flag resolution ran squarely into the reality of the victors' contestation of the meaning of victory. Sumner's opponents in that debate were as much in disagreement with him on that issue as were Wongsrichanalai's reconciliationist gentlemen on his civil rights activities, much as they would have supported his flag initiative. Indeed, Wongsrichanalai's careful reconstruction of his subjects' changing worldview across time highlights the degree to which postwar positions could draw not on wartime but on antebellum views. Much had changed for these gentlemen of honor with Sumter, but then again much changed with Appomattox. No wonder Morsman's schoolmarms found themselves, in her apt analogy, preaching to a much-reduced choir; the Massachusetts choir had been much bigger for all preachers during the war years. During Reconstruction, the Bay State had redivided.

NOTES

1. William S. Archer to William A. Graham, February 4, 1851, in *The Papers of William Alexander Graham,* ed. J. G. de Roulhac Hamilton and Max R. Williams, 7 vols. (Raleigh, N.C.: State Department of Archives and History, 1957–1984), 4:25.
2. Important recent works have highlighted the significance of other regions to the abolitionist movement. Stacey M. Robertson, for instance, has done this for the old Northwest with studies such as *Hearts Beating for Liberty: Women Abolitionists in the Old Northwest* (Chapel Hill: University of North Carolina Press, 2010). W. Caleb McDaniel, to take just another notable example from a voluminous literature, has illuminated the transatlantic nature of the movement in *The Problem of Democracy in the Age of Slavery: Garrisonian Abolitionists and Transatlantic Reform* (Baton Rouge: Louisiana State University Press, 2013). For a fuller exploration of this trend in the literature, see W. Caleb McDaniel, "The Bonds and Boundaries of Antislavery," *Journal of the Civil War Era* 4 (March 2014): 84–105. But the fact that Boston and Massachusetts abolitionists play a crucial role (albeit to varying degrees) in such works illustrates that it would be impossible to completely decenter Massachusetts and Boston from a position of peculiar importance to this movement.
3. Interestingly, there is a much fuller literature making the case for division within the antebellum and wartime South than for the North; see, for example, William W. Freehling, *The Road to Disunion,* vol. 1, *Secessionists at Bay, 1776–1854* (New York: Oxford University Press, 1990), and vol. 2, *Secessionists Triumphant, 1854–1861* (New York: Oxford University Press, 2007); Freehling, *The South vs. the South: How Anti-Confederate Southerners Shaped the Course of the Civil War* (New York: Oxford University Press, 2001); Lacy K. Ford, *Deliver Us from Evil: The Slavery Question in the Old South* (New York: Oxford University Press, 2009). For a preliminary exploration of the idea of a divided antebellum North, see Matthew Mason, "The Maine and Missouri Crisis: Competing Priorities and Northern Slavery Politics in the Early Republic," *Journal of the Early Republic* 33 (Winter 2013): 675–700.
4. Edward Everett, *Orations and Speeches on Various Occasions,* vol. 4 (Boston: Little, Brown, 1868), 652.
5. John A. Andrew to Caleb Cushing, April 27, 1861, Caleb Cushing Papers, Manuscript Division, Library of Congress.
6. As Richard R. John put it, controversies over abolitionist mailings in 1835 showed that "the very improvements [in communications] that had once knit the Union together would conspire to drive it apart." John, *Spreading the News: The American Postal System from Franklin to Morse* (Cambridge: Harvard University Press, 1998), 283.
7. Steven J. Ramold, *Across the Divide: Union Soldiers View the Northern Home Front* (New York: New York University Press, 2013). For one influential entry in a very large literature arguing that conflict characterized the Civil War North, see Mark E. Neely Jr., *The Union Divided: Party Conflict in the Civil War North* (Cambridge: Harvard University Press, 2002).

I

THE OPPOSITION TO SLAVERY

FIGURE 1. "'Marching On!': The Fifty-Fifth Massachusetts Colored Regiment Singing John Brown's March in the Streets of Charleston," *Harper's Weekly,* March 18, 1865.

The Union of Abolitionists and Emancipationists in Civil War–Era Massachusetts

JOHN STAUFFER

On April 14, 1865, William Lloyd Garrison, Massachusetts senator Henry Wilson, and other abolitionist leaders visited Charleston, South Carolina, to commemorate the end of the Civil War and of slavery.[1] Richmond had fallen and Robert E. Lee had surrendered at Appomattox. But for most Northerners, the symbolic end of the war had occurred in February, when the Massachusetts 55th Colored Regiment marched triumphantly into Charleston, the hotbed of secession, singing "John Brown's Body" as thousands of freedmen and women cheered them on (fig. 1). Garrison's son George was a lieutenant in the 55th, and the two reunited in Charleston.[2]

The highlight of the commemoration was a ceremony at Fort Sumter, in Charleston Harbor. Major General Robert Anderson presided. Exactly four years earlier, on April 14, 1861, he had lowered the American flag after surrendering the fort to Confederates. Now he raised the very same flag, which had been kept in a bank vault during the war, as a crowd of three thousand stood at attention.[3]

Attending the flag-raising with Garrison were hundreds of black soldiers, sailors, and liberated slaves from South Carolina. The most notable freedman present was navy captain Robert Smalls, who had made front-page news in 1862 while still a slave. After stowing his family and a dozen other slaves on the *Planter,* a Confederate gunboat, he had piloted it out of Charleston Harbor to a U.S. Navy fleet (fig. 2).[4] For countless Northerners, his daring feat highlighted the unbreakable link between striking out for freedom and supporting the war.

FIGURE 2. "The Steamer 'Planter' and Her Captor," *Harper's Weekly*, June 14, 1862.

Following the ceremony, Garrison gave a brief speech at the Charleston Hotel. He noted with irony that thirty years earlier he had been dragged through the streets of Boston and almost lynched by a Democratic mob for declaring himself an abolitionist, whereas now, in the marrow of the South, he was being treated as a hero and prophet. He then referred to his recent meeting with President Lincoln and said, "Of one thing I feel sure, either [Lincoln] has become a Garrisonian Abolitionist or I have become a Lincoln Emancipationist, for I know that we blend together, like kindred drops, into one."[5]

Garrison's statement wonderfully encapsulates the social revolution that accompanied the war and the role that abolitionists—especially those from Boston—played in it. Everyone understood Garrison's terms: "abolitionists" were black and white radicals who sought an immediate end to slavery *and* advocated racial equality, at least in theory. "Emancipationists," or "antislavery advocates," were liberals who sought to preserve the Union. Constituting the rank and file of the Republican Party, they too defined slavery as evil. But for emancipationists the evil inhered less in what the institution did to *slaves* than in what it did to the *Union*. They advocated practical, legal, and, preferably, gradual solutions to slavery. And, unlike the abolitionists, they opposed racial equality and were captivated by the idea of blacks' colonizing another country.[6]

But the exigencies of war had transformed Lincoln and other emancipationists into abolitionists, while Garrison and other abolitionists had become emancipationists. Preserving the Union *required* abolishing slavery, and vice versa. The categories of radical versus liberal, immediatist versus gradualist, idealist versus realist, had broken down.[7]

With the war, black and white abolitionists were transformed from a tiny group of despised fanatics into respected prophets. They were considered indispensable to the war effort and the successes of Reconstruction, notably the constitutional amendments that ended chattel slavery and guaranteed citizenship, equal protection under the law, and unrestricted male suffrage to blacks; the desegregation of federal post offices, courts, public transportation, and visitors' galleries in Congress; and the extraordinary rise of black literacy and black office holders at local, state, and national levels.[8]

Even Lincoln, who had resisted emancipation and championed colonization early in the war, recognized the importance of abolitionists. More than once, he credited the Massachusetts contingent for their crucial role in ending slavery and winning the war. At the White House reception following his Second Inaugural, he publicly greeted Frederick Douglass, who had lived in the commonwealth for nine years, by saying, "There is no man in these United States whose opinion I value more than yours." A month later, he told Massachusetts lieutenant Daniel H. Chamberlain, "I have been only an instrument. The logic and moral power of Garrison, and the anti-slavery people of the country, and the army, have done all."[9]

Lincoln also acknowledged the crucial role that black soldiers played in winning the war and ending slavery: "We can not spare the hundred and forty or fifty thousand [blacks] *now* serving us as soldiers, seamen, and laborers. This is not a question of sentiment or taste, but one of physical force," he said in September 1864. "Keep it and you can save the Union. Throw it away, and the Union goes with it."[10]

As a conservative-to-moderate Republican, Lincoln was representative of other emancipationists. He not only joined the ranks of the abolitionists in his outlook; he worked with them to end slavery and champion some form of legal equality. Shortly before he died, he endorsed limited black suffrage and began to envision racial equality. In his April 11, 1865, address from a White House window, he noted, "It is . . . unsatisfactory to some that the elective franchise is not given to the colored man. I would myself prefer that it were *now* conferred on the very intelligent, and on those who serve our cause as soldiers." John Wilkes Booth was in the crowd, listening. "That is the last speech he will ever make," he told a fellow conspirator. It was this address that convinced Booth to assassinate Lincoln, thus abandoning his plan, which the Confederacy supported, to kidnap the president in order to negotiate favorable terms for peace. A few hours after Garrison had made his speech at the Charleston Hotel, Booth put a bullet through Lincoln's head for the same reason that Garrison lauded him: because Lincoln had become an abolitionist.[11]

Garrison was right: the emancipationist *had* become the abolitionist, and vice versa. Indeed, from the 1840s through Reconstruction, abolitionists—in Massachusetts and in fact throughout the North—collaborated closely with conservative to liberal opponents of slavery. In the process they blurred the binaries of idealism versus realism, immediatism versus gradualism, pacifism versus militancy, politics versus nonresistance. They inaugurated a social revolution, which southern counterrevolutionaries soon destroyed. The Reconstruction amendments that created legal and, in some areas, social equality for blacks would not have been possible without collaboration between abolitionists and emancipationists and the breakdown of these binaries.[12]

From the end of Reconstruction to the close of the nineteenth century, Northerners recognized abolitionists' rich cooperation with more conservative antislavery advocates. They treated abolitionists as heroes who had played crucial roles in ending slavery, winning the war, and amending the Constitution to guarantee equality before the law for blacks and whites. Magisterial, multivolume histories by Massachusetts senator Henry Wilson and Hermann von Holst, the first chair of the history department at the University of Chicago and a founder of the profession, emphasized the collaborations between abolitionists and emancipationists and were highly respected.[13]

The first four volumes of James Ford Rhodes's popular *History of the United States from the Compromise of 1850* (1892–1899) also stressed these ties. In his portrayals of slavery, the Confederacy, and Reconstruction, Rhodes contributed to national reconciliation between the North and South, but at the same time he acknowledged the abolitionists' impact "in rousing the Northern conscience and laying the foundations of a triumphant Republican Party."[14] Charles Sumner, the abolitionist senator from Massachusetts, was so revered in the North that his fellow congressmen passed a diluted version of his civil rights bill in 1875, a year after he died, "mainly as a gesture to his departed spirit." *Harper's Weekly*, perhaps the most popular northern newspaper, devoted two full issues to Sumner's death and funeral and declared that his passing "more deeply touched the heart of the American people" than any other event since Lincoln's assassination. Biographers and literary men also wrote effusively about the abolitionists. In 1903 Henry James portrayed Sumner as an exemplary "statesman" and "patriot" and called his epistles "irresistible."[15]

The twentieth century, however, was not kind to the abolitionists.[16] As Peter Novick has summarized, the opening years coincided with "the racist downgrading of the Negro" by professional historians, coupled with their "need for reconciliation of the sections, and the desire to strike a posture of impartiality, fairness, detachment, and objectivity." As a result, white historians became "harshly critical of the abolitionists" and called them "irresponsible agitators." More generally, white writers and filmmakers went to great lengths to *uncouple* the links between abolitionists and emancipationists. Abolitionists were religious zealots, dangerous and often insane extremists who had helped cause an apocalyptic war, or they were pathetic figures because war had been inevitable. Emancipationists, on the other hand, were shrewd, balanced, practical statesmen, always framing their hatred of slavery in larger social and political contexts.[17]

In stark contrast to the radical reconstruction of abolitionists by white writers, *black* writers from George Washington Williams and W. E. B. Du Bois to John Hope Franklin, Benjamin Quarles, Nathan Huggins, Waldo Martin, and James Horton have been consistently charitable toward the abolitionists. They recognized that the convergence of abolitionists and emancipationists reflected a social revolution. These black writers resemble their British, French, and Brazilian counterparts, who have long remembered *their* abolitionists as heroes, working closely with political leaders to end slavery.[18]

By the middle decades of the twentieth century, a "potent, pro-Southern bias" dominated American history and literature scholarship, according to Hugh Tulloch. Indeed, white writers characterized abolitionists as communist or Nazi totalitarians. C. Vann Woodward referred to John Brown and his supporters as "fellow travelers." Robert Penn Warren argued that the abolitionists longed "for the 'total solution,' to purge in violence" existing social tensions. "Their love of *man* meant the hatred of *men*." And Frank Owsley, in his presidential address before the Southern Historical Association, singled out Massachusetts abolitionists when he said, "As far as I have been able to ascertain, neither Dr. Goebbels nor Stalin's propaganda agents have as yet been able to plumb the depths of vulgarity and obscenity reached and maintained by Wendell Phillips, Charles Sumner, Stephen Foster, and other abolitionists of note." These were among the most influential scholars of American history and literature in the twentieth century. Their perspective was clear: respectable politicians and antislavery advocates kept their distance from vulgar abolitionists. Never did the twain meet.[19]

By the end of the 1960s, owing to the successes of the civil rights movement, many historians began treating the abolitionists with sympathy, but they still referred to them as uncompromising zealots who stood totally apart from emancipationists. As Tulloch noted, New Left historians characterized *society* as mad, and abolitionists as sane in their "dedicated opposition" to it. But despite this rehabilitation, abolitionists remained uncoupled from emancipationists.[20] One sees this especially in textbooks, which began to dominate survey courses in the humanities in the 1970s. In their highly acclaimed 1973 primary source reader, the Yale team of Robert Penn Warren, Cleanth Brooks, and R. W. B. Lewis emphasized that "abolitionism was *not* the same thing as emancipationism. Jefferson, Melville, Lincoln, and Robert E. Lee were emancipationists, but they were *not* abolitionists. For an emancipationist, the problem of slavery, no matter how important, was to be treated in a general context.... But for an abolitionist the problem of slavery was paramount, central, burning, and immediate. The context did not matter." In most U.S. history textbooks, abolitionists are *still* described as "uncompromising," unwilling to collaborate with moderates and conservatives, while emancipationists are cast as balanced, practical, and heroic.[21]

Hollywood has widely disseminated the portrait of abolitionists as villains acting independently of the "good" emancipationists. This filmic uncoupling is understandable, since historical films, much like historians, reflect the ideologies and worldviews of their own era. Civil War–era films often "relate to the larger realm of discourse generated by" historians, even when they dispense with facts, as Robert Rosenstone has noted. Abolitionists have rarely been portrayed in film, and when they have appeared it has often been in contrast to the goodness of Lincoln. In fact there are rich parallels between D. W. Griffith's *Birth of a Nation* (1915) and Steven Spielberg's recent *Lincoln* (2012). In both films abolitionists are the villains, while Lincoln is the brilliant pragmatist. In *Birth of a Nation*, Lincoln is the South's "best friend," pardoning the South Carolina rebel Ben Cameron and enabling him to found the Ku Klux Klan, which redeems the nation. In contrast, Austin Stoneman (a stand-in for the abolitionist Thaddeus

Stevens), his black comrade, Silas Lynch, and his mulatto mistress, Lydia, are all demonic.[22]

Spielberg's film is much more subtle. Thaddeus Stevens champions racial equality out of self-interest: his love for his black housekeeper, Lydia, captured in a scene with them in bed together. Stevens becomes heroic only after *refusing* to acknowledge racial equality during the congressional debate over the Thirteenth Amendment. Charles Sumner reprimands Stevens for his backsliding and thus becomes a despicable idealist.[23]

In the past twenty years, some progressive writers, while lauding black militancy, cast white abolitionists as incurably racist, devoted to freedom but not equality. They thus downplay or ignore the integrated communities and the foundations of civil rights that the abolitionists established. Most recently Stephen Kantrowitz, in his superb book on Boston abolitionists, refuses to apply the label to blacks. Why? Because he says the term "abolitionist" implies a desire only for freedom and does not encompass blacks' larger vision of equality and citizenship. But virtually every one of his black characters defined *themselves* as abolitionists. To cite just one example, Frederick Douglass invoked an "abolition war" and "abolition peace" as ethical imperatives. For him and other blacks, abolitionism was a revolutionary vision of racial equality.[24]

By downplaying or ignoring interracial collaborations and friendships, progressive scholars cast whites as emancipationists who sought only freedom, not equality. In other words, they continued to *uncouple* abolitionists from emancipationists. The failure to acknowledge this collaboration highlights the degree to which white Americans, for more than one hundred years, have been either horrified by, or despairing of, a social revolution that upends segregation.

To be sure, since around 2000 there has been a dramatic change in the scholarship on the abolitionists. For the first time since Reconstruction many white Americans, especially in the Northeast, now regard the abolitionists as heroic figures who collaborated with emancipationists and helped end slavery, championed racial equality, and created the first civil rights movement. This shift is reflected in the 2013 PBS documentary *The Abolitionists*. The work of several other authors in this volume—Richard Newman, Matthew Mason, Dean Grodzins, Carol Bundy, Amy Morsman, and Peter Wirzbicki—as well as Manisha Sinha, Barbara Gannon, and Millington Bergeson-Lockwood, has contributed greatly to this transformation.

But just when abolitionists are finally beginning to receive their due, a neo-revisionist movement has emerged that is deeply critical of the "triumphalist" narrative of the Civil War, which emphasizes emancipation while downplaying the costs of the war. Several prominent scholars—Andrew Delbanco, Harry Stout, David Goldfield, and Christopher Benfey—have begun to reassess the abolitionists in light of this triumphalism. They recover themes from the prominent white scholars of the mid-twentieth century: Abolitionists were extremists who helped usher in one of the bloodiest wars in world history. They stood totally apart from pragmatic emancipationists, who respected the messiness of democratic politics and sought legal and legislative means to end slavery. Like their predecessors, these neo-revisionists downplay the institutional power of slaveholders, the violence at the heart of slavery, and the South's suppression of civil liberties.[25]

In the wake of this century-long, uncharitable assessment, I want to draw attention to the role Massachusetts abolitionists—black and white—played in secession, emancipation, and Reconstruction, emphasizing throughout their collaboration and convergence with emancipationists.

Almost every student of the Civil War era acknowledges that Massachusetts, especially Boston, was a hotbed of abolitionism and the most egalitarian state in the nation. It was one of the first states to abolish slavery, in 1783. It was one of only five states that granted unrestricted black male suffrage from 1830 through the Civil War. It was the first state to overturn a ban on interracial marriage (in 1843), the first to desegregate its public schools (in 1855), the first to admit black jurors (in 1860), and the first northern state to raise a black regiment. These "firsts" all stemmed from black and white abolitionists' working closely with antislavery allies and lawyers.[26]

Why was Massachusetts so progressive? For one thing, blacks never amounted to more than 2 percent of Boston's or the state's population, and their low numbers made them comparatively nonthreatening to whites. There was probably more prejudice against the Irish, who began flooding the state in the 1840s and comprised about 20 percent of the population by 1860. In 1856 the nativist Know-Nothing Party swept the state, and in the following year Massachusetts inaugurated a literacy test as a precondition for voting, "on the assumption that it would affect the Irish negatively." Two years later, in 1859, it imposed a two-year waiting period before new immigrants could vote.[27]

Another reason for the commonwealth's antislavery progressivism stemmed from its Puritan roots, which emphasized a sacred community devoted to social reform. This tradition persisted into the antebellum era, with the rise of religious perfectionism during the Second Great Awakening. Unitarians replaced Puritans as the spiritual and ideological drivers of the state. They sought a sacred "emotional community" through a "religion of the heart" that stressed devotional piety rather than intellectual and ritualist aspects of faith. By 1854, one Boston paper described Unitarians as "advancing towards a pure, evangelical faith" characterized by "personal communion with God through prayer."[28]

But perhaps the most important factor contributing to the state's abolitionist fervor was its constitution, which was more explicit than the Declaration of Independence in asserting the nation's revolutionary ideals. The Bill of Rights of the state's constitution, which John Adams wrote and which was passed in 1780, declared that "all men are born free and equal, and have certain natural, essential, and unalienable rights; among which may be reckoned the right of enjoying and defending their lives and liberties." Bay Staters interpreted this clause as an "organic law of the Commonwealth." It was widely quoted and inspired generations of black and white reformers.[29]

The language of the law mattered greatly, as the Quok Walker case that abolished slavery demonstrated. In a series of three trials beginning in 1781, a year after the constitution was ratified, and culminating in 1783, Quok, a twenty-seven-year-old slave, sued his master, claiming that his two former owners had promised him freedom when he turned twenty-one. Quok's lawyer, the young Levi Lincoln Sr., was one of the nation's foremost legal minds. Lincoln later became a U.S. congressman, attorney general under Jefferson, and governor of Massachusetts. In the first case he argued "on pure facts" and lost. He appealed, and in the second case he changed tactics by focusing on the morality of slavery. He cited the Massachusetts constitution and the Somerset decision that effectively abolished slavery in England in 1772. And he appealed to higher law:

> "Is it not a law of nature that all men are equal and free?" Lincoln asked the jury.
> "Is not the law of nature the law of God?"
> "Is not the law of God, then, against slavery?"[30]

It is an extraordinary brief that not only resulted in Quok Walker's freedom and emancipated the remaining slaves in Massachusetts, but also circulated widely in the 1850s, inspiring countless Bay Staters, from abolitionists to conservative opponents of slavery, to act on the law of God rather than the fugitive slave law and protect runaways. In the 1780s "an appeal to 'higher law' was *not* denounced as moral or political heresy," as a conservative Republican later noted. In the 1850s, it was. This shift reflects the counterrevolution that Southerners waged in order to nationalize slavery in the antebellum era.[31]

In one sense southern belligerence backfired. The draconian Fugitive Slave Act of 1850, part of the Compromise measures designed to preserve the Union, suspended habeas corpus and required any and all citizens to hunt down suspected fugitives; Americans were subject to a stiff fine if they refused and a prison term if they aided a runaway. The law led millions of Northerners to heed a higher law over slave law. It transformed antislavery sentiment, especially in Massachusetts, convincing Northerners that slavery was *their* problem, not just the South's. And it inspired Harriet Beecher Stowe to write *Uncle Tom's Cabin* (1852), the literary phenomenon that purportedly sold more copies than any other book in the nineteenth century save the Bible. The book was so influential that when Stowe met with Lincoln in December 1862, the president allegedly greeted her with the words, "Is this the little woman who made this great war?" *Uncle Tom's Cabin* struck a powerful chord with the British as well. During the war the Confederate diplomat William Yancey said he failed to win British support for the South because "too many Britons had read *Uncle Tom's Cabin*." Throughout Europe and America, Stowe's book inspired millions to sympathize with slaves and appeal to higher law.[32]

Significantly, Stowe was a *reluctant* abolitionist, and *Uncle Tom's Cabin* combined antislavery *and* abolitionist views. It endorsed both colonization and black citizenship. But despite her conservatism, only one black leader, Martin Delany, criticized it. Most blacks recognized the important cultural work it did. William Cooper Nell asked Stowe to write the introduction to his book *Colored Patriots of the Revolution*. Harriet Jacobs called Stowe her favorite writer and said she wished she had "one spark from her storehouse of genius and talent." Frederick Douglass called *Uncle Tom's Cabin* the "*master book*" of the nineteenth century, adding, "We doubt if abler arguments have ever been presented in favor of the 'higher law' than may be found here."[33]

Bay State resistance to the fugitive slave law dominated national news, even though only 7 of the 332 cases that it prompted occurred in Massachusetts. There was a fugitive case in almost every northern state, and in each instance abolitionists collaborated with antislavery advocates in their shared quest to free the fugitive. The most visible and transformative case was that of Anthony Burns, a Virginia slave who was arrested in Boston on May 24, 1854. Two days later the Boston Vigilance Committee, a coalition of blacks and whites, went into action. Thomas Wentworth Higginson, a Harvard-educated Unitarian minister, and Lewis Hayden, a former slave, led a biracial group that stormed the Boston Court House with axes and tried to break down the door to rescue Burns. During the assault a guard, James Batchelder, was killed. Hayden later said that he saw Higginson being attacked and, fearing for his comrade's life, fired one of his two pistols. The rescue attempt failed, however, and federal troops were called in to enforce the law and keep the peace.[34]

May 1854 was one of the most revolutionary months in Massachusetts before the Civil War, uniting countless radical abolitionists with conservative antislavery advocates. Why? Because two days before Burns was arrested, Congress passed the Kansas-Nebraska Act repealing the Missouri Compromise, which since 1820 had prevented slavery from spreading above the state's southern border (latitude 36° 30'). The act opened northern territories to slavery and, together with the Anthony Burns case, radicalized Boston's conservative textile magnates known as "Cotton Whigs." In 1848 the Boston abolitionist Charles Sumner had condemned the partnership between Cotton Whigs and slave owners, declaring it an "unhallowed union between the lords of the lash and the lords of the loom." But the lords of the loom now felt sucker-punched by their southern partners, for they had considered the Missouri Compromise a sacred covenant. Then, too, the birthplace of freedom was being overtaken by federal dragoons. Amos Lawrence, a wealthy mill owner and merchant, described the Cotton Whig transformation with only modest exaggeration: "We went to bed one night, old-fashioned, conservative, compromise Union Whigs, and woke up stark mad abolitionists."[35]

The effects of this political shift reverberated throughout the city. Lawrence approached the abolitionist Richard Henry Dana and offered him "whatever it might take" to hire an eminent lawyer to free Burns. On June 2, three days after President Pierce signed the Kansas-Nebraska Act into law, two thousand federal troops marched Burns to the waterfront, where a boat was waiting to take him back to Virginia. Some thirty thousand protesters, one-quarter of the city's population, looked on, as cries of "shame, shame" echoed through the streets (fig. 3). Seven prominent Bostonians, black and

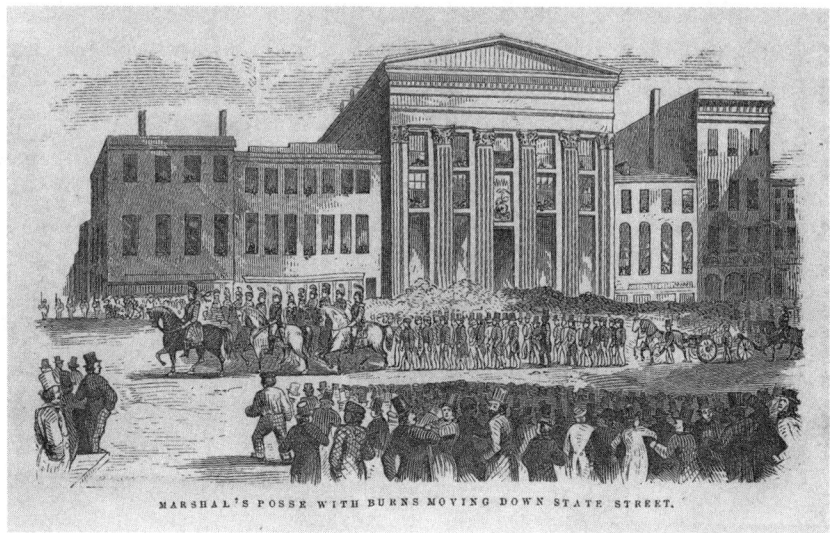

FIGURE 3. "Marshal's Posse with Burns Moving down State Street." Steel-plate engraving frontispiece to Charles Emery Stevens, *Anthony Burns: A History* (Boston: John P. Jewett and Co., 1856). Collection of Houghton Library, Harvard University.

white, were indicted for rioting, but no one was convicted. The Pierce administration spent over $40,000 to uphold the law.[36] The abolitionists won in the end, however. They quickly raised more than $1,000 to purchase Burns's freedom and paid for him to attend Oberlin College, one of the nation's few integrated schools. Burns would become an abolitionist minister.

The federal government's show of money and manpower convinced conservatives such as Lawrence that slave owners would stop at nothing to nationalize the institution. This realization further united Boston's blacks and whites, conservatives and radicals, against the Slave Power. Ulysses S. Grant was not far off when he said that the Fugitive Slave Act triggered the Civil War. It was "a degradation" that Northerners "would not permit," for "they were not willing to play the role of police for the South in the protection of this particular institution."[37]

The Kansas Territory now became the battleground. The turmoil of May 1854 prompted some of the wealthiest men in Massachusetts, who were now willing to act on higher law, to "save" Kansas from slavery. Under the leadership of Amos Lawrence, they formed the New England Emigrant Aid Society, a charitable organization that raised $200,000, sent three thousand emigrants and even more rifles to Kansas, and established

FIGURE 4. John L. Magee, *Southern Chivalry—Argument versus Club's*. Lithograph, 1856. Collection of Boston Athenaeum.

the town of Lawrence (named after Amos), which boasted a library, hotel, and newspaper. Emigrants ranged from conservative antislavery farmers and Garrisonians who abandoned their pacifism, to militants including John Brown and his sons. But Southerners sent even more men to Kansas. They controlled the territory, establishing a proslavery legislature at Lecompton, and President Pierce proclaimed their antislavery opponents "treasonous," fueling the terrorism already raging there.[38]

May 1856 was another revolutionary month. On May 21 some 750 proslavery ruffians, hoping to silence dissent and secure the admission of Kansas to the Union as a slave state, attacked the antislavery stronghold at Lawrence. Dressed in uniforms of red flannel, they burned homes, destroyed the newspaper office, and blew up the hotel. Many of them carried battle flags with the mottoes "Southern Rights," "The Supremacy of the White Race," and "Alabama for Kansas."[39]

The next day Preston Brooks, a South Carolina congressman, bludgeoned Charles Sumner almost to death on the Senate floor with a heavy cane (fig. 4). Sumner had grown up in the black neighborhood of Beacon Hill's West End, had been reading the *Liberator* since 1835, and was on close terms with William Lloyd Garrison and Wendell Phillips even though he was a political abolitionist. He knew virtually every black activist in

Boston and was friends with many of them, especially William Nell, Lewis Hayden, John Rock, Joshua Smith, and John Smith, whose barbershop he frequented almost daily when he was in town. Hayden called Sumner "the most devoted and uncompromising advocate of justice" in Congress.[40]

The provocation for the attack was Sumner's "Crime Against Kansas" speech, which accused slaveholders of raping the virgin soil of Kansas. The new Republican Party platform defined slavery and polygamy as the "twin relics of barbarism." In his speech Sumner emphasized that slavery was barbaric owing to its foundation in violence, and because it encouraged slave owners, including U.S. senators, to sleep with slave women. But Senate rules prohibited discussions of sex, so Sumner resorted to metaphor. The Kansas-Nebraska Act was "the rape of a virgin Territory," stemming from "a depraved desire, in the hope of adding to the power of slavery." He singled out Senator Andrew Butler of South Carolina, Brooks's distant cousin and an architect of the Kansas-Nebraska Act, who was rumored to have fathered slave children: "The Senator from South Carolina has read many books of chivalry, and believes himself a chivalrous knight. Of course he has chosen a mistress to whom he has made his vows and who, although ugly to others, is always lovely to him; although polluted in the sight of the world, is chaste in his sight—I mean the harlot slavery."[41]

In bludgeoning Sumner, Brooks was defending southern and family honor. He immediately became a southern hero and received thousands of commemorative canes for a deed well done. Towns and counties were named after him. His only punishment was a $300 fine. Mary Chesnut, a South Carolinian who knew Butler, was a rare Southerner who appreciated the wisdom of Sumner's speech. "Sumner said not one word of this hated institution which is not true," she wrote in her diary. "Like the patriarchs of old, our men live all in one house with their wives and their concubines, and the mulattoes one sees in every family exactly resemble the white children."[42]

Many Northerners drew a connection between the civil war raging in Kansas and in Congress, but it was Sumner's caning that sent "an unprecedented wave of indignation throughout the North." In Massachusetts people reacted physically, as though they too had been beaten. Anson Burlingame, a conservative antislavery advocate who had recently been elected to Congress on a Know-Nothing ticket, became depressed over the caning, telling his wife that he was "not very well." He overcame his despair by delivering a speech, "A Defense of Massachusetts," that responded to the assault. The Bay State was finally taking off its gloves, Burlingame declared.

He excoriated the South for its decades-long suppression of civil liberties and warned, "If we are pushed too far," he and his fellow citizens would defend their "freedom of speech on any field where we are assailed."[43]

Preston Brooks promptly challenged Burlingame to a duel. Since he considered Burlingame his social equal, the southern code of honor called for a duel, whereas Sumner, an "insulting inferior," had warranted a caning or horsewhipping. Burlingame accepted the challenge and chose the Clifton House, a hotel on the Canadian side of Niagara Falls, as the site of the confrontation. For weapons, he selected sharpshooter rifles at six paces. Raised on the Michigan frontier, he was well known as a crack shot, and he almost certainly would have killed Brooks. But the Southerner chickened out. The abortive duel launched Burlingame's national reputation as "a northern man who would fight."[44]

Lydia Maria Child also became "physically ill" when she heard the news of Sumner's caning. She, too, recovered by acknowledging that America's antagonistic elements of slavery and freedom could only be resolved through civil war. The educator Horace Mann spoke for most Bay Staters and many Northerners: "We are all not only shocked at the outrage . . . , but we are wounded in your wounds."[45] The greatest sympathy for Sumner came from African Americans. From throughout the North they sent hundreds of letters of praise and condolence. Robert Morris captured the local black sentiment: "No persons felt more keenly and sympathized with you more deeply and sincerely than your colored constituents in Boston."[46]

Sumner's caning and the sack of Lawrence, Kansas, helped whites sympathize with the plight of slaves and forced them to recognize that slavery was a state of war that must be met with force in order to preserve peace. They fractured the dichotomies of black and white, slavery and freedom, as Manisha Sinha has noted, prodding northern whites to accept biracial democracy.[47]

In the wake of these traumatic events, George Stearns, a pipe manufacturer and political abolitionist, created the Massachusetts Kansas Committee. It raised $50,000 for arms and relief in Kansas. It also served as a front for funneling money to John Brown and his biracial army, who were planning a raid on the South to free the slaves. Stearns and four other Bostonians—Samuel Gridley Howe, Theodore Parker, Thomas Wentworth Higginson, and Franklin Sanborn—along with the New Yorker Gerrit Smith, became the Secret Six, Brown's main fundraisers.[48]

Boston became Brown's adopted home in the late 1850s. He visited five times and stayed with Lewis Hayden, who supplied him with money and an additional raider, John Merriam. He twice went to Concord to raise funds. Emerson and Thoreau were quite taken with him, giving him money and opening their homes to him.[49]

His Boston friends saw in Brown a noble frontier warrior who had helped "save" Kansas from slavery. Most of them knew of his plans to invade the South, if only vaguely. But they were unaware of what he had done at Pottawatomie Creek, Kansas, since eastern papers generally had not implicated him. A few days after proslavery Kansans sacked Lawrence and murdered some abolitionists, Brown and his men retaliated by killing five unarmed settlers at Pottawatomie. Sumner had just been caned, but that news probably did not reach Kansas for another week.[50]

The assault on the senator inspired Brown in a more personal way. In 1857 he and two comrades visited Sumner, who was recuperating at his home on Hancock Street in Boston. He admired Brown and knew of his plan to invade the South. As they discussed the caning, Sumner said, "The coat I had on at the time is hanging in that closet. Its collar is stiff with blood." Brown went to the closet, took out the coat, "and looked at it as a devotee would contemplate the relic of a saint." Brown understood the power of martyrdom.[51]

Brown's Boston friends enabled him to launch his attack against slavery, which took place on October 16, 1859. With a band of five blacks and sixteen whites he captured the federal arsenal at Harpers Ferry, Virginia, about sixty miles northwest of Washington, D.C. Within two days the raiders were killed or captured, with five escaping to free soil. Brown and the others who remained in custody were tried for murder, treason, and conspiring to incite a slave insurrection and were executed, some in December 1859 and the rest in March 1860.[52]

Harpers Ferry was a crucial catalyst leading directly to secession and war. It was the South's worst nightmare realized—a slave insurrection organized by whites. The effect of the raid was profound. The eve of Harpers Ferry had been marked by comparative sectional harmony. The *Charleston Mercury,* normally zealous in its hatred of New England, had sung praises to the region in December 1858: "Give me New England's hallowed soil; / Stamped with the heraldry of toil." The vast majority of Southerners considered secession a "madman's dream," as the *Richmond Whig* put it. But John Brown's raid created a state of war, fueling the secessionist impulse. The *Richmond Enquirer* summarized the transformation in the

South: "The Harpers Ferry invasion has advanced the cause of disunion more than any other event that has happened since the formation of our government."[53]

This transformation stemmed from Brown's having been turned into a martyr. When he was hanged on December 2, 1859, church bells tolled for him throughout the North. To Southerners, "every village bell which tolled its solemn note at the execution of Brown, proclaims to the south the approbation . . . of insurrection and servile war," a South Carolina legislator declared. Southerners likened Brown to Toussaint L'Ouverture, leading slaves in an apocalyptic strike for freedom, unleashing on white men and women "a feast of blood and rapine." The murderer had become the martyr. Whatever trust had previously existed between North and South was now severed.[54]

Bay Staters were instrumental in establishing Brown's martyrdom. Initially, the response to Harpers Ferry in the North had been one of shock and condemnation. In the first week after the raid, virtually every paper in the country questioned Brown's sanity, save for the black press, whose voices remained unwavering in their support. Whites could not make sense of a white man's leading an interracial army into the South and sacrificing his life for the cause of blacks. And so they concluded that Brown must have been mad. Such was the power of racism in America.[55]

Lydia Maria Child helped initiate Brown's transformation into a martyr. After hearing of the raid and learning that he had been wounded, she wrote to Brown and to Henry Wise, the governor of Virginia, proposing to go to there to nurse the abolitionist's wounds. Though nominally a pacifist and opposed to Brown's methods, Child honored his intentions, admired his courage, and said she loved him. But neither Brown nor Governor Wise wanted her in Virginia. Brown suggested instead that she raise money for his family. As a result, Child published her correspondence with Brown, Wise, and Eliza Mason, the wife of Senator James Mason of Virginia, in newspapers throughout the country and then in a pamphlet. The letters contrasted Brown's calm eloquence with Wise and Mason's fury, and the pamphlet sold 300,000 copies in the first two months, an almost unprecedented figure. The correspondence "revolutionized public opinion."[56]

Emerson and Thoreau were also instrumental in transforming Brown into a martyr, as David Reynolds has detailed. To Thoreau, he was a man of principled action and thus exemplified the true meaning of transcendentalism. Thoreau likened Brown to Christ: "Some eighteen hundred years ago Christ was crucified; this morning Captain Brown was hung," he said in a speech that was picked up by newspapers and widely circulated. "These are the two ends of a chain which is not without its link." Emerson, one of the nation's leading public intellectuals, was even more succinct. He borrowed words from his friend Mattie Griffith, calling Brown "a new saint" who "shall make the gallows glorious like the cross." The line was picked up by the *New York Tribune* and quickly went national.[57]

Other Bay State voices now chimed in. Wendell Phillips, considered the most eloquent abolitionist orator after Frederick Douglass, said that Brown's raid had "loosened the roots of the slave system. It only breathes; it does not live hereafter." William Lloyd Garrison, while clinging to his pacifism, nevertheless called Brown a martyr and was thrilled when the church bells tolled for him: "In firing his gun, Brown has merely told us what time of day it is. It is high noon, thank God." Frederick Douglass was outraged that anyone could call John Brown insane. After all, he was only imitating "the heroes of Lexington, Concord, and Bunker Hill." To call Brown insane was to declare the Declaration insane.[58]

Just as influential, perhaps more so, was the sympathy accorded Brown by John Andrew, an attorney and rising Massachusetts Republican. Andrew knew Brown and had given him money in the late 1850s. Now he raised money for Brown's legal defense, zealously supported Brown's family, and spoke boldly in defense of Brown's actions: Whether the attempt itself was "wise or foolish, I only know that John Brown himself is right. I sympathize with the man. I sympathize with the idea because I sympathize with and believe in the eternal right."[59]

Andrew's defense of Brown catapulted him to the forefront of Massachusetts politics, as James Brewer Stewart has noted. He chaired the state delegation to the Republican National Convention, gave essential support to Lincoln, and was elected governor by a large majority, an event that further outraged Southerners. As a close friend of Jefferson Davis put it, Southerners "see the great and powerful state of Massachusetts electing by [a] 35,000 majority a man who justified the armed invasion of Virginia; and they believe that the people of Massachusetts are acting deliberately."[60]

When the Democratic National Convention met in Charleston, South Carolina, in April 1860, John Brown and his Bay State supporters remained front-page news. A Senate investigation of the raid was still under way, and *Harper's Weekly* featured an illustration of the conspirator Franklin Sanborn resisting arrest in Concord: his fellow townsmen came to his res-

FIGURE 5. "Arrest and Rescue of Frank B. Sanborn, Esq., at Concord, Massachusetts, on the Night of April 3, 1860," *Harper's Weekly,* April 14, 1860, 235.

cue as he kicked a U.S. marshal (fig. 5). These circumstances galvanized secessionists. Prior to Harpers Ferry, Stephen Douglas had been the clear front-runner for the 1860 presidency. One of the preeminent politicians in the country, he had almost won the Democratic nomination in 1856. His chief political aim was to preserve sectional harmony.[61] But in the wake of Harpers Ferry, secessionists set out to defeat Douglas and split the Democratic Party. Allan Nevins's analysis remains compelling: "Southern hysteria after John Brown was directed against the Douglas Democrats." Secessionists accused Douglas of treating slavery as evil, even though he refused to take a moral position on it. And they demanded a "slave code" to protect slavery in every territory, which undermined Douglas's doctrine of popular sovereignty.[62]

The turning point of the convention came on April 28 in a speech by William Yancey of Alabama, another leading secessionist and one of the South's best orators. Yancey invoked the specter of John Brown, in effect saying that a vote for Stephen Douglas was a vote for allowing more radicals to invade the South. Douglas delegates refused to abandon their doctrine of popular sovereignty, and Southerners walked out. Although they reconvened in Baltimore in June, almost everyone recognized that the national party had been destroyed. The split in the Democratic Party resulted in a four-way race for the presidency, virtually ensuring the election of a Republican president, as Republicans themselves acknowledged. John Brown's raid, and the blacks, whites, conservatives, and radicals in Massachusetts who championed him as a martyr, paved the way to secession and war.[63]

In August 1861 Robert Winthrop, a conservative merchant who would soon become a Copperhead Peace Democrat, bemoaned the prominent role that Massachusetts was playing in the war: "Sumner at the head of Foreign Affairs, [Henry] Wilson at the head of Military Affairs, [Benjamin] Butler commanding one wing [of the army], [Nathaniel] Banks commanding another wing, [Charles] Adams Minister to London, Burlingame to Pekin [China], Motley to Vienna, Regiment after Regiment of Mass volunteers hurrying to the conflict—all this tends to keep up the idea that this is a Mass. war and provokes increased hostility and exasperation at the South."[64]

Winthrop was right. Indeed, he might also have noted that General Butler, formerly an antiabolitionist Democrat, had recently joined the growing list of Bay Staters who refused to return fugitives. In May 1861 he had famously declared them "contraband of war," which meant that slaves were practically, though not legally, free. "Contraband" became a keyword of the war, prompting tens of thousands of slaves to flock to Union lines. In August 1861, Butler's proclamation led Congress to pass the First Confiscation Act, which authorized the army to seize all slaves aiding the Confederacy who reached Union lines. From the beginning, Bay Staters sought to turn the conflict into an emancipation war.[65]

John Brown became a mascot of the Union army in the summer of 1861. In April, Governor Andrew had ordered the Massachusetts Second Battalion, known as the "Tigers," to garrison Fort Warren in Boston Harbor, where they drilled, cleaned the compound, and sang to pass the time. One of the Tigers was a Scottish immigrant named John Brown, whose comrades needled him for his illustrious name. "This cannot be John Brown," they sang; "His body lies mouldering in the grave." Soon the men had created five stanzas, set to the lyrics of a camp-meeting hymn, "Say, Brothers, will you meet us, on Canaan's happy shore." The hymn had originated as a *slave* spiritual, as an 1807 North Carolina hymnbook has revealed. In June the Boston abolitionist C. S. Hall published the "John Brown song" to the "Say Brothers" tune. By August this black hymn had become the most popular tune in the Union army, inspiring soldiers throughout the North to remain steadfast in their efforts to vanquish the proslavery enemy, even if their efforts would cost them their lives.[66]

Later that year, Bostonians formed a new organization that brought together abolitionists and conservative Republicans in order to champion emancipation and Union more effectively. The Emancipation League reunited all abolitionists for the first time since their split in 1840. It also forged rich collaborations between abolitionists and the Republican Party in the hopes of pressuring the Lincoln administration to free the slaves. Abolitionists knew that Republican support would give them greater power in molding public opinion and shaping policy. Republicans, meanwhile, recognized the power of abolitionist rhetoric and morality. The league obtained the support of most of the leaders in both groups. To cite just one example, Frederick Douglass "rejoiced" in its formation and delivered one of its keynote lectures.[67]

Garrison had helped form the Emancipation League. He and most other pacifists, including most Quakers, endorsed the war. Unlike "peace" Democrats, they recognized that opposing the conflict meant supporting the Confederacy. As the Boston Quaker John Greenleaf Whittier observed, there could be no "durable peace" until slavery was destroyed: "We must be 'first pure' before we can be peaceable." Garrison abandoned his principles of pacifism and disunion immediately after Fort Sumter: "When I said I would not sustain the Constitution, because it was a 'covenant with death and an agreement with hell,' I had no idea that I would live to see death and hell secede." Wendell Phillips echoed him: "I was a Disunionist for twenty years," he told audiences. "I hated the Union when it meant making white men hypocrites and black men slaves." But with the war, the Union now represented the "justice" of emancipation that would enable it to survive.[68]

Three Bostonians—a conservative and two radicals—worked together to shape the terms of the final Emancipation Proclamation. In August 1862 George Livermore delivered a talk at the Massachusetts Historical Society on Tremont Street. A merchant, bibliophile, and friend of Sumner, he had engineered the gift of the Thomas Dowse Library to the society in 1856. Consisting of almost five thousand beautifully bound volumes, it was one of the preeminent private libraries in New England (fig. 6). Livermore was

FIGURE 6. H. Wright Smith, after H. Billings, *The Dowse Library*. Lithograph, ca. 1857. Collection of the Massachusetts Historical Society.

himself a brilliant collector and purportedly read every book he acquired. His talk addressed the central question of the war that summer: whether or not to emancipate and arm blacks. A month earlier, Congress had passed the Second Confiscation Act, which declared all slaves of rebel masters within Union lines "forever free" and authorized the president to "employ" blacks "in such a manner as he may judge best for the public welfare." (Blacks had been serving in the navy since the beginning of the war.)[69] Many Bostonians were growing impatient with Lincoln. Two local soldiers, Morris Copeland and Robert Gould Shaw, had gone to Washington in May, hoping to raise a black regiment. But Secretary of War Edwin Stanton refused their request and then cashiered Copeland. Wendell Phillips became so frustrated with Lincoln that he called him "a first-rate *second-rate man*."[70]

Livermore answered the question by calling on history. His talk and the book that followed emphasized the precedent and virtues of emancipating and arming slaves, from the Revolution through the early Republic. An extraordinary work of scholarship, it was partly inspired by William Cooper Nell's *Colored Patriots of the American Revolution* (1855), which Sumner had told him to read and which was "now out of print," as Livermore noted (fig.

FIGURE 7. "Are Colored Men Citizens? A Book for the Times." Broadside advertisement, ca. 1855, for William Cooper Nell, *Colored Patriots of the American Revolution* (1855). Collection of Houghton Library, Harvard University.

7). During his talk at the historical society, he even displayed a flag from a Revolutionary War company of black soldiers, the "Bucks of America," which Nell had loaned him (fig. 8). While Nell's book had emphasized blacks' right to citizenship, however, Livermore's focused on the benefits to the *nation*

FIGURE 8. Bucks of America, flag. Oil painting on silk, ca. 1789. Collection of the Massachusetts Historical Society.

of emancipating and arming blacks. The books were in fact written for different audiences, Livermore's for mainstream Republicans. Indeed, he was appalled by some radicals. Shortly before delivering his address he posed a question to Sumner: Can you influence "some of Wendell Phillips' friends and have him sent to a *madhouse* before he's *arrested* for a *traitor*?"[71]

Sumner loved Livermore's book and sent it to Lincoln in November 1862, after the president had already issued his preliminary Emancipation Proclamation. "I call your especial attention to the last half," he told Lincoln. "You'll find it learned, thorough, and candid. The author is a *conservative* Republican, and his paper was read before the Mass. Historical Society, which is one of the most *conservative* bodies in our country."[72]

There are two main differences between the preliminary and final Emancipation Proclamations: the former does not explicitly call for using blacks in the army, while the latter does, and it urges colonization, whereas the final Proclamation is silent on that topic. As James Oakes noted, "Lincoln's final draft lifted the long-standing ban on black troops in the Union army."[73]

Livermore, with help from Nell and Sumner, influenced Lincoln's decision to arm blacks in the final Proclamation. On December 24, as the president prepared the document, he met with Sumner, referred to Livermore's

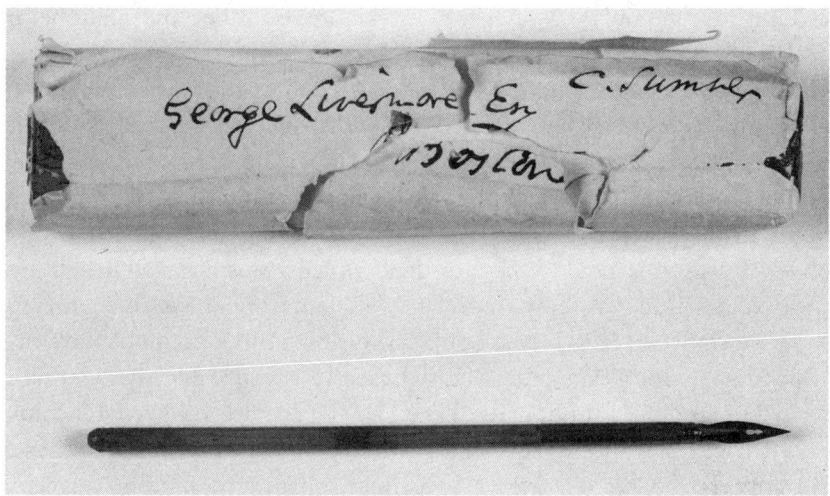

FIGURE 9. Pen used by Abraham Lincoln to sign the Emancipation Proclamation, January 1, 1863. Pen by Blanzy Poure & Cie, Paris; nib by B. & P. Lawrence, mid-nineteenth century. Collection of the Massachusetts Historical Society.

book, and "said that his copy was mislaid and that he wished to consult it now." Sumner gave Lincoln his own copy. Attorney General Edward Bates also "acknowledged his obligation" to the book in determining that Lincoln's final proclamation was constitutional. Livermore's publication "cannot be forgotten," Sumner said.[74]

Livermore was thrilled that Lincoln found his book useful. He asked Sumner if he could obtain the pen "with which he signs this Declaration of Independence": "Can it be done without impropriety? Can you get it for me? I so much desire to have that precious instrument come to Massachusetts, that I would do almost anything to get it." Livermore also asked about receiving a signed copy of the final Proclamation. "That would be still better than the pen," he said.[75]

Sumner forwarded Livermore's request to Lincoln. "If nobody has yet spoken for" the pen, "let me," on behalf of Livermore, Sumner said, adding that Livermore "also inquires about the E.P. I hope you will be able to gratify him at least in part." Lincoln satisfied Livermore's requests. He gave him a signed copy of the final Proclamation and the pen he had used to sign it. Livermore eventually gave the pen to that "most conservative body," the Massachusetts Historical Society (fig. 9).[76]

Lincoln's gifts and the influence of Livermore's book became public news on January 12, 1863. As *Frank Leslie's* reported, Sumner "read to the president . . . an eloquent letter from George Livermore, of Boston, acknowledging the receipt of the steel pen . . . with which the president signed the New Year's proclamation. Mr. Livermore's claim to its possession is founded upon his 'historical research' as to the opinions of the founders of the Republic respecting negroes as slaves, citizens and soldiers, a copy of which was presented to the president while he was engaged in writing the Proclamation."[77] A few months later, William Cooper Nell, recognizing the importance of Livermore's book and his own influence on it, gave his "Bucks of America" flag to the Massachusetts Historical Society.[78]

In January 1863, around the time that Livermore received Lincoln's pen, Governor Andrew requested permission to raise a black regiment. He appointed George Stearns, a former conspirator in John Brown's raid, to spearhead recruitment, and Stearns hired Frederick Douglass to raise the 54th Massachusetts (Colored) Infantry. The nation's preeminent black leader, Douglass had been an early and ardent advocate for arming blacks. He immersed himself in the project, emphasizing the intimate link between black soldiers and citizenship. If blacks contributed to a Union victory, then the government would feel compelled to grant them equal rights. Douglass's sons Lewis and Charles were among his earliest recruits.[79]

Douglass wrote and circulated a recruiting broadside highlighting the state's crucial role in ending slavery and winning the war. "We can get at the throat of treason and slavery through the state of Massachusetts," he told prospective recruits. "She was first in the War of Independence; first to break the chains of her slaves; first to make the black man equal before the law; first to admit colored children to her common schools, and she was first to answer with her blood the alarm cry of the nation, when its capital was menaced by rebels. You know her patriotic governor, and you know Charles Sumner. I need not add more."[80]

One final indication of the degree to which abolitionists' struggle for freedom and equality had been mainstreamed comes from *Harper's Weekly*. In 1863, following the Massachusetts 54th attack on Fort Wagner, the magazine paired two illustrations that contrasted the heroism of blacks with the cowardice of whites (fig. 10). The top image depicts the execution of three deserters from the 46th Pennsylvania regiment, while the bottom illustration shows the Massachusetts 54th storming Fort Wagner under

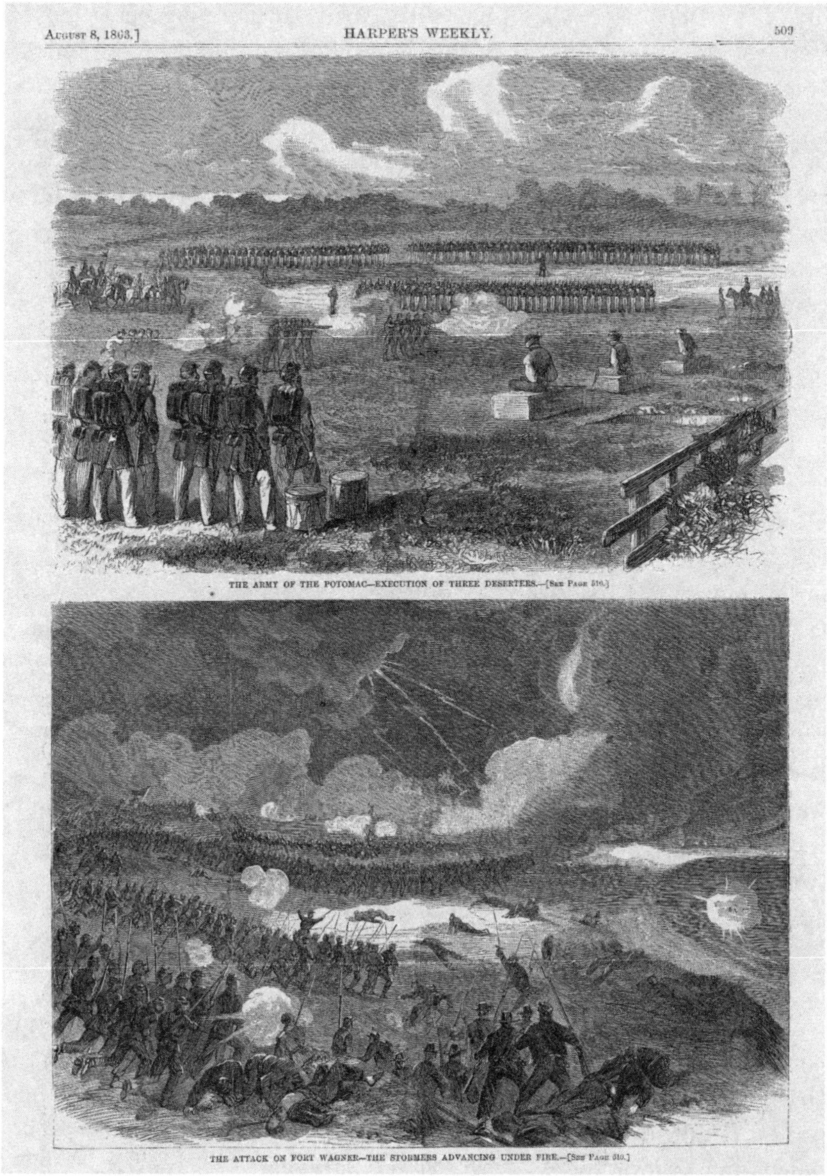

AUGUST 8, 1863.] HARPER'S WEEKLY. 509

THE ARMY OF THE POTOMAC—EXECUTION OF THREE DESERTERS.—[SEE PAGE 510.]

THE ATTACK ON FORT WAGNER—THE STORMERS ADVANCING UNDER FIRE.—[SEE PAGE 510.]

FIGURE 10. “The Army of the Potomac—Execution of Three Deserters” and “The Attack on Fort Wagner—The Stormers Advancing under Fire,” *Harper's Weekly,* August 8, 1863, 509.

fire. The latter image is apocalyptic, with fateful lightning being loosed from the heavens at the enemy. It is a visual counterpart of "The Battle Hymn of the Republic," the Union anthem that Julia Ward Howe adapted from "John Brown's Body" in late 1862. A New Yorker and an Episcopalian by birth, Howe had settled in Boston and became a Unitarian after marrying Samuel Gridley Howe. In the *Harper's* engraving of the 54th, God is marching on. His work is visible. The contrast between the two images is profound: in the one, white deserters are ignominiously executed by their comrades as they sit, blindfolded, on their coffins; in the other, black soldiers "deal with their contemners" in return for God's—and the nation's—grace. In essence, black soldiers *out-citizen* whites, and are thus more deserving than whites of equality before the law.[81]

On the evening of April 15, 1865, Holy Saturday as it was already being called, because it was the day Lincoln died, Garrison visited the camp of the Massachusetts 55th, three miles from Charleston, to see his son George. The regiment had recently convoyed some twelve hundred plantation slaves from the interior to the coast. Garrison had never before seen plantation slaves, and he was shocked at the sight. Indeed, he had never conceived that a picture of such "rags and wretchedness, . . . of the misery and degradation of slavery," could exist. The slaves had no idea who he was, but they gathered around him after being told by some officers that he was their friend. After some awkward attempts at communication, Garrison tried to end the meeting on a triumphal note. "Well, my friends, you are free at last—let us give three cheers for freedom."

He led off with the first cheer, but there was no response.

He gave the second and third cheers. Again, no response.

His son George, who witnessed the scene, concluded that the contrabands "*did not know how to cheer.*"[82] More probably, they did not *want* to cheer, recognizing in their plight that freedom was a struggle rather than the endpoint implied by Garrison's facile "free at last." As Harriet Jacobs noted after visiting the sick and dying contrabands at Duff Green's Row in Washington, D.C., their "tearful eyes often looked up to [her] with the language, 'Is this freedom?' "[83]

Garrison had spent thirty years advocating an immediate end to slavery. Like many other abolitionists, he had assumed that with freedom, equality before the law and citizenship would quickly follow. But his meeting with the contrabands no doubt made him wonder, "How long? How long?" It also likely made him consider how long the revolutionary time in which he lived, and which he had helped usher in, would last. How long before this revolutionary moment would perish?[84]

Not long, as it turned out. For the counterrevolution was already under way, and the voices seeking to uncouple abolitionism from emancipationism were gaining power.

NOTES

1. Congress had passed the Thirteenth Amendment in January 1865, and by April 1865 nearly three-quarters of the states had ratified it. See "Banquet in Charleston," *Liberator*, May 12, 1865; and especially Michael Vorenberg, *Final Freedom: The Civil War, the Abolition of Slavery, and the Thirteenth Amendment* (Cambridge: Cambridge University Press, 2001), chap. 6.
2. "'Marching On!': The Fifty-Fifth Massachusetts Colored Regiment Singing John Brown's March in the Streets of Charleston," *Harper's Weekly*, March 18, 1865; Henry Mayer, *All on Fire: William Lloyd Garrison and the Abolition of Slavery* (New York: St. Martin's, 1998), 577.
3. Mayer, *All on Fire*, 579.
4. "The Steamer 'Planter' and Her Captor," *Harper's Weekly*, June 14, 1862; Mayer, *All on Fire*, 578.
5. "Banquet in Charleston"; Thomas E. Schneider, *Lincoln's Defense of Politics: The Public Man and His Opponents in the Slavery Crisis* (Columbia: University of Missouri Press, 2006), 105.
6. On the distinctions between antislavery advocates and abolitionists, see David Brion Davis, "The Emergence of Immediatism in British and American Antislavery Thought," in *From Homicide to Slavery: Studies in American Culture* (New York: Oxford University Press, 1986), 238–57; John Stauffer, "Fighting the Devil with His Own Fire," in Andrew Delbanco et al., *The Abolitionist Imagination* (Cambridge: Harvard University Press, 2012), 57–80. "Emancipationist" was coined in 1862 by the *Continental Monthly*. See *Continental Monthly* 1 (January–February 1862): 97–98, 113–14; James M. McPherson, *The Struggle for Equality: Abolitionists and the Negro in the Civil War and Reconstruction* (1964; repr., Princeton: Princeton University Press, 1992), 90–93.
7. John Stauffer, *Giants: The Parallel Lives of Frederick Douglass and Abraham Lincoln* (New York: Twelve, 2008); James Oakes, *The Radical and the Republican: Frederick Douglass, Abraham Lincoln, and the Triumph of Antislavery Politics* (New York: Norton, 2007).
8. Edward J. Blum, *Reforging the White Republic: Race, Religion, and American Nationalism, 1865–1898* (Baton Rouge: Louisiana State University Press, 2005), 5; McPherson, *Struggle for Equality*, 81–90, 99–133, 229–32, 341–66, 417–32; McPherson, "Abolitionists and the Civil Rights Act of 1875," *Journal of American History* 52 (December 1965): 493–510; Vorenberg, *Final Freedom*, chaps. 3–7; Garrett Epps, *Democracy Reborn: The Fourteenth Amendment and the Fight for Equal Rights in Post–Civil War America* (New York: Henry

Holt, 2006), chaps. 6–11; Philip Dray, *Capital Men: The Epic Story of Reconstruction through the Lives of the First Black Congressmen* (Boston: Mariner Books, 2010); Eric Foner, *Freedom's Lawmakers: A Directory of Black Officeholders during Reconstruction* (Baton Rouge: Louisiana State University Press, 1996); Foner, *Reconstruction: America's Unfinished Revolution, 1863–1877* (New York: Harper & Row, 1988), chaps. 1–2, 6–10. On the significance of the Reconstruction amendments, see Akhil Reed Amar, *The Bill of Rights: Creation and Reconstruction* (New Haven: Yale University Press, 1998), part II; and Amar, *America's Constitution: A Biography* (New York: Random House, 2006), chap. 10.

9. Frederick Douglass, *Life and Times of Frederick Douglass* (1892; repr., New York: Collier, 1962), 366; Daniel H. Chamberlain quoted from *New York Tribune*, November 4, 1883, in *William Lloyd Garrison, 1805–1879: The Story of His Life, Told by His Children*, vol. 4 (New York: The Century Co., 1889), 132n. Chamberlain said he quoted Lincoln "in exact substance, and very nearly in words." For corroboration of Lincoln's statement to Douglass at the reception following the Second Inaugural, see *Memorial of Sarah Pugh: A Tribute of Respect from Her Cousins* (Philadelphia: J. B. Lippincott, 1888), 107.

10. *The Collected Works of Abraham Lincoln*, ed. Roy P. Basler, vol. 8 (New Brunswick, N.J.: Rutgers University Press, 1953), 2.

11. Ibid., 8:403; William A. Tidwell, *Come Retribution: The Confederate Secret Service and the Assassination of Lincoln* (Jackson: University Press of Mississippi, 1988), 408, 421; John Rhodehamel and Louise Taper, eds., *"Right or Wrong, God Judge Me": The Writings of John Wilkes Booth* (Urbana: University of Illinois Press, 1997), 154; Henry Louis Gates Jr., "Abraham Lincoln on Race and Slavery," in *Lincoln on Race and Slavery*, ed. Henry Louis Gates Jr. and Donald Yacovone (Princeton: Princeton University Press, 2009), xxv, xlix–l; David Herbert Donald, *Lincoln* (New York: Simon & Schuster, 1995), 585–88.

12. James Oakes, *Freedom National: The Destruction of Slavery in the United States, 1861–1865* (New York: Norton, 2013), xix–xxi, 284, 450–51, 489–92; McPherson, *Struggle for Equality*, 81–90, 99–133, 229–32, 341–66, 417–32; McPherson, "Abolitionists and the Civil Rights Act," 493–510; Vorenberg, *Final Freedom*, chaps. 3–7; Epps, *Democracy Reborn*, chaps. 6–11; Foner, *Reconstruction*, chaps. 1–2, 6–10. On distinctions between legal and social equality in Reconstruction, see Kate Masur, *An Example for All the Land: Emancipation and the Struggle over Equality in Washington, D.C.* (Chapel Hill: University of North Carolina Press, 2010), 9–11.

13. Henry Wilson, *History of the Rise and Fall of the Slave Power in America*, 3 vols. (Boston: James R. Osgood, 1872–77); Hermann von Holst, *The Constitutional and Political History of the United States*, 8 vols. (Chicago: Callaghan, 1876–92), esp. vols. 7–8; John L. Myers, "The Writing of *History of the Rise and Fall of the Slave Power in America*," *Civil War History* 31 (June 1985): 144–62; Peter Novick, *That Noble Dream: The "Objectivity Question" and the American Historical Profession* (Cambridge: Cambridge University Press, 1988), 25; Thomas L. Haskell, "Objectivity Is Not Neutrality: Rhetoric vs. Practice in Peter Novick's *That Noble Dream*," *History and Theory* 29 (May 1990): 137n13; Eric F. Goldman, "Hermann Eduard von Holst: Plumed Knight of American Historiography," *Mississippi Valley Historical Review* 23 (March 1937): 511–32; Eric F. Goldman, "Importing a Historian: Von Holst and American Universities," *Mississippi Valley Historical Review* 27 (September 1940): 267–74.

14. James Ford Rhodes, *History of the United States from the Compromise of 1850*, 8 vols. (New York: Macmillan, 1892–1919), esp. vol. 1, chaps. 1, 3, 5, and vol. 2, chap. 7; Hugh Tulloch, *The Debate on the American Civil War Era* (Manchester: Manchester University

Press, 1999), 74 (quotation); David W. Blight, *Race and Reunion: The Civil War in American Memory* (Cambridge: Harvard University Press, 2001), 357–59.
15. James M. McPherson, *The Abolitionist Legacy: From Reconstruction to the NAACP* (Princeton: Princeton University Press, 1975), 14 (quotation); McPherson, "Abolitionists and the Civil Rights Act of 1875," *Journal of American History* 52 (December 1965): 506; "Charles Sumner," *Harper's Weekly*, April 4, 1874, front page (quotation); *Harper's Weekly*, June 20, 1874; Henry James, *William Wetmore Story and His Friends: From Letters, Diaries, and Recollections*, 2 vols. (Boston: Houghton, Mifflin, 1903), 1:30–31, 234, 2:31; David Herbert Donald, *Charles Sumner* (1960, 1970; repr., New York: Da Capo, 1996); Stauffer, "Fighting the Devil with His Own Fire," 64. The first full biography of Sumner, exhaustive in scope and magisterial in style, remains the best: Edward L. Pierce, *Memoir and Letters of Charles Sumner*, 4 vols. (Boston: Roberts Brothers, 1893). On nineteenth-century memories of the abolitionists, see McPherson, *Abolitionist Legacy*, 3–142; Tulloch, *Debate*, 71–74; Blight, *Race and Reunion*, 231–37; Julie Roy Jeffrey, *Abolitionists Remember: Antislavery Autobiographies and the Unfinished Work of Emancipation* (Chapel Hill: University of North Carolina Press, 2008).
16. It should be clear that I refer to the "modern" or "immediate" abolitionists. Sympathetic treatment of the early, pre-1830s generation of abolitionists begins with David Brion Davis, *The Problem of Slavery in Western Culture* (New York: Oxford University Press, 1967); and Davis, *The Problem of Slavery in the Age of Revolution, 1770–1823* (Ithaca, N.Y.: Cornell University Press, 1975).
17. Novick, *That Noble Dream*, 76–77; Tulloch, *Debate*, chap. 3. Although Tulloch does not distinguish between abolitionists and emancipationists in his historiography, it is clear from his narrative that the two categories are separate.
18. George W. Williams, *History of the Negro Race in America, 1619–1880* (New York: G. P. Putnam's Sons, 1883), chaps. 9–21; W. E. B. Du Bois, *John Brown* (Philadelphia: G. W. Jacobs, 1909); Du Bois, *The Gift of the Black Folk: The Negroes in the Making of America* (Boston: Stratford, 1924); Du Bois, *Black Reconstruction: An Essay toward a History of the Part Which Black Folk Played in the Attempt to Reconstruct Democracy in America, 1860–1880* (New York: Russell & Russell, 1935); John Hope Franklin, *From Slavery to Freedom: A History of American Negroes* (1947; repr., New York: Knopf, 1971), 242–70; Benjamin Quarles, *The Negro in the Civil War* (1953; repr., New York: Da Capo, 1989); Quarles, *Black Abolitionists* (New York: Oxford University Press, 1969); Dudley Taylor Cornish, *The Sable Arm: Negro Troops in the Union Army, 1861–1865* (1956; repr., Lawrence: University Press of Kansas, 1987); Nathan Huggins, *Black Odyssey: The Afro-American Ordeal in Slavery* (New York: Pantheon, 1977); Waldo E. Martin Jr., *The Mind of Frederick Douglass* (Chapel Hill: University of North Carolina Press, 1984); James Oliver Horton and Lois E. Horton, *Black Bostonians: Family Life and Community Struggle in the Antebellum North* (1979; repr., New York: Holmes & Meier, 1999), chaps. 7–9; Horton and Horton, *In Hope of Liberty: Culture, Community and Protest among Northern Free Blacks, 1700–1860* (New York: Oxford University Press, 1997), chaps. 9–10. On British abolitionists, see for example the synthesis by Adam Hochschild, *Bury the Chains: Prophets and Rebels in the Fight to Free an Empire's Slaves* (Boston: Houghton Mifflin, 2005). On French abolitionists see Lawrence C. Jennings, *French Anti-Slavery: The Movement for the Abolition of Slavery in France, 1802–1848* (Cambridge: Cambridge University Press, 2000); and Seymour Drescher, *Abolition: A History of Slavery and Antislavery* (New York: Cambridge University Press, 2009).

19. Tulloch, *Debate*, 10; C. Vann Woodward, "John Brown's Private War" (1952), reprinted in *The Burden of Southern History*, 3rd ed. (Baton Rouge: Louisiana State University Press, 1993), 51; Robert Penn Warren, *The Legacy of the Civil War* (1961; repr., Lincoln: University of Nebraska Press, 1998), 22; Frank L. Owsley, "The Fundamental Cause of the Civil War: Egocentric Sectionalism," *Journal of Southern History* 7 (February 1941): 16. See also Oakes, *Freedom National*, xv–xvii.
20. Tulloch, *Debate*, 89–100, quotation on 93; Merton L. Dillon, "The Abolitionists: A Decade of Historiography, 1959–1969," *Journal of Southern History* 35 (November 1969): 500–522.
21. Cleanth Brooks, R. W. B. Lewis, and Robert Penn Warren, eds., *American Literature: The Makers and the Making*, vol. 1 (New York: St. Martin's, 1973), 335; James A. Henretta et al., *America: A Concise History*, 3rd ed., vol. 1 (Boston: Bedford / St. Martin's, 2006), 368.
22. Robert Rosenstone, "Does a Filmic Writing of History Exist?," *History and Theory* 41 (December 2002): 134–44, quotation on 137; Casey King, "Abolitionists in American Cinema: From the Birth of a Nation to Amistad," in *Prophets of Protest: Reconsidering the History of American Abolitionism*, ed. Timothy Patrick McCarthy and John Stauffer (New York: The New Press, 2006), 268–93; Robert Lang, ed., *The Birth of a Nation* (New Brunswick, N.J.: Rutgers University Press, 1994), 93.
23. Stevens's enemies and most biographers have asserted that he had a sexual relationship with his housekeeper, Lydia Hamilton Smith. Smith was probably a "confidante," but there is no evidence that she was his mistress. The most sustained allegation of a sexual relationship is by Fawn Brodie. In her biography she accuses Stevens of acting little different from slave owners who kept concubines. Her evidence of a sexual liaison is based on the following: Smith worked for Stevens for twenty years and lived in his house; he bequeathed her money after his death ($500 a year or $5,000 in a lump sum) and deeded her property; he insisted on being buried in an interracial cemetery; and he commissioned a portrait of her. The first three were common arrangements between trusted housekeepers and employers in the nineteenth century. It is also understandable that Stevens, a bachelor, would commission a portrait of his confidante. And most abolitionists insisted on being buried in interracial cemeteries. Stevens and Smith were buried in different cemeteries—Smith in the cemetery of St. Mary's Catholic Church, where she had long been a member, and Stevens in Shreiner's Protestant Cemetery, both in Lancaster, Pennsylvania.

    The most compelling evidence, which no one has pursued, of intense spiritual, emotional, and possible sexual intimacy, is that just before Stevens died he received the Roman Catholic rite of baptism, possibly at the request of Smith. Perhaps Smith wanted to be buried beside Stevens, and so had him baptized in her faith. Stevens was probably not "fully aware of what was going on." See Hans L. Trefousse, *Thaddeus Stevens: Nineteenth-Century Egalitarian* (Chapel Hill: University of North Carolina Press, 1997), 69–70, 240 (quotation); Fawn M. Brodie, *Thaddeus Stevens: Scourge of the South* (New York: Norton, 1959), 17, 20, 52–53, 86–93.
24. Stephen Kantrowitz, *More Than Freedom: Fighting for Black Citizenship in a White Republic, 1829–1889* (New York: Penguin, 2012), 4; Frederick Douglass, "The Mission of the War," in *The Frederick Douglass Papers*, ser. 1, vol. 4, ed. John W. Blassingame and John R. McKivigan (New Haven: Yale University Press, 1991), 11, 24; David W. Blight, *Frederick Douglass' Civil War: Keeping Faith in Jubilee* (Baton Rouge: Louisiana State University Press, 1989), 175–78. Joseph Yanielli cites other recent uncharitable assessments of white

abolitionists in his article "George Thompson among the Africans: Empathy, Authority, and Insanity in the Age of Abolition," *Journal of American History* 96 (March 2010): 980.

David Walker is the only major figure in Kantrowitz's book who does not define himself as an abolitionist. This is because he bridged the gradualist and immediatist movements, indeed helped to launch the immediatist, or modern abolitionist, movement that embraced racial equality and integration. As I note elsewhere, "In essence, the liberal abolitionists of the early Republic became the colonizationists and 'liberal' anti-slavery advocates of the antebellum era. They distanced themselves from the radical immediatists." See my response to Andrew Delbanco, "Fighting the Devil with His Own Fire," in Delbanco et al., *Abolitionist Imagination*, 74.

25. Delbanco et al., *Abolitionist Imagination*; Harry S. Stout, *Upon the Altar of the Nation: A Moral History of the Civil War* (New York: Penguin, 2006); David Goldfield, *America Aflame: How the Civil War Created a Nation* (New York: Bloomsbury, 2011); Christopher Benfey, "Terrorist or Martyr," *New York Review of Books*, March 7, 2013; Benfey, introduction to Allen Tate, *Collected Poems, 1919–1976* (New York: Farrar Straus Giroux, 2007), xiii–xix. Although much more subtle, Sean Wilentz echoes C. Vann Woodward by characterizing the abolitionists as "fellow travelers." See Wilentz, *The Rise of American Democracy: Jefferson to Lincoln* (New York: Norton, 2005), 650. See also Yael A. Sternhell, "Revisionism Reinvented? The Antiwar Turn in Civil War Scholarship," *Journal of the Civil War Era* 3 (June 2013): 239–56.

On the belligerence of southern slaveholders, see Manisha Sinha, *The Counter-Revolution of Slavery: Politics and Ideology in Antebellum South Carolina* (Chapel Hill: University of North Carolina Press, 2000); David Brion Davis, *Inhuman Bondage: The Rise and Fall of Slavery in the New World* (New York: Oxford University Press, 2006), chaps. 9, 10, 14; William W. Freehling, *The Road to Disunion*, vol. 2, *Secessionists Triumphant, 1854–1861* (New York: Oxford University Press, 2007).

26. Arthur Zilversmit, *The First Emancipation: The Abolition of Slavery in the North* (Chicago: University of Chicago Press, 1967), chap. 5; Leon F. Litwack, *North of Slavery: The Negro in the Free States, 1790–1860* (Chicago: University of Chicago Press, 1961), 94, 106; Donald M. Jacobs, ed., *Courage and Conscience: Black and White Abolitionists in Boston* (Bloomington: Indiana University Press, 1993), 1–46; James Brewer Stewart, *Abolitionist Politics and the Coming of the Civil War* (Amherst: University of Massachusetts Press, 2008), 3–32; Bruce Laurie, *Beyond Garrison: Antislavery and Social Reform* (Cambridge: Cambridge University Press, 2005), 153–73; Stephen Kendrick and Paul Kendrick, *Sarah's Long Walk: The Free Blacks of Boston and How Their Struggle for Equality Changed America* (Boston: Beacon, 2004).

In practice, Massachusetts was the first state to abolish slavery. In the 1790 census, Massachusetts (including Maine, its territory), was the only state listed with no slaves. Although Vermont passed the first constitution in history abolishing slavery (in 1777), it called for gradual abolition, emancipating male slaves at age twenty-one and female slaves at age eighteen. The 1790 census lists sixteen slaves in Vermont. For a critique of the 1790 Massachusetts census, see Margot Minardi, *Making Slavery History: Abolitionism and the Politics of Memory in Massachusetts* (New York: Oxford University Press, 2010), 18–19.

27. Eric Foner, *Free Labor, Free Soil, Free Men: The Ideology of the Republican Party before the Civil War* (New York: Oxford University Press, 1970), 250–53; Laurie, *Beyond Garrison*, 285–87, quotation on 286.

28. Timothy L. Smith, *Revivalism and Social Reform: American Protestantism on the Eve of the Civil War* (New York: Harper & Row, 1957), 31–32, 87–88, 95–102, quotations on 32, 95; Daniel Walker Howe, *The Unitarian Conscience: Harvard Moral Philosophy, 1805–1861* (1970; repr., Middletown, Conn.: Wesleyan University Press, 1988), 151–73, quotations on 151, 152; Jacobs, *Courage and Conscience*, 1–8; Conrad Wright, *The Beginnings of Unitarianism in America* (Boston: Starr King Press, 1955); David M. Robinson, "'A Religious Demonstration': The Theological Emergence of New England Transcendentalism," in *Transient and Permanent: The Transcendentalist Movement and Its Contexts*, ed. Charles Capper and Conrad Edick Wright (Boston: Massachusetts Historical Society, 1999), 49–72; Conrad Wright, introduction to *Three Prophets of Religious Liberalism: Channing, Emerson, Parker* (1961; repr., Boston: Beacon, 1986), 3–46.
29. George Livermore, *An Historical Research Respecting the Opinions of the Founders of the Republic on Negroes as Slaves, as Citizens, and as Soldiers. Read before the Massachusetts Historical Society, August 14, 1862* (Boston: John Wilson and Son, 1862), 32; Hon. Emory Washburn, "Extinction of Slavery in Massachusetts," *Proceedings of the Massachusetts Historical Society*, vol. 3 (1855–58), 196; Minardi, *Making Slavery History*, 39–41.
30. Washburn, "Extinction," 201; Livermore, *Historical Research*, 30–32; Robert M. Spector, "The Quock Walker Cases (1781–83)—Slavery, Its Abolition, and Negro Citizenship in Early Massachusetts," *Journal of Negro History* 53 (January 1968): 12–32, quotation on 13; Arthur Zilversmit, "Quok Walker, Mumbet, and the Abolition of Slavery in Massachusetts," *William and Mary Quarterly* 25 (October 1968): 614–24; Elaine MacEacheren, "Emancipation of Slavery in Massachusetts: A Reexamination, 1770–1790," *Journal of Negro History* 55 (October 1970): 289–306.
31. Washburn, "Extinction," 201; Livermore, *Historical Research*, 30 (quotation).
32. Allan Nevins, *Ordeal of the Union*, vol. 1, *Fruits of Manifest Destiny, 1847–1852* (1947; repr., New York: Collier, 1992), 380–86; Robert M. Cover, *Justice Accused: Antislavery and the Judicial Process* (New Haven: Yale University Press, 1975), 175–91; Wendy F. Hamand, "'No Voice from England': Mrs. Stowe, Mr. Lincoln, and the British in the Civil War," *New England Quarterly* 61 (March 1988): 22; J. E. B. Munson, "A Book Forming a Foreign Policy: Uncle Tom in England," *Civil War Times Illustrated*, January 1983, 40; David S. Reynolds, *Mightier Than the Sword: Uncle Tom's Cabin and the Battle for America* (New York: Norton, 2011), x, chap. 4; Joan D. Hedrick, *Harriet Beecher Stowe: A Life* (New York: Oxford University Press, 1994), 218–71; Annie Fields, "Days with Mrs. Stowe," *Atlantic Monthly* 78 (August 1896): 148. Daniel R. Vollaro discusses Lincoln's alleged remark in "Lincoln, Stowe, and the 'Little Woman / Great War' Story: The Making, and Breaking, of a Great American Anecdote," *Journal of the Abraham Lincoln Association* 30 (Winter 2009): 18–34.
33. *The Harriet Jacobs Family Papers*, ed. Jean Fagan Yellin, vol. 1 (Chapel Hill: University of North Carolina Press, 2008), 200 (quotation), 296; *The Life and Writings of Frederick Douglass*, ed. Philip S. Foner, 5 vols. (New York: International Publishers, 1950–1955), 2:227; untitled article, *Frederick Douglass' Paper*, April 8, 1852 (quotation); Hedrick, *Stowe*, 208–23; Reynolds, *Mightier Than the Sword*, chaps. 3–4; Robert S. Levine, *Martin Delany, Frederick Douglass, and the Politics of Representative Identity* (Chapel Hill: University of North Carolina Press, 1997), 72–74; William Cooper Nell, *The Colored Patriots of the American Revolution . . .* (Boston: Robert F. Wallcut, 1855), 5–6.
34. Stanley W. Campbell, *The Slave Catchers: Enforcement of the Fugitive Slave Law, 1850–1860* (1968; repr., New York: Norton, 1972), 124–30, 199–207; Albert J. Von Frank, *The*

Trials of Anthony Burns: Freedom and Slavery in Emerson's Boston (Cambridge: Harvard University Press, 1998); Kantrowitz, *More Than Freedom*, 205–13; James Batchelder, Official Death Certificate, in *Boston Slave Riot, and Trial of Anthony Burns* (Boston, 1854), Thomas Wentworth Higginson Papers, Houghton Library, Harvard University; William Channing to Thomas Wentworth Higginson, April 7, 1874, Higginson Papers.

35. Von Frank, *Trials of Anthony Burns*, 53–68, 203–19; Richard H. Abbott, *Cotton and Capital: Boston Businessmen and Antislavery Reform, 1854–1868* (Amherst: University of Massachusetts Press, 1991), 24–27, quotation from Lawrence on 26; Kantrowitz, *More Than Freedom*, 184.
36. Von Frank, *Trials of Anthony Burns*, 53; Campbell, *Slave Catchers*, 129–30; Kantrowitz, *More Than Freedom*, 205–13.
37. Abbott, *Cotton and Capital*, 25–30; Kantrowitz, *More Than Freedom*, 184; Stewart, *Abolitionist Politics*, 24–25; Ulysses S. Grant, *Memoirs and Selected Letters* (1886; repr., New York: Library of America, 1990), 773.
38. Abbott, *Cotton and Capital*, 28–62; David S. Reynolds, *John Brown, Abolitionist: The Man Who Killed Slavery, Sparked the Civil War, and Seeded Civil Rights* (New York: Knopf, 2005), 148–58.
39. Reynolds, *John Brown*, 156–57; Abbott, *Cotton and Capital*, 38–45.
40. Robert Morris to Sumner, June 11, 1856, Charles Sumner Papers (MS Am 1), Houghton Library, Harvard University (hereafter cited as CSP); Lewis Hayden to Sumner, January 24, 1870, CSP; John Daniels, *In Freedom's Birthplace: A Study of the Boston Negroes* (Boston: Houghton Mifflin, 1914), 57; Manisha Sinha, "The Caning of Charles Sumner: Slavery, Race, and Ideology in the Age of the Civil War," *Journal of the Early Republic* 23 (Summer 2003): 235–38.
41. Sumner, "Crime Against Kansas," *Congressional Globe*, 34th Cong., 1st Sess. (1856), 530; Sinha, "Caning," 233–62; Michael D. Pierson, "'All Southern Society Is Assailed by the Foulest Charges': Charles Sumner's 'The Crime Against Kansas' and the Escalation of Republican Anti-Slavery Rhetoric," *New England Quarterly* 68 (December 1995): 533–34; Akhil Reed Amar, "Women and the Constitution," *Harvard Journal of Law and Public Policy* 18 (Spring 1995): 466–67; Amar, "Child Abuse as Slavery: A Thirteenth Amendment Response to Deshaney," *Harvard Law Review* 105 (April 1992): 1366; Sumner to Samuel Gridley Howe, March 31, 1856, CSP.
42. Mary Chesnut, *The Private Mary Chesnut: The Unpublished Civil War Diaries*, ed. C. Vann Woodward and Elisabeth Muhlenfeld (New York: Oxford University Press, 1994), 42; Donald, *Charles Sumner*, chap. 11.
43. William E. Gienapp, *The Origins of the Republican Party, 1852–1856* (New York: Oxford University Press, 1987), 299; Gienapp, "The Crime Against Sumner: The Caning of Charles Sumner and the Rise of the Republican Party," *Civil War History* 25 (September 1979): 218–45; David L. Anderson, "Anson Burlingame: Reformer and Diplomat," *Civil War History* 25 (September 1979): 299, 300.
44. Anderson, "Burlingame," 300–302. The Clifton House was rich in symbolism. Built on the site of the Battle of Lundy's Lane in 1814, it divided the farms of two Quaker brothers, whose relative, Benjamin Lundy, became a famous antislavery editor and mentor to Garrison. The Clifton House thus symbolized brotherly peace being severed by war. See Wendell Phillips Garrison and B. C. Lundy, "In Lundy's Land," *Pennsylvania Magazine of History and Biography* 19.3 (1895): 340–43.
45. *Lydia Maria Child: Selected Letters, 1817–1880*, ed. Milton Meltzer and Patricia Holland

(Amherst: University of Massachusetts Press, 1982), 283, 287, 289; Mann quoted in Gienapp, *Origins,* 300.
46. Robert Morris to Sumner, June 11, 1856, CSP.
47. Sinha, "Caning," 235, 252, 262.
48. Abbott, *Cotton and Capital,* 33–59; Reynolds, *John Brown,* 209–10, 236–49.
49. John Stauffer and Zoe Trodd, eds., *The Tribunal: Responses to John Brown and the Harpers Ferry Raid* (Cambridge: Harvard University Press), xxix–xxx.
50. John Stauffer, *The Black Hearts of Men: Radical Abolitionists and the Transformation of Race* (Cambridge: Harvard University Press, 2002), 195–200; Robert E. McGlone, *John Brown's War against Slavery* (Cambridge: Cambridge University Press, 2009), 74, 350n11.
51. James Freeman Clarke, *Anti-Slavery Days* (1883; repr., New York: Negro Universities Press, 1970), 153–54. See also Clarke's earlier and almost identical but a bit wordier description in *Memorial and Biographical Sketches* (Boston: Houghton, Osgood, 1878), 101–2.
52. Reynolds, *John Brown,* 288–333; Tony Horwitz, *Midnight Rising: John Brown and the Raid That Sparked the Civil War* (New York: Henry Holt, 2011), esp. 291–92.
53. "New England Society," *Charleston Mercury,* December 23, 1858; *Richmond Whig,* November 22, 1859; *Richmond Enquirer,* October 25, 1859; Allan Nevins, *Ordeal of the Union,* vol. 4, *Prologue to Civil War, 1859–1861* (1950; repr., New York: Collier, 1992), 114–15; David M. Potter, *The Impending Crisis, 1848–1861* (New York: Harper & Row, 1976), 383–84; Stauffer and Trodd, *Tribunal,* xxi, xxxix.
54. Stauffer and Trodd, *Tribunal,* xxxviii, xl, 322–23, 330–31. See also Matthew J. Clavin, *Toussaint Louverture and the American Civil War: The Promise and Peril of a Second Haitian Revolution* (Philadelphia: University of Pennsylvania Press, 2010), chap. 2.
55. Stauffer and Trodd, *Tribunal,* xxxiv–xxxv; Reynolds, *John Brown,* 339–44.
56. *Correspondence between Lydia Maria Child and Gov. Wise and Mrs. Mason, of Virginia* (New York: American Anti-Slavery Society, 1860), 14; Carolyn L. Karcher, *The First Woman of the Republic: A Cultural Biography of Lydia Maria Child* (Durham, N.C.: Duke University Press, 1994), 423.
57. Reynolds, *John Brown,* 363–69; Stauffer and Trodd, *Tribunal,* 109, 113.
58. Stauffer and Trodd, *Tribunal,* 117–19, 175; William Lloyd Garrison, "Speech at the Annual Meeting of the Massachusetts Anti-Slavery Society" (January 27, 1860), *Liberator,* February 17, 1860.
59. Stauffer and Trodd, *Tribunal,* 126–27; Henry Greenleaf Pearson, *The Life of John A. Andrew, Governor of Massachusetts, 1861–1865,* 2 vols. (Boston: Houghton, Mifflin and Co., 1904), 1:95–101, quotation on 100.
60. Franklin Pierce, "A Letter on the Secession Movement" (November 23, 1860), in "Some Papers of Franklin Pierce, 1852–1862," *American Historical Review* 10 (January 1905): 365; James Brewer Stewart, "John Albion Andrew," *American National Biography Online,* www.anb.org.
61. "Arrest and Rescue of Mr. Frank B. Sanborn, Esq., at Concord, Massachusetts, on the Night of April 3, 1860," *Harper's Weekly,* April 14, 1860, 235. The Senate investigation, which lasted through May 1860, was published as *Mass Violence in America: Invasion at Harper's Ferry* (New York: Arno Press and the New York Times, 1969). On Stephen Douglas, see Robert W. Johannsen, *Stephen A. Douglas* (1973; repr., Urbana: University of Illinois Press, 1997).

62. Nevins, *Prologue to Civil War,* 177.
63. William Lowndes Yancey, speech to the National Convention, *Proceedings of the Conventions at Charleston and Baltimore* (Washington, D.C.: National Democratic Executive Committee, 1860), 69, 78; Eric H. Walther, *William Lowndes Yancey and the Coming of the Civil War* (Chapel Hill: University of North Carolina Press, 2006), 237–43; Nevins, *Prologue to Civil War,* 217–19; Stauffer and Trodd, *Tribunal,* xliv–xlvi.
64. Quoted in Edith Ellen Ware, "Political Opinion in Massachusetts during Civil War and Reconstruction," *Studies in History, Economics and Public Law* 74 (1917): 5.
65. Oakes, *Freedom National;* Kate Masur, "'A Rare Phenomenon of Philological Vegetation': The Word 'Contraband' and the Meanings of Emancipation in the United States," *Journal of American History* 93 (March 2007): 1050–84.
66. John Stauffer and Benjamin Soskis, *The Battle Hymn of the Republic: A Biography of the Song That Marches On* (New York: Oxford University Press, 2013), chaps. 1–2.
67. Frederick Douglass, "The Black Man's Future in the Southern States," in *The Frederick Douglass Papers,* ser. 1, vol. 3, ed. John W. Blassingame (New Haven: Yale University Press, 1985), 496–97; McPherson, *Struggle for Equality,* 77–98, 178–91; Matthew Furrow, "Samuel Gridley Howe, the Black Population of Canada West, and the Racial Ideology of the 'Blueprint for Radical Reconstruction,'" *Journal of American History* 97 (September 2010): 344–70.
68. *The Letters of William Lloyd Garrison,* vol. 5, *Let the Oppressed Go Free, 1861–1867,* ed. Walter M. Merrill (Cambridge: Harvard University Press, 1979), 59; "Drafting—What Is the Duty of the Abolitionists?," *Liberator,* September 26, 1862; Garrison, *The Abolitionists, and Their Relation to the War; A Lecture Delivered at the Cooper Institute, New York, January 4, 1862,* Pulpit and Rostrum, no. 26 (New York: E. D. Barker, 1862), 46; Wendell Phillips, "The War for the Union" (December 1861), in *Speeches, Lectures, and Letters* (Boston: Lee & Shepard, 1870), 440; Samuel T. Pickard, *Life and Letters of John Greenleaf Whittier,* vol. 2 (Boston: Houghton Mifflin, 1894), 441, 450.
69. "Death of George Livermore," *Proceedings of the Massachusetts Historical Society,* vol. 8 (1864–65), 443–58; Thomas Boylston Adams, "Here We Have Lived: The Houses of the Massachusetts Historical Society," *Proceedings of the Massachusetts Historical Society,* 3rd ser., vol. 78 (1966), n.p. [first page]; Louis Leonard Tucker, "Thomas Dowse," *American National Biography Online,* www.anb.org; Charles Sumner, "The Death of George Livermore, Esq.," *Boston Daily Advertiser,* September 2, 1865; "Second Confiscation Act" (July 1862), in *The Civil War: The Second Year Told by Those Who Lived It,* ed. Stephen W. Sears (New York: Library of America, 2012), 320, 321; Oakes, *Freedom National,* 224–55.
70. Russell Duncan, ed., *Blue-Eyed Child of Fortune: The Civil War Letters of Colonel Robert Gould Shaw* (Athens: University of Georgia Press, 1992), 23–25, 125, 202; *Statement of R. Morris Copeland . . . , Discharged from Service, August 6, 1862* (Boston: Prentiss & Deland, 1864); McPherson, *Struggle for Equality,* 113.
71. Livermore, *Historical Research,* 206–7; Livermore to Sumner, April 10, 1862, August 10, 1862, and July 14, 1862, all in CSP; McPherson, *Struggle for Equality,* 113. On Nell's loaning Livermore his "Bucks of America" flag, see Livermore, *Historical Research,* 206.

Other scholars have acknowledged the influence of Livermore's *Historical Research* on Lincoln's final Emancipation Proclamation: Louis P. Masur, *Lincoln's Hundred Days: The Emancipation Proclamation and the War for the Union* (Cambridge: Harvard University Press, 2012), 169–72; John Burt, *Lincoln's Tragic Pragmatism: Lincoln, Douglas, and Moral Conflict* (Cambridge: Harvard University Press, 2013), 753n76; Mark E. Neely,

The Last Best Hope of Earth: Abraham Lincoln and the Promise of America (Cambridge: Harvard University Press, 1995), 111. Only Henry Louis Gates Jr. and Donald Yacovone have acknowledged the role of William Cooper Nell, though they don't go into detail about the connections between Sumner, Livermore, Nell, and Lincoln. See Gates and Yacovone, *Lincoln on Race and Slavery,* xxxix–xl, 265, 270.

72. Sumner to Lincoln, November 28, 1862, CSP.
73. Oakes, *Freedom National,* 317–28, 340, quotation on 340. Oakes notes that in the western theater, Sherman and Grant interpreted Lincoln's Preliminary Emancipation Proclamation as authorizing them to pay blacks as laborers, but not to arm them as soldiers.
74. Sumner to Livermore, December 25, 1862, CSP; Sumner, "Death of Livermore," *Boston Daily Advertiser,* September 2, 1865; Charles Deane, "Memoir of George Livermore," *Proceedings of the Massachusetts Historical Society,* vol. 10 (1867–1869), 464.
75. Livermore to Sumner, December 25, 1862, CSP.
76. Sumner to Lincoln, December 28, 1862, CSP; Livermore to Sumner, January 5, 1863, CSP; "Epitome of the Week," *Frank Leslie's Illustrated Newspaper,* January 31, 1863, 291.
77. *Frank Leslie's Illustrated Newspaper,* January 31, 1863, 291.
78. On the gift of Nell's "Bucks of America" flag to the Massachusetts Historical Society, see "Report on the Cabinet" (April 9, 1863), *Proceedings of the Massachusetts Historical Society,* vol. 7 (1863–1864), 24.
79. Pearson, *Life of John A. Andrew,* 2:63–90; Duncan, introduction to *Blue-Eyed Child,* 20–28; Stauffer, *Giants,* prologue.
80. Douglass, "Men of Color, To Arms!," in Foner, *Life and Writings of Frederick Douglass,* 3:318.
81. "The Army of the Potomac—Execution of Three Deserters," and "The Attack on Fort Wagner—The Stormers Advancing under Fire," *Harper's Weekly,* August 8, 1863, 509, 510. On "Battle Hymn," see Stauffer and Soskis, *Battle Hymn,* chap. 3. *Harper's Weekly* endorsed blacks as soldiers and as citizens from mid-1862. Blacks are "the only allies we have thus far met among the Southerners," it declared in June 1862. See "Our Black Friends Down South," *Harper's Weekly,* June 14, 1862, 373.
82. *Garrison: Story of His Life,* 4:148–49; Mayer, *All on Fire,* 583–85.
83. Harriet Jacobs ["Linda"], "Life among the Contrabands," *Liberator,* September 5, 1862. See also Jean Fagan Yellin, *Harriet Jacobs: A Life* (New York: Basic Books, 2004), 157–74; Frederick Douglass, *My Bondage and My Freedom,* ed. John Stauffer (New York: Modern Library, 2003), 201–2.
84. On the perishability of revolutionary time, see especially Davis, *The Problem of Slavery in the Age of Revolution,* 306–26.

"Constitution or No Constitution, Law or No Law"
The Boston Vigilance Committees, 1841–1861

DEAN GRODZINS

Boston antislavery activists established three successive, distinct vigilance committees, in 1841, 1846, and 1850, each dedicated to protecting fugitive slaves. Why did they favor this particular kind of organization for this purpose? Vigilance committees style themselves "committees of the whole," because they claim to act in the name of an entire people. On this basis, they assume a mandate to maintain law and order when the government, for reasons of incompetence, corruption, or bias, fails to do so.[1]

Boston activists were struggling with a dilemma. Two political values they cherished, human rights and rule of law, were in conflict, because the U.S. Constitution and federal legislation protected slavery. Some abolitionists resolved this dilemma by rejecting the authority of the Constitution and even advocating forceful resistance to federal law, but most friends of the fugitive refused to do either. Instead, they created vigilance committees, which allowed them to operate outside of legally established institutions and even to some degree in defiance of them, while still claiming to act in the name of the law, and made possible coalitions of activists with contradictory constitutional and political views. Yet such coalitions proved unstable, and, for antislavery purposes, vigilance committees turned out to have inherent limitations.

Vigilance committees have appeared at different times and in many places over the course of American history, and many, perhaps most, have had nothing to do with slavery. Two San Francisco vigilance committees, organized in 1851 and 1856, respectively, lynched criminals in the name of ending lawlessness in a Wild West boom town.[2] Two of the first recorded vigilance committees in Massachusetts were organized in response to anti-Catholic riots in August 1834 in which the Ursuline convent in Charlestown was burned; the nuns moved to Roxbury but were pursued by threats that a mob would come from Boston to attack them again. Prominent local men in Charlestown set up a vigilance committee to track down the original perpetrators, while others in Roxbury established a "Committee of Vigilance and Protection," which guarded the nuns' new house for weeks, until the threat of violence had passed.[3]

African Americans in New York City organized the first antislavery vigilance committee in November 1835 as a response to the failure of local courts to enforce laws that protected free black people from enslavement. According to its published charter, the objectives of the committee were to "ascertain . . . the extent to which the cruel practice of kidnapping . . . was being carried on" in New York—that is, to what extent free blacks were being seized under the "pretext of being fugitive slaves"—and to provide anyone under threat of enslavement with "such protection as the law will allow." The committee was not formally dedicated to helping fugitive slaves, except to guarantee that they were "claimed or proved as slaves by legal process."[4]

The committee operated publicly and in the name of the law. It therefore had nothing to do, officially, with the informal networks of activists that helped slaves escape to freedom and that came to be called (around 1840) "the Underground Railroad." Men and women involved in the latter activity knew that they were breaking the law, which is why they kept their doings clandestine. Yet individual members of the New York Committee of Vigilance were very active in the Underground Railroad. Its secretary and dominant figure, David Ruggles, personally helped hundreds of runaways to escape capture, among them the young Frederick Douglass.[5] This contradiction between the professed lawfulness of the New York committee and the willingness of its leaders to break the law seems to have produced little controversy in the organization, probably because most of its leaders, members, and donors were African Americans. Among free blacks, for whom enslavement represented an existential threat, a broad consensus existed that individuals had to be kept out of slavery by any means necessary, whether legal or illegal.

The New York committee served as the model for the vigilance committees of Boston. Here the black community was much smaller, however, both in absolute numbers and proportionally: not 16,000 African Americans making up 7 percent of the total city population, but only 2,000, making up 2 percent. It was also relatively poorer. As a consequence, Boston blacks never had enough people or the money to run an effective vigilance committee on their own. The only organization they founded and led that dealt with runaways, the New-England Freedom Association (NEFA), concentrated its efforts on raising money from white abolitionists to provide "destitute fugitives" with cash, food, clothing, and temporary housing. Boston blacks had long given fugitives such assistance, but only by straining their own limited resources. Starting in 1843, NEFA organized a series of successful charity concerts, "levees," and public lectures; then, in 1845, its secretary, Robert Wood, was accused of mishandling funds. The resulting controversy seems to have produced a fatal decline of white support. In August 1846, a NEFA spokesman announced that its treasury was "exhausted." Shortly afterward, its work was taken over by the second Boston Vigilance Committee.[6]

Whites provided most of the funds, leadership, and membership for all three Boston vigilance committees, and among whites no consensus existed over means and ends. The vigilance committee concept seems, in fact, to have had enduring appeal in Boston in part because ideologically divergent factions within the white antislavery movement found it useful and could, at least potentially, rally around it.

The legal problem of fugitive slaves in Massachusetts was defined by the U.S. Constitution, which declares, "No person held to service or labour in one state, under the laws thereof, escaping into another, shall, in consequence of any law or regulation therein, be discharged from such service or labour, but shall be delivered up on claim of the party to whom such service or labour may be due" (article 4, section 3, clause 2). In the 1840s and 1850s, antislavery leaders in Massachusetts would object that this "fugitive slave clause" imposed slave law upon them, but in February 1788, when a convention in Boston debated whether to ratify the Constitution, the provision excited no remark.

At the time, antislavery sentiment was rising in Massachusetts, and slavery would be declared extinct there in 1790. Some convention delegates objected strongly to two other proslavery provisions in the proposed constitution: the "three-fifths clause," by which slaves were counted toward representation in the House of Representatives and Electoral College, and the clause forbidding Congress to outlaw slave importations until at least 1808. Unlike these provisions, however, the fugitive slave clause seemed at the time to have no sectional implications. Two states bordering Massachusetts, Connecticut and New York, had substantial black slave populations, while significant numbers of indentured servants, to whom the clause might apply, lived in Massachusetts—many of them, in fact, emancipated slaves. Moreover, the wording of the fugitive slave clause and its placement in article 4, which details the obligations states owe to one another, suggested that each state would determine, according to its own laws, the process by which a "person held to service or labour" would be "delivered up."

As a result, no one seemed to fear that the clause would be abused by southern masters or their agents coming north to make false claims to ownership of free black residents. Instead, the principal threat to black freedom was seen as coming from "evil-minded" Yankees, especially merchants and seamen involved in the African or domestic slave trade, who might try to entrap local black sailors and offer them for sale out of state. To prevent such activity seems to have been the principal object of the state anti-kidnapping law enacted in 1785 and a law passed in 1787 that guaranteed to Massachusetts citizens the right to use the ancient common-law writ of personal replevin, which when served on someone holding a person "in duress" on the claim of owing labor, forced him to turn the detainee over to a sheriff until the claim could be adjudicated in claims court, which meant before a jury. Bay State kidnappers were also the focus of a law passed just weeks after the ratification convention concluded, which forbade Massachusetts citizens or residents from participating in the African slave trade, and granted "Relief to the Families of such unhappy Persons as may be kidnapped or decoyed away from this Commonwealth," by allowing families of the victims to sue the perpetrators for damages.[7]

The fugitive slave clause only became an issue in Massachusetts in 1793, when Congress approved the first federal Fugitive Slave Act.[8] It empowered slave holders or their agents to come into any free state, get a warrant, and "seize or arrest" their runaways. The slave holder or agent was then supposed to go before a magistrate—a federal judge or, as these were few and far between, a state judge or even a justice of the peace—to obtain a certificate authorizing the removal of the fugitive from the state. If after a summary hearing the magistrate was "satisfied" that the alleged fugitive really did "owe labor," he would issue the certificate. The law also established a stiff fine for anyone who "should obstruct or hinder" a fugitive's arrest or attempt a rescue, and it made anyone who "harbored or concealed" a known fugitive liable for a damage suit from the master.[9]

This law was never popular in Massachusetts, and no fugitive was ever returned from the state under its provisions. Only four attempts to do so were even made, and all failed. In 1794 and again in 1837, mobs rescued the alleged fugitives during the certificate hearings in Boston.[10] In 1820, Camillus Griffith, the agent of a Virginia slaveholder, tried to seize a man named Randolph in New Bedford, only to find himself arrested and convicted of assault, battery, and false imprisonment. Although the Massachusetts Supreme Court eventually overturned the conviction, ruling that Griffith had acted within his constitutional rights, Randolph remained a free man.[11] Again, the right to the writ of personal replevin stayed on the statute books in Massachusetts, despite efforts to repeal it as a relic of medieval English law, because its promise of a jury trial to alleged runaways made the Fugitive Slave Act potentially more cumbersome and expensive for claimants to invoke.[12]

Most fugitive slave cases in the state, however, appear not to have involved the 1793 law. They concerned stowaways on Massachusetts ships that traded with southern ports. One such case helped prompt the creation of the first Boston vigilance committee.[13]

In May 1841, a rough-hewn Cape Cod sailor named Higgins walked into the Marlboro Chapel in Boston, where the Massachusetts Abolition Society was holding its annual meeting. He spoke with a number of those assembled, among them the Reverend Charles T. Torrey. From Higgins, Torrey learned to his dismay that a fugitive slave had just been taken out of Boston.

Higgins had served as first mate on a Boston-based schooner, the *Wellington*, which traded regularly in North Carolina. On the return leg of its latest voyage, the crew had found a slave named John Torrence hidden in the hold. The captain, Higgins's brother, feared that he would be charged with slave stealing and so decided to bring Torrence back to the South after finishing his business in Boston. While the *Wellington* lay at anchor in the harbor, Torrence had been locked below deck, but he escaped, dove overboard, and tried to swim to shore. Instead, he was picked up by sailors who thought he was a seaman jumping ship. They brought him back to the *Wellington*, where the captain had him clapped in irons, set armed crew members to guard him, and placed a keg of powder on the deck, ready to be lit if anyone made a rescue attempt. The night before Higgins talked to Torrey, the *Wellington* had sailed with Torrence for North Carolina. Higgins now wanted abolitionists to give him $700 so he could buy Torrence's freedom.

Torrey suspected not philanthropy but a swindle, and he was outraged that Torrence had been illegally detained; none of the *Wellington* crew was an agent of his master, and so none of them had the authority, under the terms of the Fugitive Slave Act, to arrest him. Torrey promptly went to the police and charged Higgins and his brother, the captain, with violating the 1785 Massachusetts statute against kidnapping, yet a Suffolk County grand jury refused to indict. Torrey accused the jurors of having "DISREGARDED THE LAW *and the facts*."[14] Just as this case was unfolding, David Ruggles, secretary of the New York Committee of Vigilance, visited Boston to raise money for the *Mirror of Liberty*, his magazine devoted to the fugitive slave issue. On June 2, Boston black leaders welcomed him at a public meeting at which they passed resolutions praising him and his work. The conjunction of his visit and the Torrence case seems to have inspired Torrey to "do as our New-York brethren have done."[15]

In response to Torrey's call, a "representation from various classes of our citizens, white and colored, (the latter of whom were quite numerous)," gathered in Marlboro Chapel on June 4. They voted unanimously to establish a vigilance committee authorized to "secure persons of color the enjoyment of their constitutional and legal rights" through the use of "legal, peaceful, and christian methods." The group appointed at least thirteen men to the committee, three of them black. Torrey dominated the proceedings, proposing all the resolutions, and was named secretary, the position Ruggles held in New York. He was appointed agent as well, making him responsible for fundraising, but he apparently decided not to become the overall leader of the committee. Instead, he steered the group to offer the chairmanship to Francis Jackson, a prominent white abolitionist businessman who was not present.[16]

Torrey promptly began soliciting contributions and issued a call for abolitionists in other Massachusetts seaport towns to create auxiliary committees, but he almost immediately ran afoul of antislavery factions that had recently emerged over questions of strategy and policy. On one side were abolitionists allied with William Lloyd Garrison, a founder of the movement and the editor of the influential antislavery weekly *The Liberator*. On the other were those who rejected Garrison's leadership, owing partly to his anticlericism and advocacy of woman's rights, but above all to his rejection of electoral politics and his denunciation of the U.S. Constitution as a proslavery document. In 1840, Garrison's critics had withdrawn from the various antislavery societies that his allies controlled and had established new ones.

Torrey was an evangelical preacher who favored electoral activism—he had helped to found the small, radically antislavery Liberty Party—and he numbered among Garrison's harshest critics. He had broken with the Massachusetts Anti-Slavery Society (MASS), which Garrisonians controlled, and played a large role in establishing the rival Massachusetts Abolition Society (MAS).[17] He knew that other MAS members would support his vigilance committee and in late June convinced some of them, notably the Baptist revivalist Nathaniel Colver, to hold a rally at the Tremont Chapel in support of the project.[18] Yet he also knew that the committee could not do its work effectively without help from Garrisonians, who had money, strong connections to the Underground Railroad, and the support of most Boston black leaders.

Torrey therefore took pains in a public letter to explain that his committee had "no connection" with either the MASS or the MAS and to urge that abolitionists unite on the fugitive slave issue, which was of "*common interest.*"[19] He made sure that the African American journalist William C. Nell, who worked closely with Garrison at the *Liberator*, received a seat on the executive committee. His most important gesture, however, was to offer the chairmanship of his committee to Jackson, who was president of the MASS and personally so close to Garrison that the latter would one day name a son after him.

These attempts at bridge building worked only with Garrison's black allies. The most prominent of them, Nell, agreed to serve on Torrey's committee and wrote sympathetically about it for the *Liberator*. Among white abolitionists, the story was different. Jackson refused the chairmanship, while Garrison signaled to other friends to keep their distance. It was "unfortunate for the prosperity of this committee," he wrote in the *Liberator*, "that one so decidedly objectionable as is Charles T. Torrey to so large a portion of abolitionists of this Commonwealth, should be its Secretary and Agent."[20]

Garrisonian opposition seems to have killed Torrey's vigilance committee, which apparently had ceased operations by December 1841, when Torrey left Massachusetts to continue elsewhere his work on behalf of fugitive slaves. His committee never got to prove its public commitment to lawful action, which, in truth, seemed rather weak. Torrey was active in the Underground Railroad, and he appears to have been none too careful about separating his legal and illegal activities. In his first public statement as secretary, he expressed the desire to "establish an active correspondence with the friends of the slave, on the *great lines of northern travel,* through New England"—in other words, to build an Underground Railroad line. After leaving Massachusetts, Torrey moved to the Washington, D.C., area, where he helped to run scores of slaves to freedom. Eventually, he was arrested in Baltimore and convicted of slave stealing. He died in a Maryland prison in May 1846.[21]

The year after the failure of the first Boston Vigilance Committee, a final attempt was made to enforce the Fugitive Slave Act of 1793 in Massachusetts. In October 1842, James Gray, a young Virginia slaveholder, came to Boston in pursuit of George Latimer, who had run away from him a month earlier. According to the law, Gray should have applied for a warrant and tried to arrest Latimer himself. Instead, he charged Latimer with theft, so that the Boston authorities could make the arrest. Only after Latimer was in custody did Gray claim him as his slave. On October 22, following the 1793 procedure, he applied to Joseph Story, the U.S. Supreme Court justice presiding over the federal Circuit Court in Boston, for a certificate of removal. Story ruled that Gray would need an affidavit from Virginia and gave him until November 5 to obtain it. In the interim, he ordered Gray to keep Latimer in his custody; Gray promptly hired the sheriff of Suffolk County to detain Latimer on his behalf in the Leverett Street jail. Story then fell ill, however, and the certificate hearing was postponed. After various legal maneuvers, it was rescheduled for November 21 before the federal district judge, Peleg Sprague.[22]

Agitation against Latimer's detention started immediately upon his arrest and grew as the weeks passed. A large, raucous protest meeting was held in Faneuil Hall on October 28; angry crowds milled continually around the jail and followed Gray through the streets; abolitionists started a special newspaper devoted to the case, *The Latimer Journal and*

North Star, which circulated widely; and antislavery lawyers repeatedly challenged Latimer's detention. Finally, on November 17, the sheriff, under enormous political pressure and fearing a riot, ordered Latimer returned to Gray's personal custody, declaring that he would never again allow a fugitive slave to be held in his jail. Gray knew that he could not restrain Latimer himself, so he reluctantly accepted an offer to sell him his freedom for just $400—Gray complained that Latimer was worth nearly twice that—and left town.[23]

The uproar over Latimer's detention grew so large in part owing to resentment over a decision that the U.S. Supreme Court had handed down seven months earlier. The author of the principal opinion in *Prigg v. Pennsylvania* was the same jurist who had ordered Latimer into Gray's custody, Justice Story. Prigg, a slave catcher from Maryland, had seized Margaret Morgan and her children as runaway slaves in Pennsylvania and, following the procedures of the federal law, had applied to a local justice of the peace for a certificate of removal. The justice of the peace had refused to grant him one, however, because a state anti-kidnapping law required that Morgan be given the chance to prove herself and her children free. In response, Prigg had defiantly taken his captives to Maryland without a certificate. A Pennsylvania grand jury had indicted him for kidnapping, but Maryland had refused to extradite him. Story ruled that Prigg's indictment could not stand because the Pennsylvania law was unconstitutional. He argued that it obstructed the working of a federal law, the act of 1793, and violated the right of slaveholders, guaranteed in the fugitive slave clause, to seize their human property wherever in the United States they found it.[24]

Story had long been hailed as the greatest legal mind from Massachusetts, but his decision provoked dismay in his home state. It seemed to void all legal limitations to slave catching, including the Massachusetts law guaranteeing fugitives the right to the writ of replevin and therefore to jury trials. Story's ruling was so proslavery that it may have inspired Gray to seek him out when requesting a certificate to remove Latimer from the state.

Antislavery activists, however, took note of remarks that Story made in his argument that the rendition of fugitive slaves should be regarded as exclusively a federal matter.[25] By this logic, the U.S. government could not require state officials to assist in the return of runaways. After Latimer's release, Massachusetts antislavery activists seized on this idea. They held conventions in every county and organized the largest petition drive in state history, sending one appeal to the legislature and another to the U.S. Congress. In the end, more than sixty thousand people signed the first petition and nearly as many the second. The "Great Massachusetts" petition resulted in an act known as the Latimer Law, written by Charles Francis Adams, a state representative and the son and grandson of presidents. Enacted in March 1843, it forbade any public official in Massachusetts from "aiding or abetting the arrest or detention of any person claimed as a fugitive from slavery" and barred any jail or public building in Massachusetts from being used to detain runaways.

In Massachusetts, the Latimer Law hampered the operation of the Fugitive Slave Act of 1793, which relied primarily on state and local resources, both for officials who would execute it and, since no federal prisons yet existed, for jails where fugitives could be detained. Another major demand of the Latimer petitions, however, required action from Congress and so went nowhere: the passage of "such amendments to the Constitution of the United States as shall forever separate the people of Massachusetts from all connection with slavery."[26]

During the months of agitation surrounding Latimer's case, no one proposed reviving the Boston vigilance committee. Antislavery activists apparently saw no reason to do so. The basic problem exposed by Latimer's detention, they believed, was less that state laws to protect fugitives were not being enforced, but that the Supreme Court had unjustly interpreted the U.S. Constitution. The creation of a new vigilance committee would have to wait until September 1846, when another stowaway case occurred.

George had been found hidden in the hold of the brig *Ottoman* as it carried goods back to its home port of Boston from New Orleans. The captain, James Hannum, feared that he would be charged with slave stealing if he did not return "the darkey," as Hannum called him, to Louisiana. He ordered George confined with the intention of transferring him to a South-bound ship, but the *Ottoman* encountered none before reaching Boston. When Hannum got there, he feared trouble from abolitionists and so told no one what he was doing except his employer, the Boston merchant Jonathan Pearson, who approved his actions. Meanwhile, Hannum had made sure to get George off the *Ottoman* before it sailed into the harbor. He had him taken, by pilot boat, to Light House Island, and then to Spectacle Island, where Hannum and his crew guarded him.

Things went smoothly until George slipped away and stole the captain's boat. Hannum spotted him sailing it to nearby South Boston Point, seized another boat and, with his crew, gave chase. George got ashore, but his pursuers landed right behind him. They ran hot on his heels for two miles "through corn fields and over fences." Just as he reached a bridge to downtown Boston, they tackled him. Onlookers gawked. The captain shouted that George was a thief, and George, distrusting whites and seeing no black faces in the crowd, hung his head. Hannum had him carried back to Spectacle Island.

Yet the captain's scheme had been exposed. One of the handful of island residents realized that George was a fugitive slave and alerted the city police. By the next morning, abolitionists had obtained a warrant to arrest Hannum for kidnapping, but the Suffolk County sheriff delayed serving it. Meanwhile, an interracial crew of armed men steamed into the harbor on the *General Lincoln* to effect a rescue. They were too late. Hannum had already put George on a swift ship heading south.[27]

When news of what had happened spread, the scale of the public reaction showed the impact of the Latimer agitation in 1842–1843; it also indicated rising concern over the spread of slavery as a consequence of the annexation of Texas in December 1845 and the resulting war with Mexico, which had been declared the following May. While the Torrence case had attracted only a small gathering of abolitionists in Marlboro Chapel, on September 22 the George case produced an "immense" assembly in Faneuil Hall, the moot hall of Boston since the Revolution. Calling the meeting to order was none other than the aged congressman and former U.S. president John Quincy Adams, father of Charles Francis, the author of the Latimer Law, who also spoke. Although the two Adamses and others at the meeting were obviously upset that a fugitive had been returned from Boston at all, the resolutions that the meeting approved and most of the speeches did not object to the act as such, only to its having been undertaken "without any pretence of legal authority."[28]

One of the speakers, however, questioned whether any law could have sanctioned George's return to slavery. The aristocratic orator Wendell Phillips was a close ally of Garrison who, like him, rejected the authority of the Constitution because it was a "pro-slavery compact." He pointed out that if Hannum had only carried in his pocket an affidavit signed by George's master, everything he did would have been lawful. The time had come, Phillips declared, "when self-respect, duty to the slave, and duty to

God demand of us to announce that, Constitution or no Constitution, law or no law, *humanity* shall be paramount in Massachusetts." Yet his views did not reflect those of the meeting. When he dismissed the Constitution as a "farce," the audience turned on him, shouting and hissing.[29] Nonetheless, when the meeting voted to establish a new vigilance committee, it appointed him one of the forty members. He declined to take part, however, as did two other white Garrisonians; a fourth, the MASS president, Francis Jackson, who had refused to chair Torrey's vigilance committee, did agree to serve on this one, as did Garrison's black ally William C. Nell, but neither man appears to have been active in its affairs.[30]

Garrison's friends probably kept their distance from the organization because of the political beliefs of its dominant figure, the social reformer Dr. Samuel Gridley Howe. Howe had headed the committee of arrangements for the Faneuil Hall meeting and written the resolutions approved there, including the one that created the vigilance committee; he became overall chairman of the new committee as well as of its executive committee. Not only did Howe despise Garrison, his ambition for the vigilance committee was that it would use the fugitive slave issue to recast electoral politics in the North along antislavery lines. Many of Garrison's allies, like Jackson and Phillips, refused to vote and so did not consider this task their proper work.

Garrisonian opposition had scuttled Torrey's vigilance committee, which had relied exclusively on the support of abolitionists—that is, those who supported "immediate emancipation" in the South. Howe's committee was more politically diverse. He was very active in the antislavery or "conscience" wing of the Massachusetts Whig Party and so could get support from his political friends, who hated slavery but were not abolitionists, because they believed they had no constitutional right to interfere with slavery in the states. Among those on his committee who held this position were two lawyers and rising Massachusetts political stars: Charles Sumner, who would become the leading opponent of slavery in the U.S. Senate, and John A. Andrew, who would serve as governor during the Civil War. Of the four African Americans on Howe's committee, all apparently were active in electoral politics. Like Howe himself, all would support the antislavery Free Soil Party when it was organized in 1848: Nell, who voted and would even run as a Free Soil candidate for the legislature in 1850, despite his close association with the nonvoting Garrison; the wealthy caterer J. B. Smith, later a state senator; the lawyer Robert Morris Jr.; and the pamphleteer Benjamin Weeden.[31]

Howe laid out his ambitions for the vigilance committee in an "Address to the People of the Northern States," which he wrote in October. The committee endorsed and published it, sending copies to newspaper editors across New England, all members of the Massachusetts legislature, all Massachusetts representatives in Congress, and every merchant listed in the Boston City Directory, among others.[32] Howe's "Address" conceded that the committee had a mandate only to prevent "fugitive slaves from being illegally carried away from Boston" but insisted that "our sense of duty, our love of our fellow-beings, and our obligations to God . . . bid us not to stop here." Howe therefore laid out a broad political agenda: free state voters must "oppose the election" of any candidate for any office not pledged "to strive for the immediate abrogation of all laws and constitutional provisions by which the Free States are involved in the guilt of slavery," and Northerners must organize a "NATIONAL LEAGUE FOR FREEDOM, uniting in a permanent organization all who would strive to realize the IDEAL OF AMERICAN LIBERTY."[33]

In regard specifically to fugitive slaves, Howe's "Address" made equally grand proposals. It called on the free states to repudiate *Prigg v. Pennsylvania* and pass new antislavery laws, the most ambitious of which was to confiscate "all ships in which human beings shall be illegally carried from a free State into slavery." Yet when the "Address" considered what to do with runaway slaves in the North, its proposals were modest. It recommended that free people avoid giving slave catchers any "aid or counsel" while offering "comfort and help to any fugitive slaves who may be thrown upon our hospitality."[34] Neither action was obviously illegal. The Fugitive Slave Act required no one to assist a slave catcher and only condemned the concealment or "harboring" of a runaway. Although southern courts tended to interpret "harboring" broadly, as referring to any form of assistance, in northern and even federal courts, "harboring" seems to have been construed more narrowly, as assisting a fugitive to evade capture. Simply giving a runaway slave "comfort and help"—food, clothing, money, even employment—was not seen as a criminal act outside of the South.[35]

The direct dealings that Howe's vigilance committee had with fugitives fell into this legal gray area, until recently occupied by the New-England Freedom Association, in which three of the four black members of the committee, Weeden, J. B. Smith, and Nell, had been active. The committee assigned its general agent, John W. Browne, to handle fugitive cases, and he recorded his efforts in an account book that he kept from November

1846 to April 1847. The runaways who came to him (all men, mostly young) sometimes got clothing, sometimes small sums of money, and most often help finding jobs. He would set them up with prospective employers and track their progress for weeks or months. Browne functioned, as one historian has aptly remarked, like a one-man Urban League. Over six months, he worked with nineteen runaways, seventeen of whom he helped, and two of whom he came to suspect were actually imposters—free blacks claiming to be fugitives to trick the committee out of money.[36]

These are not large numbers and almost certainly did not represent all of the fugitives who came to or through Boston that winter. Perhaps some did not approach Browne because he was not authorized to help them with their most pressing need—to escape. Hiding fugitives or helping them to leave the country would have been, after all, against the law. The records of the committee show that it considered helping only one runaway slave get to Canada, and his was a special case.

George Kirk, a fugitive from Georgia, had stowed away on a ship to New York but was discovered and detained by the captain. When New York abolitionists challenged the detention in federal court, Judge Halmer Emmons ordered Kirk released, because the captain had no authority to detain him under the 1793 law. The police then arrested Kirk under an old New York state fugitive slave statute. Abolitionists challenged the arrest before Judge Emmons, who ruled that because the *Prigg* decision made renditions exclusively a federal matter, the state law was unconstitutional. Kirk was released again and abolitionists hurried him to Boston. There, the vigilance committee received word that Kirk's master was going to send a properly authorized agent to claim him under the Fugitive Slave Act. Howe therefore called a meeting to debate the "propriety" of giving Kirk money for a ticket to Canada. This would have been an illegal act, yet it would have been in support of two judicial decisions that committee members liked. Finally, they decided to tell Kirk what they knew, and if he elected to flee they would help him. No record indicates whether Kirk took them up on the offer.[37]

Meanwhile, none of Howe's grand political plans were coming to fruition, largely because his fellow Whigs would not support them. In October 1846, the committee authorized Howe to ask John Quincy Adams to become president of his proposed National League of Freedom. At the next meeting, however, he reported back that eminent "friends of the cause" (meaning antislavery Whigs) had "induced" him not to call on the former president, telling him that "the time had not arrived for the formation of a League." In February 1847, the committee got up a petition to the Whig-controlled Massachusetts legislature urging it to pass a ship-confiscation law, but soon learned that "the Judiciary Committee of the Legislature were not prepared to bring in any bill like that suggested by the Committee."[38] Howe's frustration with the Whigs' caution would lead him to abandon them in 1848 and help to establish the antislavery Free Soil Party.

The committee did not even succeed with its more modest goal of getting Captain Hannum prosecuted for kidnapping. In September and October 1846, Browne spent several days collecting statements from a large number of witnesses to Hannum's detention of George in Boston. The testimony was presented to a Massachusetts grand jury, which, however, refused to hand down an indictment. "It is evident," complained Howe, "that the question of personal liberty, at least in the case of a colored man, is considered of little moment in Massachusetts."[39] By the spring of 1847, the committee was only doing welfare work for fugitives, which must have seemed a letdown. Browne resigned as general agent and handed his records over to J. B. Smith, who assumed the new title of "Relief Agent." Not long afterward, the vigilance committee stopped holding meetings.[40]

On September 18, 1850, a new federal Fugitive Slave Act took effect. Southerners in Congress had designed it to correct what they considered to be major flaws in the 1793 legislation. It relied not on state judges and local magistrates to issue arrest warrants and certificates of removal, but on commissioners of the federal circuit courts, who were under federal supervision and could be dismissed immediately for showing antislavery tendencies. Like the judges and magistrates of the old law, a commissioner would hold a summary hearing to determine the validity of a slaveholder's claim to a fugitive, but now the fugitive's testimony would be explicitly excluded as evidence, and the commissioner would receive a financial incentive, in the form of a higher fee—$10 versus $5—to decide for the claimant over the fugitive. The 1793 law had required the claimant himself to execute the arrest warrant against a fugitive and personally to detain him; now, federal marshals could execute the warrant and hold the fugitive in custody on the claimant's behalf. The new law also substantially increased penalties for helping a runaway to escape or resist capture. Members of the Underground Railroad, who previously had to worry about going to prison only if they were arrested in the South, now could be sentenced in federal court to six months behind bars.⁴¹

In response to this legislation, "colored citizens" of Boston met at the Belknap Street Church on October 4 and unanimously approved a series of defiant resolutions. These called for the "citizens of Boston," black and white, to gather in Faneuil Hall and "send forth, in the ear of all Christendom, their opinion of the Fugitive Slave Bill, and their intention to DISOBEY its decrees." The resolutions also called for the creation of "a League of Freedom, composed of all those who are ready to resist the law, rescue and protect the slave at every hazard."⁴² By implication, the Faneuil Hall meeting would establish the new body.

William C. Nell wrote these resolutions. A veteran of both the 1841 and 1846 vigilance committees, he may have proposed a "League of Freedom" because by this point he associated the name "Vigilance Committee" with failure. His resolutions indicate, however, that he had a deeper reason for offering the new name. Vigilance committees claimed to uphold the law when the government failed to do so; in this case, the government was threatening to enforce an unjust law. Nell's resolutions therefore demanded outright resistance to the law and the government—in other words, revolution. His address prefacing the resolutions commended the examples of "the Revolutionary Fathers, in resisting British oppression," the "Poles, Greeks, and South Americans, in their struggles for freedom," and the 1848 republican uprisings in France, Italy, and Hungary. Unlike the "League of Freedom" Howe had proposed four years before, Nell's version was for revolutionists. Although Nell's resolutions did not explicitly endorse violent resistance to the law, they did so implicitly, and J. B. Smith, who also spoke at the Belknap meeting, was loudly cheered when he "urged every fugitive to arm himself with a revolver."⁴³

As Nell wanted, Bostonians, both black and white, soon did hold a meeting in Faneuil Hall and there did create a resistance organization. It was not, however, the "League of Freedom," but the "Committee of Vigilance and Safety." This new vigilance committee was principally the brainchild of the white pastor of the largest congregation in Boston—a racially integrated "free church" where Nell often worshipped—the Reverend Theodore Parker. Parker had served with Nell on the failed 1846 vigilance committee, yet he evidently thought the concept still had life in it. In particular, he hoped that it would help him to accomplish a longstanding ambition to bridge the major divide between antislavery activists such as Garrison, Jackson, and Phillips, who rejected the authority of the U.S. Constitution and, by extension, electoral politics, and those such as Howe and John A. Andrew, who accepted its authority and worked within the electoral system.

Parker viewed the Constitution as a particular historical expression of what he called "the American Idea" of freedom and democracy. He saw it as a valuable national charter worthy of allegiance, especially because the governmental system it established, characterized by federalism, checks and balances, and democracy, accomplished what he considered to be an extraordinarily difficult yet worthy feat: that of balancing "national unity of action" with "individual variety of action." Nonetheless, he thought that Americans were morally obligated to disregard the Constitution where it contradicted the American Idea, as in the fugitive slave clause; he was sure that, eventually, they would perfect the Constitution by rewriting it. Parker's flexible outlook enabled him to declare irenically to an antislavery convention in 1848, "Some men will try political action. The action of the people, of the nation, must be political action. It may be constitutional, it may be unconstitutional. I see not why men need to quarrel about that."[44] Moreover, he had forged pastoral connections with antislavery leaders on both sides of the constitutional and political split. For example, he had baptized one of Howe's daughters in 1846 and, two years later, had helped to conduct the funeral service for one of Garrison's daughters. Both men and their wives attended his preaching.

Personally, Parker agreed with Nell that the new Fugitive Slave Act should be defied. In "A Sermon of Conscience," preached on September 22, just days after the law took effect, he explained that one's obligation to obey the law of God as it was revealed to one's own conscience trumped any obligation to uphold human law, even if one had pledged to do so under oath. Parker also declared that the "man who attacks me to reduce me to slavery, in that moment of attack alienates his right to life, and if I were the fugitive and could escape in no other way, I would kill him with as little compunction as I would drive a mosquito from my face."[45] Privately, he seems to have resolved to use lethal force, if necessary, to protect any fugitive placed under his protection. In late October 1850, when the famous runaway slave Ellen Craft hid in his house, he kept a sword and loaded gun handy.

Yet Parker knew that many potential allies, particularly white political abolitionists active in the Free Soil Party, thought differently than did he or Nell. Free Soilers continued to accept the authority of the U.S. Constitution and eschewed law-breaking and violence. Although they opposed the Fugitive Slave Act, they admitted, at least theoretically, the obligation that the fugitive slave clause of the Constitution imposed on them. Parker seems to have recognized that such people would never join a "League of Freedom" but could be persuaded to join a vigilance committee—a resistance organization committed, officially at least, to legal action.

In the weeks leading up to the Faneuil Hall meeting, Parker carefully built support for such an organization. In the "Sermon of Conscience," he declared, "I will do all in my power to rescue any fugitive slave from the hands of any officer who attempts to return him to bondage. . . . I will serve as head, as foot, or as hand to any body of serious and earnest men, who will go with me . . . in this work." Parker made sure to emphasize that they would use "no weapons but their hands."[46] He reiterated this call on October 6 in a special church announcement: "I will act with any body of serious or decent men . . . in any mode not involving the use of deadly weapons, to nullify and defeat the operation of this law."[47] Parker wrote the call for the Faneuil Hall meeting, which appeared in the Boston papers on October 7; it was endorsed by 384 prominent Bostonians, white and black, although interestingly not by William Nell.[48] At about this time, Parker also drafted resolutions to propose to the meeting. Three of them presented objections to the Fugitive Slave Act, while the fourth called for the creation of a "Committee of Vigilance & Safety."[49]

Calling this a "Vigilance & Safety" committee, as opposed to a committee simply of "Vigilance," seems to have been an ideological maneuver on Parker's part. "Committees of Safety" had appeared throughout the colonies during the Revolutionary War, their mission to find and punish Loyalist traitors. With the words "& Safety," therefore, Parker claimed the mantle of the founding fathers and implicitly charged slave catchers with betraying their ideals. At the same time, he seemed to be signaling his sympathy with Nell's claim that the current situation was revolutionary.[50]

Yet Parker's draft resolutions avoided such inflammatory language. They condemned the new Fugitive Slave Act as unconstitutional and unjust, but did not directly call for people to disobey it. Instead, they asserted, "we will not entertain the opinion that any Citizen can be found in this city . . . so destitute of love for his country & his race, & so devoid of all sense of Justice as to endeavor to return a fugitive slave under this law." This wording dodged any responsibility for defying the law—it seemed to say "resistance happens"—and was deliberately vague about what such resistance should look like. Nell's proposed League would have been authorized to "resist the law," whereas Parker's "Committee" would merely attempt by all "just means" to "secure the fugitives & colored inhabitants of this city . . . from any invasion of their rights by persons acting under this new law."

In the end, Parker presented to the Faneuil Hall meeting only his fourth resolution, which created the new committee. In crafting its final form, he made its language even more ambiguous. It now authorized the organization to "take all measures which [its members] shall deem expedient to protect the colored people of this city in the enjoyment of their lives and liberties." Did these "measures" involve law breaking? Had the committee been authorized to protect the liberty of "fugitive slaves," the answer would have been "Probably." Had it been authorized to protect the liberty of "colored citizens of Massachusetts," in other words, to keep those blacks who were legally free from being falsely seized as slaves, the answer would have been "No." But Parker used the words "the colored people of this city." This formulation both challenged the assumption of the Fugitive Slave Act that all blacks were slaves unless proven otherwise and, as Parker intended, gave the new vigilance committee a hazy mandate.

Parker turned over the task of writing the other resolutions, which criticized the Fugitive Slave Act, to the young attorney Richard Henry Dana Jr., who was already highly regarded in the Boston legal world and had a history of interest in fugitive slaves. One of his first cases before the bar, in 1841, had been to work with Charles Torrey to try to indict Higgins and his brother for kidnapping. Yet Dana firmly believed in upholding the U.S. Constitution and, more generally, law and order. He would endorse only legal acts on behalf of fugitives. Dana was exactly the kind of ally that Parker feared alienating with language of "resistance." Letting him write the final version of the resolutions was apparently a bid for his support.

Dana's resolutions resembled those of Parker—they also express incredulity that any Massachusetts citizen would "take part in returning a fugitive under this law"—but with some notable shifts of emphasis. They were more legalistic in tone, denouncing the Fugitive Slave Act for depriving "men of their liberty without due process of law" and for being "inconsistent with the purposes of the Constitution . . . which was ordained to establish justice, and secure the blessings of liberty." Dana's resolutions pledged "aid, co-operation, and relief" specifically "to our colored fellow-citizens who may be endangered by this law." Because fugitives were not "fellow citizens," this wording suggests that Dana's major concern was with the kidnapping of those who were legally free. Finally, Dana added a resolution calling for the "INSTANT REPEAL" of the Fugitive Slave Act at the next session of Congress—a demand that neither Parker nor Nell had made, in part because they were less committed than Dana to legal process, but also because they knew that a repeal would not happen any time soon. In fact, the Fugitive Slave Act would stay on the books until 1864.

By the time the Faneuil Hall gathering took place on October 14, the success of Parker's coalition-building strategy was apparent. The "immense" meeting enthusiastically passed Dana's resolutions and cheered denunciations of the Fugitive Slave Act from across the antislavery political spectrum. As at the Faneuil Hall meeting in 1846 that created Howe's vigilance committee, Charles Francis Adams played a prominent role. This time, the author of the Latimer Law, who was as firmly committed as Dana to upholding the U.S. Constitution and law and order, presided over the proceedings and gave one of the major speeches. He criticized the new legislation for placing "one entire class of our population . . . out of the pale of the law's protection," yet he conceded that the fugitive slave clause of the Constitution "inhibits legislation in the free states which would cut off the slave relation," or the personal power of masters to "recover" their slaves. He urged "no measures of violence or excess" but called on the meeting "to consider a course of measures to secure the houses of many of our citizens who have been filled with anguish," and, "above all," to "nerve yourselves to the duty of labouring without ceasing for the repeal of this odious law."[51]

Wendell Phillips also spoke. At the 1846 Faneuil Hall meeting, he had caused a stir by insisting that fugitives should never be returned to their masters, regardless of the law, and for dismissing the Constitution as a "farce." Although his views on the Constitution had not changed, he now denounced the Fugitive Slave Act as "utterly unconstitutional": "We are not here for other issues; we beg, on our knees, for the poor boon of the constitution."[52] Perhaps Parker, Phillips's neighbor and friend, had persuaded him to be conciliatory.

As the meeting drew to a close, Parker got what he wanted. He offered his resolution calling for the creation of the Committee of Vigilance and Safety, and it passed without dissent.[53] As the audience began to file out, the Baptist evangelist Nathaniel Colver, pastor of the Tremont Temple, rose to speak. Perhaps this old friend of Charles Torrey had been asked to give a benediction, but he had something else in mind. He was evidently frustrated with Parker's success in keeping the meeting from making a clear pronouncement on whether the return of a fugitive slave was ever legally or constitutionally justified. Colver had led a series of highly successful "revivals of religion" and had learned from that experience how to force people to make a choice by stating the alternatives in stark terms.[54] He therefore spontaneously proposed an additional resolution: "*Constitution or no Constitution, law or no law, we will not allow a fugitive slave to be taken from Massachusetts.*"[55]

When Phillips had made a similar declaration at the 1846 meeting, the audience had turned on him. Now the crowd, or at least those still in the hall, thundered "AYE!" and the meeting adjourned.[56]

Parker's Committee of Vigilance and Safety grew far larger than the previous two Boston vigilance committees combined. The Faneuil Hall meeting appointed 50 members, authorizing them to "add to their numbers, if future exigencies shall require it." A few months later, the committee published a broadside listing 157 members, and eventually, the number topped 200.[57] Under Parker's leadership as the de facto permanent chair of its executive committee, the group successfully reached out to a range of abolitionists who either had never worked together before, or had not done so in a long time. Dana became a member, as did other political abolitionists such as Howe and John A. Andrew; abolitionists who rejected the authority of the Constitution also joined, including Phillips, who agreed to sit on the executive committee, and Francis Jackson, who became treasurer and the chair of the finance committee. African American leaders, all dedicated to forceful resistance to the law, became very active in the organization, among them Nell, J. B. Smith, Robert Morris, and Lewis Hayden. Non-resistants, who eschewed violence, were also on the committee, most notably Garrison himself.

The ideological diversity of this committee would prove to be both its great strength and its great weakness. It had wide appeal, attracting ministers, newspaper editors, publishers, lawyers, and politicians. Not committed to one mode of action to help fugitive slaves, it came to perform a dizzying variety of functions, which kept it busy until the outbreak of the Civil War. On the one hand, it operated as a legal, public organization. It printed the names of its members in the newspapers, organized public meetings, and even took care to get its accounts audited. It lobbied the state legislature for new laws to protect fugitive slaves, paid lawyers to defend runaways and those prosecuted for rescuing them, and collected money in churches across the commonwealth in order to provide destitute fugitives with food, shelter, clothing, and firewood. It also organized three successful rescues of runaways being illegally detained on ships in Boston Harbor. On the other hand, the committee incited antislavery mob action, arranged to hide fugitives from the authorities, helped to alert the black community when slave catchers were discovered in town and paid spies to watch them, and gave nearly a hundred fugitives money explicitly and specifically for the purpose of fleeing to Canada.[58]

Yet despite its effectiveness, the committee would also be wracked by internal ideological strife that would paralyze it at critical junctures. Among the most vocal dissenters turned out to be Richard Henry Dana, who resigned from the committee in 1851 to protest its willingness to endorse the use of force to accomplish its goals.[59] The organization had the greatest trouble, however, deciding what to do when fugitives in Boston were arrested.

In February 1851, the fugitive Shadrach Minkins was captured and brought before a commissioner, but rescued by a black mob. The federal government would prosecute three members of the vigilance committee for this "flagitious offense"—Lewis Hayden, Robert Morris, and the white newspaper editor Elizur Wright—and the committee would create a special legal committee to defend them. The vigilance committee did not, however, organize the rescue, which appears to have been Hayden's own, spontaneously conceived plan.[60] In April 1851, when another fugitive, Thomas Sims, was arrested, and again in May 1854, when Anthony Burns was seized, some members of the committee wanted to assault the Boston Court House, where each was held, or at least try to bribe the jailors into freeing them, but as a whole the membership could never reach a consensus, and both Sims and Burns were returned to bondage.

In both cases, antislavery opinion generally blamed the vigilance committee and its leaders for indecisiveness. As the abolitionist Anne Weston remarked sarcastically after the Sims rendition, "Theodore Parker has shrunk in the *wetting*."[61] Eventually, even Parker stopped trying to get all the different antislavery factions to work together in a single organization. He continued, however, to support divergent approaches to antislavery action. In the late 1850s he campaigned for the Republican Party, which was deeply committed to a constitutional approach, while secretly giving money and weapons to John Brown, who aimed to overthrow the "Slave Power" with revolutionary violence.

Another Brown backer, the Worcester abolitionist Thomas Wentworth Higginson, recalled in a memoir that during the Sims case he had been invited to attend an emergency meeting of the Boston vigilance committee at the office of the *Liberator*. The question had come up whether to effect a rescue, but no decision was made. Higginson complained that he could not

> conceive of a set of men, personally admirable, yet less fitted on the whole than this committee to undertake any positive action in the direction of forcible resistance to authorities. In the first place, half of them were non-resistants, as was their great leader, Garrison, who stood composedly by his desk preparing his next week's editorial, and almost exasperating the more hotheaded among us by the placid way in which he looked beyond the rescue of an individual to the purifying of a nation. On the other hand, the "political Abolitionists," or Free-Soilers, while personally full of indignation, were extremely anxious not to be placed for one moment outside the pale of good citizenship. The only persons to be relied upon for action were a few whose temperament prevailed over the restrictions of non-resistance on the one side, and of politics on the other; but of course their discussion was constantly damped by the attitude of the rest.[62]

Although Higginson remembered one point incorrectly—only a handful of committee members were non-resistants—he was right about the committee's paralysis. How could it resolve on forceful resistance to the government? Doing so overtly ran counter to the fundamental claim of a vigilance committee, that it acted in the name of law and order.

NOTES

1. The term "vigilance committee" could also refer to an organized group that monitored and encouraged the progress of a specific cause or measure. Political parties, for example, occasionally organized vigilance committees to mobilize their voters before an election. The definition given in the text, however, was the prevailing one.
2. Jennet Kirkpatrick, *Uncivil Disobedience: Studies in Violence and Democratic Politics* (Princeton: Princeton University Press, 2008), 40–50. My argument in this essay has been influenced by Kirkpatrick's useful distinction between revolutionary and vigilance organizations. Both operate outside the government, but one aims to overthrow it, the other to preserve law and order.

3. "The Outrage," *Boston Evening Transcript,* August 13, 1834; Committee of Vigilance and Protection Records (Ms. S-110), Massachusetts Historical Society, Boston (MHS), published in *Proceedings of the Massachusetts Historical Society,* vol. 53 (1919–1920), 325–31.
4. *The First Annual Report of the New York Committee of Vigilance* (New York: Committee of Vigilance, 1837), 3, 4, 9, 19.
5. Graham Russell Hodges, *David Ruggles: A Radical Black Abolitionist and the Underground Railroad in New York City* (Chapel Hill: University of North Carolina Press, 2010); Fergus M. Bordewich, *Bound for Canaan: The Underground Railroad and the War for the Soul of America* (New York: HarperCollins, 2005), 171–74, 179–81.
6. For the history of the New-England Freedom Association, see the *Liberator:* "Juvenile Concert," May 5, 1843; "Juvenile Colored Concert," May 26, 1843; "New-England Freedom Association," April 12, 1843; "Caution to Abolitionists," September 6, 1845; "Notice," January 3, 1845; "Notice," January 10, 1845; "Notice," January 17, 1845; "Notice," March 7, 1845; "Notice," August 22, 1845; "New-England Freedom Association," December 12, 1845; "Help the Fugitive," January 16, 1846; "Grand Anti-Slavery Festival," January 23, 1846; "The Fugitive," August 28, 1846.
7. Thomas D. Morris, *Free Men All: The Personal Liberty Laws of the North, 1780–1861* (Baltimore: Johns Hopkins University Press, 1974), 11, 220. See "An Act Directing the Process in *Habeas Corpus*" (March 16, 1785), section 10; "An Act establishing the right to, and the Form of the Writ *De Homine Replegiando,* or writ for replevying a man" (February 19, 1787); and "An Act to prevent the Slave-Trade, and for granting relief to the families of such unhappy Persons as may be kidnapped or decoyed away from this Commonwealth" (March 26, 1788), in *The Perpetual Laws of the Commonwealth of Massachusetts* (Boston: I. Thomas & E. T. Andrews, 1801), 1:239–40, 361–65, 407–9.
8. Paul Finkelman, "The Kidnapping of John Davis and the Adoption of the Fugitive Slave Law of 1793," *Journal of Southern History* 56.3 (August 1990): 397–442.
9. 1 Stat. 302.
10. Marion Gleason McDougall, *Fugitive Slaves (1619–1865)* (Boston: Ginn, 1891), 35; Leonard Levy, "The 'Abolition Riot': Boston's First Slave Rescue," *New England Quarterly* 25.1 (March 1952): 85–92.
11. *Commonwealth v. Camillus Griffith* (2 Pickering 11).
12. Morris, *Free Men All,* 76–79. In 1836, as part of a general revision and modernization of the Massachusetts legal code, the legislature repealed the right to the writ of replevin, but reinstated it the following year with "An Act to restore the Trial by Jury, in questions of personal freedom." See *The Revised Statutes of the Commonwealth of Massachusetts* (Boston: Dutton & Wentworth, 1836), 660; *Laws of the Commonwealth of Massachusetts Passed Subsequently to the Revised Statutes, 1836 to 1849 Inclusive* (Boston: Dutton & Wentworth, 1849), 44–47.
13. The first vigilance committees in Massachusetts devoted to helping fugitive slaves were organized not by Boston abolitionists but by a meeting of the Anti-Slavery Society of Worcester County, North Division. In October 1839, it authorized the creation of three-person vigilance committees in each of twenty-five towns in northern Worcester County, among them Leominster, Boylston, Harvard, and Athol. The committees were "to inquire after, and take measures to recover, those of our free citizens who may be stolen from their homes." See *Christian Reflector,* October 16, 1839.
14. "Extraordinary Case of Kidnapping!," *Liberator,* June 11, 1841; Charles Torrey, "The Illegal Conduct of the Grand Jury of Suffolk County Exposed!," *Liberator,* June 18, 1841.

15. William Cooper Nell, "Meeting on Behalf of the Mirror of Liberty," in *Selected Writings, 1832–1874*, ed. Dorothy Porter Wesley and Constance Porter Uzelac (Baltimore: Black Classics Press, 2002), 98–99; J. P. Bishop and Charles T. Torrey, "To the Friends of the Slave, in New-England," *Liberator,* June 11, 1841.
16. Nell, "Boston Vigilance Committee," *Selected Writings,* 99–100. In determining the race of vigilance committee members, I have generally relied on the Boston Athenaeum's BOSBLACK database, which compiles those identified as "colored" in various sources, including the city directories and tax records, and federal and state censuses. See http://app.bostonathenaeum.org/BosBlack.
17. Torrey was one of the managers of the Massachusetts Anti-Slavery Society and apparently one of the authors of its *Second Annual Report* (Boston, 1841), severely critical of Garrison, which he helped to read before the society's annual meeting in May 1841.
18. Charles T. Torrey, "The Boston Vigilance Committee," *Liberator,* July 2, 1841.
19. Bishop and Torrey, "To the Friends of the Slave, in New-England."
20. "The Boston Vigilance Committee," *Liberator,* June 18, 1841.
21. Bishop and Torrey, "To the Friends of the Slave, in New-England"; Stanley Harrold, "On the Borders of Slavery and Race: Charles T. Torrey and the Underground Railroad," *Journal of the Early Republic* 20.2 (Summer 2000): 273–92.
22. E. G. Austin, counsel for Gray, gives his account of events in "To the Public," originally in the Boston *Atlas,* republished in the *Liberator,* November 25, 1842.
23. Morris, *Free Men All,* 109–11; [Zachariah Chandler], "The Latimer Case," *Monthly Law Reporter* 5 (March 1842): 481–98, 524.
24. 41 U.S. 539 (1842); Joseph C. Burke, "What Did the Prigg Decision Really Decide?," *Pennsylvania Magazine of History and Biography* 93.1 (January 1969): 73–85; Paul Finkelman, "Story Telling on the Supreme Court: *Prigg v Pennsylvania* and Justice Joseph Story's Judicial Nationalism," *Supreme Court Review* (1994): 274–94.
25. Paul Finkelman, "*Prigg v. Pennsylvania* and Northern State Courts: The Anti-Slavery Use of a Pro-Slavery Decision," *Civil War History* 25.1 (March 1979): 5–35.
26. "The Latimer and Great Massachusetts Petition," http://edison.rutgers.edu/latimer/petition.htm. This Latimer Petition is addressed to the Massachusetts legislature; a second Latimer Petition, which received nearly 52,000 signatures, was addressed to Congress, requesting it pass laws and constitutional amendments separating Massachusetts from slavery; it was presented to the U.S. House of Representatives by John Quincy Adams. See "General Intelligence," *New York Evangelist,* February 23, 1843.
27. Samuel Gridley Howe et al., *Address of the Committee Appointed by a Public Meeting, Held at Faneuil Hall, September 24, 1846, for the Purpose of Considering the Recent Case of Kidnapping from Our Soil, and of Taking Measures to Prevent the Recurrence of Similar Outrages* (Boston: White & Potter, 1846), 34–38.
28. Ibid., 2, 6. In response, the meeting voted to create a "Committee of Vigilance," authorized "to take all needed measures to secure the protection of the laws" for those who may be "in danger of abduction from this Commonwealth" (4).
29. Ibid., 16, 18, 20.
30. Besides Phillips, the two other Garrisonians who were appointed at the meeting but declined to serve were Cornelius Bramhall and A. B. Phelps. Jackson attended the first meeting of the vigilance committee, on September 30, but he does not appear in the records thereafter and did not sign the "Address" that Howe prepared. Nell did sign the "Address," but he does not seem to have attended any of the meetings. Ibid., 39, 8;

Boston Vigilance Committee Records [1846], in the Boston Anti-Man Hunting League Records (Ms. N-1875), MHS.
31. The names of Smith, Morris, and Weeden appear on the "Free Soil Roll" (MS Am 521), Houghton Library, Harvard University, a list of all Free Soil voters in 1852–1853. Nell's name does not appear there, but Martin Delaney mentions his running for office on the Free Soil ticket in 1850 in *The Condition, Elevation, Emigration, and Destiny of the Colored People of the United States* (Philadelphia: Martin Delaney, 1852), 123.
32. Boston Vigilance Committee Records [1846].
33. Howe et al., *Address of the Committee*, 4, 6–8.
34. Ibid., 6–8.
35. In *Jones v. Van Zandt*, 46 U.S. (1847) 215, 232, the U.S. Supreme Court would rule that "any overt act so marked in its character as to show an intention to elude the vigilance of the master or his agent, and which is calculated to attain such an object, is a harboring of the fugitive within the [Fugitive Slave Act]." In 1854, the Alabama Supreme Court, interpreting a state fugitive slave statute that also forbade "concealing" and "harboring," would rule that merely feeding or furnishing shelter to a runaway constituted "harboring." *McElhaney v. State*, 24 Ala. 71, 74.
36. "Committee of Vigilance, Agent's Record and Subscription Book" (1846–47), Wendell Phillips Papers / Crawford Blagden Papers (bMS Am 1953, nos. 1573, 1574), Houghton Library, Harvard University; this manuscript is transcribed and published in Irving H. Bartlett, "Abolitionists, Fugitives, and Imposters in Boston, 1846–1847," *New England Quarterly* 55.1 (March 1982): 97–110. Bartlett makes the Urban League comparison.
37. Finkelman, "*Prigg v. Pennsylvania* and Northern State Courts," 30–31; Boston Vigilance Committee Records [1846].
38. Boston Vigilance Committee Records [1846].
39. Howe et al., *Address of the Committee*, 41–42.
40. Boston Vigilance Committee Records [1846].
41. 9 Stat. 462.
42. "Declaration of Sentiments of the Colored Citizens of Boston," in Nell, *Selected Writings*, 272–73.
43. Ibid., 272.
44. Theodore Parker, "Doings of the Abolitionists" (May 31, 1848), in *Speeches, Addresses, and Occasional Sermons*, 2 vols. (Boston: W. Crosby & H. P. Nichols, 1852), 2:116. For the theological underpinnings of Parker's constitutional opinions, see Dean Grodzins, "Why Theodore Parker Backed John Brown: The Political and Social Roots of Support for Abolitionist Violence," in *Terrible Swift Sword: The Legacy of John Brown*, ed. Peggy Russo and Paul Finkelman (Athens: Ohio University Press, 2005), 6–9.
45. Parker, "A Sermon of Conscience" (September 22, 1850), in *Speeches, Addresses, and Occasional Sermons*, 2:258.
46. Ibid., 2:257; "Rocking the Old Cradle of Liberty," *Liberator*, October 18, 1850.
47. "A Good Testimony from the Pulpit," *Boston Chronotype*, October 7, 1850.
48. "Rocking the Old Cradle of Liberty."
49. Parker, "*Resolved*" (draft resolutions, 1850), Mss., Joel Myerson private collection. An edited version of these draft resolutions appears in John Weiss, *The Life and Correspondence of Theodore Parker*, 2 vols. (New York: D. Appleton, 1864), 2:94.
50. Committees of "vigilance and safety" had been created before. Citizens in Baltimore, for example, organized one during the War of 1812, after the British army burned

Washington, D.C. Parker seems to have been unaware of the Baltimore case, although if he had, he might have liked it; he often claimed that Boston was being threatened with conquest by the "Slave Power."
51. "Rocking the Old Cradle of Liberty."
52. Ibid.
53. The *Liberator* article "Rocking the Old Cradle of Liberty" does not specifically say that Parker proposed this resolution, but he claims he did (and there is no reason to doubt him) in Theodore Parker, *The Trial of Theodore Parker, for the "Misdemeanor" of a Speech in Faneuil Hall against Kidnapping with the Defence* (1855; repr., New York: Negro University Press, 1970), 186.
54. On Colver's career, see Justin Almerin Smith, *Memoir of Rev. Nathaniel Colver, D.D.* (Boston: Durkee & Foxcroft, 1873).
55. "Rocking the Old Cradle of Liberty." The italics and small capitals appear in this report.
56. Ibid.
57. Ibid.; "Members of the Committee of Vigilance" (Boston: John Wilson, 1850), broadside (Bdses-Sm 1850), MHS. The two most comprehensive lists of members are what I call the "Doorman's List" and the "Secretary's List." The Doorman's List, of 211 names, was maintained by Austin Bearse, who among his many jobs for the committee would call members to meetings and, when closed meetings were held, would watch the door to make sure that nonmembers did not enter. The Doorman's List is the best known, because Bearse published it in *Reminiscences of Fugitive Slave Law Days in Boston* (Boston: Warren Richardson, 1880), 3–6. The Secretary's List, of 210 names, was maintained by the secretary of the Vigilance Committee, a position filled by Charles List, until his death in 1855, and then by William F. Channing and John W. Browne; it can be found in a notebook, "Records of the Vigilance Committee of Boston" (Ms B.17), Garrison Collection, Boston Public Library (BPL). A few names appear on the Doorman's List that do not appear on the Secretary's List and vice versa.
58. See *Account Book of Francis Jackson, Treasurer, the Vigilance Committee of Boston* (1850–61), facsimile reproduction (Boston: Bostonian Society and the Boston Public Library, [1924]); "Records of the Vigilance Committee of Boston"; Theodore Parker, "Memoranda of the Troubles in Boston Occasioned by the Infamous Fugitive Slave Law, Kept from Day to Day" (Ms E.2.10 [1851]), BPL.
59. Parker, "Memoranda," 15.
60. Gary Collison, "'This Flagitious Offense': Daniel Webster and Shadrach Rescue Cases, 1851–1852," *New England Quarterly* 68.4 (December 1995): 609–25. See also Collison, *Shadrach Minkins: From Fugitive Slave to Citizen* (Cambridge: Harvard University Press, 1997), 124–33.
61. A. W. Weston to C. D. Weston, April 15, 1851 (Ms. A.9.2), BPL.
62. Thomas Wentworth Higginson, *Cheerful Yesterdays* (Cambridge, Mass.: Riverside Press, 1900), 139–40.

"Today Abolitionist Is Merged in Citizen"
Radical Abolitionists and the Union War

PETER WIRZBICKI

"New occasions," William Lloyd Garrison wrote as the Civil War began, "teach new duties."[1] In earlier years, Garrison had been an outspoken pacifist whose belief in the proslavery nature of the Constitution and the federal government had led him to reject participation in formal politics. Now, like other abolitionists, he was pinning his hopes for emancipation on the bayonets of the Union army. This essay will focus on the transition in the attitude of abolitionists such as Garrison toward the federal government and the entire American national project. How did radicals who had conceived of their political identity in opposition to the American state accommodate themselves to a war that dramatically expanded that state? How did abolitionists who for years had been calling for the dissolution of the American Union become cheerleaders for a war designed to protect that very union? How did black intellectuals, many of whom had seriously considered emigrating to Haiti or elsewhere, become outspoken patriots? I will argue that while the start of the war did dramatically change abolitionists' attitudes toward the American nation, they drew on old ideas, even those rooted in their earlier embrace of disunionism, to adjust to the new state of affairs. The Union war effort, they hoped, could come to realize the very virtues that the earlier American state had lacked. Drawing on cultural aspirations as well as political ones, they projected onto the new Union the values that they had seen as latent but unrealized, in New England in particular.

As is well known, many Massachusetts abolitionists were hostile to the U.S. Constitution and the federal government during the years before the

Civil War. The most obvious manifestation of this was the disunionist platform of William Lloyd Garrison and his allies. According to Garrison, the Constitution, the document upon which federal power was based, was a "covenant with death and an agreement with Hell" because it contained numerous clauses supporting slavery. Starting primarily in the 1840s, Garrison and his allies, such as Wendell Phillips, began advocating disunionism, the peaceful separation of the northern free states from the southern slave states. This was both a practical political platform that addressed the abolitionist conviction that the Constitution was inherently proslavery, and a moral, almost metaphysical, argument that Northerners should avoid at all costs any personal connection with slavery.[2] Just as abolitionists would "come out" of churches that upheld the institution, so would northern states come out of the slaveholding Union. It reflected, then, the morally absolutist impulse that animated many radicals.

This abolitionist opposition to the federal government should not be confused with the antimajoritarian states' rights doctrine of John C. Calhoun and other southern conservatives, even if it shared some superficial similarities. Calhoun's position was partly pragmatic, as devolving power to the states made a general slave emancipation less likely, but it also reflected a more abstract conservative ideology, one that distrusted democracy itself. The public power of the federal government was to be stymied, thus upholding and strengthening the private domination of master over slave. While Calhoun sought to disempower the national government because it threatened the agency of a minority—southern planters—Garrison was convinced that the problem was exactly that it allowed that minority too much power and influence. Abolitionists were not, on principle at least, opposed to central federal power. Instead, as committed believers in black and female suffrage, they led the most consistently democratic movement in antebellum America. Garrison even declared that Calhoun's "state sovereignty" was nothing but "slave sovereignty."[3] But Garrisonians did believe that, in practice, the national government was controlled by the Slave Power and that the Constitution held explicit protections for slavery; thus, for very different reasons than Calhoun espoused, they opposed the power of the federal government.

Historians are increasingly realizing the degree to which abolitionists were important figures, not just in the fight for emancipation and civil rights, but for the definition of democracy itself. Caleb McDaniel has restored the abolitionist vision of democracy, one that he argues drew from transatlantic sources as diverse as John Stuart Mill, Alexis de Tocqueville, and Giuseppe Mazzini.[4]

Casting themselves as both advocates and protectors, McDaniel notes, abolitionists were anxious to defend the legitimacy of the American democratic project from European skeptics, who pointed to slavery as evidence of the failure of democracy. At the same time, they confronted American mobs and politicians, who sought to shut down the free speech necessary for a democratic society—albeit in the name of defending the democratic Union! Moreover, abolitionists were the only significant group in America who supported women's suffrage and had close ties to the broader movement for women's rights. Thus abolitionists settled on a message that defended the necessity of constant agitation for a healthy democracy. Democratic institutions, in other words, required political movements that were constantly challenging the status quo in order to prevent democracy from descending into a "tyranny of the majority." In particular, abolitionists focused on a disunionist platform, hoping to create a free northern government cleansed of the compromises with slavery that marked the current nation. Disunionism, which even its adherents admitted was unlikely to be put into action, was every bit as much a rallying cry, a reminder of the moral compromises that came with the Constitution—indeed, a call for moral and democratic regeneration—as it was a realistic political project.[5]

Not all abolitionists agreed with Garrison that the Constitution was essentially proslavery; Garrison's onetime friend and ally Frederick Douglass split with him on exactly this issue. Douglass worried, with good cause, that Garrison's disunionism, were it successful, would abandon the southern slaves to the mercy of the slaveholders. For Douglass and other political abolitionists, disunionism was an unfortunate privileging of abolitionist moral purity over the welfare of the slave.

But even among non-Garrisonians there was a widespread sense that the federal government as currently constituted was a bulwark of support for slavery. Thus the practical disagreements among abolitionists were not as large as their heated rhetoric on the constitutionality of slavery would sometimes suggest. After all, the idea that a conspiracy of slave owners had taken control of the federal government—the "Slave Power" theory—was strong among political abolitionists such as Douglass and Gerrit Smith. The difference between them and Garrisonians such as Wendell Phillips, Thomas Wentworth Higginson told an audience in 1857, was that "one [group] thinks the Constitution is pro-slavery; the other thinks the *existing interpretation* of the Constitution is pro-slavery."⁶ In other words, political abolitionists like Douglass differed from Garrison only in believing that the Constitution could *someday* be put to good use, but they agreed that, as it was currently implemented, it was largely a force for evil. Since the success of an abolition-driven campaign for disunion was nearly unthinkable, both types of abolitionists ended up advocating for many of the same policies in the short term, among them the repeal of the Fugitive Slave Act, the admission of Kansas as a free state, and the overturning of the Dred Scott decision.

Political fights in the antebellum period, especially those involving fugitive slaves, dramatically increased abolitionist hostility toward the federal government. The use of federal agents to capture African Americans off the streets of Boston was a direct insult to Yankee pride, symbolizing a loss of sovereignty and a betrayal of regional identity. In the wake of a series of high-profile slave renditions and rescue attempts in Massachusetts, including those of Thomas Sims in 1851 and Anthony Burns in 1854, the state government passed a series of personal liberty laws prohibiting the use of state resources and personnel in the capture of fugitive slaves. Southerners charged, probably correctly, that this action effectively nullified the Fugitive Slave acts of 1793 and 1850, as well as the clauses of the Constitution mandating slave rendition. In fact, Southerners would repeatedly cite the passage of personal liberty laws and the general inability of the federal government to enforce the Fugitive Slave Act in their declarations of secession. Meanwhile, the fact that northern black sailors were being denied equal protection in southern ports, where they were being jailed or even sold into slavery, seemed to illustrate to abolitionists that even those good parts of the Constitution—providing, for example, that each state should respect the privileges and immunities of citizens from other states—were effectively meaningless in a slave republic.

Their sense that mainstream American patriotism was nothing but a cynical facade for the self-interest of those who profited from southern trade contributed to abolitionists' distrust of the Union. In 1859, Wendell Phillips condemned the "men who prate about 'nationality,'" as simply those whose "minds rise no higher than some petty mass of white States making money out of cotton and corn."⁷ The pro-Union rioter who, while attempting to prevent Phillips from speaking, exclaimed, "Damn him! He has depreciated stocks $3,000,000 by his slang" confirmed the abolitionists' suspicion that at least some of the support for the Union came from less than noble impulses.⁸ Even Ralph Waldo Emerson declared in his journal that "cotton thread holds the union together, unites John C. Calhoun & Abbott Lawrence." Yet the idea that American nationalism was little more than a crude ideological veil for the interests of the textile industry did not stem entirely from abolitionist paranoia. Even the Democratic *Boston Post,* in the aftermath of Abraham Lincoln's election, frantically warned readers that secession would result in economic collapse, a loss of "thirty millions of capital," if the "unwise and useless agitation" of the abolitionists continued.⁹

The Idea of New England and Cultural Disunionism

While political calculations contributed to the abolitionists' alienation from the federal government, powerful cultural currents were also helping to convince many New England antislavery intellectuals to question their allegiance to the United States. The strong role that New England regional pride played in the abolitionist moment in general, and disunionism in particular, has not been fully appreciated by historians. Even abolitionists who did not embrace disunion helped to raise tensions with the South by celebrating the cultural superiority of New England. As early as the colonial era, strong cultural currents had identified these states as a region distinct from the rest of the country, constituting an imagined community of those who shared religious, cultural, and political norms separate from the rest of the nation and world. And from the Revolution onward, the South was increasingly the foil against which New England defined itself.

Like all notions of identity, New Englandism was rent with disagreements and contradictions, but a couple of general themes were clear: the region was Puritan, hard-working, orderly, and educated; Virginia and South Carolina were marked by religious laxity, ruling class idleness, the degradation of both slaves and poor whites, and a general disorder of home and state. As New England freed its slaves after the Revolution, it re-imagined its past as one in which slavery played no significant role in its society and in which black people themselves were largely absent.¹⁰ These were mainstream cultural and political values, expressed in Sunday sermons and Fourth of July speeches, in newspaper columns and public monuments, and were not necessarily associated with abolitionism or radical politics.¹¹

Radical abolitionists, though, had a conflicted view of this regional pride and would eventually articulate their own variation on it, one that more clearly put them at odds with the rest of the nation. Abolitionists' pride in New England was always tempered by their awareness that many in the region continued personally to profit off of slavery. Especially in industrializing New England, the textile industry was reliant on cheap, slave-picked cotton, giving rise to the "Cotton Whigs," who dominated the political landscape in antebellum Massachusetts. Prominent Massachusetts politicians such as Daniel Webster played conspicuous roles in the passage of the Fugitive Slave Act, while business-friendly newspapers urged that the mollification of the cotton states was more important than abstract ideas about freedom or human equality. The abolitionist minister Theodore Parker compared Massachusetts leaders to the greatest of New England villains. "It would be cruel to Benedict Arnold," Parker declared, "to compare him with certain other sons of New England now in high official place."[12] Complicating, then, any sense of New England pride was the abolitionists' realization of the sordid nature of the region.

While pride in a slave-holding nation was a non-starter for abolitionists, and New England remained compromised by slavery, white abolitionists increasingly began to celebrate their cause as a manifestation of the "idea" of New England, an idea that persisted despite the fact that it was yet to be manifested in society. This appeal to an as yet unrealized transcendent "idea" of New England allowed abolitionists to begin celebrating the region, even while they vigorously attacked the compromises made by its leaders. Parker often argued that the true idea of the North, despite the corruption of its leading men, could be found in the spirit of liberty and equality that supposedly had animated the Puritans.[13] Emerson, in his journal, commented that the "true Boston" was found in its lyceums, railroads, and "love of German literature," not in Hunker "talks of Union, & fevers into pro-slavery," that constituted the transient surface-play of the city. And Wendell Phillips could describe Anson Burlingame, an unsuccessful antislavery politician in Boston, as "the representative of an idea," adding that "the city that rejected him disgraced only herself."[14]

Celebrating the idea of New England implied that there were virtues in the region's essence that had not yet been manifested in society. Theodore Parker developed an elaborate theory of reform in which social change started with "sentiment," passed through an "idea," and was finally realized by "fact." The job of reformers such as Parker was to turn the unarticulated sentiment of a community (for instance, a preference for liberty) into coherent ideas (the antislavery movement), cultivating and popularizing them until they bore fruit in fact (emancipation). The true essence of a society, its unique telos for which the region existed, could lie underground for years as sentiments before becoming realized as social fact.[15]

According to Parker and other abolitionists, one distinguishing mark of New Englanders was their willingness to abide by abstract ideas. In Parker's mind, that meant they were more progressive, more able to turn sentiments for liberty or equality into ideas and then facts and thus push forward human history. It also imparted them with a certain moral absolutism: a "fanatic" willingness to follow abstraction. Such an impulse had led Puritans to behead their king in 1649 and led their descendants to join John Brown. In 1859, for example, Wendell Phillips warned the South that "there is an element even in the Yankee blood which obeys ideas[,] . . . an impulsive, enthusiastic aspiration, something left to us from the old Puritan stock."[16]

The celebration of abstract ideals had its roots, perhaps, in the Transcendentalist privileging of the world of Reason over the material world of Understanding. But a celebration of the New England ability to "follow ideas" was particularly appealing to radical abolitionists for two other reasons. First, it was an explicit criticism of the compromising Northerners, Hunkers, who were letting their material interest prevail over ideas such as equality and justice. This implied that the mobs in Boston and the aristocrats on Beacon Street had betrayed the true meaning of New England. Even more, though, a celebration of New England "fanaticism" fit the mood of the time, as many discouraged abolitionists, disgusted by the compromises and cowardice of northern leaders, strove to identify a Cromwellian figure, a "fanatic" such as John Brown or Toussaint L'Ouverture, whose absolute dedication to freedom would lead them to an uncompromising war on slavery. It was in these terms that Henry David Thoreau defended John Brown, whom he described as "by descent and birth a New England farmer," "a transcendentalist above all, a man of ideas and principles,—that was what distinguished him."[17] This desire for a violent redemptive abolitionist hero was often expressed in language that drew on new abolitionist ideals of manhood, ideals that began to call into question abolitionist dedication to feminism.[18]

Sometimes explicitly and sometimes implicitly, this appeal to New England values went hand in hand with a skepticism about a greater federal nationalism. For instance, when Thomas Wentworth Higginson advertised a Disunion Convention in 1857, he based his argument not on the immorality of the Constitution, but rather on the "fundamental difference in education, habit, and laws" that existed between North and South. New England's supposed economic and cultural superiority demonstrated that a new nation would be strong, more economically viable, and certainly more morally righteous than the old one. When defending disunionism, Wendell Phillips racialized the region, proudly noting that "our blood is largely Yankee" as an explanation for why a northern nation would be strong.[19]

The "idea" of New England may have been about abstract dedication to equal rights and antislavery, but it was unclear, at a practical level, where black Northerners were supposed to fit into this equation. If the region was marked by its "Puritan" legacy, what happened to the descendants of the slaves whom the Puritans had imported?[20] Most New Englanders, even if they grudgingly conceded citizenship to free blacks, did not consider them within the affective embrace of New Englandism.

Many radical white abolitionists even contributed to this racial exclusion. Theodore Parker, as dedicated to nineteenth-century racial science as he was to abolitionism, was the most prominent spokesman of a racially exclusive notion of abolitionist New England identity. Parker wrote of the "superiority of New England civilization" and became one of the biggest proponents of the notion that the particularly antislavery "idea" inherent in New England life had its roots in the Anglo-Saxon race.[21] A central part of the "genius" of that race, according to Parker, was its love of liberty and democracy, specifically, the "old Teutonic spirit, the love of individual liberty."[22] Parker frankly considered people of African and Irish descent to be inferior to Anglo-Saxons, even if he maintained that they should retain formal equality. Even white abolitionists less interested in racial science than Parker contributed to the association of New England "blood" with abolition. Wendell Phillips, who by all accounts treated African Americans with respect and never engaged in the type of crude stereotyping that Parker did, still sometimes appealed to the "blood" of the New Englanders and the "sacred soil of the Puritans."[23]

As historians have long been aware, New Englanders and other Northerners partly conceived of their difference from the South in gendered terms. Abolitionists criticized the sexual practices of southern planters— because of both the rape that was common on plantations and the more generalized sexual disorder that southern slavery seemed to encourage.[24] The orderly monogamous northern household was a potent symbol of the "civilization" that the South lacked. Abolitionists played a complicated game: they used such ideas about a superior northern culture to appeal to a wider public while also criticizing the lack of women's rights even in the North. Parker, for instance, both celebrated what he called the "Domestic Function" of women and advocated an enlarged "Public Function," which would include philanthropic, reform, and religious activity. Proslavery sentiment, he implied, was upheld in the North because women were not consulted on moral issues.[25]

Black intellectuals in Massachusetts responded to this New Englandism forcefully. William C. Nell and Charlotte Forten articulated probably the most common response by attempting to correct the erasure of black people from the idea of New England, reminding white abolitionists, as well as the broader public, of the contributions and presence of black New Englanders. By doing so, they attempted to decouple New Englandism from any racial or ethnic identification. Nell did this in his historical work, especially in his *Colored Patriots of the American Revolution,* in which he recovered the story of Crispus Attucks and other black Revolutionary War heroes. Nell explicitly saw his histories as serving to counter the widespread white idea—given legal sanction by the Dred Scott decision—that black people had not been members of the American community at its founding. Since the Revolution loomed large in rhetoric about New Englandism, Nell's celebrations of Crispus Attucks and black contributions to the American Revolution were his way of connecting black history to the national community and strongly arguing for the inclusion of black people in the making of the New England values of freedom and equality.[26]

Charlotte Forten, for her part, wrote a revealing essay for the *National Anti-Slavery Standard* called "Glimpses of New England," which seemed to be participating in the same celebratory construction of New England regionalism. Filled with pastoral scenes of rambling walks in the woods, visits to eccentric local notables, and pleas for the preservation of historic buildings, it might appear almost as an apolitical exercise in localism and nostalgia. But unlike Parker, Forten was particularly attuned to the racial attitudes of white New Englanders; on the one hand she celebrated how much less racially hostile they were than her native Philadelphians, while on the other hand she attacked the "aristocrats" in her adopted hometown of Salem who were "pro-slavery people."²⁷ Rather than fight the narrative of "Yankeedom," both Nell and Forten tried to integrate it, reminding white New Englanders of the presence of black people and their importance to the meaning of the region.

Black intellectuals such as Nell and Forten were shifting the meaning of New Englandism, stripping it of any racial implications even as they adopted many of its symbols. Frederick Douglass's reaction when he was mobbed by a Boston crowd in the aftermath of Lincoln's election expressed well a similar ambivalence toward the idea that the region was particularly devoted to liberty. Douglass had lived in Massachusetts for almost a decade before moving to upstate New York and had close, if often tense, relations with many of its leading white and black abolitionists. On December 3, 1860, a violent mob shut down a celebration of John Brown's life at which Douglass had been invited to speak. A week later, reflecting on the event, Douglass pointed out that "even here, in Boston, the moral atmosphere is dark and heavy." He traded on the pride his audience would feel in symbols of Boston's Revolutionary history—reminding them that while "Faneuil Hall and Bunker Hill Monument *stand,* freedom of speech is struck down." White Bostonians were privileging the symbolism of liberty, Douglass suggested, over the actual practice of it. While acknowledging that the idea of Boston represented liberty—"Boston is a great city," he declared—he pointed out the dark side of this belief: by holding to the ideal of the city's liberty, white citizens were deceiving themselves about the true nature of its compromises. He ended his remarks with an appeal for free speech, emphasizing that society had an especially urgent responsibility to protect the speech of the "poor and humble."²⁸

Dr. John Rock represented another tactic. In a dramatic public debate with Theodore Parker, he pointed to the heroism of the black Revolutionary martyr Crispus Attucks and the Haitian revolutionaries to refute Parker's suggestion that Anglo-Saxons were uniquely brave and capable of martial prowess. In the South, the supposedly democratic Anglo-Saxons were too scared of the lynch mob even to advocate for the principles of their own Declaration of Independence. Rock also reminded the audience that Cicero had cautioned against buying slaves from the British Isles "on account of their stupidity."²⁹ It was a popular line among black intellectuals, who were particularly eager to repeat this quotation, as it served to hoist whites—obsessed as they were with the genius of the classical Romans and Greeks—by their own petard while simultaneously suggesting that racial stereotypes were a product of environment and history and not of biology.[30] Rock thus attacked the very foundations of racial superiority that underwrote Parker's New England essentialism.

If some black intellectuals looked to integrate New England, they were competing with a growing number of black activists who were advocating emigration out of the country. The years right before the war saw an interest in Haitian emigration among black intellectuals rise to levels not seen since the 1820s. If many white radicals were looking inward to celebrate New England, a unit smaller than the nation, many black intellectuals looked outward, articulating notions of nationhood and community that extended beyond American borders to encompass the Caribbean and Africa. The variety and complexity of colonization, emigration, and nationalist ventures proposed in the years immediately before the Civil War demonstrates well the sense of alienation that existed among prominent black intellectuals and their search for alternative national communities. As one black Rhode Islander said, "I have held in *utter contempt* the United States flag, because it gave us no protection."[31] Even Charlotte Forten, who never was interested in emigration, acknowledged her "prejudice against everything *Am.*[erican]," in her journal.[32]

Pushed by the Dred Scott decision and pulled by an active campaign of recruitment by Haitian government officials, an increased number of black intellectuals, including Henry Highland Garnet, Alexander Crummell, and Martin Delany, advocated various alternative nationalisms. Crummell, employed as a missionary in Liberia, continued to work within the white-dominated American Colonization Society. Predicting the eventual decay of "Anglo-Saxon civilization," he told a black audience that his experience in Liberia had convinced him that "the negro is rising; and will rise."[33] Meanwhile Douglass's old partner, Martin Delany, formed the African Colonization Society, a black-led organization that sought to take the African emigration movement out of the control of the conservative, white-led American Colonization Society. Delany's name change—switching "American" to "African"—illustrated his desire to build on "the principles of an African Nationality, the African race being the ruling element of the nation."[34]

The movement to which African Americans in Boston were most sympathetic was the renewed push for Haitian emigration that began in the 1860s. Haitian government officials had recruited James Redpath, a white editor well known for his close connections with John Brown, to lead the Haitian Emigration Bureau, which was headquartered in Boston. The racial politics of Redpath's movement were complicated. Some of its most prominent leaders and advocates, including Redpath, Richard Hinton, and John Brown Jr., were white men, albeit ones whose association with John Brown gave them an egalitarian credibility that the leaders of the American Colonization Society lacked. At the same point, the Haitian government funded the bureau and a number of prominent black activists, including Garnet, William Wells Brown, and H. Ford Douglas worked as its paid agents.[35] Even Frederick Douglass, a lifelong foe of emigration, initially warmed to the movement, temporarily putting aside his qualms and writing that "we can raise no objection to the present movements toward Hayti."[36] Douglass was even planning a trip there to assess the viability of emigration before the outbreak of the Civil War disrupted his travel plans.

Black reactions in Boston to the movement were mixed. Some New England black leaders, such as George T. Downing, were vehemently opposed, arguing that "positions of commercial and other commanding influences" were slowly opening up to black men of ability in New England.[37] William Lloyd Garrison, who retained moral authority among black Bostonians, was skeptical of the new Haitian effort, arguing that it would be detrimental to the overall effort to end American slavery.[38] On the other hand, black thinkers with deep roots in black Boston, such as William Wells Brown, were far more sympathetic. Even William C. Nell, often seen as one of the most consistently "integrationist" black leaders in antebellum America, was a subscriber to the *Pine and Palm,* the official newsletter of Redpath's organization, suggesting that he held more than a passing interest.[39] While most black Bostonians may not have been interested personally in emigrating to Haiti or Africa, they were well aware of emigration as a possibility and as an alternative to either a New England or an American national identity.

Their interest in emigration demonstrated a profound alienation from the American national project. Widespread skepticism of the Republican Party fueled it and other forms of black nationalism, since even black opponents of emigration agreed that the mainstream Republicans were woefully conservative on issues of race and slavery. In Boston, black activists were particularly incensed by the proposed Crittenden Compromise, the last-minute attempts to avoid the Civil War through concessions to the South that many prominent Republicans, including William Seward and the local leader Charles Francis Adams, entertained.[40] Nor did black abolitionists initially warm to Lincoln, widely seen as representing the less radical wing of the Republican Party. The *Weekly Anglo-African*, a prominent black newspaper, declared, "We gather no comfort from the Inaugural of President Lincoln. . . . The Republican party is for the *white* man. We must rely on ourselves."[41] Other black intellectuals, such as Frederick Douglass, were likewise initially skeptical of Lincoln's prospects.

The Secession Crisis and Abolitionists

On the eve of the war, then, alternatives to the federal state and to American nationalism abounded among Massachusetts radicals. The start of the secession crisis did not, at first, dramatically change the position of many abolitionists in regard to the federal government. In fact, the degree to which many Boston radicals resisted the "rally around the flag" mentality that otherwise dominated the city was notable. In the immediate aftermath of the 1860 election, Phillips celebrated that "for the first time in our history the *slave* has chosen a President," even as he cautioned that Lincoln was "not an Abolitionist, hardly an antislavery man" and recounted the various assurances Lincoln had given that he would maintain white supremacy. Interpreting the victory of the Republican Party as evidence of the increasing antislavery sentiment of the North, Phillips predicted that antislavery Northerners would increasingly come to value liberty over the Union, decoupling Daniel Webster's famous dyad. "Their motto will soon be," he declared, " 'Liberty first,' a long pause, then 'Union afterwards.' "[42]

Abolitionists had long been accustomed to a hostile public, but they were unprepared for the violence and mob activity that confronted them during the secession crisis. By the late 1850s, they took pride in the fact that they were no longer the target of vicious antiabolitionist mobs, as they had been in the 1830s. Just a month before Lincoln's election Garrison had boasted that "the struggle for freedom of speech and of the press has everywhere been fought, and the victory won."[43] That they could now conduct meetings in peace and rely on a degree of public support was one of the few tangible signs of abolitionist success. As the secession crisis began, though, this all seemed to crumble, as violent mobs in Syracuse, Ann Arbor, and elsewhere attacked abolitionist meetings and shouted down antislavery voices. The black abolitionist George T. Downing called this mob activity a "rowdy feeling, which now rules Boston."[44]

In December, one month after Lincoln's election, abolitionists became victims of mob violence for the first time in decades. On December 3, 1860, a mob (Phillips sneered that they were the "snobbish sons of fathers lately rich, anxious to show themselves rotten before they are ripe") took control of an abolitionist meeting commemorating John Brown and used the platform to pass resolutions conciliatory to the South.[45] This was not a mob of drunk rowdies or the desperate poor; rather, as abolitionists emphasized, it was the business community that had come out to silence the antislavery speakers. One abolitionist declared, "They looked like the frequenters of State street, and of the avenues of wholesale trade in cotton goods."[46] After abolitionists retreated to the Joy Street Church to continue their meeting, black attendees were followed home by what Douglass described as a well-dressed mob of "gentlemen" who threw stones at black passersby and attacked a number of prominent black abolitionists with clubs.[47] In the aftermath of these assaults, well-known abolitionists took to arming themselves when they walked the streets of Boston, and young men such as Oliver Wendell Holmes Jr. and the German-American members of the *Sozialistischer Turnerbund* volunteered to act as bodyguards for abolitionist speakers.

For many northern conservatives, abolitionists' eager embrace of disunionism, or their fiery rejection of the compromises supposedly necessary to keep the Union together, which seemed to be the same thing, put New England abolitionists in the same camp as the southern rebels. In New York the inventor and nativist Samuel Morse headed the reactionary American Society for Promoting National Unity, dedicated to combating the ideas of the "visionary reformers," who were taking the Declaration of Independence too seriously and creating "a feeling of hostility between the North and the South."[48] Even Richard Henry Dana Jr., a thinker with solid reformist, if not radical, credentials, compared Garrison and Phillips to the southern rebels, claiming that the New England radicals had "seceded long ago."[49] The conservative Democratic *Boston Post*, bending over backward to be fair-minded to what it called the "justly aggrieved South," claimed that Massachusetts had often been disloyal to the Constitution, especially the "traitors here, who, for years, have been proclaiming our Constitution and Union to be a covenant with death."[50] The *Post* piously disclaimed any involvement in the mob activity in Boston, but along with other Democratic presses it had played a significant role in legitimizing antiabolitionist violence.

During the winter of 1860–1861, abolitionist responses to the secession crisis, like those of most Americans, were mixed, as they attempted to keep up with the rapidly changing political landscape and assess whether the South's threats were serious. Even after South Carolina seceded, many Northerners continued to suspect that the region was simply bluffing, once again playing the secession card and hoping for concessions from a North that, up to now, had been all too willing to cave to southern bluster. Given the seeming conservatism of Lincoln, who promised to protect slavery in the South and abide by the Fugitive Slave Act, Garrison thought that slaveholders would be mad to abandon the protection of the federal government. Instead, he reminded his readers, "By their bully and raving, they have many times frightened the North into base submission to their demands—and they expect to do it again!"[51] In December a correspondent wrote to the *Liberator* hoping that abolitionists would concede nothing to the "pointless irony of Southern braggadocio."[52]

Remembering the proslavery compromises to which the North had agreed in 1850, the last time that the South had threatened to secede, abolitionists made resistance to any compromise the centerpiece of their strategy. For years they had been railing against actual compromises—the constitutional clauses that protected slavery, deals with the South that allowed slave states in the Union, the concessions made by the North in 1850, the opening up of Kansas and Nebraska to slavery—and often against the very idea of moral compromise itself.[53] A central part of the abolitionist imagination, one that distinguished men and women such as Garrison or Phillips from antislavery politicians such as Seward or Lincoln, was their disdain for the horse-trading and "any-means-to-an-end" logic of antebellum politics. The abolitionist and Transcendentalist James Freeman Clarke, in a widely circulated pamphlet written after Lincoln's election, articulated how this anti-instrumental idealism motivated abolitionist resistance. He condemned the northern politicians who became so invested in designing new means to preserve the Union that they had forgotten the ends for which the Union existed. "Surrendering any principles of liberty or justice," Clarke warned, was a foolish privileging of the "value of methods, but not the superior values of principles."[54] Now, as some northern politicians contemplated another concession to the South—among the proposals were plans to pass unrepealable constitutional amendments that would guarantee slavery where it existed, strip northern blacks of civil rights, and mandate colonization—abolitionists had to mobilize against the most dangerous compromises ever proposed.

Black abolitionists were especially concerned with addressing these developments, as white politicians eagerly volunteered to trade away black civil rights. On February 14, just days after Jefferson Davis became president of the Confederacy, a massive meeting of the "colored citizens of Massachusetts" convened at the Joy Street Church to respond to the Peace Conference currently being held in Washington. J. Sella Martin called the Crittenden Compromise, the era's most prominent attempt to restore the Union by forever cementing slavery, "one of the most atrocious onslaughts on human liberty" ever contemplated. Black abolitionists all agreed that any compromise would be a disaster, but they were split on the degree to which they should trust their white neighbors in the North. Dr. J. B. Smith of New Bedford felt that "the colored man had placed too much confidence in the non-slaveholding States and placed too little reliance on themselves," and Martin agreed that the North was willing to "sacrifice those few colored men who have received a portion of the common liberty." On the other hand, William Wells Brown and Robert Morris both argued that there were encouraging signs despite the dark national climate. To Morris, Massachusetts politics appeared "progressive," slowly improving over the last twenty-five years.[55]

After South Carolina and the cotton states announced their secession, Garrison articulated a concrete position: the North should peacefully allow the South to leave the Union rather than accede to its demands. Resisting compromise was a win-win for Garrisonian radicals: if Southerners folded after the North called their bluff, the abolitionists would have prevented another terrible compromise; if the South in fact seceded, then they would have realized the long-term abolitionist goal of disunion. Even before secession, Henry Ward Beecher, not a Garrisonian but associated with radical antislavery politics, had responded to threats of secession by declaring, "I don't believe they will; and I don't care if they do!" Wendell Phillips even praised the South for their courage, declaring on January 20, 1861, that he wished New England "could count one State as fearless" as South Carolina, and he seemed to equate the disunionism of southern fire-eaters with that of northern abolitionists. Southern leaders were using a similar strategy, Phillips argued, albeit for different ends. In March, the *Liberator* responded to Lincoln's inauguration by calling, in bold capital letters, for a peaceful "SEPARATION BETWEEN THE FREE AND SLAVE STATES." The *National Anti-Slavery Standard* declared, with a mix of fatalism and excitement, that "the Revolution of the seven States is perfect and complete, and that it is the duty of our government to acknowledge their independence and proceed to make the best treaty it can with them."[56]

Meanwhile, abolitionists began fantasizing about the creation of a "Northern Free Confederacy" that could be built without the slaveholders. This brought out the utopian streak in New England abolitionists, who began imagining a Constitution that would "omit, in all its basis papers both the words *male* and *white*," creating an egalitarian nation no longer marked by hierarchies of race and gender.[57]

After Sumter

Then, on April 12, the war began, and immediately it seemed as if everything changed. If the rumors of secession in the fall had pushed the northern political climate to the right as politicians made one last desperate attempt to mollify the South, Fort Sumter pushed it dramatically in the opposite direction as Northerners reacted with patriotic fury to the assault on federal troops. One observer described Boston's political climate in biblical terms: "The lion of Democracy has lain down with the lamb of Free Soilism, and a little negro is leading them," he told the *National Anti-Slavery Standard*.[58] James Freeman Clarke gushed, "If the *moral* condition of a nation is its *true* condition, then we may say that this nation of free States was never in a better condition than it is to-day."[59] Voices that had urged conciliation one week earlier now called for the recruitment of soldiers and the violent suppression of southern rebellion the next. Sensing the changed political climate, abolitionists dramatically adjusted their positions. Lydia Maria Child declared herself "glad to witness the universal enthusiasm for the U.S. Flag."[60]

While their impressions of the federal government and its emancipatory potential were changing, they did not jettison their earlier intellectual concerns and cultural politics. Instead they drew on earlier ideas about freedom and nationality rooted in their versions of New England identity to frame their stance. In the end, abolitionists would come to combine an appreciation for federal centralization with the old idea of New England as a repository of antislavery cultural values, projecting outward onto the entire nation the regional values of equality and freedom.

The most closely watched and dramatic conversion was that of Wendell Phillips, who on April 21 publicly endorsed the war effort. Three months earlier Phillips had told a hissing crowd, "All hail, then, Disunion!" but now he appeared in front of the Twenty-Eighth Congregational Society,

Theodore Parker's old church, on a platform festooned with American flags to "make the welcome I give this war hearty and hot." In an indication of his newfound patriotism, he declared that "to-day Abolitionist is merged in citizen—in American."[61]

Phillips claimed that he was motivated now, as he had been before, solely by concern for the slave. When discussing secession, though, he walked a fine line so as not to appear a hypocrite. He now maintained that, constitutionally, secession was disallowed; it could only be claimed as a revolutionary right, an expression of the one source of power—the people—that was greater than the Constitution. But South Carolina could only legitimately assert that it was expressing the will of its people if it had allowed both the 384,000 white men and the 484,000 black men of its population to have a say. Phillips thus distinguished his earlier support for disunion, which presumably would have resulted from a true democratic vote, from the current southern rebellion.[62] Garrison made a similar argument, suggesting that abolitionists had never claimed the right to secede without cause, but had believed that the action could be taken only for a democratic and just reason, a reason that the South lacked.[63]

At the end of his speech, Phillips revealed what may well have been his and other abolitionists' real motive for accepting the war. The one thing that Fort Sumter had settled, he told the audience, was "that there never can be a compromise." Abolitionists, in fact, were shocked at the degree to which the attack changed the political atmosphere of the North, forever scuttling any talk of a settlement between the regions. Phillips admitted his surprise, declaring, "the only mistake I have made, was in supposing Massachusetts wholly choked with cotton-dust and cankered with gold."[64] In an important editorial following Fort Sumter, the *Liberator* marveled that "for the first time, we find our State governments and our Federal government united in active and hearty opposition to the power that upholds slavery," and the paper declared that abolitionists' duties as "lovers of justice" were beginning to collide with their duties as citizens.[65]

Although Garrison and Phillips would remain vocal critics of many aspects of the North's policies, especially regarding the slow pace of emancipation and the arming of black troops, they were increasingly a loyal opposition, one pledged to work within the framework of the national state.[66] As Garrison wrote, "the old Union is *non est inventus,* and its restoration, with its pro-slavery compromises, well-nigh impossible. The conflict is really between the civilization of freedom and the barbarism of slavery."⁶⁷ On December 13, 1861, the veteran abolitionist symbolically changed the masthead of the *Liberator*, Boston's preeminent abolitionist newspaper: "The United States Constitution is 'a covenant with death, and an agreement with hell,'" was removed and replaced with the more prosaic "Proclaim Liberty throughout all the Land, to all the inhabitants thereof."⁶⁸

The European Left and the Birth of "Homogeneous" Institutions

In early April 1861, as Lincoln debated whether to come to the aid of the blockaded Fort Sumter, the *Liberator* ran a lengthy translation of a German pamphlet by the revolutionary theorist Karl Heinzen. In a work of abstract political philosophy, Heinzen, an unfairly forgotten abolitionist intellectual, was making a crucial intervention into antislavery thought, strongly arguing in favor of what he called a "unitarian" government, a centralized democratic state. Translated into English just as the war began, Heinzen's bold predictions of 1853, that slavery would inevitably cause the federal system to split, gave credence to his theories and played a significant role in reconciling Massachusetts abolitionists to a more powerful centralized government.

An atheist and avowed advocate of political violence, Heinzen seems like an odd character to have been given significant space in the Garrisonian *Liberator* during such a crucial time. Heinzen was a "48er," one of the German revolutionaries who had moved to America following the failed rebellions. He and Karl Marx had been drinking buddies, and Heinzen contributed to Marx's *Rheinische Zeitung*. By 1847, though, the two had parted ways over a series of doctrinal and philosophical issues. Marx thought Heinzen misunderstood Hegel and was angry that he preached revolution to the peasant masses, rather than the urban proletariat. Like most of Marx's friendships, their relationship ended amid a series of vicious polemics over doctrinal purity. Heinzen interpreted the failure of the 1848 revolutions as a result of the insufficient rigor and violence of revolutionaries, and he became a prominent advocate of political terrorism—of the necessity of the violent repression of counterrevolutionaries as well as tyrannicide as a political strategy. After relocating to America, Heinzen became a victim of political violence himself, as slaveholders repressed his antislavery activities in Texas. He eventually found his way to Boston, where he began publishing a radical and influential German-language paper, *Der Pionier*.⁶⁹

Marx may have dismissed Heinzen's philosophical pretensions, but in his essay in the *Liberator* Heinzen sounded like a good Hegelian, declaring his object to be "subjecting the federative system to a rational and radical critique." He argued that, just as individuals judged their own lives by abstract standards of rationality, it was the task of activists to subject the state to similar rational criticisms and then to "strive for its realization."[70] The recent failure of revolutions in Germany, where the endless squabbling of provisional governments in each state had allowed absolutist counterrevolutionaries to regroup, was no doubt on Heinzen's mind. He admitted that federal systems—governments in which power is devolved to local authorities—were often associated with republicanism in nineteenth-century Atlantic thought. But states that required divided authority, Heinzen argued, were "defective" ones that would, inevitably, end in either division or eventual consolidation. The devolution of power was necessary, he wrote, where governments were controlled by undemocratic executive powers; there local forms of power could act as bulwarks against centralizing tyranny. But in "ideal" states, where the people could properly express their democratic wishes, a "unitarian" state was better able to give voice to the "general interest."

The *Liberator*, no doubt, found Heinzen's text attractive because of the role he assigned slavery and slaveholders in dividing the American republic. His prediction that "the sectional policy of the slave States . . . *will sooner or later secede, or compel the Union to a forced reconstruction,* and the result of that reconstruction must be a unitarian State," was remarkably prescient. Local forms of power, Heinzen argued, were necessarily particular and irrational, incapable of administering the general will according to "prevailing reason." Centralized authority was tied to the democratic expression of rational and universal ideas, just as Parker and other abolitionists had declared. True democracy, Heinzen argued, would be possible only if America became a consolidated state, while under the current federal system, "*it is and will remain more or less in the hands of the aristocrats and slaveholders.*"[71] This attack on the undemocratic power of local authority was a good example of the liberal nationalism that Thomas Bender sees as representative of Atlantic thought in the age of the Civil War. Throughout the Atlantic world liberals and radicals responded to this "federative crisis" by counseling a more unified state in which one's national citizenship would be the primary guarantor of civil rights.[72]

Much has been written about the abolitionists' embrace of the war powers clause as a tool for emancipation.[73] It is important to note, though, that the rediscovery of John Quincy Adams's arguments about the president's powers came at a time in which abolitionists were increasingly associating democratic freedom with a strong national government. In celebrating Heinzen abolitionists embraced a political theory in which democratic politics were tied to the construction of national states that alone were capable of upholding the general democratic will against the various particularistic powers of local authorities. By removing the mediating influence of local "egotistic" forms of authority, this system would increase the democratic potential of the national government. Moreover, abolitionists were as likely to draw on sources tied to the European left as they were to draw on American sources such as Adams when they began to advocate a strong central government. The antiabolitionist press certainly believed that centralization derived from the European left, declaring the "notion that these United States are a consolidated nation," to be a "French red republican theory" that was "common among higher law devotees, and the unreflecting youths who are educated by anti-slavery lecturers."[74]

In the coming months Wendell Phillips, in particular, would develop an analysis of the war that seemed to combine Heinzen's distrust of local authority with the old abolitionist view that there was an idea of liberty—now associated with the whole North, not simply New England—that could be made real if the North won the war. The conflict was fundamentally between democracy and aristocracy, he told audiences. His idea that the nation had split into two sides, one devoted to liberty, another to slavery, was old; what was new was his solution. If the North and South were not going to split, it made sense for the free states to exert dominance over the slave states, a process that required central control.

Taking a cue from Heinzen, he declared that the result of the war must be to "remove that cause which divides us, to make our institutions homogeneous."[75] The language of "homogeneity" was the clearest way in which Heinzen's support for a "unitary" state made itself felt. As the Transcendentalist minister O. B. Frothingham declared, "Heterogeneous Europe may support a hundred differing dynasties. Homogeneous America can only support one." And the antislavery preacher made it clear that the prevailing "idea" of that homogeneous America would be liberty.[76] Ending slavery would provide justice to the slave, but it would also enable America to achieve an ideal and unified nationality. The *Commonwealth*, an antislavery Boston newspaper, declared that the "unity and homogeneity" of

America's geography were environmental evidence of the divine plan—"the great currents and survey and system of Eternal Laws"—mandating emancipation and unified institutions.[77]

Meanwhile black abolitionists also began to adopt the imagery of American patriotism. On April 23, ten days after they first received word of the southern attack on Sumter, black Bostonians held a meeting to discuss the formation of a drill company. As the meeting commenced, "a beautiful American flag" was hoisted onto the stage, an event greeted "with tumultuous enthusiasm."[78] Still unable to join either the U.S. Army or the Massachusetts militia, the 125 black residents who signed up for the "Home Guard" intended that their show of patriotism would shame racist policymakers. The Home Guard served as a bridge between the earlier forms of black militant communal organizations, such as the Liberty Guards and the Massasoit Guards, and future black military organizations such as the famous 54th Massachusetts Regiment.[79]

Even as the *Liberator* proudly reported on blacks' donations to the Union cause and their pro-Union meetings, significant discontent continued to boil beneath the facade of black patriotism.[80] When black activists attempted to demonstrate this fidelity, they were rewarded not with gratitude but with racial fury. When black Bostonians attempted to hold a meeting to organize aid to the Union war effort, a white policeman told them, "We want you d—d niggers to keep out of this; this is a white man's war."[81] And when a similar group in New York tried to hold a meeting "for the purpose of tendering their services to the Government," they were dispersed by the police, who feared that such a display of black citizenship might "exasperate the South."[82] Thus when the *Anglo-African* used the language of America as a "homogenous people," it was as a counterfactual; the black newspaper was well aware of how stark divisions of race split the nation.[83] In fact, the paper largely resisted the rush to unthinking jingoism. Although the editors were confident that war would ultimately benefit the cause of black freedom, they mocked what they referred to as a "national hypnotism," an affliction they diagnosed as "a mania for red, white and blue, and frantic demonstrations over the Flag of our Union."[84] This skepticism, which the *Anglo-African* displayed at the start of the war, foreshadowed the later conflicts that occurred when many abolitionists pushed their reluctant black colleagues to enlist in the U.S. Army, even though black soldiers received lower pay and served under white officers.[85]

An Ideology for the War

As soon as the war began, Boston abolitionists sought to imbue the conflict with an ideological purpose. In this they struggled against the Democratic Party, which wanted a conservative war that would restore the Union "as it was," and even many Republicans, who shrunk from openly declaring the war to be antislavery. Abolitionists argued that only armies with "ideas" at their back could conquer the South; only by inspiring troops with principles and a sense of purpose could the North win the war. As James Freeman Clarke told his congregation, "An army is not as strong as a principle—*Ideas* lie back of armies, back of guns and cannon. Cannon and guns fight as the idea directs. . . . An army fighting without ideas and convictions is the unmagnetized nail." Throughout the war, Boston antislavery activists would argue that each setback had been caused by what the *Commonwealth* called the "Want of Ideas in the Army."[86]

If, according to the abolitionists, the army needed ideas, those same abolitionists knew exactly what could provide them: the unique cultural heritage of New England. They began projecting onto the entire nation virtues they had once reserved for only the region. "The two great ideas of the war," declared the *Commonwealth*, "that of the Union, and that of freedom to every inhabitant—have in reality become one. That we cannot have the former if we do not have the latter, is a settled point."[87]

Emerson expressed this new nationalism well in the *Atlantic Monthly*. He had once declared that "nationality is babyishness for the most part," but now found himself writing a paean to "American Civilization."[88] For Emerson the Civil War was a grand conflict between the ideas embodied in northern and in southern civilization. Defining civilization in terms of both technological advancement and racial characteristics, he was particularly interested in the "genius" of each region, as well as its ability to follow ideas. The central quality of civilization, he declared, was morality, and quoting Kant he defined moral action as the ability to follow abstract and universal ethical codes. A civilized man, Emerson wrote, "leans on a principle, when he is the vehicle of ideas." The war was thus one of civilization versus barbarism, as the "Southern States have introduced confusion into the moral sentiments of their people, by . . . denying a man's right to his labor." Southern life was feudal, expressed in regular violence, aristocratic disdain for labor, and low levels of education and industry. Thus "emancipation is the demand of civilization." Turning the Civil War into a war of freedom would serve to spread the "best civilization" over the whole continent.[89]

In its context, of course, Emerson was lending his prestigious voice to the Radical Republican position, demanding immediate emancipation and "justice" for the newly freed blacks. But he was also doing so in language drenched with racial assumptions. Failure to emancipate the slaves, he warned, could lead to the "Africanization" of the country, the result of an inevitable race war. Moreover, as scholars of imperialism have well demonstrated, this language of violently spreading civilization over barbarous people would have an ignoble impact in the coming years. Emerson, of course, was implying that southern whites, despite their own racial self-conceit, were the ones who lacked civilization and needed the guidance of the Union army. But his association of civilization with the "genius" of certain races, and with their ability to improve technologically and economically, also allowed him to condemn Native Americans and Africans, whom he falsely claimed had remained in the same status for centuries.

Emerson's position developed out of the ideas that were prevalent among abolitionists before the war. The rigors of war would make real the "idea" of New England—ideals of liberty and equality—that had previously lay hidden beneath the various compromises of the cotton elite. Meanwhile the Union army would carry New England civilization south, spreading these ideas throughout the nation. Their preexisting preference for these cultural values convinced many white abolitionists to join in the war effort. But at the same point, the old racial language that had complicated this message before the war re-emerged, now cloaked in a language of civilization and the "genius" of the American people, a community often explicitly defined as white.

Black intellectuals, meanwhile, constantly sought to reinsert the idea of racial equality into abolitionist discourse, to strip from this new American nationalism its exclusivity. In 1862, J. Sella Martin published a poem titled *The Hero and the Slave* that captured well the black activists' ambivalent embrace of the Union. The bulk of the poem's action takes place during the Baltimore Riot of 1861, when pro-southern rioters attacked Union troops from Massachusetts as they passed through to Washington, D.C. The protagonist, an unnamed ex-slave, stumbles upon a wounded Union soldier and shelters him from the fury of the mob. The black man does this not out of national pride, but because as a slave he had long heard that Massachusetts was uniquely dedicated to liberty, the "first to give the negro freedom."⁹⁰ Later, having escaped from bondage, the slave makes his way to Boston, where he is rudely treated by a racist crowd. They call him a "nigger" and want to throw him out of the celebration for the returning Massachusetts soldiers, until the man he saved recognizes him. The poem ends with a rhetorical question and warning:

> Shall our hatred of the negro
> Bred by those who *hate us* worse,
> Make our State, and race, and nation,
> Subjects of their double curse?
> Love of masters—we have lost it—
> Love of slaves we too may lose.⁹¹

Even as he called for expanding the scope of the war to include emancipation, Martin was privileging the position of Massachusetts over that of the nation. The anonymous slave protects the soldier not out of dedication to the Union cause, nor because the soldier is able to offer him emancipation, but because he is associated with Massachusetts, and therefore with the idea of liberty. Although Martin embraced the idea that New England was particularly devoted to antislavery (or, equally plausibly, saw that employing this language would be a useful way to appeal to white Yankees), he was not uncritical of the Union project or Boston society. Until the white soldier intervenes, the black hero is in danger of being thrown out of a Union celebration, symbolically enacting the exclusion from the war effort that was then occurring. Moreover, the last line implies that the Union is in danger of losing any support that slaves might offer. Martin's poem captured the ambivalence that black activists felt during the Civil War toward both nation and state, as they worried that they were being left out of the new nationalism.

This tension between Emerson's nationalistic readings of liberty, in which freedom and equality were described as the particular possessions of Americans, a group coded as white and northern, and the broader and more universal notion of rights that black abolitionists articulated would continue to haunt northern political life. The self-satisfied complacency of Gilded Age New England elites—who appealed to their legacy as abolitionists to obtain moral authority even as their ethical and political vision narrowed, their idealism devolved into self-righteousness, and their Transcendentalism turned into irrelevant mysticism—was a logical consequence of this earlier celebration of the antislavery cultural values of New England. Meanwhile, black abolitionists kept alive their attempts to make real a commitment to equal rights and protections, even as the political climate moved to the right in the aftermath of Reconstruction.

NOTES

1. "New Occasions Teach New Duties," *Liberator*, May 3, 1861.
2. Historians today have largely agreed with the Garrisonian position that the Constitution contained significant protections for slavery. See, for instance, David Waldsreicher, *Slavery's Constitution: From Revolution to Ratification* (New York: Hill & Wang, 2010).
3. Quoted in Henry Mayer, *All on Fire: William Lloyd Garrison and the Abolition of Slavery* (New York: Norton, 1998), 522.
4. W. Caleb McDaniel, *The Problem of Democracy in the Age of Slavery: Garrisonian Abolitionists and Transatlantic Reform* (Baton Rouge: Louisiana State University Press, 2013).
5. Ibid.
6. Thomas Wentworth Higginson, *The New Revolution: A Speech before the American Anti-Slavery Society, at Their Annual Meeting in New York, May 12th, 1857* (Boston: R. F. Wallcut, 1857), 7.
7. Wendell Phillips, "Idols" (1859), in *Speeches, Lectures, and Letters* (Boston: James Redpath, 1863), 243.
8. Quoted in James McPherson, *The Struggle for Equality: Abolitionists and the Negro in the Civil War and Reconstruction* (Princeton: Princeton University Press, 1967), 43.
9. Ralph Waldo Emerson, *Selected Journals, 1841–1877*, ed. Lawrence Rosenwald (New York: Library of America, 2010), 324; "A New Way to Settle the Cotton Question" and "Northern Agitation—Is It to Stop?," *Boston Post*, December 3, 1860.
10. Joanne Pope Melish, *Disowning Slavery: Gradual Emancipation and "Race" in New England, 1780–1860* (Ithaca, N.Y.: Cornell University Press, 1998).
11. Joseph Conforti, *Imagining New England: Explorations of Regional Identity from the Pilgrims to the Mid-Twentieth Century* (Chapel Hill: University of North Carolina Press, 2000), 123–202.
12. Theodore Parker, "A New Lesson for the Day: A Sermon Preached at the Music Hall, in Boston, on Sunday, May 25, 1856," in *The Collected Works of Theodore Parker*, ed. Frances Power Cobbe, 14 vols. (London: Trübner, 1876), 4:291.
13. See, for instance, Parker, "The State of the Nation, Considered in a Sermon for Thanksgiving Day—Preached at the Melodeon, November 28, 1850," in *Collected Works*, 4:253–57.
14. Emerson, *Selected Journals*, 2:554–55; Phillips, "Lincoln's Election" (1860), in *Speeches, Lectures, and Letters*, 297.
15. Parker, "The State of the Nation," 4:258, and Parker, "Speech at a Meeting of the American Anti-Slavery Society, to Celebrate the Abolition of Slavery by the French Republic, April 6, 1848," in *Collected Works*, 5:86.
16. Phillips, "Harper's Ferry" (1859), in *Speeches, Lectures, and Letters*, 281.
17. Henry David Thoreau, "A Plea for Captain John Brown" (1859), in *Collected Essays and Poems* (New York: Library of America, 2001), 399.
18. Stephen Kantrowitz, "Fighting Like Men: Civil War Dilemmas of Abolitionist Manhood," in *Battle Scars: Gender and Sexuality in the American Civil War*, ed. Nina Silber and Catherine Clinton (New York: Oxford University Press, 2006), 20–21.

19. Thomas Wentworth Higginson to F. W. Bird, January 7, 1857, Francis William Bird Papers (MS Am 1851), box 175, Houghton Library, Harvard University; Phillips, "Disunion" (1861), in *Speeches, Lectures, and Letters*, 360.
20. There was no clear role for Catholic immigrants, either. These were mostly antiabolitionist Irish, who in many ways posed a larger ideological threat to the image of idealist antislavery New England.
21. Quoted in Henry Steele Commager, *Theodore Parker: Yankee Crusader* (Boston: Beacon Press, 1947), 147.
22. Theodore Parker, *The Nebraska Question: Some Thoughts on the New Assault upon Freedom in America and the General State of the Country* (Boston: Benjamin Mussey, 1854), 23.
23. Quoted in Austin Bearse, *Reminiscences of Fugitive Slave Law Days in Boston* (Boston: Warren Richardson, 1880), 13.
24. See Michael Pierson, *Free Hearts and Free Homes: Gender and American Antislavery Politics* (Chapel Hill: University of North Carolina Press, 2003). John Ashworth makes a similar argument—that industrial capitalism had encouraged different family structures and sexual practices in the North and that many Northerners understood their opposition to slavery through such gendered critiques of the slave South. John Ashworth, *Slavery, Capitalism, and Politics in the Antebellum Republic*, vol. 2, *The Coming of the Civil War, 1850–1861* (New York: Cambridge University Press, 2007), 173–338.
25. See "Speech of Wendell Phillips, Esq., at the Convention Held at Worcester, October 15 and 16, 1851," in Phillips et al., *Woman's Rights Tracts* (Boston: Robert Wallcut, 1854), 1–23.
26. For Nell on Attucks see Stephen Kantrowitz, "A Place for 'Colored Patriots': Crispus Attucks among the Abolitionists, 1842–1863," *Massachusetts Historical Review* 11 (2009): 97–117.
27. Charlotte Forten, "Glimpses of New England," *National Anti-Slavery Standard*, June 19, 1858.
28. "Frederick Douglass at Music Hall," *Liberator*, December 14, 1860.
29. Quoted in "The Boston Massacre, March 5th, 1775: Commemorative Festival in Faneuil Hall," *Liberator*, March 12, 1858.
30. See, for example, William Wells Brown, *The Black Man: His Antecedents, His Genius, and His Achievements* (Boston: R. F. Wallcut, 1863), 34.
31. Quoted in "Meeting of Colored Citizens of New Bedford," *National Anti-Slavery Standard*, October 26, 1861.
32. Charlotte Forten Grimké, *The Journals of Charlotte Forten Grimké*, ed. Brenda Stevenson (New York: Oxford University Press, 1988), 307 (May 2, 1858).
33. Rev. Alexander Crummell, "A Lecture on Liberia," *Pine and Palm*, June 8, 1861.
34. "The African Civilization Society," *Weekly Anglo-African*, November 16, 1861.
35. John R. McKivigan, *Forgotten Firebrand: James Redpath and the Making of Nineteenth-Century America* (Ithaca, N.Y.: Cornell University Press, 2008), 71.
36. Quoted ibid., 72.
37. George T. Downing, "Why Go to Hayti," *Weekly Anglo-African*, March 9, 1861.
38. Although Garrison eventually came out against the Haitian emigration scheme, he was willing to "believe it is intended for your good, and for the good of those who shall go to Hayti," and he added, "So far, then, as this emigration, inaugurated by the government of Hayti, and its official agent, Mr. Redpath, are concerned, I have no censure whatever to bestow, and no quarrel to make, here or anywhere else." "William Lloyd Garrison's

Address, Delivered at Rev. Mr. Grimes's Church, Boston, Sunday Evening, July 21, 1861," *National Anti-Slavery Standard*, August 3, 1861.
39. The Carl A. Kroch Library at Cornell University holds William C. Nell's copies of the *Pine and Palm*.
40. "Affairs about Boston," *Weekly Anglo-African*, March 2, 1861.
41. "President Lincoln's Inaugural," *Weekly Anglo-African*, March 16, 1861.
42. Phillips, "Lincoln's Election," 294, 314.
43. Quoted from an October 11, 1860, letter reprinted in the *Liberator*. See "Letter from William Lloyd Garrison," *Liberator*, November 9, 1860.
44. "Affairs about Boston," *Weekly Anglo-African*, March 2, 1861.
45. Phillips, "Mobs and Education" (1860), in *Speeches, Lectures, and Letters*, 325.
46. "Notes on the Tremont Temple Mob," *Liberator*, December 14, 1860.
47. "Mobocratic Assault upon an Anti-Slavery Meeting in Boston," *Liberator*, December 7, 1860; "Frederick Douglass at Music Hall," *Liberator*, December 14, 1860.
48. Samuel B. Morse et al., *American Society for Promoting National Unity* (New York: John Trow, 1861), 3, 6.
49. "The Abolitionists of the North," *Liberator*, March 29, 1861.
50. "The American Union" and "Massachusetts and the Constitution," *Boston Post*, November 12, 1860.
51. "Southern Desperation," *Liberator*, November 16, 1860.
52. "Principle versus the Spirit of Fear," *Liberator*, December 14, 1860.
53. Andrew Delbanco criticizes this spirit of absolutism in his essay "The Abolitionist Imagination," based on a lecture he delivered at Harvard in 2010. See his *The Abolitionist Imagination* (Cambridge: Harvard University Press, 2012), which also contains critiques of his position by Manisha Sinha, John Stauffer, Darryl Pinckney, and Wilfred McClay.
54. "What Ought the North to Concede," *Liberator*, March 1, 1861.
55. "Affairs about Boston," *Weekly Anglo-African*, March 2, 1861.
56. "Henry Ward Beecher on the Dissolution of the Union," *Liberator*, December 7, 1860; Phillips, "Disunion," 343–44; "Mr. Lincoln's Inaugural Address," *Liberator*, March 8, 1861; "Probabilities and Possibilities of Secession," *National Anti-Slavery Standard*, March 23, 1861.
57. "A Northern Free Confederacy," *Liberator*, March 29, 1861; "Address to the American People," *Liberator*, April 12, 1861.
58. "Our Boston Correspondence," *National Anti-Slavery Standard*, April 27, 1861.
59. "The State of the Nation," *National Anti-Slavery Standard*, May 4, 1861.
60. Lydia Maria Child, *Letters of Lydia Maria Child, with a Biographical Introduction by John G. Whittier and an Appendix by Wendell Phillips* (New York: Houghton, Mifflin, 1882), 150.
61. Phillips, "Disunion," 370, and "Under the Flag" (1861), in *Speeches, Lectures, and Letters*, 396.
62. Phillips, "Under the Flag," 406.
63. "Southern Disunionists and Northern Disunionists," *Liberator*, April 19, 1861.
64. Phillips, "Under the Flag," 407, 397, 411.
65. "New Occasions Teach New Duties," *Liberator*, May 3, 1861.
66. As an example of an early criticism of Union policy see Garrison's disappointed editorial: "'The Flag of Our Union'—What Does It Symbolize?," *Liberator*, June 7, 1861. Garrison argued that "the idea of fighting the slaveholders without the help of the slaves,

without the help of God and Refuge of the enslaved, is a daring one and an ambitious one. So was the idea of the arch rebel described by Milton, but it proved an impractical one."

67. William Lloyd Garrison, "The Relation of the Anti-Slavery Cause to the War," *National Anti-Slavery Standard,* May 18, 1861.
68. *Liberator,* December 13, 1861.
69. Carl Wittke, *Against the Current: The Life of Karl Heinzen* (Chicago: University of Chicago Press, 1945).
70. Karl Heinzen, "The People and the State; or the Unitarian State and the Federative State," *Liberator,* April 5, 1861.
71. Karl Heinzen, "The People and the State; or the Unitarian State and the Federative State," *Liberator,* April 12, 1861.
72. Thomas Bender, *A Nation among Nations: America's Place in World History* (New York: Hill & Wang, 2006), 116–50.
73. James Oakes, *Freedom National: The Destruction of Slavery in the United States, 1861–1865* (New York: Norton, 2013), 36.
74. "Ignorance of American Institutions; Massachusetts Heresies," *Boston Post,* November 15, 1860.
75. Phillips, "The War for the Union" (1861), in *Speeches, Lectures, and Letters,* 429.
76. "Union and Disunion," *National Anti-Slavery Standard,* May 11, 1861.
77. "Union Foundations," *The Commonwealth,* April 10, 1863; "The New Birth of the Nation, a Discourse, before the 28th Congregational Society, Boston, Sunday, April 26, 1863, by Samuel Johnson, Minister of the Free Church at Lynn," *The Commonwealth,* May 1, 1863.
78. "Meeting in Boston," *Weekly Anglo-African,* May 4, 1861.
79. "Meeting of Colored Citizens," *Liberator,* May 3, 1861; for more on the black militias in Massachusetts, see Stephen Kantrowitz, *More Than Freedom: Fighting for Black Citizenship in a White Republic, 1829–1889* (New York: Penguin, 2012), 198–204, 214–19.
80. "Meeting of Colored Citizens," *Liberator,* May 3, 1861.
81. Quoted in Kantrowitz, *More Than Freedom,* 263.
82. "Attack on the Constitution," *Weekly Anglo-African,* April 27, 1861.
83. "What We Are Fighting For," *Weekly Anglo-African,* September 14, 1861.
84. "National Hypnotism," *Weekly Anglo-African,* April 27, 1861.
85. Kantrowitz, *More Than Freedom,* 282–99.
86. James Freeman Clarke, "The Plagues of Egypt and America: A Sermon, Preached in Boston, Sept. 26th, 1862, Being the Sunday following the President's Proclamation," *The Commonwealth,* October 11, 1862; "Want of Ideas in the Army," *The Commonwealth,* November 15, 1862.
87. "Motives in the War," *The Commonwealth,* April 3, 1863.
88. Emerson, *Selected Journals,* 2:537.
89. Ralph Waldo Emerson, "American Civilization," *Atlantic Monthly* 9 (April 1862): 502–9.
90. Rev. J. Sella Martin, *The Hero and the Slave: Founded on Fact* (Boston: W. F. Brown, 1862), 6.
91. Ibid., 11.

The Rise and Fall of the Abolitionist Republic

RICHARD S. NEWMAN

On the eve of sectional war, Massachusetts abolitionists confronted a question lurking deep inside their collective psyche: What would success mean? While Bay State reformers could agree that the end of slavery nationally was a necessary precondition to any declaration of victory, they nevertheless fell into often acrimonious debate about the precise meaning of an abolitionist republic—what a nation without slavery would look like, how it would operate, and on what political, economic, and cultural terms black freedom might move forward.

Of course, abolitionists had decades of experience dissenting from one another. Yet the matter of abolition's potentially successful future now seemed less theoretical, more palpable, even imminent. With the Republican Party steadily gaining adherents throughout the North and Midwest, and with Massachusetts Republicans leading the charge against both the western expansion of slavery and the Slave Power's encroachments on white Northerners' rights, the question of just how a movement of "passionate outsiders" would become felicitous insiders pressed hard on the Bay State's antislavery faithful.[1] At the Massachusetts Anti-Slavery Society's annual convention in 1859, William Lloyd Garrison battled Garrisonians, while friends who had survived countless schisms fought among themselves with a passion that surprised even the most grizzled abolitionist. As Garrison remarked to the ever dour Parker Pillsbury (with whom he would soon break), he was tired of Massachusetts reformers' "somber and discouraging views of the state of our cause." With Jubilee nigh, Garrison believed that it was time for "a little sunshine" in the abolitionist movement.[2]

He would soon get his wish, of course, for Civil War emancipation came in a seeming flash. That meant Garrison had to change his views of the sinful nation against which he had fought tirelessly for decades. As he observed to English friends feting him in 1868, he had never been prouder than when raising the U.S. flag over Confederate Charleston—a shroud on the coffin of southern slavery—at the war's end. To see an abolitionist republic ascend was a miracle to Garrison.[3] His colleagues were not so sanguine, however. No sooner had the war ended than Garrison's onetime friend and now friendly nemesis, Frederick Douglass, called for a renewal of radical abolitionist commitments. True, Douglass conceded, slavery had been vanquished and an abolitionist nation proclaimed, but he feared that this new republic would not fully protect African Americans' rights. As Douglass yelled during a convention of black activists in Boston in 1865, "Peace for the southern white men [has] meant war against the Negro."[4] With those words, Douglass offered a keynote to his next phase of heroic activism. He would now struggle to reform a still imperfect American nation.

As these vignettes indicate, the prospect and reality of emancipation in the Civil War era prompted deep reflection among Massachusetts abolitionists broadly conceived. Having long fought for national emancipation, Bay State reformers surprised even themselves by so hotly contesting that much-hoped-for but elusive entity known as the abolitionist republic. John Stauffer has argued that antebellum abolitionists believed in their hearts and minds that slavery could in fact end on any given day.[5] Yet the suddenness of slavery's destruction in the 1860s created a wave of concern as well as jubilation among the antislavery faithful. Just what would the future bring? Would the looming abolitionist republic end bondage but not racial injustice? Would the reconstructed Union grant full equality, especially voting rights, to emancipated persons in the South and free blacks in the North? Would reconstruction be based on the liberal economic imperatives of free labor or the communitarian values of mutual responsibility—and would reunion's dreams sacrifice blacks' struggle for justice in either case? Then there was the matter of time. Should reformers demand that a pure abolitionist republic take shape immediately at war's end? Or should they recognize that an antislavery Union was the best that could be accomplished in wartime and that the nation's moral fabric would only slowly arc toward justice?

In answering these questions, abolitionists remained a querulous lot.[6] So whither the abolitionist republic? Perhaps more than any other group of reformers, Bay Staters constantly debated this vexing question throughout the 1860s, with their often competing visions of economic, military, and cultural reconstruction framing Union emancipation policies. From a throng of congressional and military abolitionists who hailed from Massachusetts (Nathaniel P. Banks, Charles Sumner, and Joseph Wilson, to name just a few) to well-known native sons and daughters who had long defined abolitionism nationally (Garrison, Wendell Phillips, Samuel J. May, Lydia Maria Child, Maria Weston Chapman, and even Douglass), Massachusetts in no small way shaped Americans' vision of a post-slavery United States. As George Loring told a Salem audience rather bluntly in 1865, the entire Civil War could be reduced to a rather simple query: Would South Carolina slavery or Massachusetts abolitionism define American society in the future? That question had now been answered firmly, Loring proclaimed, for "Massachusetts has carried the day."[7]

Yet the dual promises of Union victory and national emancipation created for Bay Staters what scholars would call a "republican moment": a time of intense debate over a society's ideal "civic personality."[8] While it may raise eyebrows to refer to the bloody Civil War as just such a moment, the analysis is more than apt. Indeed, much like Revolutionary and early national debates over the ideals of American governance, political economy, and social relations, Civil War debates over race, rebellion, and reunion all had at their core idealist notions of the American republic.[9] Having argued for years that their struggle aimed at restoring the American promise of liberty for all, black and white abolitionists took full advantage of military chaos in the 1860s to argue on behalf of a republic of racial virtue. Little wonder that modern Civil Rights reformers such as Martin Luther King would return to the promises laid down by abolitionists and others in the second founding of the 1860s. That era remains not just the ur-moment of American emancipation but a fertile time of nation building and political imagination.

In a very real way, abolitionists' republican moment flowed from antebellum sectional battles over the place of slavery in American culture. Then, as during the war, Bay State activists meditated thoughtfully on the nature of democracy, politics, and republics past, present, and future. By the early 1860s, however, abolitionists knew that time itself had shifted, providing them a hitherto unseen opportunity to work with politicians, military leaders, and citizens alike for a more perfect Union. Here, classical republicanism and the Republican Party met, as wartime abolitionists argued that the antislavery struggle stood for many of the same essential values that a reconstructed Union would: the expansion of liberty, the saliency of free labor markets, and the destruction of American slave powers in economic and political realms. When Union leaders listened, many Massachusetts abolitionists rejoiced at the prospect of converting their grand ideals into practical programs and policies: an American abolitionist republic.

Bay State reformers were not unmindful of this republic's foreign policy implications either. From the advent of the radical antislavery struggle onward, abolitionists situated their movement in a world of emancipation struggles all bending toward absolute justice. During the 1830s and 1840s, for instance, Garrisonians and their allies used British emancipation to shame Americans into confronting southern bondage. Though he was no hardcore race reformer, even Ralph Waldo Emerson referred to British emancipation as evidence of global humanity's moral uplift.[10] August First celebrations, which marked the formal unfurling of emancipation in the British Caribbean in 1834, remained on the abolitionist calendar well into the Civil War era. Each summer in the early 1860s, for instance, Bay Staters gathered in Abington to commemorate emancipation overseas while simultaneously pushing for complete abolition in the war-torn United States.[11] Massachusetts abolitionists also used the example of Francophone emancipation for inspiration in building a new republic: in 1862 the Bostonian Mary Booth, a Republican operative, translated the first volume of French political writer Augustin Cochin's treatise *L'Abolition de l'esclavage* (as *The Results of Emancipation*) in order to spur military and political attacks on Confederate slavery in the United States. Cochin hailed both French and British emancipation in the Caribbean over and against antiabolitionists who had created a whirl of doubts about black freedom globally. Led by the rabble-rousing New York physician John Van Evrie, antiabolitionists argued vociferously in the 1850s and early 1860s that emancipation had never worked anywhere in the Atlantic world. Building on abolitionists' studies of post-slavery society in the Caribbean, Cochin argued otherwise. By making Cochin's work readily available to members of the Lincoln administration who eagerly read her translation, Booth hoped to show that the only relevant lesson of international abolition was that it should have occurred sooner. Following Booth's and Cochin's lead, antislavery advocates in and beyond Massachusetts began touting Civil War emancipation as the fulfillment of global abolitionist dreams, with American freedom now presaging black liberty in Cuba and Brazil, the lone holdouts in the Atlantic world after the Confederacy's fall. As the Massachusetts politician and abolitionist George Boutwell argued, wartime abolition was thus not only expedient but morally necessary and just.[12]

No sooner had slavery been smashed, however, than reformers wondered again about their republican moment. As the religious reformer Lyman Abbott put it perceptively in 1867, "The abolition of slavery and the establishment of freedom are not one and the same thing."[13] Freedom was grand but it remained a tricky reality for black as well as white activists. Here, abolitionists' disagreements flowed not only from longstanding concerns about the means and ends of racial justice in American society but also from the launching of an abolitionist republic on the ashes of Union military victory. Indeed, the vice of military abolition was in its virtue, for watching slavery suddenly crumble around them meant that race reformers had precious little time to build an abolitionist republic from scratch. They had to trust that might had made right and that white Americans in both the North and South wanted an abolitionist republic after the war.

In short, while Massachusetts reformers could claim many victories on the road to final freedom, they remained divided over the shape and contours of a new republic. With this thought in mind, it may make sense to see national reconstruction's weaknesses as part and parcel of the rise and fall of abolitionism and not separate from it.

Toward an Abolitionist Republic

Although they often defined themselves as social agitators outside the political mainstream, many Massachusetts abolitionists came to see the Civil War through the lens of a political and social revolution that would bring them inside politics and the process of nation building. Eschewing previous understandings of political activism, Garrison, May, Lydia Maria Child, and for a while Wendell Phillips, among others, argued that the great slaveholder's rebellion of 1860–61 had shattered the antebellum politics of abolition, in which antislavery activists were cast as outsiders. Indeed, the violent nature of the war compelled many abolitionists to reexamine both their peace principles and their political commitments, if for no other reason than that war had become the most effective vehicle of national emancipation. When Charles Sumner argued in the early 1860s that the slaveholders' rebellion had erased the political legitimacy of both the planter class and the Confederate states—the Union as it was—it became easier for Garrison and others to jump on the Union bandwagon.[14] That does not mean there was in fact an antislavery Union at the start of the war. But Garrison in particular came to believe that, in a revolutionary time, social radicals had to commit to the political cause most closely aligned with right and might: that of the Union.[15]

The politics of sectionalism paved the way for an abolitionist republic, many Bay State reformers believed. During the 1850s, abolitionists everywhere girded for more direct confrontations with slaveholders, compelling them to articulate the broader political and philosophical meaning of the antislavery struggle. Massachusetts had been the self-styled home of radical abolitionism for more than a generation, and its proud abolitionists reasserted their leadership role in a changing antislavery struggle. Sensing that a broad swath of Northerners had tired of the "Slave Power," Bay Staters did more than criticize particular laws such as the Fugitive Slave Act of 1850, the Kansas-Nebraska Act, and the Dred Scott decision. They also appealed to the first principles of republican ideology: free speech, free markets, bodily liberty, open government, open society, and an open press.

Moreover, like the revolutionary founders, late antebellum abolitionists were obsessed with notions of decaying liberty in American culture: the nation's fall from republican grace that slavery and slaveholders' power had instigated within the United States. Indeed, with American slavery expanding economically and geographically and slaveholders' power pervading all branches of national government, Massachusetts abolitionists vigorously asserted that American freedom itself was in jeopardy. In 1856, May catalogued the "victims" of slavery by noting that the Fugitive Slave Act harmed not only black and white Americans but the very idea of just law. Referring to the sensational case of Solomon Northup, a free black man in New York who had been kidnapped into Deep South bondage for a dozen years before being liberated, May noted that it exhibited the tenor of the times: while "not under the Fugitive Law" per se, Northup's struggle offered a "striking illustration of the [slave] power which created that law."[16] There were untold numbers of Northups in American society, May indicated; in fact, he argued that American law itself, which had been intended to protect and not restrict liberty, had been entirely corrupted by slavery and slaveholders. Abolitionists likewise highlighted slavery's impact on another key republican institution, the free press. As one of May's colleagues noted, of the hundreds of American papers in existence in the 1850s, only a precious few (perhaps forty) were truly dedicated to free discourse rather than protecting slavery and the sinful status quo.[17] For abolitionists, the moral of the story was that slavery overwhelmed a potentially virtuous American republic.[18]

By the mid-1850s several Bay State reformers thought that Americans were finally ready to embrace abolitionists' critique of the Slave Power. Even Theodore Parker, who reveled in his identity as a disturber of American peace, noted that radicals might well be on a new path to civic power. Indeed, many Northerners realized that abolitionists had not been agitators so much as prophets. Look no further than the Republican Party, Parker observed, which had been winning antislavery friends in a staggeringly short time. Many Bay Staters, he proclaimed, took part in this Republican juggernaut. Through the Republican Party, slavery and not freedom was now under broad attack. For the first time since radical abolition emerged in the 1830s, abolitionists were part of a mainstream movement. There was, Parker concluded, great hope for an abolitionist future.[19]

Nevertheless, Parker pointed out, revolutions were not animated by ideas alone. To be consummated, they must be followed by "action," which, as he put it, meant making "the thought a thing."[20] A preview of Parker's "thought in action" came in January 1861, when the Republican Party marshaled enough political might in the midst of the secession crisis to admit Kansas—that long-embattled western territory—as a free state. Abolitionists everywhere rejoiced, feeling that they had created the framework for such political action. The Slave Power had been defeated because radicals and politicians had taken advantage of a crisis to advance American liberty. In many ways, it was the first victory for the abolitionist republic.

Sectional war did something similar: it offered abolitionists the chance to form alliances with Unionists and ground antislavery thinking in concrete political and military steps that would lead to the demise of bondage. Throughout the war years, many Bay State abolitionists justified their brash Unionism by arguing that they had actually been fighting a "moral war" against bondage for thirty years. Backing military emancipation now was no contradictory step for reformers to take. As the longtime Boston radical Maria Weston Chapman noted in September 1861, the Civil War brought the prospect of abolition so close to the nation that abolitionists should urge the government to use every bit of its military power to smash bondage *inside* the South, a move that even arch-radicals often avoided advocating before 1860.[21] But times had changed, and Chapman did more than talk: she circulated a petition to female abolitionists elsewhere "requesting the government, under the war power, to proclaim the abolition of slavery as the speediest and most efficient means for quelling the rebellion."[22] Like the founders of 1776, Chapman and her allies realized that revolutionary moments and republican experiments came around only once in a great while. Garrison certainly agreed, telling abolitionists to back the Union as perhaps the last best hope of immediate emancipation.

Or maybe not. For other Bay State reformers, wartime abolitionism potentially compromised antislavery goals by mistaking the power of force for the power of ideals. Lydia Maria Child captured this sentiment perfectly when she wrote in 1861 that, though "emancipation would be the result of the war," it would be a "forced result" and "not the chosen one."[23] While sure that American moral sentiment was shifting in favor of emancipation, Child agreed with others that the abolitionist republic had to be established on a much firmer footing than violent expediency in order to succeed. Parker Pillsbury agreed with Child, noting that wartime abolitionism might fool Americans into thinking that slavery was merely a southern labor problem and not a national moral disgrace.[24] Speaking at the July 1862 picnic of the Essex County Antislavery Society, Henry Wright echoed some of these thoughts, too, arguing that unless and until racial prejudice had been destroyed, the American Union—and not merely the Confederacy—must be smashed as well.[25]

In Boston that same summer, Wendell Phillips urged reformers to return to the social movement philosophy that had defined immediate abolitionism in the 1830s. By pressuring but not joining the political mainstream, Phillips argued, abolitionists could best promulgate the struggle for racial justice.[26] Clearly, the comments of Child, Phillips, Pillsbury, and Wright, coming as they did before Lincoln's Emancipation Proclamation took effect, registered deep dissatisfaction with the Union's piecemeal antislavery policies of 1861 and 1862. The dawning of mass black freedom in 1863 changed the abolitionist calculus somewhat, for Child and Wright would for a time become champions of Lincoln's Union. But Phillips, like Pillsbury, would become an even more vocal critic of both Lincoln and the Union in subsequent years. In Phillips's eyes, during the 1860s only a fatally flawed abolitionist republic was in the works, and it was something he could not support.

As these diverging positions indicate, Civil War reformers' first task was to decide whether or not a true republican moment had appeared in the wake of military and political emancipation. As longtime critics of the founders' fatal compromises on slavery, many Massachusetts abolitionists were not necessarily friendly to the idea of walking with slaveholding founders of 1787; instead, they hoped to smash the limits of the old republic by returning to the virtuous spirit of 1776. But as students of history, Bay State reformers knew that republics were fragile and often elusive. Indeed, antebellum abolitionists emerged just as western territorial development renewed debates over republican experiments through time and space. In art, literature, and political discourse, Americans wondered if they were imbedded in the cycles of history or beyond them.[27] For black abolitionist thinkers such as the Bostonian David Walker, American republicanism had long since been compromised by racial oppression. When Garrisonians emerged in the 1830s, they optimistically assumed that a massive social movement could overwhelm the corrupted nation and bring Americans back to the founding republican ideals of equality and justice for all, laid down in 1776.[28] That did not happen. When a seemingly better republican moment came around in the 1860s, then, Garrison jumped at it.

But the history of antislavery taught another lesson: there were few good national or global models to follow. While the idea of an abolitionist republic had tantalized reformers since the eighteenth-century beginnings of the movement, race reformers had often been disappointed in the results of post-emancipation societies in the Atlantic world, particularly those in the northern United States. Pennsylvania, for example, had drained slavery from its midst but rescinded blacks' suffrage. Among Atlantic-world powers, Great Britain had created a towering example of imperial abolition in the 1830s—yet the compensation it awarded to slaveholders appalled many American reformers.

Even Massachusetts, perhaps the closest thing to an abolitionist republic before the Civil War, had limitations. Though it was deemed a relatively safe state for radicals, fugitives, and free blacks alike, black reformers believed that Massachusetts suffered from a resilient brand of racism. When he returned to Massachusetts in the midst of the war, Frederick Douglass told a Boston audience that "every time I come to these [antislavery] meetings I feel that I have lost a great deal by making my home west of Boston, West of Massachusetts." For "if anywhere in the country there is to be found a sense of justice," he continued, "I look for it in the East, I look for it here."[29] Nevertheless, battles over prejudice and "racial chauvinism" (in Margot Minardi's words) haunted Bay State reformers.[30] Douglass believed that any abolitionist republic had to confront these racial demons before moving forward.

Other black leaders agreed. Samuel Ringgold Ward used the word "dictation" to refer to white Garrisonians' antebellum propensity for barking orders at blacks. Writing to Frederick Douglass from London in 1855, Ward rebuked white reformers who preached racial equality but refused to embrace it within the movement proper. Having left the United States for Canada, where like Douglass he edited his own antislavery newspaper, Ward believed that building an abolitionist republic in America was difficult if not impossible precisely because white antislavery friends would not examine their own prejudices. Many black activists disavowed such views. Nevertheless, that Douglass published Ward's version of antislavery heresy nearly a decade after breaking away from Garrisonians speaks to the steady undercurrent of resentment among black abolitionists in and beyond New England.[31] Would war finally break down these racial barriers? Or had the antislavery struggle proved that a color-blind abolitionist republic was an unattainable goal?

The Massachusetts Miracle: Bay Staters and the Economic Republic

These were not the only questions looming when Civil War reformers debated the possibility of living in a republican moment. Indeed, for a significant segment of reform-minded Bay Staters, the advent of an abolitionist republic depended on economic changes in a reconstructed American union, especially the success of southern free labor experiments, in which formerly enslaved people would work for wages under the tutelage of northern reformers and businessmen. By establishing free labor economies in the emancipating South, race reformers hoped that former slaves would be integrated into a national political economy. And that would lead not only to economic but to racial uplift, a wide range of abolitionists believed. In fact, free labor success below the Mason-Dixon line would keep former slaves from streaming north, where fears of migrating blacks had pervaded public discourse during the war, making the new economic order a bulwark against racial chaos nationally.

The leading advocates of economic reconstruction were Bay Staters, whose experiences with early factory systems and free labor forces in Massachusetts framed their understanding of the nation's postwar political economy. In their eyes, the "Massachusetts Miracle" of contract labor would work wonders in the New South. According to Edward Pierce, two questions dominated northern discussions of wartime emancipation in slave country: Would former slaves "fight for their freedom"? And would "the people of African descent work for a living"?[32] A Free Soiler and then a Republican operative who counted ardent abolitionists such as Charles Sumner and Wendell Phillips as friends, Pierce—the Stoughton-born son of an old Puritan family—had a Zelig-like career that lent weight to his musings on these matters. He went from the harried abolitionist scene of Harvard Law School in the 1840s to heated debates over sectional politics in Salmon Chase's law offices in the 1850s. He witnessed the calls for a free labor frontier at Lincoln's nominating convention in Chicago in 1860 as well as debates about Union abolitionist policy that occurred amid the throng of fugitive slaves at Fort Monroe in secessionist Virginia in 1861. By the time he arrived at Union-occupied South Carolina, where thousands of liberated slaves lived, he believed that abolitionists needed projects to demonstrate the vitality of southern emancipation. And that meant proving African Americans' desire to work for wages beyond bondage.

Indeed, Pierce became famous for his advocacy of black economic uplift in the emancipating South. Port Royal, a wealthy cotton island off the South Carolina coast, he described as a world without slavery and virtually without whites. Yet with this single area of the Confederacy experiencing what some northern newspapers termed a "sudden" emancipation—larger than almost any gradual emancipation edict of the early republic—white fears about free blacks took flight above the Mason-Dixon line.[33] Some worried that freed people would head North and compete with white laborers for various jobs. Others feared that the cotton crop would fail for lack of black workers, leaving northern industry bereft of its heady antebellum profits.

More generally, whites worried that free blacks would become unruly. Though white Massachusetts soldiers often supported emancipation, more than a few registered deep concerns about black freedom because they could not imagine how African Americans would live and work without the hard hand of bondage. "I think I should make a harsher master than most of these slaveholders do," a Springfield lumberman named Orrin Cook wrote after serving with the Massachusetts 22nd Regiment in slave country. "I should not bear with these impudent, lying, thieving niggers.

I am as strongly antislavery as ever, and even more anti-nigger."[34] Cook was not alone. Indeed, with the war causing economic dislocation in many Bay State towns and cities—from disruptions of the whaling industry to the loss of textile markets in the South—the mere prospect of southern emancipation caused concern in Massachusetts.[35] Attempting to neutralize such fears, Garrison himself would encourage nervous white Unionists to engage in "hope, trust and patience" when thinking about the great trend toward the "abolishment" of slavery in the wartime South.[36]

Members of the Lincoln administration wanted more concrete policies than hope, trust, and patience. They looked north to men with experience in iconic free labor settings such as Boston.[37] Treasury Secretary Salmon Chase thus dispatched Pierce to Union-controlled South Carolina to study black freedom. "The Freedmen at Port Royal," as Pierce's seminal *Atlantic* essay of September 1863 was called, did just that, examining African Americans' industriousness, productivity, and educability beyond bondage. Though it also considered freed people's religion and character, Pierce's essay pivoted on potential black industriousness. From the moment that slaves in the North had first been freed, blacks' industry had been a major concern of post-emancipation politicians. As Joanne Melish has illustrated, white New Englanders worried that northern abolition might very well lead to a dependent class of African Americans, who would become "slaves to the community."[38] Black and white abolitionists fought hard against such stereotypes, but fears of black economic debility remained strong in northern culture. As Garrison himself would famously remark in 1862, many white Americans wanted to know what would happen when abolition "philosophy becomes practical." Pierce's report would tell all.[39]

As Pierce illustrated, white northerners' guidance in South Carolina had helped liberated blacks to move not only from bondage to freedom but from the immoral economy of slavery to the promised land of free labor production.[40] Visiting freedmen's camps, schools, and churches, he found former slaves eager to embrace the principles of free labor. "As to industry," he wrote, African American "laborers, during their first year under the new [free market] system, have acquired the idea of ownership, and of the security of wages, and have come to see that labor and slavery are not the same thing." Young and old alike were amenable to "voluntary" labor, Pierce continued; in other words, freed people did not have to be coerced to work (as many northern whites believed). At one school,

Pierce talked with young pupils about the free labor lessons of the hour. "Children, what are you going to do when you grow up?" Pierce asked. "Going to work, Sir," the children replied. "On what?" Pierce asked. "Cotton and corn, Sir." The dialogue continued in rapid-fire fashion. "What are you going to do with corn?" "Eat it." "What are you going to do with the cotton?" "Sell it." "What are you going to do with the money you get for it?" "Put it in my pocket, Sir." "That won't do," Pierce corrected them, asking "What's better than that?" "Buy clothes, Sir." Better. "What else will you buy?" "Shoes, Sir." With that, Pierce reported, the children connected the dots of the free labor world: their hard work and earnings paid for churches, schools, and businesses, North and South. "One who listens to such answers can hardly think that there is any natural incapacity in these children to acquire with maturity of years the ideas and habits of good citizens."[41] By extension, Pierce explained elsewhere, there was little doubt that liberated blacks would be productive and trusted free laborers.

Pierce's soothing analysis of Civil War freedom became a talking point for abolitionist politicians and reformers throughout the Union. By underscoring the centrality of a stable labor force in the South, Massachusetts abolitionists imagined a harmonious, integrated national economy with black and white citizens literally working together across the color line. The *Liberator* ran ads supporting free labor concerns in the South. Pierce's program became the template for an entire style of race reform, one linking freed people's educational and religious values to a free labor world. For instance, Pierce spurred the creation of the New England Educational Commission for Freedmen, which one Massachusetts manufacturer hailed as "the first society organized in the North to take charge of the emancipated slaves in their transition from slavery to freedom."[42] Soon, groups in Pennsylvania and New York signed on to help advance economic reconstruction as a vital part of the wartime abolitionist struggle.

Pierce was far from being the lone advocate of a "Massachusetts Miracle" in the South. Both Edward Philbrick and Edward Atkinson touted the virtues of free labor experiments among freed people. With the blessings of the Union, Philbrick, a Harvard man and an engineer by profession, bankrolled a series of plantation investments on captured Confederate land in South Carolina, hoping to reap the rewards of black free laborers. But he also talked publicly about his conversion from skeptic of black industriousness to advocate of free labor experiments in and beyond Port Royal. His endorsement encouraged more Northerners to back the Massachusetts

Miracle. Atkinson, the scion of a well-heeled Brookline family who had been educated below the Mason-Dixon line, became perhaps the leading exponent of economic reconstruction in the wake of the Port Royal experiment. A cotton manufacturer who joined the Free Soil Party before supporting both John Brown and the Republican Party, Atkinson came to see slavery as an unlawful restriction on African Americans' free labor activities. In his view, by utilizing uncompensated black laborers southern masters engaged in inefficient and ineffectual business practices that harmed people and environments in equal measure. Just as slavery gobbled up black bodies, so too did it tarnish bountiful southern landscapes, since masters merely moved on to new territory without worry about the destruction they left behind. For Atkinson, slavery was bad business in every sense of the phrase.

In Atkinson's eyes, the Civil War offered northern businessmen no less than reformers a chance to build a better economic model in the South. As he wrote in a series of fascinating essays on the political economy of emancipation, Confederate slaveholders' mad dash from the Union made southern abolition a sure bet, for it broke Northerners' belief in coddling masters and by extension their destructive economic as well as human practices. Yet Atkinson also realized that a prospective Union victory meant that "the Negro Question" would replace the slavery problem as the nation's next great social debate in the eyes of many northern whites. Never fear, he explained, because a reconstructed Union would feature "New England ideas" applied to the nation as a whole. "It is already evident," he wrote in 1864, "that the whole cotton industry must be permeated and regenerated by New England men" and their free labor programs. Only then would the nation and the South be rejuvenated in equal measure. For Atkinson, the war offered black and white Americans a chance to reinvent the American republic on the solid economic ground of New England mercantilism.[43]

Women added an important domestic dimension to the Massachusetts Miracle. By the end of the war, hundreds of female schoolteachers from the Bay State had poured into the conquered regions of the Confederacy to work in burgeoning freedom schools. They did much more than offer literacy and numeracy instruction in cramped and creaky schoolhouses; they also emphasized the saliency of the domestic economy in former enslaved women's lives.[44] Arguing that stable homes bolstered free labor systems, white women urged African American women to maintain neat, orderly, and efficient houses. Local branches of the New England Freedmen's Aid Society (launched in 1862 and based in Boston) constantly raised awareness about the need to fund and facilitate programs of black domestic uplift. No project was too small to support. For instance, some New England teachers championed freedom gardens as a means of supplying not only needed nourishment to the growing male free labor workforce in the South but discipline to black women on the home front. As a female teacher wrote from Jacksonville, Florida, Northerners were missing a "golden opportunity" to inculcate the lessons of free labor in southern homes because African American women did not have enough seed for crops. If northern women would speedily send seedlings southward, however, they would provide "the women and children honest work."[45]

This sentiment became an article of faith for the hundreds of female schoolteachers working in the South, who learned (if they did not already know) that they were representatives not only of educational achievement but of northern economic superiority. As *The Freedmen's Record* quipped, "free labor [served] as a missionary" in the former Confederacy.[46] And it was winning converts. "The thrift, industry, and general prosperity exhibited by the colored freedmen in many quarters of the South, during the last three or four years, have surprised many," the paper proclaimed several months after Appomattox. Yet northern teachers had important work to do in the years ahead, for African Americans still showed the "ill effects" of bondage.[47] If women could raise more money throughout Massachusetts (where they dominated local freedmen's aid societies), they could further spread the gospel of the Massachusetts Miracle: that freedom was hard work.

Needless to say, some black and white abolitionists registered concerns about the Massachusetts Miracle. Worried that liberated blacks might become the pet project of northern reformers, black leaders contested descriptions of freed people as dependents in need of white paternal guidance. While both *Douglass' Monthly* and the *Christian Recorder* reported favorably on free labor experiments, they also made clear that African Americans were merely continuing their industrious habits from antebellum times.[48] Borrowing from a jeremiad tradition that had linked black work to American nation building—the famed black abolitionist Richard Allen wrote in 1828 that blacks had long since made fortunes for whites[49]—Douglass argued that black runaways had long demonstrated their utility to the Union cause; now they wanted equal treatment under the law (their rights and liberties) as well as the same economic support as soldiers fighting in the war.

African American women were particularly important bearers of this message. Charlotte Forten, who hailed from a founding black family in Philadelphia before moving to Salem, offered perhaps the most moving analysis of African American uplift in the reconstructing South. From her teaching post on the Sea Islands of South Carolina, she issued two missives on free black educational and work initiatives in the former heart of slave country. Published in the *Atlantic Monthly* in May and June 1864, Forten's essays portrayed African Americans as eager and honest (if sometimes naive) pupils of democracy, education, and industry who deserved to be viewed as equals to the "haughty Anglo-Saxon race." Indeed, after "centuries" of horrible treatment, she argued that liberated blacks deserved every "right and privilege" of freedom rather than lectures about their need to overcome degradation. Given time and support, free blacks would thrive.[50] Harriet Jacobs, the former slave whose 1861 narrative (published first in Boston) alerted northern audiences to the sexual predation of southern masters, agreed. During the war, she served as a roving correspondent with Lydia Maria Child, who pushed Jacobs's words into the public realm. Jacobs asked Bay Staters to see liberated blacks as industrious fellow citizens who were "full of the spirit of freedom." As she toured contraband camps outside Washington in the wake of the Emancipation Proclamation, Jacobs met former slaves who worked hard, sought "employment," and wanted to help win the war against bondage. Yet while they aided and even "freely fed" Union soldiers coming into Virginia, self-liberated blacks now faced "insults" and "beatings" from white men who castigated them as beggars and paupers. Jacobs wanted Northerners (particularly in Massachusetts, the home of abolition) to see African Americans as more than mere parts in freedom's machine; they were the heart and soul of the abolitionist republic.[51]

Still other abolitionists raised concerns about the hidden agendas of free labor. Nathaniel P. Banks's plan to reconstruct Louisiana along the lines suggested by Pierce and Atkinson became a major flashpoint in wartime abolitionist debates over the post-slavery future. In the second half of the war, the Massachusetts general had essentially dictated labor contracts to Louisiana's freed people as a way to steady the unstable regional economy. Blacks would get an annual wage but were contractually required to stay on their plantations for a year. Moreover, freed blacks did not have a say in the political system; without voting rights, they would not be cofounders of the new civic order. The abolitionist press hotly debated Banks's decisions. Though he offered a mild defense of the general, Garrison opened the columns of the *Liberator* to Banks's critics. Wendell Phillips served as perhaps the main voice of an anti-Banks faction, but he was far from alone.[52] Lydia Maria Child again spoke for many of her comrades when she wrote, "I agree with most of your views, friend Garrison; but I cannot accept your apology for Gen. Banks' system in Louisiana." A wise policy was not necessarily a moral one, she explained. And to her, Banks's labor system offered "a dangerous precedent" for the future—a form of unholy coercion if not servitude.[53] When Garrison subsequently told others that even the great Frederick Douglass had achieved freedom before equality— and would not have remained a slave because he did not yet have the right to vote—that hardly eased the deeper concern among abolitionists that free labor experiments now valorized order over rights.

And so the question lingered: Would the Massachusetts Miracle derail the new abolitionist republic before it started?[54]

Blood Sacrifice: The Black Abolitionist Republic

Perhaps because post-slavery economic debates imagined black liberty as in some way contingent on white aid and free labor successes, black reformers emphasized a different foundation for the abolitionist republic, one that claimed African Americans' rights and liberties through martial means. Here, black soldiers generally, and the Massachusetts 54th in particular, became the living symbol not only of an emancipation war but of an abolitionist peace. As the *Christian Recorder*, one of the leading African American journals, reported when the famous black regiment returned to Boston at the close of the war, "the demonstrations of respect [for black soldiers] were more than have usually been awarded to returning regiments, even in Massachusetts, which cherishes her soldiers with an unforgetting affection." The hyperbole in this statement was matched by the correspondent's acute insight into blacks' great and to some extent tragic hope that their martial sacrifices would lead to a more perfect Union. In some ways, African Americans felt that they were the only true republicans for their triple commitment to racial, national, and global human equality. Indeed, according to the *Christian Recorder*, the Massachusetts 54th's finest hour had not occurred on the battlefield but was represented by its firm commitment to egalitarian principles in refusing to accept unequal pay from the Union. "It was sublimer heroism," the correspondent wrote, "than that which inspired them at Fort Wagner."[55]

The rediscovery of the Massachusetts 54th in our time makes any claims to its historical importance seem bland. But it is well to remember that the very prospect of armed black soldiers scared the hell out of many white Unionists. That black soldiers and their families would thus turn to military means as a way to secure abolitionist ends should not be taken for granted. That many white reformers came to support black soldiers as a way to destroy the slaveholding republic and usher in a new abolitionist polity provides a double lesson in the way that war changed the calculus of antislavery activism.[56] For many white radicals had often opposed even black self-defense claims. In Massachusetts and elsewhere, antebellum reformers had long debated means and ends, with some offering grudging support of tactical violence. But relatively few white activists came out firmly in favor of armed conflict as a strategic pathway to universal black freedom. Once again, the war changed that.

African Americans in and beyond Massachusetts had long since embraced practical perspectives on the use of force. By the 1850s, Douglass, who had previously decried Henry Highland Garnet's appeal to southern slaves' uprising as too violent, began touting the connections between bloodshed and black freedom. In October 1851, for instance, he reprinted a letter approving of the black runaway William Parker's physical defense of his freedom in Christiana, Pennsylvania. After a white man lay dead for trying to recover him, Parker refused to apologize for his physical tactics, later noting that he had the same rights to self defense as anyone else. Linking the names of Parker's associates to those "brave patriots who fell at Bunker Hill," the writer—and Douglass—gloried in blacks' grasp of "the right of revolution."[57] Black writers around the nation agreed.

Significantly, there was no place in the antebellum nation that sanctified blacks' full equality as citizen soldiers. Even Massachusetts prohibited African Americans from forming militia companies. The Fugitive Slave Act of 1850 compelled black activists to claim more firmly what might be termed martial rights. An 1852 petition campaign to the state legislature, which more than sixty African Americans signed, demanded blacks' right to form an independent militia. It fell on deaf ears.[58] When the campaign was renewed the following year, one of its ringleaders, William J. Watkins, defended blacks' right to bear arms on the grounds that they were "law-abiding, tax-paying, liberty-loving, native-born, American citizens." When blacks again failed to gain legislative support for self-defense tactics, Watkins steamed that African Americans were viewed as nothing more than "lunatics, paupers, and common drunkards."[59]

Not until the Civil War would African Americans be viewed as competent military figures, and then, of course, Massachusetts played a pivotal role in establishing the image of blacks as freedom fighters. No longer slave rebels, they were now Union heroes. African Americans who had been making the case for emancipation were thrilled to find many white reformers falling in behind them as they celebrated black soldiers' contributions to building an abolitionist republic. At the presentation ceremony in Boston that sent the Massachusetts 54th into battle, black and white men shared the stage. Leonard Grimes, a legendary black activist, offered the opening prayer before giving the floor to Governor John A. Andrew. The ceremony conveyed the state colors to the black regiment—an incredibly powerful moment of civic belonging. As Amy Greenberg has shown, the ideal of "martial manhood" dominated mid-nineteenth-century American conceptions of self and nation, linking brave, strong men to brave, strong nations.[60] Although they often understated the heroic service of black female nurses and runaways, a large collection of African American writers celebrated black soldiers. So, too, did whites, who connected America's civic rebirth with black military service, which Governor Andrew highlighted as "an opportunity for a whole race of men" both to kill slavery and to "strike a blow" for equal citizenship. And the standard they fought under was "*their* country's flag now as well as ours."[61] A bit of doggerel that a member of the Massachusetts 54th produced captured the enthusiasm of African Americans for the regiment's heroic exploits. With "old Abe" literally wallowing in his Union-losing "fears," it seemed as if "every hope was lost but the colored volunteers."[62]

Despite its valorization, the reality of black action was not only predictably bloody but horribly savage. African Americans were more likely than white Unionists to be tortured and summarily executed by Confederates; they faced a horrible death rate; and their dead bodies were more subject to ritualistic violence than anyone else's. Yet, as Carole Emberton and Kate Masur have reminded us, African Americans turned from celebrations of heroic military contributions to the metaphor of black sacrifice as a way to make the case for national equality.[63] Particularly on the matter of voting rights, African American soldiers and their allies emphasized black suffering and pain as a tragic ingredient for a more perfect Union. Indeed, well before Lincoln's Second Inaugural connected national redemption to the salving of enslaved peoples' centuries of pain, the Massachusetts 54th symbolized this transmutation of Union values. By pointing to bloodshed on battlefields south and west, black and white abolitionists along with reform-minded politicians could argue that African Americans no less than whites had literally suffered and died for "their" country.

In this way, the Old Testament jeremiad tradition that decried black blood spilled for white wealth became a New Testament vision of black and white men together drinking the blood of Christ for a better republic. The *Christian Recorder* began printing lists of the black dead and wounded, hoping to show the cost of black glory. Lewis Douglass, son of the famous abolitionist, wrote from Morris Island, South Carolina, in late July 1863 that black military men actually courted danger and death for the greater good. Though "the splendid 54th is cut to pieces," he observed after the bloody assault on Fort Wagner, black soldiers' refusal to back down from battle was nothing short of inspiring. The senior Douglass published his son's searing letter in his newspaper the following month, hoping to spread Lewis's ode to black sacrifice.[64] So too did the poet Frances Ellen Watkins Harper, who wrote in the familiar tones of blood: "And from the soil drenched with their blood, / The fairest flowers of peace shall bloom; / And history cull rich laurels there, / To deck each martyr hero's tomb."[65]

With blacks making such a powerful case for national blood sacrifice, even some non-resistants supported violence as a means of creating the abolitionist republic. This alarmed hardcore peace advocates. One writer observed to "Brother Garrison" in the *Liberator* that it seemed as if all the "peace men generally have become warriors."[66] Garrison knew it was true. He watched his son join the Massachusetts 55th Regiment, formed after the famous 54th overflowed with volunteers, while his friend Thomas Wentworth Higginson volunteered to lead former South Carolina slaves in perhaps the very first United States Colored Troops regiment, colloquially known as the "first South." Lydia Maria Child corresponded with the mother of Robert Gould Shaw, who led the 54th and died at Fort Wagner. Though she worried that the Emancipation Proclamation had been secured merely as "a war measure," Child still thrilled at stories of black and white soldiers' overcoming the limits of racial oppression in the 1860s. In 1864, she told a friend the stirring story of an African American soldier who, when verbally assaulted on a train between Boston and Roxbury, found a white soldier at his side. For Child, that was clear evidence of "a change in public opinion."⁶⁷

But by war's end discord again loomed. Massachusetts abolitionists who considered violence an expedient did not necessarily envision its utility in the future. The *Liberator* ratified a call in *Harper's* magazine for "Peace"—and the "Prince of Peace"—as keys to Reconstruction.⁶⁸ While opposing the traitorous Copperhead peace of 1864, several Massachusetts abolitionists began touting postwar peace as a patriotic means of conducting American reform after 1865. The formation of peace wings of the abolition movement by the mid-1860s signaled many white reformers' distaste for both the moral stain of military emancipation and the immorality of violent tactics. Henry C. Wright, who had condemned Democratic peaceniks in 1864, held forth at an American Peace Society meeting in Boston in December 1865 on the virtues of pacifism henceforth. "Human rights cannot be protected by force," Wright proclaimed, noting that among the "first principles" of moral action was the disavowal of violence.⁶⁹

For African Americans, the obverse held true: the lesson of the hour was that black liberty, like the promises of an abolitionist republic, was fragile and must be protected by any means available. As an Ohio woman commented in the *Christian Recorder* near the end of the war, blacks desired peace but "not a peace like 1776—not like that of 1812—not a peace which holds four and a half millions of human beings in worse than Egyptian bondage."⁷⁰ That kind of peace meant war. Where would white reformers stand then?

Cultural Reconstruction: Abolitionists' Civilizing Missions

That question shadowed American Reconstruction for years, but it became pertinent well before the Confederacy's demise, as black and white abolitionists struggled to define the essential values undergirding an emancipated society in the South. As slavery withered, many white reformers called for much more than black economic uplift or military action against slaveholders. They counseled the educational, spiritual, and social uplift of recently liberated blacks as well. Though clearly related to economic reconstruction—for the language of uplift suffused free labor ideology—this brand of thinking is perhaps best understood under the umbrella term "cultural reconstruction." Indeed, while looking forward to a future abolitionist republic in which black and white citizens would enjoy equal liberty, white advocates also prized a form of emancipation tutelage for African Americans that was nothing less than a civilizing mission. For a host of Bay State reformers, who organized the earliest and in many ways most powerful group of freedmen's aid organizations, cultural reconstruction in former Confederate strongholds was absolutely essential to making freedom work.[71] From its wartime founding, the New England Freedman's Aid Society noted that "all [northern reformers who work in the South] are expected to give instruction in those arts of civilized life which the negro needs quite as much as book-learning." Instructional courses spanned a wide range of topics, from the "lessons of industry," to "domestic management and thrift," to the importance of "truth and honesty." Taken together, these areas of study would "help [black] pupils (children and adults) to unlearn the teachings of slavery." By inculcating republican rules and responsibilities in former bondspeople, the group concluded, "our New-England men and women are striving to introduce into our Southern States" a proper understanding of liberty.[72]

Unlike the Massachusetts Miracle, which emphasized a speedy buildup of black free labor colonies in the wartime South (as well as the necessity of quickly inculcating lessons of domestic economic uplift among black women and children), cultural reconstruction emphasized a brand of gradualism. Though reformers realized that military emancipation had been rather sudden, they argued that abolitionists had prompted broader "changes in public sentiment during the past fifteen years," changes that would also lead to a full reconstruction of race relations in the former heart of slave country if reformers could unfold their civilizing programs. In fact, with white reformers skillfully schooling blacks in the arts of uplift, even the most skeptical white master would someday see African Americans as equals. Thus, as the *Freedmen's Record*, the house organ of the New England Freedmen's Aid Society, put it in 1865, African Americans would "need all our help to raise [them] up to education and free civilization."[73] But it would take time.

To be sure, advocates of cultural reconstruction invested their educational missions and civilizing programs with a sense of urgency, yet even longtime abolitionists such as Garrison saw no conflict between his former advocacy of immediatism and his new belief that a gradual cultural reconstruction of race relations would be the best way to secure an abolitionist republic. Dissenting from former allies such as Wendell Phillips, Garrison argued that such key citizenship initiatives as voting rights should not be granted to African Americans at once. Rather, blacks should enter the school of freedom first, learning from white and black Northerners about living with liberty. "When was it ever known that liberation from bondage was accompanied by a recognition of political equality?" he vehemently asked a correspondent critical of early reconstruction policies in Louisiana that denied blacks full civil and voting rights.[74] For him, cultural reconstruction—education, the gospel, the arts of civilized life—would prove much more useful to African Americans in the short run.

Toward this end, Garrison supported the American Freedmen's Aid Commission (AFAC), which provided further direction to advocates of cultural reconstruction. As the group noted in its constitution, the AFAC would "promote the education and elevation" of liberated blacks through a variety of missionary activities.[75] While recognizing the often dire threats to black freedom in the reconstructing South, the AFAC resolved to fight fire with words—words about education, words about uplift. After taking shape in Philadelphia in September 1865, the group encouraged the federal government to intervene on behalf of endangered southern blacks. Yet it focused on "education and religion" as essential to race reform. By being pious, virtuous, and self-reliant, the group argued, African Americans would prove their fitness for freedom and dispel any lingering concerns about emancipation.[76] And with that peace plank firmly in place, many white reformers believed, reunion would proceed much more smoothly for all.

In some respects, abolitionist motives were complex. More than a few whites believed that African Americans had fought for the Union—as they put it, "our rights"—during the Civil War and now deserved white educational support in return.[77] White teachers, especially women, would not only teach former slaves the arts of civilization but stand with them physically in any hour of need. "Let us have a cordon of school-houses and a regiment of teachers so strong that they cannot be sacrificed without arousing the indignation of the whole country," the *Freedmen's Record* put it starkly in 1865.[78]

Moreover, even military commanders conceded that postwar reunion required a sea change in white attitudes toward blacks. General Rufus Saxton, a proud Bay State native who became famous for his wartime abolitionist views, closely studied racial interactions along the conquered South Carolina coast, always with an eye to their future meaning. After

Union troops swept into the Sea Islands, Saxton took control of a vast military district stretching from South Carolina to Florida. While he shared many of the biases of his white comrades—Saxton wanted to make sure, for example, that liberated African Americans learned free labor ways and did not become an economic drain on the Union—he supported many vanguard measures, from the marshaling of black regiments early in the war, including the First South Carolina Volunteers, to land allotments for former slaves at affordable rates. He also advocated cultural reconstruction, believing that it provided a pathway to progress for a long oppressed group.

Still, Saxton knew that many white Unionists, let alone Confederates, did not share his concern for black uplift and equality. When a white sergeant looking to advance in the army asked Saxton if he was raising more "African Regiments," Saxton testily replied that he hoped "to raise regiments of Native Americans, who are not less Americans, because their skin has the [darker] hue."[79] More ominously, Saxton fielded reports about white Unionists' harassment of black civilians and soldiers in the conquered South. On several occasions, he responded to complaints from African Americans by asking that white troops be cordoned off from black settlements or that military guards be assigned to protect those communities. From these experiences, Saxton knew that even northern whites would need time to adjust to black liberty across the nation.

Yet cultural reconstruction had another, often hidden, agenda: a retreat to peaceful reunion as a healing gesture after the brutal war. As the *Freedmen's Record* observed, abolitionists must now fight for "liberty, equality, and *unity*" in the former Confederacy. That meant treating conquered Confederate whites, the onetime enemies of both enslaved people and Unionists, as allies and friends. African Americans had a special duty to help advance this part of cultural reconstruction, for only when liberated blacks acted as whites wanted them to would they become equal citizens. According to the *Freedmen's Record*, certain "truths must be borne in mind" in the postwar world, including the idea that blacks' "ignorance" had accentuated prejudice among whites North and South.[80] In a circular distributed among "the colored people of the South" by the New England Freedmen's Aid Society in the fall of 1865, even Gov. John A. Andrew, the hero of the famed 54th, agreed. Though he addressed liberated blacks as true "fellow citizens," Andrew warned that much work remained to be done *for* and to them. "Abraham Lincoln decreed your emancipation from slavery," he observed; now "let us complete the work, and emancipate the mind from ignorance."[81]

Harkening back to founding debates over responsibilities as well as rights, Andrew argued that liberty entailed a wide range of freedoms, including the freedom to be educated and instructed by others. "You are now free to receive help in becoming intelligent citizens. But not even God can make you so unless you help yourselves." Andrew emphasized the principles of self-help and moral uplift as critical adjuncts to postwar abolitionism. As he put it, "the enjoyment of every right hangs on education," including such essential civic rights as suffrage. "Thus far," Andrew lectured, "the colored people have nobly fulfilled the hopes of their true friends." But, he indicated, there was much work to do, both in their name and in that of national unity.[82]

Frederick Douglass had strong words for advocates of cultural reconstruction, leveling them at abolitionist friends gathered at the thirty-second annual meeting of the Massachusetts Anti-Slavery Society. Even if the rest of the nation rushed toward a reconstruction policy that put heavy responsibilities on blacks for the success of southern emancipation, Douglass argued passionately that Massachusetts reformers must surely not go and do likewise. For him, cultural reconstruction, including education, temperance, and Bible training, like economic uplift, must follow rather than precede blacks' assumption of national political rights, voting rights in particular. That would be the only sound basis for an abolitionist republic. "I look over this country at the present time," he commented, "and I see educational societies, sanitary commissions, freedmen's associations, and the like—all very good." But, he intoned, the vote would be better. And getting it would require a social movement that returned to the days of abolitionist outrage, that would thunder for equal *"justice,"* that would not equivocate, and that would not worry about the consequences of being heard.[83]

Beyond 1865: Imperfect Nation or Abolitionist Republic?

Indeed, when black Bostonians convened a regional meeting in Massachusetts in December 1865, they sought to follow Douglass's advice and invest the postwar era with a sense of activist urgency reminiscent of the 1830s. Planned at virtually the same time that the American Peace Society gathered in the city and as William Lloyd Garrison prepared for the *Liberator*'s end after nearly two thousand issues, the convention would mark the first statewide gathering of Bay State blacks since 1859. Though slavery had been slain, and the Thirteenth Amendment banning bondage was now a constitutional reality, black abolitionists nevertheless worried that racial equality remained a distant dream. In fact, with new forms of racial oppression settling in northern as well as southern areas of the reconstructing Union, black activists wondered what had actually changed. Did 1865 represent the dawning of a true abolitionist republic? Or was it an opportunity missed?[84]

Douglass returned to Boston to stir white as well as black audiences. Although he had been giving speeches around the North telling whites that they should do "nothing" with former slaves except treat them equally, Douglass knew that such rhetoric would not solve what he called a looming "disaster" in southern race relations. Blacks must realize that, far from living in a peaceful and righteous abolitionist republic, they were still navigating a time of war and desolation. Members of the convention agreed, passing a resolution that African Americans everywhere deprecated the return to the Justice Taney principle of 1857: the idea that whites did not have to respect black rights in the least. Perhaps this resolution would convince white reformers to join them in a new crusade for equality.[85]

While Douglass and black Bostonians certainly recognized that something fundamental had changed in American culture with the demise of slavery, they worried that the abolitionist republic, which depended on white and black unity as a means of overcoming the vestiges of slavery, would be lost before it had begun. With key white allies moving on, the republic was in trouble. Douglass and other blacks would have scathing words for reformers who embraced any brand of abolitionist gradualism. For his part, Douglass still believed in a liberal republic that protected rights at the national as well as the state level. He deprecated race reform struggles that instructed blacks to engage in cultural uplift as a means of winning white hearts and minds in conquered southern states. Blacks wanted nothing less than equality, North and South, and they should stop at nothing until they got it.

As Stephen Kantrowitz has brilliantly shown, Douglass's concerns about the potential failures of national reconstruction echoed in Massachusetts during the 1860s and 1870s. While African Americans would get a taste of political and social equality (with a very small number of blacks elected to local and statewide office), and while they certainly influenced definitions of national citizenship, black abolitionists felt increasingly disappointed in the Bay State's version of an abolitionist republic. By the 1880s, in fact, many viewed the Civil War as an incomplete revolution. North of Dixie, racial discrimination remained strong.[86]

Thus for many blacks the end of the Civil War brought an end to the dream of building a pure abolitionist republic. With so many reformers arguing that their job was done, or had changed, or that blacks must prove their fitness for freedom all over again, all that remained was the *American Republic*—glorious and imperfect, changed and unchanged in nearly equal measure. Now as in the past, black abolitionists had to lead the charge against the nation's imperfections. As hope mixed with dread, at least they could reflect that they had years of practice on that score.

More broadly, abolitionist reformers remained divided over their strategic future. Universal suffrage was a major point of contention, with Bay State women often dissenting from their former activist comrades nationally over the Fifteenth Amendment, which granted black men but not black or white women voting rights. While Lydia Maria Child was saddened that the abolitionist republic would not sanction female suffrage, she remained horrified that Susan B. Anthony and Elizabeth Cady Stanton—who had supporters in various parts of Massachusetts—had joined forces with antiblack Democrats in opposition to African American men's suffrage. Similarly, Lucy Stone, who moved back to Massachusetts after the war and helped lead the New England Women's Suffrage Association (launched in 1868), recoiled at Anthony and Stanton's willingness to betray former antislavery friends, even as she too remained concerned about women's voting rights during Reconstruction.[87]

Even at the organizational level, Bay Staters quarreled over whether to continue serving in the abolitionist cause. The Massachusetts Anti-Slavery Society engaged in vociferous debates over whether or not to shutter its fabled group at war's end. Like abolitionists around the country, many white reformers wondered if their formal antislavery charge had ended with the arrival of national emancipation. Garrison certainly thought so, arguing in meetings, in print, and in private communications that abolition and black uplift were interconnected but distinct phases of American race reform. He made a powerful point, noting that white and black reformers had to claim some victories to move forward and inspire younger generations of activists. And how could any abolitionists argue that they had been unsuccessful, Garrison wondered, when the world's largest slave system had been shattered? With "slavery being constitutionally abolished and prohibited," as he observed in an 1866 letter to a New York paper, "the work of agitating for its overthrow is ended. There is no need of any more anti-slavery journals, anti-slavery lectures, anti-slavery speeches, [or] anti-slavery tracts." The only task that remained, he continued, was that "of educating, elevating, protecting, and vindicating the emancipated millions."[88]

Wendell Phillips vehemently disagreed with his friend's postwar pleadings. "We have never had a democracy yet," he cautioned in the summer of 1862, arguing that abolitionists must not become mere adjuncts of the Republican Party, thereby losing their moral standing as reformers.[89] Agreeing with black abolitionists such as Douglass at war's end, Phillips proclaimed that while slavery was now dead, racial oppression remained vibrantly alive in political, economic, and social realms. In short, abolitionists had helped win the war but they might very well lose the peace if they blindly supported reunion. As for Garrison's advocacy of cultural reconstruction, Phillips, again like Douglass, felt that it did not meet the demands of the hour. Without a renewed abolitionist push after 1865, Phillips proclaimed, reunion itself would proceed on the backs of African Americans, who already experienced new forms of slavery. A majority of the Massachusetts Anti-Slavery Society, like the American Anti-Slavery Society, agreed with Phillips's reasoning: both stayed in existence until the Fifteenth Amendment was passed in 1870. And even then, some abolitionists felt that their job was not complete. Little did they know that it would take four score and many more years to get anything like a true abolitionist republic of equality and justice for all.

NOTES

I would like to thank Matt Mason, John Stauffer, Manisha Sinha, Donald Yacovone, and Drew McCoy, among many others, for their insightful questions and commentaries. A hearty thank you, as well, to Conrad Edick Wright, Kate Viens, and Matt Mason for their terrific editorial suggestions.

1. See John Stauffer, *The Black Hearts of Men: Radical Abolitionists and the Transformation of Race* (Cambridge: Harvard University Press, 2002), 15.
2. William Lloyd Garrison to Parker Pillsbury, June 3, 1859, and Garrison to Abby Kelley Foster, July 25, 1859, in *The Letters of William Lloyd Garrison*, ed. Walter M. Merrill

and Louis Ruchames, 6 vols. (Cambridge: Harvard University Press, 1975), 4:627–30, 642–46.
3. See Garrison's remarks of June 29, 1867, in *Proceedings at the Public Breakfast Held in Honour of William Lloyd Garrison, Esq.*, ed. F. W. Chesson (London: William Tweedie, 1868), 40–50.
4. "The Convention of the Colored People of New England" (December 1, 1865), in *Proceedings of the Black National and State Conventions, 1865–1900*, vol. 1, *New York, Pennsylvania, Indiana, Michigan, Ohio*, ed. Philip S. Foner and George E. Walker (Philadelphia: Temple University Press, 1986), 199–208.
5. John Stauffer on the PBS television series *American Experience: The Abolitionists* (2013), episode 1, transcript available at www.pbs.org.
6. Aileen Kraditor's perspective has long provided the framework for understanding abolitionist tactical and strategic debates before the war and in some ways after it. See Kraditor, *Means and End in American Abolitionism: Garrison and His Critics on Strategy and Tactics, 1834–1850* (1970; repr., Chicago: Ivan R. Dee, 1989), introduction. For a more recent perspective on abolitionists as democratic philosophers between the 1830s and 1870s, see W. Caleb McDaniel, *The Problem of Democracy in the Age of Slavery: Garrisonian Abolitionists and Transatlantic Reform* (Baton Rouge: Louisiana State University Press, 2013).
7. Dr. George B. Loring, "The Present Crisis, A Speech . . . at Lyceum Hall" (April 26, 1865), reprinted in *The Radical Republicans and Reconstruction, 1861–1870*, ed. Harold M. Hyman (Indianapolis: Bobbs-Merrill, 1967), 231–42, quotation on 236.
8. For the most famous definition of the "republican moment," see J. G. A. Pocock, *The Machiavellian Moment: Florentine Political Thought and the Atlantic Republican Tradition* (Princeton: Princeton University Press, 1975), viii.
9. See Drew R. McCoy, *The Elusive Republic: Political Economy in Jeffersonian America* (Chapel Hill: University of North Carolina Press, 1980).
10. See, for instance, Emerson's Concord speech (August 1, 1844), published as *An Address Delivered in the Court-House in Concord, Massachusetts . . . On the Anniversary of the Emancipation of the Negroes in the British West Indies* (Boston: James Munroe, 1844). See also Franklin Sanborn's pamphlet *Emancipation in the West Indies* (Concord: n.p., 1862).
11. For reports on August First ceremonies in Abington, see William Lloyd Garrison to Wendell Phillips Garrison, August 9, 1861; Garrison to Oliver Johnson, July 31, 1862; and Garrison to Oliver Johnson, July 14, 1863, all in Merrill and Ruchames, *Letters of William Lloyd Garrison*, 5:30–31, 100–103, 165–66.
12. See the announcement for Boutwell's Boston speech, "The Justice, Expediency and Necessity of Emancipation," *Liberator*, December 13, 1861.
13. Lyman Abbott, "Results of Emancipation in the United States of America," in *Special Report of the Anti-Slavery Conference, Held in Paris . . . , August 1867* (London: Committee of the British and Foreign Anti-Slavery Society, 1867), reprinted in Hyman, *The Radical Republicans and Reconstruction*, 216–29, quotation on 217.
14. E. L. Pierce, ed., *Memoir and Letters of Charles Sumner*, 4 vols. (Cambridge: Roberts Brothers, 1893), 4:73.
15. On an antislavery Union, see James Oakes, *Freedom National: The Destruction of Slavery in the United States, 1861–1865* (New York: Norton, 2013). On Garrison's growing and ardent Unionism, see Henry Mayer's epic biography of the abolitionist leader, *All on Fire: William Lloyd Garrison and the Abolition of Slavery* (1998; repr., New York: St. Martin's, 2008).

16. [Samuel May], *The Fugitive Slave Law and Its Victims* (New York: American Anti-Slavery Society 1856), 31.
17. "Free Democratic Press" listing, in *Thirteenth Annual Report of the American and Foreign Anti-Slavery Society, . . . May 11, 1853* (New York: American Anti-Slavery Society, 1853), 132–33.
18. *Catalogue of Anti-Slavery Publications in America* (New York: American Anti-Slavery Society, 1864).
19. Theodore Parker, *The Great Battle between Slavery and Freedom* (Boston: Benjamin H. Greene, 1856), 6.
20. Ibid.
21. Though they called for the immediate end of slavery, most antebellum Garrisonians agreed that slaveholders had constitutional, if not moral, rights to retain human property in the United States; this perspective constantly informed Bay Staters' moral suasion campaigns, which called on masters to eliminate bondage in their midst.
22. Weston petition quoted in the September 25, 1861, meeting record of the Philadelphia Female Anti-Slavery Society, in PFASS Executive Committee Minute Books 1856–1870, Pennsylvania Abolition Society Papers, Historical Society of Pennsylvania, microfilm, reel 31.
23. Child to Henrietta Sergeant, August 24, 1861, in Lydia Maria Child, *Letters of Lydia Maria Child, with a Biographical Introduction by John G. Whittier and an Appendix by Wendell Phillips* (New York: Houghton, Mifflin, 1882), 156. On Child, see Carolyn Karcher, *The First Woman in the Republic: A Cultural Biography of Lydia Maria Child* (Durham, N.C.: Duke University Press, 1998).
24. Stacey M. Robertson, *Parker Pillsbury: Radical Abolitionist, Male Feminist* (Ithaca, N.Y.: Cornell University Press, 2000), esp. chap. 8.
25. "Essex County Antislavery Society Picnic," *Liberator*, July 25, 1862.
26. "Address of Wendell Phillips, Delivered before the Twenty-Eighth Congregational Society, at Music Hall, July 6," *Liberator*, July 11, 1862.
27. Roger G. Kennedy, *Mr. Jefferson's Lost Cause: Land, Farmers, Slavery, and the Louisiana Purchase* (New York: Oxford University Press, 2003).
28. See Robert Fanuzzi, *Abolition's Public Sphere* (Minneapolis: University of Minnesota Press, 2003).
29. Frederick Douglass, "What the Black Man Wants" (January 26, 1865), reprinted in *The Frederick Douglass Papers*, ser. 1, vol. 4, *1864–1880*, ed. John W. Blassingame and John R. McKivigan (New Haven: Yale University Press, 1991), 59–69, quotation on 61.
30. Margot Minardi, *Making Slavery History: Abolitionism and the Politics of Memory in Massachusetts* (New York: Oxford University Press, 2011), 7–8.
31. Samuel Ringgold Ward to Frederick Douglass, March 1855, *Frederick Douglass' Paper*, April 13, 1855, reprinted in *The Black Abolitionist Papers*, vol. 1, *The British Isles, 1830–1865*, ed. C. Peter Ripley et al. (Chapel Hill: University of North Carolina Press, 1985), 417–22, quotation on 418–19.
32. Edward L. Pierce, "The Freedmen at Port Royal," *Atlantic Monthly* 12 (September 1863): 291–315, quotations on 291.
33. See the *Philadelphia Inquirer*, October 4, 1861; *Franklin County (Penn.) Valley Spirit*, November 27, 1861, and June 11, 1862.
34. Quoted in "Resisting Slavery: Springfield and the Civil War," http://ourpluralhistory.stcc.edu.

35. See, among more recent works, Earl Mulderink III, *New Bedford's Civil War* (New York: Fordham University Press, 2012), esp. chaps. 5 and 7; William Hallett, *Newburyport and the Civil War* (Charleston, S.C.: History Press, 2012), chaps. 8–9. The classic treatment of northern mill owners' concerns about abolition and emancipation remains Thomas H. O'Connor, *Lords of the Loom: The Cotton Whigs and the Coming of the Civil War* (New York: Scribner, 1968).
36. William Lloyd Garrison, "Hope, Trust and Patience," *Liberator,* June 27, 1862.
37. On free labor policies generally, see Bruce Levine, *The Fall of the House of Dixie: The Civil War and the Social Revolution That Transformed the South* (New York: Random House, 2013).
38. Joanne Pope Melish, *Disowning Slavery: Gradual Emancipation and "Race" in New England, 1780–1860* (Ithaca, N.Y.: Cornell University Press, 1998), vii.
39. Garrison, "Hope, Trust and Patience."
40. *Christian Recorder,* November 23, 1861.
41. Pierce, "The Freedmen at Port Royal," 308, 306–7.
42. Edward Atkinson, *The Future Supply of Cotton* (Boston: Crosby & Nichols, 1864), 11.
43. Ibid.
44. For an essential analysis of gendered understandings of economic Reconstruction, see Amy Dru Stanley, *From Bondage to Contract: Wage Labor, Marriage, and the Market in the Age of Slave Emancipation* (New York: Cambridge University Press, 1998), chap. 4.
45. Letter of "E. H. H." (Esther H. Hawkes), September 8, 1865, published in *Freedmen's Record,* October 1865, 164.
46. "Free Labor as a Missionary," *Freedmen's Record,* October 1865, 165.
47. "The Free Colored People," *Freedmen's Record,* October 1865, 154.
48. *Christian Recorder,* November 23, 1861; *Douglass' Monthly,* July 1861. On Douglass's wartime activism, see esp. John Stauffer, *Giants: The Parallel Lives of Frederick Douglass and Abraham Lincoln* (New York: Twelve, 2008).
49. On Allen, see Richard S. Newman, *Freedom's Prophet: Bishop Richard Allen, the AME Church, and the Black Founding Fathers* (New York: New York University Press, 2008).
50. Charlotte Forten, "Life on the Sea Islands," *Atlantic Monthly* 13 (May 1864): 587–96, quotations on 591.
51. Harriet Jacobs to Lydia Maria Child, March 18, 1863, in *The Harriet Jacobs Family Papers,* ed. Jean Fagan Yellin, 2 vols. (Chapel Hill: University of North Carolina Press, 2008), 2:468–70.
52. See James Brewer Stewart, *Wendell Phillips: Liberty's Hero* (Baton Rouge: Louisiana State University Press, 1998), introduction.
53. "Letter from Mrs. L. M. Child," March 15, 1865, *National Anti-Slavery Standard,* April 1, 1865.
54. Child to Garrison, *Liberator,* March 24, 1865; see Garrison's reprint of Banks's speech in Lawrence, Massachusetts, on his views of Reconstruction, *Liberator,* October 6, 1865.
55. *Christian Recorder,* September 23, 1865.
56. On the 54th as a fighting unit, see esp. Donald Yacovone, ed., *A Voice of Thunder: A Black Soldier's Civil War* (Champaign-Urbana: University of Illinois Press, 1997).
57. *Frederick Douglass' Paper,* October 2, 1851.
58. See esp. Stephen Kantrowitz, *More Than Freedom: Fighting for Black Citizenship in a White Republic, 1829–1889* (New York: Penguin, 2012).
59. Quoted in Jeffrey R. Kerr-Ritchie, *Rites of August First: Emancipation Day in the Black Atlantic World* (Baton Rouge: Louisiana State University Press, 2007), 174.

60. Amy S. Greenberg, *Manifest Manhood and the Antebellum American Empire* (New York: Cambridge University Press, 2005).
61. "Presentation Speech of Gov. Andrew," reprinted in *William Wells Brown: A Reader*, ed. Ezra Greenspan (Athens: University of Georgia Press, 2008), 355–64, quotation on 357.
62. Greenspan, *William Wells Brown: A Reader*, 363–64. The poem was originally printed in the *Boston Transcript* and then reprinted in William Wells Brown, *The Negro in the American Rebellion* (1867).
63. Carole Emberton, *Beyond Redemption: Race, Violence, and the American South after the Civil War* (Chicago: University of Chicago Press, 2013); Kate Masur, *An Example for All the Land: Emancipation and the Struggle over Equality in Washington, D.C.* (Chapel Hill: University of North Carolina Press, 2010).
64. Sgt. Lewis H. Douglass to Frederick and Anna Murray Douglass, July 20, 1863, *Douglass' Monthly*, August 1863.
65. "The Massachusetts 54th," originally published in the *New York Weekly Anglo-African*, October 10, 1863, reprinted in *Freedom's Journey: African American Voices of the Civil War*, ed. Donald Yacovone (Chicago: Lawrence Hill Books, 2004), 352.
66. *Liberator*, February 12, 1864.
67. Child to John Greenleaf Whittier, September 10, 1861; to Lucy Searle, December 21, 1862; to Mrs. S. B. Shaw, circa 1863; to Miss Eliza Scudder, circa 1864, in Child, *Letters of Lydia Maria Child*, 150–51, 157–61, 170, 171, 180.
68. *Liberator*, February 24, 1865.
69. *Liberator*, December 22, 1865.
70. *Christian Recorder*, April 8, 1865.
71. For a perspective on the radical nature of women's activism, in particular, in the postwar South, see Carol Faulkner, *Women's Radical Reconstruction: The Freedmen's Aid Movement* (Philadelphia: University of Pennsylvania Press, 2004).
72. "Second Annual Report of the New-England Freedmen's Aid Society," *Freedmen's Record*, April 1865, 49.
73. "Prospects for the Future," *Freedmen's Record*, November 1865, 169.
74. Garrison to Prof. Francis W. Newman, July 22, 1864, in Merrill and Ruchames, *Letters of William Lloyd Garrison*, 5:228–34, quotation on 228.
75. "Constitution of the American Freedmen's Aid Commission," *Freedmen's Record*, October 1865, 153.
76. "American Freedmen's Aid Commission," *Freedmen's Record*, November 1865, 176.
77. Ibid.; "Prospects for the Future," 169–70.
78. "Prospects for the Future," 169.
79. General Rufus Saxton to Sergeant Joseph H. Williams, April 4, 1863, box 1, folder 2, Rufus and S. Willard Saxton Papers (MS 431), Manuscripts and Archives, Yale University Library.
80. "Prospects for the Future," 170 (emphasis added), 169.
81. "Letter from Gov. Andrew of Massachusetts to the Freedmen," September 1, 1865, reprinted as a "Circular," *Freedmen's Record*, October 1865, 164.
82. Ibid., 164–65.
83. Douglass, "What the Black Man Wants" (January 26, 1865), in Blassingame and McKivigan, *Frederick Douglass Papers*, ser. 1, vol. 4, 67–68.
84. "The Convention of the Colored People of New England" (December 1, 1865), in Foner and Walker, *Proceedings of the Black National and State Conventions*, 1:199–208.

85. Ibid., 1:202–3.
86. Kantrowitz, *More Than Freedom*, 8–9.
87. On Child, see Karcher, *The First Woman in the Republic*, 532–44. On Stone, Garrison, and the New England Women's Suffrage Association, see Garrison to Isabella Beecher Hooker, November 12, 1869, and Garrison to Theodore Tilton, April 2, 1870, in Merrill and Ruchames, *Letters of William Lloyd Garrison*, 6:144–48, 167–72.
88. Garrison to Theodore Tilton, editor of the New York *Independent*, February 3, 1866, in Merrill and Ruchames, *Letters of William Lloyd Garrison*, 5:377–81, quotation on 379.
89. "Address of Wendell Phillips, Delivered before the Twenty-Eighth Congregational Society, at Music Hall, July 6," *Liberator*, July 11, 1862.

THE WAR YEARS

The Politics of Unionism

*Edward Everett, the
Constitutional Union Party,
and the Election of 1860*

MATTHEW MASON

Looking back on the fun and frolics of student life, one Harvard alumnus recounted how, during the historic presidential election of 1860, "our crowd" vigorously supported the Constitutional Unionist Party ticket of Tennessee's John Bell and Massachusetts's own (and former Harvard president) Edward Everett. He recalled that his coterie's "motto proud," which they proclaimed while "carry[ing] torches Sixty miles," was "Bell and the Belles."[1] One of innumerable plays on Bell's name that issued from his supporters, this particular witticism spoke to the close association of Everett with the patriotic ladies of the United States. The Harvard graduate's reminiscence also spoke to a level of popular involvement by young people that confounds many scholars' stereotypes of the Constitutional Unionist cause of 1860. Being willing to carry torches up to sixty miles for the cause is something we associate more readily with the Republican Party's young foot soldiers, the Wide Awakes.

But in March 1860, when Everett encountered real Wide Awakes, his reaction forecast what would be the chief electoral weakness of Unionism. He was in New Haven, Connecticut, to repeat his oration "The Character of Washington," which he had been delivering to popular acclaim around the country for years. All the proceeds of this effort went to purchasing Mount Vernon on behalf of the nation, so that both by holding up Washington as an example and by preserving his home as a mecca for Unionism, Everett hoped to help preserve the Union itself. But on the evening of his performance, he reported to his daughter, "it happened that there was a tremendous rally of both political parties, ... accompanied by bands of music & torchlight processions." He and those who had invited him thought that "this was not a very auspicious circumstance for my audience," worrying "that we should not 'take enough' to pay expenses." One organizer quipped to Everett "as a consolation that the 'wide awakes' (a club) would parade all night, with a band of music, & would no doubt serenade me." Everett retorted, "After travelling a couple of hundred miles, and speaking, I should prefer to be left with the 'sound asleeps.'" Instead of his usual packed house, Everett spoke to what could only be described as "a decent audience, considering."[2] His jest about the Wide Awakes was amusing, but was very much an old man's response.

More to the point, before 1860 neither Republican nor southern fire-eater had been able to dent Everett's Mount Vernon campaign significantly, but this was an election year. In that setting, this quiet, dignified movement stood little chance of competing with both parties' loud theatrics and masculine appeal. Both friend and foe often referred to the Constitutional Unionist Party (CUP) in general and Everett in particular as "the ladies' candidate(s)." For friends, that bespoke the enormous cultural power of emotional, disinterested Unionism. For foes, it was a backhanded compliment at best, given that, as much as women helped shape political culture, they did not vote. These two anecdotes encapsulated both the cultural strength of Unionism and the limits of its appeal at the polls in 1860.

Most historians of the election of 1860 have emphasized the limits rather than the strength. Distinguished scholars have taken the CUP and its political appeal seriously.[3] But to many other historians the CUP is a curious footnote, an irrelevance in a campaign that was about the Republicans and the divided Democratic Party. In an era characterized by sectional polarization, the CUP's evasive platform and reliance on the statesmanship of its candidates made it fatally old-school. As such, the aged, ivory-towered Everett was a perfect choice for the bottom of the ticket.[4] The CUP, however, merits close scrutiny because its influence and fate in 1860 and thereafter illuminate much about the most important election in American history as well as its aftermath. Such a study suggests a strange paradox: the majority of Northerners proved unwilling to vote for straight Unionism in 1860, but willing to kill and die for the Union cause thereafter.

By the time of Edward Everett's awkward encounter with the Wide Awakes, he was nearly sixty-six years old and entering the latest phase of a distinguished political career. Best known today for preceding Abraham Lincoln on the program to dedicate the national cemetery at Gettysburg in November 1863, he had in fact had a long career seeking to build American nationalism and find a middle ground on divisive issues such as slavery. From the time he accepted the post as preacher at the eminently fashionable Unitarian Brattle Street church at the ripe age of nineteen until his death in 1865, Everett's star remained prominently fixed in the New England firmament. After resigning Brattle Street to accept the inaugural chair in Greek literature at Harvard, he took a leave of absence to study in Germany and become the first American to earn a Ph.D., returning to Boston to teach at Harvard and edit the *North American Review*. At the age of thirty he traded these promising scholarly careers for politics, serving from 1825 to 1835 as the Massachusetts Middlesex District's Congressional representative. From 1836 to 1839 he served as his state's governor, and then from 1841 to 1845 represented the United States at the Court of St. James's in London. After returning to America he took up the presidency at Harvard from 1846 to 1849, and upon his good friend Daniel Webster's death in 1852 Everett succeeded him as secretary of state in the waning days of the Millard Fillmore administration. In 1854 the Massachusetts legislature sent him to the U.S. Senate, where his participation in the debate over the Kansas-Nebraska Act proved a political disaster for him. He opposed the legislation but without the emotional fire many of his constituents expected, and when he had the great misfortune to miss the crucial vote on the bill, both his political and physical well-being took a great step backward. He soon resigned his Senate seat and returned to Boston to recover his health and ponder his future career.

By a happy coincidence for Everett, in the 1850s the material decline of the Mount Vernon property had become intolerable to many Americans. Women playing their role as paragons of patriotic virtue launched a fundraising campaign to purchase and preserve the estate for the nation. Eventually incorporated in 1856 as the Mount Vernon Ladies Association of the Union (MVLAU), they succeeded spectacularly, purchasing the estate from the family for $200,000 in 1858. As their name suggested, their idea was to leverage Unionist sentiment to save Mount Vernon while leveraging the memory of Washington to save the Union.[5] Everett was a natural choice to become the lead fundraiser for the MVLAU. He enjoyed the reputation of being the greatest living exemplar of the orator's art of linking the rational to deep emotionalism. Moreover, his devotion to both Washington and the Union had been a decades-long theme in his public career.[6]

When MVLAU officials approached him to support them, therefore, Everett found his post-senatorial calling. The scheme was for him to deliver his "Character of Washington" speech throughout the Union and donate the proceeds (which in the end amounted to nearly $90,000) to the MVLAU. Between 1856 and 1860, Everett delivered the oration 131 times. In the midst of a recession, throngs of people paid a minimum of fifty cents each to hear the speech. In some towns Everett had to deliver it twice to accommodate the demand. One contemporary asserted plausibly that more people had heard this oration than any other speech "since the beginning of time." In late 1858, realizing what a hot property Everett had become, Robert Bonner, editor of the *New York Ledger,* offered to donate $10,000 to the fund if Everett would author a year-long weekly series for his newspaper. This was an offer Everett could not refuse, both for the fund's sake and because it would give him a weekly audience of up to a million readers for his Unionist gospel.[7]

This gospel constituted an emotional appeal to the historical ties that bound the Union together, with the great unifier George Washington as its patron saint. The restored Mount Vernon, Everett enthused, would house "a collection of all the personal relics and memorials" of the sainted founder and would feature a mausoleum "to enshrine the sacred ashes of the First of Men." God had plainly raised up Washington—"THE GREATEST OF GOOD MEN AND THE BEST OF GREAT MEN"—to effect the founding of the American Union, Everett argued. And perhaps the crowning achievement of his efforts was his Farewell Address, with its prescient rebuke of sectionalism that spoke so directly to the 1850s. Everett claimed for that Farewell "marvellous discernment and unerring wisdom."[8] In the "Character of Washington" oration, Everett taught that to study Washington's career was to learn that he was "the greatest man of our own or of any age," "a man toward whom affection rises into reverence, and reverence melts back into childish, tearful love." In evangelical tones, he bore witness that "I believe, as I do in my existence, that it was an important part of the design of Providence in raising him up," to give Americans "a living example" of the sort of public and private virtues that could save the Union. Unionism's Mecca would be Mount Vernon, for "while it stands the latest generations of the grateful children of America will make this pilgrimage to it as to a shrine." Everett also proposed that this sect "make a national festival and holiday of his birthday" which would unite congregants as they realized that their "fellow-citizens on the Hudson, on the Potomac, from the Southern plains to the Western lakes, are engaged in the same offices of gratitude and love." Finally, this cult of Washington had a sacred text in the Farewell Address, to which parishioners must give "practical deference" by "the preservation of the Union of these States." Should Americans forget the Farewell, boats on "the Potomac may toll their bells with new significance as they pass Mount Vernon; they will strike the requiem of constitutional liberty for us,—for all nations. But . . . by the sacred dust enshrined at Mount Vernon; no, by the dear immortal memory of Washington,—that sorrow and shame shall never be."[9]

The popularity of both Everett and his cause bespoke the deep emotional resonance the idea of the Union had for Americans in the late 1850s. As Elizabeth Varon has shown, even as disunion rhetoric and programs became more commonplace, attacking one's enemies as disunionists remained a winning political tactic.[10] One of the more dramatic manifestations of this came in the northern response to John Brown's October 1859 raid on Harpers Ferry. In large cities and small towns throughout the North, Unionists called mass meetings to reassure southern Unionists (and warn abolitionists) that Northerners would stand by the sacred Union. The Union gatherings that attracted the most attention were the "Monster Meetings" in Boston, New York, and Philadelphia, whose turnouts refuted the notion that old-school Unionism, with its emotional appeals to Washington and the founding, was limited to a few fossilized patricians.[11]

These meetings tapped the masses' deep emotional attachment to the founding fathers' Union. At the Philadelphia gathering, held December 7, 1859, a series of speakers lauded the Constitution as nothing less than "a divine revelation for the political regeneration of man." "Let the Union," urged one, "formed by the wisdom of sages and patriots, and sanctified by the breath and blood of sainted heroes, be guarded like the holy altar of the temple." And as if all these echoes of the Mount Vernon cause were not enough, a number of Philadelphia ladies joined—and thus helped to consecrate—the cause by sending a flag emblazoned with suitable Unionist sentiments to Virginia's governor.[12] Speakers and letter writers addressing the New York Unionist assembly repeatedly exhorted the roughly thirty thousand attendees that "the voluntary affection and loyalty of the people" must be yielded to the Union as "the greatest political blessing ever conferred upon mankind." This meeting was especially fruitful in circulating rhetoric that equated the Union to the sacrament of marriage. A banner on the hall's stage excerpted the Farewell Address, as did the last of the resolutions. One speaker pointed out that after a national separation, "the dividing line would take from us the grave of Washington." It would be a poor trade, he gibed, to "lose the grave and lose all connection with the name of Washington" and be left only with the "memory of John Brown in its place."[13]

From the opening prayer forward, the religious rhetoric of the Boston assemblage rivaled the extravagance of the others. "With the deepest emotions of veneration" for Washington, the meeting's final resolution reiterated the warning against sectionalism in his Farewell Address. Everett, one of the headline speakers, received an enthusiastic response from both the crowd and his fellow orators. He led by recounting his involvement in the "congenial" and "useful" Mount Vernon cause, "seeking to rally the affections of my countrymen North and South, to that great name and precious memory which is left almost alone of all the numerous kindly associations, which once bound the different sections of the country together." His predominant purpose was "to inculcate the blessings of the Union," consecrated as they were by "the memory of our Fathers" who had passed them to the next generations. Those who could not attend the meeting but who sent letters participated fully in such histrionics, such as one who thanked "God we have Everett . . . and a host of others, fit priests to serve at altars, whose fires were lighted by pilgrim hands." Should someone strike up "a grand chorus to the tune of the 'Constitution and the Union,'" he continued, it would "find a response in more hearts than you dream of." A newspaper reporter remarked on "the frequent tears in the eyes and on the faces of multitudes touched by a common sympathy, as some patriotic emotion was awakened by the sentiments of the several speakers." Indeed, attendees' "hearts were swelling with pent-up emotions, longing to find adequate expression."[14] The memory of Washington may have been one of the few threads holding the Union together, but this meeting testified that it was tied tightly to countless heartstrings.

Many Unionists sought to carry the sentimental appeal of these Union meetings into electoral politics, looking ultimately to the presidential election of 1860. Sectional moderates, especially those in the Upper South, had long desired a Union party, and they hoped these meetings would provide momentum. Well-wishers predicted that the meetings would awaken "honest men everywhere," who would in future elections "frown down all attempts to sunder those whom a beneficent Providence has joined together." They would open "a new era in the political history of the country ... by kindling the flames of enthusiasm" for a "conservative and Union ticket" as an alternative to the morally bankrupt Democratic and treasonable Republican parties. As sectional moderates organized the CUP in late 1859 and early 1860, successes in local elections showed them that the border states of the South would be their center of strength, although they harbored hopes for New York, New Jersey, and Pennsylvania.[15]

On May 9, 1860, CUP delegates gathered in Baltimore to craft their platform and nominate their presidential ticket. On that first day, Leslie Coombs of Kentucky mockingly proposed platforms for the Democratic and Republican parties, and for the CUP, "the Constitution of the United States as it is"—which provoked hearty applause—"and the Union under it now and forever"—which prompted an even greater ovation. Another delegate asserted that the electorate was "heartsick and head-sick" of party platforms, so the convention agreed to have no platform other than the Constitution and the Union.[16] Various statesmen, all of whom were from the Upper South but the Texan Sam Houston, had support for the presidential nomination, but on the second day the convention settled on John Bell, a Tennessee Whig who had had a long career of moderate Unionism in Congress.[17]

Given his association with Washington and the Union, Everett was a natural choice for the vice-presidential slot, so after naming Bell the convention nominated him by acclamation. The delegates, who met underneath a full-length portrait of Washington, recognized Everett's connection with the first president as a universally accepted Unionist talisman. Everett's selection was thus a high point of an emotional meeting that repeatedly and loudly cheered every mention of party shibboleths. Speakers knew the Washington hagiography by heart and argued that to reject the Union would be to "scatter the sacred dust of Washington ('Never,' 'never,'), teach your boys to forget his name, and never let the pilgrim's foot tread the consecrated groves of Mount Vernon." As for Everett himself, one supporter recorded that his nomination "heaved the breast; it kindled the cheeks; it broke from the eyes in warm, gushing, irrepressible tears." His association with both Washington and the ladies was the touchstone for this response. Because Everett "has studied the character of Washington," a delegate from Mississippi enthused, his patriotism "is enough of itself to save the Union." His Mount Vernon activities also rendered Everett wildly popular with the women in the galleries, and another Mississippian cracked that "the delegates were mostly married men, and must know very well that it was no use to oppose the ladies." A representative from Tennessee invoked the aid of women who had "participated with the illustrious gentleman who has just been nominated by such loud acclaim, in that great work of redeeming the grave of Washington." He assumed they were "to the last man, 'Everett men.'" More seriously, he continued, "If we have domestic discord and civil war, does it not visit the household? Does it not overspread the hearthstone?"[18] Douglas Egerton has recently strained to understand Everett's appeal to the women, assigning it to his good looks.[19] But the party convention, with the Mount Vernon campaign as its crucial context, made it clear that as an avatar of domesticity, Everett epitomized the nightmare of disunion as well as the virtues of the Union.

For all that, Everett proved torturously ambivalent about this nomination. He had instructed George S. Hillard, his close friend and representative at the convention, to withdraw his name from consideration for the top of the ticket, but had not anticipated the vice-presidential nod. And that movement on the floor happened so suddenly that Hillard had no time to react even had he been prepared to do so.[20] Everett also harbored almost no hope for the success of the ticket, which only reinforced his apparently sincere distaste for the scramble of partisan politics at this point of his life. He thus resented the degree to which "this terrible nomination" was a harassing distraction from his "ordinary pursuits."[21] Then there was his pride. He admitted to being "deeply touched with the cordiality of feeling, with which my name was received" at the convention. But he also candidly, if privately, stated that he took being the subordinate to the younger and less accomplished Bell—as opposed to the acknowledged elder statesman of the CUP, Crittenden—as something like an insult. Contemporaries and subsequent historians have agreed that this was not merely Everett's ego talking. One editor dubbed the CUP's the "kangaroo ticket," having longer hind legs than front legs.[22]

While Everett tried to keep his anguish over accepting the nomination private, his delay in deciding was very public, and damaging to the CUP. For this problem to crop up in the party's very infancy could prove fatal to its already slim hopes. Sober observers agreed that the best the CUP could hope for was to throw the election to the House of Representatives by preventing any other party from gaining a majority in the Electoral College, but Everett's dithering threatened even this limited goal as it gained a wide circulation by word of mouth.[23] The party's General Executive Committee insistently urged him to accept, citing his ability to attract conservative voters and the high stakes for the Union of the election. Everett's declining, they lectured him, would be "disastrous" given that his nomination had "been received with the greatest satisfaction by *all* the conservative men of the country both South and North." His acceptance would thus advance the CUP's efforts "to furnish a basis on which the patriotic and national and Union loving men of all parties could unite." A banding together of such men would result in "a great and permanent good to the country" even if the CUP did not win the election. "It was for these unselfish and important objects that the Union organization was formed," they wrote, but Everett's refusal "would greatly impair if not destroy our chances of success and produce serious if not irremediable mischief . . . to the whole country," especially since his nomination was already public. It was a powerful appeal to his "patriotism and sense of duty," hitting him where he lived.[24]

And it worked. On May 29, Everett finally wrote a public letter accepting the nomination. He excused his delay by explaining that his Mount Vernon activities had benefited from his "known and recognized disconnection from party politics," so that rather than thinking he was "speaking one word for Mount Vernon and two for myself," his audience gave him "credit for having a single eye to that meritorious object." And there was still work to do: there were still parts of the country—the Gulf states of the Deep South, in particular—to which to take the message. And

> in holding up to the admiring veneration of the American people the peerless name of Washington, (almost the only bond of fraternal sentiment which the bitterness of our sectional controversies has left us,) I feel as if I was doing more good, as far as I am able to do any good, and contributing more to revive the kindly feeling which once existed between North and South, and which is now, I grieve to say, nearly extinct, than I could possibly do by being engaged in the wretched scramble for office, which is one great source of the dangers that threaten the country.

After diagnosing the many maladies of sectional politics, Everett's prescription was that "a spirit of patriotic moderation must be called into action throughout the Union, or it will assuredly be broken up." Americans must look to 1776 and 1787 for their models rather than seek as sections to predominate over the other, for the Union must be one of consent and harmony rather than force, and the spirit of domination "comes loaded with the death smell from fields wet with brothers' blood."[25] It was a remarkable acceptance letter, yet another microcosm of the strengths and weaknesses of the CUP appeal. Affective Unionism had little hope of reaching its full political potential when its most effective proponent was so openly hesitant to put it to partisan purpose.

Still, the CUP was hardly dead on arrival. Party rallies and literature wielded the double-edged sword of feelings associated with the Mount Vernon cause, and those sentiments attracted passionate support, especially in the Upper South. This was far from being exclusively an elite affair, as the spelling in one supporter's letter highlighted: "Thar is a grait stur about the Presedential Election," a North Carolinian wrote his brothers. "We go for the unin the constitunion & the in forsement of the law & Bel & Everit to cary them out." One young Baltimorean grew his whiskers in hopes of a Bell and Everett win.[26] On a rather grander scale, CUP mass meetings were large, emotional affairs laying direct claim to the legacy of the warning against sectionalism in Washington's Farewell Address. At a CUP rally in Mississippi, when a speaker appealed to "our battle-fields, . . . our heroes, . . . our statesmen, and . . . the Father of his Country," it "warmed every heart and gave inspiration to those who have enlisted for the war." "Few could have failed to record a vow to Heaven that come weal come woe we will stand by the glorious Union of our fathers," the newspaper account concluded. Party faithful in North Carolina resolved that the party platform, which had been "approved and recommended by the illustrious Washington and his compeers, is National and broad enough for all true patriots."[27] The old-time religion was good enough for Washington, and therefore good enough for them.

Because "Mr. Everett's name is destined to be indissolubly connected with that of Washington," not only in America but also abroad, CUP leaders took great pride in having Everett on their ticket. Their standard practice of referring to their nominees both privately and publicly as the "Bell and Everett" ticket typified this satisfaction. By contrast, they directly mentioned rival presidential candidates but only very rarely other vice-presidential nominees.[28] Party publications highlighted Everett's Mount Vernon activities, which gave both "popularity" and "nationality" to "his fame" and made him better known and loved to women than Bell was, even in the Upper South. Everett's candidacy thus embodied all the disinterested patriotism associated with the ladies. But the party also claimed to embody "the courage and the manliness to stand firm" and defend the damsel in distress that was the Union. One of Everett's fans at the party convention got closer to this idea when he proclaimed that his state was "in love with Edward Everett." Still, in the rough-and-tumble of electoral politics, with all its masculine posing for exclusively male voters, a candidate might not benefit from being so closely tied to "feminine" ideals.[29]

Be that as it may, Everett was not about to run away from the Mount Vernon legacy in the midst of this election. He was the last man who would have violated the era's expectations that candidates refrain from stumping for votes, but he did give a few public speeches after accepting the nomination. In them he found every opportunity, no matter how much a stretch it might seem, to insert Washington's legacy and the Union into the proceedings. He had no need to make such a reach when Boston's city authorities invited him to give them a Fourth of July address in 1860. Everett noted that the founders "are gone, but their work remains." Thus it was appropriate that Bostonians had "escaped from . . . the dissensions of party, from all that occupies and all that divides us, to celebrate, to *join* in celebrating, the birthday of the nation, with one heart and with one voice." His theme was the question of "whether the great design of Providence, with reference to our beloved country," was succeeding, or failing as British critics in particular had recently asserted. He set out to vindicate American institutions, and his ultimate trump card was that his countrymen

> may proudly boast of one example of Life and Character . . . of which all the countries and all the ages may be searched in vain for a parallel. I need not—on this day I need not—speak the peerless name. It is stamped on your hearts, it glistens in your eyes, it is written on every page of your history, on the battle-fields of the Revolution, on the monuments of your Fathers, on the portals of your capitols. It is heard in every breeze that whispers over the fields of Independent America. And he was all our own.[30]

The CUP's strength was evident in other parties' nomination conventions, particularly the Republican conclave in Chicago. While in 1860 the leaders of rival parties knew they must reckon with the affective Unionism that the CUP sought to harness in the election, Bell and Everett's nomination gave William Henry Seward's opponents within the Republican Party encouragement. With a reputation as a radical, Seward would render his party vulnerable to the CUP in the Upper South and border regions of the North. Nominating a moderate, however, would not only unify the Republicans; it would also allow them to triangulate the CUP's one attractive issue. When their convention assembled, as Eric Foner has pointed out, one-fifth of the delegates represented southern states. Republican leaders thus had reasons "for believing that, as one Connecticut delegate put it, many southerners agreed with their party 'if they dare express it.'"[31]

One of the men who had made himself most electable on this score was Abraham Lincoln. Repeatedly in the late 1850s he had insisted on "the identity of" the Republican Party's stance on slavery "with the doctrines of the Fathers of the Republic" as well as with those of Henry Clay. He would not cede the legacy of the fathers to the conservative Unionists. For instance, he declared the mass Union meetings of late 1859 and early 1860 "a humbug—they reverse the scriptural order, calling the righteous" antislavery men of the North "and not sinners" (southern disunionists) "to repentance." And in his February 1860 speech at New York's Cooper Institute, which propelled him toward the Republican nomination, Lincoln went out of his way to address those who "delight to flaunt in our faces the warning against sectional parties given by Washington in his Farewell Address." Reminding his audience that the first president had signed legislation enforcing the Northwest Ordinance's ban on slavery, he asked, "Could Washington himself speak" (as Everett had so often wished), "would he cast the blame of that sectionalism upon us, who sustain his policy, or upon you who repudiate it? We respect that warning of Washington, and we commend it to you, together with his example pointing to the right application of it." In his peroration he urged wavering Republican Unionists to "be diverted by none of those sophistical contrivances wherewith we are so industriously plied and belabored—contrivances such as groping for some middle ground between the right and the wrong." Such tactics included "beseeching true Union men to yield to Disunionists," as well as "invocations to Washington, imploring men to unsay what Washington said, and undo what Washington did." Instead, "LET US, TO THE END, DARE TO DO OUR DUTY AS WE UNDERSTAND IT."[32]

Such rhetoric was the stuff with which to meet the CUP's appeal to conservatives both within and without the Republican Party. "Lincoln's choice" as the nominee, as Douglas Egerton has astutely summarized, "allowed the Chicago delegates to hold fast behind their party's core ideals while reaching out to northern moderates and winning over the states necessary to an electoral victory."[33]

The electioneering contest between the CUP, the Republican Party, and the divided Democratic Party (the largely northern wing behind Stephen A. Douglas and the largely southern wing behind John C. Breckinridge) revealed the CUP's electoral flaws. All three of its rivals dismissed the CUP platform as an irrelevancy and an evasion of the central issue of the campaign, the expansion of slavery into the territories, even as they triangulated the platform. As the CUP floundered to respond to these attacks and dismissals, its internal as well as its electioneering weaknesses revealed themselves.

Rival parties' assaults on the CUP shared much in common but also varied by region and party. From the latter point of view, nominating statesmen rather than politicians and refusing to adopt a platform was key to the strategy of saving the Union from the maladies of the 1850s. But both Democratic and Republican papers, in the South as well as the North, flailed at the CUP on these very points. Its lack of a platform was a weaselly—even unmanly—dodge of the defining issue of the day. Everett's image as a detached scholar played right into this line. Given that none of the parties rejected either the Constitution or the Union, one editor spoke for many when he mocked that the CUP "might as well have taken the multiplication table and the Decalogue for its platform." For his part, Frederick Douglass quickly dismissed the CUP, jabbing that "a party without any opinion need have no opinion expressed of it."[34]

Both Douglas Democrats and Republicans repeatedly sought to steal the CUP's stance on the Union and thus chip away at its natural constituency in the contested border regions of both North and South.[35] The Republicans were particularly effective in pursuing this tactic. Edward Bates, a former Whig from Missouri, dealt the CUP a blow by endorsing Lincoln as "*a sound, safe, national man*" who "could not be sectional if he tried." Other party stump speakers followed suit, echoing Lincoln's claim to the legacy of the founders. The Republicans, their arguments went, were the true conservatives by this measure, rather than the CUP men whose noncommittal stance would maintain the 1850s' violations of the founders' original intent.[36] As one frustrated CUP operative in New York groaned, the widespread view that by nominating Lincoln the Republican Party "is becoming more conservative... operates upon many persons who are disposed to follow the current and take refuge in what they consider a strong and prosperous party."[37]

The Republicans seemed to many undecided voters to offer an escape from having to choose between their Unionism, their antislavery principles, and their desire for victory. Such was the strength this built for the Republicans in large parts of the North that in later years one party stalwart recalled the election of 1860 as a "three-cornered contest... between Lincoln, Douglas, and Breckinridge," with the latter standing no chance in the North.[38] Taken as a whole, the image of the CUP in other parties' literature was as a nullity, if a respectable one with a prized issue on its side.

For their part, the Breckinridge Democrats found it most useful to light into the CUP in a distinctly southern accent. They tussled with the party over how to frame the true issues of the campaign. For the southern Democrats, "the real issue of this canvass is not union or disunion; but the effort on the part of the State Rights Democracy" to limit the power of the meddlesome Republicans.[39] A common tactic against Everett, for instance, was to use his friendly public correspondence with abolitionists while governor of Massachusetts to paint him as an abolitionist himself. "Indeed," one Breckinridge publication reminded readers, "so well known was Mr. Everett as an Abolitionist, that the legislature of Georgia passed, in 1841, a resolution censuring one of their Senators, Mr. Berrien, for voting to confirm his nomination" to the Court of St. James's. In light of this and more recent evidence of Everett's sympathies for rank abolitionists, this pamphlet asked, "can any man point out the difference between Edward Everett and [the Republican vice-presidential nominee] Hannibal Hamlin? And is this the man whom the Southern people would feel safe in supporting?"[40]

In response to the general lines of criticism, the CUP had little to offer besides reiterations. They were neither unmanly, they protested, nor fossilized relics from a bygone age. The Republicans by their own admission and principles were a sectional, even a disunionist, party—they had even removed the word "National" from their name at the Chicago convention. The Union was in mortal danger from secessionists and from the eternal agitation of the slavery issue. The sectional breakup of the Democratic Party dashed its hopes for power and killed its claims to being national. Washington, as the CUP's literature restated countless times, opposed such sectional parties as all three rivals represented. The CUP's large, enthusiastic rallies were evidence that it was becoming the great net gathering conservative men fleeing the breakup of the Democracy and the radicalism of the Republicans—indeed, the other parties were the unelectable ones. And make no mistake: "THE REAL ISSUE [was]: UNION OR DISUNION." Or "THE TRUE ISSUE [was]—BELL OR LINCOLN—PEACE OR STRIFE!"[41]

As unsatisfying as these bland and repetitive generalities were, however, they were the CUP's only chance to preserve unity as a national party. So effective were the Republicans' triangulation efforts, in particular, that Crittenden and other potential speakers declined invitations to stump for the ticket in New York and Pennsylvania, writing them off to the Republicans.[42] Such calculations led many CUP efforts to slant so southerly as to kill any attempt to regain the border North. In the most prominent of these efforts, a small group of Constitutional Unionists met in Selma, Alabama, and drew up their own platform in the absence of a national one. They pledged allegiance to the Union but also their determination that all territories be free for slavery expansion. The publication of this counterplatform led to the defection of many northern CUP men to the Republicans.[43]

Desperate to refute the charges that Everett was an abolitionist, southern Constitutional Unionists bombarded him with requests for clarification that were bound to offend one whole bloc of voters either way. A Virginia man, writing on behalf of his friends, begged Everett to "say whether the sentiments imputed to you are *now* entertained by you; and if modified in any respect, please say to what extent and in what particular." He had high hopes for the CUP in his state, but bluntly informed Everett that "to propound" the antislavery sentiments ascribed to Everett "as *our creed* would be fatal to our cause." "Unless you recant the doctrines attributed to you by" Breckinridge's supporters, another CUP man in Virginia lectured Everett, "or make some explanation satisfactory to the people of the South, I will owe it to myself—my section & the Union—to abandon the advocacy of you, & thousands in my state will do likewise."[44]

Everett was becoming a drag on the ticket in its heartland, but if he assuaged such concerns too decidedly, he would kill whatever slim chances the party had in the North. Some CUP papers countered Breckinridge Democrats' narrative of Everett's past by emphasizing an 1826 Congressional speech in which he had defended slavery—a speech that had made him notorious in the North.[45] When an Alabamian Constitutional Unionist described to Everett how he defended him there, the dilemma was plain. When the state's Democrats, he wrote, "charge you with being an abolitionist I cut & slash in reply to the right and the left. Among many other things I tell them you left your own quiet happy home to travel thousands of miles to eulogize the memory of a slave holder [Washington] & toiled night & day to earn money to purchase slave territory [Mount Vernon] to present it to the wives & daughters of slave holders, when there was no slave holder willing or able to do the tenth part you did."[46] Everett, who had seen his Mount Vernon activities as consciously nonsectional, must have been mortified to see this sectional spin on them, necessary as such an approach was in Alabama.

Everett, of course, could control the message by responding himself, but at first he resisted doing so. In July, an exasperated Everett confided to a friend: "Our Southern friends must understand that whatever is gained *there* is lost *here,* by demanding of me decidedly Southern principles: the very basis of our party is to unite the two sections." "What a mess we should make" if Bell or Everett were to give in to either section's demands "for explanations!"[47] His logic was irrefutable, but it would not do either to ignore or wish away the sectionalism that drove the election of 1860. So by the time fall arrived, Everett had drafted his own response, one that leaned southern. He led by staking his just claim to "the entire confidence not merely of the conservative men of his own section . . . , but also that of conservative men throughout the country." He wrapped himself in the mantle of Daniel Webster and Henry Clay at every opportunity. Among the living, he cited evidence that both Breckinridge himself and Jefferson Davis had named him "as one of 'the noble band of northern conservatives.' " He explained away his antislavery expressions as governor by asserting that in the 1830s "similar views were not only universal at the North, but they extensively prevailed at the South." He admitted to having opposed the Kansas-Nebraska Act, but he argued that he did so on eminently conservative ground: "We do not believe there is a candid man at the South of any party, who really differs from him" in seeing that bill and its aftermath as "the Pandora's box of all the evils which now distract the country."[48] This southern-friendly reply proved satisfactory to Constitutional Unionists in the Upper South, but the whole episode illustrated perhaps better than anything else that, as a historian of the CUP has put it, "the slavery question simply would not be downed."[49]

Under assault from without and fissuring from within, the CUP's possible paths to the presidency seemed to narrow with every passing day. Its travails led to a failure to reach many voters in its natural constituency of conservative Unionists, especially in the North. Sidney George Fisher, for instance, a conservative member of Philadelphia's elite, harbored serious reservations about the Republicans' sectionalist stance, and he had always hated the Democrats. He also approved of Bell and Everett personally as men of the highest respectability. "And yet," he regretted in his diary, "their merits are the only argument the convention offers in their favor." The party claimed to uphold the Constitution, but "as each party says the same thing, this assertion amounts to nothing." Slavery comprised "the overwhelming and exciting subject now before the country," and "by its side all other issues are insignificant." "How," he wondered, "can a party which passes this question by hope for success"? Because the party was so out of touch with popular passions on the slavery issue, Fisher wrote, "it is common to hear men say they prefer Bell & Everett, but to vote for them would be useless." "I shall therefore probably vote for Lincoln," he concluded, "if I vote at all." He ended up not voting, because "I do not entirely like the animus of the Republican Party," but that mattered little to the CUP, which had lost his vote.[50] Others in the CUP base offered a simpler rationale for begging off: they thought the ticket unelectable. Ex-president Millard Fillmore probably swayed none of these when he vowed in a public letter to "vote for Bell and Everett, whether any one else does so or not."[51] Even Everett's own sister, Sarah P. E. Hale, confessed to one of her sons that if she had had the franchise she would have voted Republican![52]

In this dire scenario, one hope was that the CUP might coalesce with the Douglas Democrats to rally northern Unionists. This became a central theme in the CUP story in potential swing states including New York, New Jersey, and Pennsylvania—and to a much lesser degree in the Upper South. But actual fusions of this sort were short-lived, and many others were only rumored or dreamed of. Old partisan divisions plagued these attempts, with ex-Whigs chronically suspicious of Democrats and vice versa. And given how divided among themselves the Democrats were in 1860, the Whig–Democrat rupture was but one of many running through the fusion scene. Common hatred of the Republicans was simply not enough to overcome all of that.[53] The house divided unto itself that was conservative Unionism in 1860 was bound to fall.

Historians argue over whether the sectional moderates could have defeated Lincoln had they joined forces.[54] As it was, the CUP carried only 12.6 percent of the popular vote. It did outdistance Douglas in the Electoral College by carrying Tennessee, Kentucky, and Virginia for a total of thirty-nine electoral votes. But its failure in the North was total. Lincoln carried the vast majority of former Whigs in the North, whereas Bell and Everett polled only 13.1 percent of the overall vote in Massachusetts, even though it was Everett's home state. Lincoln carried every county in New England, the only time anyone did that between 1832 and 1896. So beleaguered was the Bell and Everett Association in Philadelphia that it was constantly in search of a meeting place, since the owner of the building containing one of its rooms would not remove his Lincoln and Hamlin flag.[55]

If Northerners had voted in the same way that they had supported the Mount Vernon cause and the Union meetings, it would have been more prophecy than the standard partisan hyperbole when a Virginian wrote in March 1860, "I firmly believe the Union Conservative party will sweep the whole country."[56] But the Republican Party's triangulation of Unionism and the legacy of the founders, aided by the CUP's own maddeningly nebulous non-platform, made the electorate's options far from clear. "A voter's choice is often difficult," Egerton has observed. In 1860, they "had to decide whether to vote with their heads or their hearts."[57] Many whose hearts were with the affective Unionism that the CUP sought to harness found their heads leading them to cast a more electable ballot. Constitutional Unionists pictured Americans as torn between the angel of Unionism on one shoulder and the devil of sectionalism on the other. Everett himself declared that everywhere he had traveled, he had found that Americans "have their sectional loves and hatreds, but before the dear name of Washington they are all absorbed and forgotten."[58] The Republicans' nomination of Lincoln convinced many Northerners that they could respond to their anger at and fear of the South without completely brushing off the Unionist creed.

Everett's brand of Unionism, then, was dazed and programmatically confused, not dead, in 1860. Its continuing force was evident when President-elect and then President Lincoln framed the issues of secession and war in terms reminiscent of the Mount Vernon cause and the Union meetings. On his way from Springfield to Washington, he complained that those who balked at forcibly upholding the Union treated it as nothing "like a regular marriage at all, but only as a sort of free-love arrangement." More soberly in his First Inaugural, he again compared the Union to a marriage and appealed to disgruntled Southerners to consider not only the "benefits" but also the "memories" associated with it. "Though passion may have strained, it must not break our bonds of affection," he implored in his peroration. "The mystic chords of memory, stretching from every battle-field, and patriot grave, to every living heart and hearthstone, all over this broad land, will yet swell the chorus of the Union, when again touched, as surely they will be, by the better angels of our nature."[59] The whole passage had channeled Everett for very much the same cause that Everett had channeled Washington.

When northern soldiers marched south to prosecute the Civil War, they did so with a holy zeal for preserving the Union uppermost in their minds. And the "religious feeling, that this war is a crusade for the good of mankind" to be wrought by putting down "this hell-begotten conspiracy" sustained those who stayed through four bloody years of conflict at least as much as did hatred for the South.[60] Union soldiers wrote letters on stationery featuring a variety of patriotic, Unionist slogans, including "THE UNION, THE CONSTITUTION—AND THE ENFORCEMENT OF THE LAWS." "The Founders," Gary Gallagher has shown, "appeared on envelopes in various ways, most often in the person of George Washington." "Think of the Union they have helped to preserve," one of the regimental histories published soon after the war waxed, "with all its blessings, all its memories, and all its hopes."[61] The fact that they used such terms to describe why they were willing to fight for so long was in part a testament to the cultural work people like Edward Everett had done in perpetuating and increasing a deeply emotional attachment to the Union.

When Everett died in January 1865, the former candidate whose party had done so pitifully in his native state was widely honored for his contributions to the Union cause. One eulogist remembered that "no person who came under the influence of" his "Character of Washington" oration "can imagine that he failed in rekindling the fire of patriotism on a thousand, thousand altars; that he failed in . . . preparing many noble hearts to offer themselves in generous sacrifice for its preservation and perpetuity."[62] With all due allowance for eulogistic hyperbole, this speaker captured the truth that Everett's affective Unionism fed consciously on the memory of Washington. So nourished, it could not stave off secession, but it helped to assure that secession meant civil war.

NOTES

1. Nathan Appleton, Jr., scrapbooks, Nathan Appleton Scrapbooks, 1845–1895 (Ms. N-58), Massachusetts Historical Society, Boston (MHS).

2. Everett to Charlotte Wise, March 29, 1860, Everett-Hopkins Papers, 1813–1921 (Ms. N-1203), MHS.
3. Douglas R. Egerton, *Year of Meteors: Stephen Douglas, Abraham Lincoln, and the Election That Brought on the Civil War* (New York: Bloomsbury Press, 2010), esp. 85–101; John Ashworth, *Slavery, Capitalism, and Politics in the Antebellum Republic*, vol. 2, *The Coming of the Civil War, 1850–1861* (Cambridge: Cambridge University Press, 2007), 592–606; Peter Knupfer, "Aging Statesmen and the Statesmanship of an Earlier Age: The Generational Roots of the Constitutional Union Party," in *Union and Emancipation: Essays on Politics and Race in the Civil War Era*, ed. David W. Blight and Brooks D. Simpson (Kent, Ohio: Kent State University Press, 1997), 57–78; Daniel W. Crofts, *Reluctant Confederates: Upper South Unionists in the Secession Crisis* (Chapel Hill: University of North Carolina Press 1989), esp. 75–81; John B. Stabler, "A History of the Constitutional Union Party: A Tragic Failure" (Ph.D. diss., Columbia University, 1954).
4. For just a very few examples ranging across time and genres, see Allan Nevins, *Ordeal of the Union*, vol. 4, *The Emergence of Lincoln: Prologue to Civil War, 1859–1861* (New York: C. Scribner, 1950), 261–62; Michael A. Morrison, *Slavery and the American West: The Eclipse of Manifest Destiny and the Coming of the Civil War* (Chapel Hill: University of North Carolina Press, 1997), esp. 232; Sean Wilentz, *The Rise of American Democracy: Jefferson to Lincoln* (New York: Norton, 2005), 745–91; and even Thomas Brown, "Edward Everett and the Constitutional Union Party," *Historical Journal of Massachusetts* 11 (June 1983): 69–81.
5. *The Illustrated Mount Vernon Record, The Organ of the Mount Vernon Ladies' Association of the Union* . . . , vol. 1 (Philadelphia: Devereux, 1859), 1; Scott E. Casper, *Sarah Johnson's Mount Vernon: The Forgotten History of an American Shrine* (New York: Hill & Wang, 2008), 63–71; Jean B. Lee, "Historical Memory, Sectional Strife, and the American Mecca: Mount Vernon, 1783–1853," *Virginia Magazine of History and Biography* 109.3 (2001): 255–300; Elizabeth Varon, *We Mean to Be Counted: White Women and Politics in Antebellum Virginia* (Chapel Hill: University of North Carolina Press, 1998), 10–70, 124–36.
6. Daniel Walker Howe, *The Political Culture of the American Whigs* (Chicago: University of Chicago Press, 1979), 219–31; Garry Wills, *Lincoln at Gettysburg: The Words That Remade America* (New York: Simon & Schuster, 1992), 42–52.
7. Stuart J. Horn, "Edward Everett and American Nationalism" (Ph.D. diss., City University of New York, 1973); Paul Revere Frothingham, *Edward Everett, Orator and Statesman* (Boston: Houghton Mifflin, 1925), 373–407; Varon, *We Mean to Be Counted*, 130; Edward Everett, *The Mount Vernon Papers* (New York: D. Appleton, 1860), 53–71; Edward Everett, *Orations and Speeches on Various Occasions*, vol. 4 (Boston: Little, Brown, 1868), 3–17; Ronald F. Reid, *Edward Everett: Unionist Orator* (New York: Greenwood Press, 1990), esp. 1–3, 79–85, 214–15; George B. Forgie, *Patricide in the House Divided: A Psychological Interpretation of Lincoln and His Age* (New York: Norton, 1979), 171 (quotation). For more on this phase of Everett's career, see Matthew Mason, " 'The Sacred Ashes of the First of Men': Edward Everett, the Mount Vernon Ladies Association of the Union, and Late Antebellum Unionism," in *Remembering the Revolution: Memory, History, and Nation-Making from Independence to the Civil War*, ed. Michael A. McDonnell et al. (Amherst: University of Massachusetts Press, 2013), 265–79.
8. Everett, *Mount Vernon Papers*, quotations on 4, 124; Edward Everett, *The Life of George Washington* (New York: Sheldon and Co., 1860), 99–103, 211–22, 262–72.
9. Everett, *Orations and Speeches*, 4:20–51.

10. Elizabeth Varon, *Disunion! The Coming of the American Civil War, 1789–1859* (Chapel Hill: University of North Carolina Press, 2008), 9–11, 128, 151, 174, 208–9, 227–28, 263–64, 273–87, 327–28, 344.
11. *Great Union Meeting, Philadelphia, December 7, 1859: Fanaticism Rebuked* (Philadelphia: Crissy & Markley, 1859), 3–7; *Boston Courier Report of the Union Meeting in Faneuil Hall, Thursday, Dec. 8th, 1859* (Boston: Clark, Fellows, and Co., 1859), 3–8, 10, 12, 13, 20, 22, 24–26, 30; *Official Report of the Great Union Meeting Held at the Academy of Music, New York, December 19, 1859* (New York: Davies & Kent, 1859), 3, 41, 43–44, 86–89, 93–176; *North American and United States Gazette* (Philadelphia), December 8, 1859; *Frank Leslie's Illustrated Newspaper* (New York), December 31, 1859; Stabler, "History of the Constitutional Union Party," 273–300.
12. *Great Union Meeting, Philadelphia*, 14–21, 27, 34, 42–43, 46–47, 55–59.
13. *Official Report*, esp. 9–10, 19, 27–28, 47–48; quotations on 47 and 27. For crowd estimates ranging from 20,000 to 40,000, see *Daily National Intelligencer* (Washington, D.C.), December 21, 1859; *Fayetteville (N.C.) Observer*, December 22, 1859; *Dover (N.H.) Gazette & Strafford Advertiser*, December 24, 1859.
14. *Boston Courier Report*, 10–17, 23–24, 28–30.
15. Thomas A. R. Nelson to John Bell, January 10, 1851, and Neill S. Brown to John Bell, August 10, 1858, John Bell Papers, Manuscript Division, Library of Congress; *North American and United States Gazette*, December 8, 1859; *Daily National Intelligencer*, December 9, 1859; *New York Herald*, December 21 and 23, 1859; Stabler, "History of the Constitutional Union Party," 349–415; Daniel W. Crofts, "The Southern Opposition and the Crisis of the Union," in *A Political Nation: New Directions in Mid-Nineteenth-Century American Political History*, ed. Gary W. Gallagher and Rachel A. Shelden (Charlottesville: University of Virginia Press, 2012), 85–111. For an especially rich documentary trail of the founding of the CUP, see the correspondence of the man who became the chair of its National Executive Committee in Alexander R. Boteler Papers, 1729–1924, Rubenstein Rare Book and Manuscript Library, Duke University.
16. Quoted in William B. Hesseltine, ed., *Three against Lincoln: Murat Halstead Reports the Caucuses of 1860* (Baton Rouge: Louisiana State University Press, 1960), 124–25.
17. Joseph H. Parks, *John Bell of Tennessee* (Baton Rouge: Louisiana State University Press, 1950), esp. 349–55; Stabler, "History of the Constitutional Union Party," 416–40.
18. *Union Guard*, July 12, August 23 and 30, 1860; Hesseltine, *Three against Lincoln*, 121–22, 127, 131–40; Stabler, "History of the Constitutional Union Party," 465–68.
19. Egerton, *Year of Meteors*, 96; see also 189. It is also difficult to ascribe too much power to the physical charms of a sixty-six-year-old man.
20. Everett to Joseph Barbour [or Barbiere?], May 16, 1860, Edward Everett Papers, 1832–1865, American Antiquarian Society, Worcester, Mass. (AAS); Everett to Washington Hunt, May 14, 1860, Everett to Hillard, May 15, 1860, and Everett to John J. Crittenden, May 28, 1860, Edward Everett Papers, 1675–1910 (Ms. N-1201), MHS; Everett to Henry A. Wise, May 14, 1860, Everett-Hopkins Papers, MHS.
21. Everett to W. W. Corcoran, June 6, 1860, Edward Everett Papers, Manuscript Division, Library of Congress; Everett to Mrs. Charles Eames, June 29, 1860, Edward Everett Papers, MHS. Everett to Charlotte Wise, May 7, 1860; Everett to Henry A. Wise, May 18 and 28, 1860; and Everett to Henry A. Wise, June 2, 1860 (quotations), Everett-Hopkins Papers, MHS.
22. Everett to Hillard, May 15, 1860, Edward Everett Papers, MHS (first quotation); Everett

to Henry A. Wise, May 14, 1860, Everett-Hopkins Papers, MHS; Everett to John J. Crittenden, June 2, 1860, John J. Crittenden Papers, Rubenstein Rare Book and Manuscript Library, Duke University; David M. Potter, *The Impending Crisis, 1848–1861* (New York: Harper & Row, 1976), 417; Egerton, *Year of Meteors*, 97 (second quotation).

23. [No author] to Everett, May 25, 1860, Edward Everett Papers, AAS; Amos A. Laurence [or Lawrence] to John J. Crittenden, May 25, 1860, John J. Crittenden Papers; Everett to Henry A. Wise, May 18, 1860, Everett-Hopkins Papers, MHS; Stabler, "History of the Constitutional Union Party," 480–92, 520–25, 693–98.

24. John J. Crittenden et al. to Everett, May 25, 1860, Edward Everett Papers, MHS.

25. *Union Guard*, July 12, 1860.

26. Wm. B. Brock to "Dear Brothers," 1860, William Clark Doub Papers, 1778–1899 (quotation), and Ned to Joseph S. Williams, December 5, 1860, Joseph S. Williams Papers, 1857–1882, both in Rubenstein Rare Book and Manuscript Library, Duke University.

27. *New York Herald*, February 5, September 6 and 17, October 7–8, 25, and 28, and November 3, 1860; *Daily National Intelligencer*, September 19 and October 10, 1860; *Weekly Raleigh (N.C.) Register*, July 11, September 26, October 17 and 31, and November 7, 1860; *Hinds County Gazette* (Raymond, Miss.), March 21, 1860; *Virginia Free Press* (Charlestown, Va.), August 30, 1860. For a fascinating window into the earnestness of CUP organizers, see Friends of Bell and Everett Association Minute Book, 1860–1862, Historical Society of Pennsylvania, Philadelphia.

28. See *Union Guard*, passim (quotation from September 27, 1860); Alexander R. Boteler Papers.

29. *Address of the National Executive Committee of the Constitutional Union Party to the People of the United States* ([1860]), 1, 4; *The Life, Speeches, and Public Services of John Bell, Together with a Sketch of the Life of Edward Everett* (New York, 1860), 97–101; Varon, *We Mean to Be Counted*, 144–46; *Union Guard*, August 23 and 30, 1860. For more on gendered rhetoric and the sectional crisis, see Varon, *Disunion!*, 186–91, 196, 201, 203, 221.

30. Everett, *Orations and Speeches*, 4:283–310, quotations on 283–85, 295; see also 277–82, 315–16, 319.

31. Eric Foner, *The Fiery Trial: Abraham Lincoln and American Slavery* (New York: Norton, 2010), 141; see also David Herbert Donald, *Lincoln* (New York: Simon & Schuster, 1995), 247; Nevins, *The Emergence of Lincoln*, 240; Wilentz, *Rise of American Democracy*, 758.

32. *The Collected Works of Abraham Lincoln*, ed. Roy P. Basler, 8 vols. (New Brunswick, N.J.: Rutgers University Press, 1953), 3:333; 4:13; 3:536–37, 550. See also 3:19, 29, 87, 93, 117, 220, 276, 307–8, 374–76, 398, 407, 414–17, 436, 439, 464–66, 484, 489, 496, 498, 502, 522–54, 4:30.

33. Egerton, *Year of Meteors*, 110–48, quotation on 147.

34. Samuel Bowles quoted in Thomas J. O'Connor, *Lords of the Loom: The Cotton Whigs and the Coming of the Civil War* (New York: Scribner, 1968), 141; *The Frederick Douglass Papers, Series One: Speeches, Debates, and Interviews*, vol. 3, *1855–1863*, ed. John W. Blassingame (New Haven: Yale University Press, 1985), 384–86. See also *The Public Record and Past History of John Bell and Edward Everett* (Washington, D.C.: National Democratic Executive Committee, 1860); Egerton, *Year of Meteors*, 191; Stabler, "History of the Constitutional Union Party," 553–55. For a good discussion of the CUP worldview in this respect, see Ashworth, *Slavery, Capitalism, and Politics*, 2:592–606.

35. For examples from the Douglasites, see Joel H. Silbey, ed., *The American Party Battle: Election Campaign Pamphlets, 1828–1876*, 2 vols. (Cambridge: Harvard University Press, 1999), 2:82–113. For a good secondary discussion of the CUP's opponents' strategies and tactics, see Parks, *John Bell*, 361–88.
36. Silbey, *American Party Battle*, 2:114–50, quotation on 119; Charles Sumner, *Charles Sumner: His Complete Works, with Introduction by George Frisbie Hoar*, 20 vols. (1900; repr., New York: Negro Universities Press, 1969), 6:313–14, 330–31, 355–58, 7:7–19, 26–40, 74–75, 83, 86–87; Egerton, *Year of Meteors*, 186.
37. Washington Hunt to John Bell, May 24, 1860, John Bell Papers.
38. Abram J. Dittenhoefer, *How We Elected Lincoln: Personal Recollections* (1916; repr., Philadelphia: University of Pennsylvania Press, 2005), 33; see also 40.
39. Dwight L. Dumond, ed., *Southern Editorials on Secession* (1931; repr., Gloucester, Mass.: P. Smith, 1964), 191–95, quotation on 193.
40. *Public Record and Past History*, 29–32; see also John M. Speed to Edward Everett, July 17, 1860, Rare Books and Manuscripts, Boston Public Library (BPL).
41. *Union Guard*, passim, quotations on 184, 252; see also Dumond, *Southern Editorials*, 159–62, 166–67, 195–98, 214–18.
42. Egerton, *Year of Meteors*, 190; Joshua J. Bell to John Bell, September 20, 1860, John Bell Papers.
43. Egerton, *Year of Meteors*, 100–101.
44. John M. Speed to Edward Everett, July 17, 1860, and John H. McCue to Edward Everett, July 25, 1860, BPL. See also T. J. Anderson to Everett, June 12, 1860, Edward Everett Papers, MHS.
45. *Weekly Raleigh (N.C.) Register* and *Daily Register* (Raleigh, N.C.), October 17 and 31, 1860.
46. Andrew H. H. Dawson to Edward Everett, July 26, 1860, BPL.
47. Everett to Hillard, July 21, 1860, Edward Everett Papers, MHS.
48. "Mr. Everett" [1860], a long undated document in Everett's own hand, Alexander R. Boteler Papers. For the published version, see *Union Guard*, October 4 and 18, 1860.
49. John M. Speed to Edward Everett, July 27, 1860, BPL; Stabler, "History of the Constitutional Union Party," 731.
50. Jonathan W. White, ed., *A Philadelphia Perspective: The Civil War Diary of Sidney George Fisher* (New York: Fordham University Press, 2007), 34–35, 38, 46–47, 56–57.
51. *Daily National Intelligencer*, June 11, 1860 (quotation); typescript of William Appleton Diary Notes, September 15, 1860, Appleton Family Papers, 1539–1941 (Ms. N-1778), MHS; Henry M. Fuller to Bell, June 22, 1860, John Bell Papers.
52. Quoted in Ronald J. Zboray and Mary Saracino Zboray, *Voices without Votes: Women and Politics in Antebellum New England* (Durham: University of New Hampshire Press, 2010), 205. This was only in part due to the "insult" she perceived in Everett's receiving the second slot on the ticket.
53. Stabler, "History of the Constitutional Union Party," 640–712; Nevins, *The Emergence of Lincoln*, 285–86, 297–98; Jean H. Baker, *Affairs of Party: The Political Culture of Northern Democrats in the Mid-Nineteenth Century* (1983; New York: Fordham University Press, 1998), 46, 325–27; Crofts, *Reluctant Confederates*, 75–81. For press coverage of fusion attempts that, even in the most enthusiastic pieces, underscores the difficulties, see *Virginia Free Press* (Charlestown, Va.), September 27, 1860; *Weekly Raleigh (N.C.) Register*, September 26 and October 17, 1860; *New York Herald*, October

7–8, 25–28, November 3, 1860; *Daily National Intelligencer,* October 10, 1860. The John Bell Papers, Library of Congress, also contain a vivid account of the rise and fall of the fusion cause in 1860. For an excellent exploration of northern Democrats' internal divisions that roots them in the late 1850s, see Allen C. Guelzo, "Houses Divided: Lincoln, Douglas, and the Political Landscape of 1858," *Journal of American History* 94 (September 2007): 391–417. Jefferson Davis, interestingly enough, was an early proponent of fusion against the Republicans; see Jefferson Davis, *The Rise and Fall of the Confederate Government,* 2 vols. (New York: D. Appleton, 1881), 1:52, 577–78.

54. For a strong statement that this was possible, see Peter B. Knupfer, *The Union as It Is: Constitutional Unionism and Sectional Compromise, 1787–1861* (Chapel Hill: University of North Carolina Press, 1991), 208–11. For a strong statement of doubt, together with a useful review of this historiographical debate, see Egerton, *Year of Meteors,* 335–37.

55. Egerton, *Year of Meteors,* 212; Foner, *Fiery Trial,* 144; entry for September 13, 1860, Friends of Bell and Everett Association Minute Book, 1860–1862, Historical Society of Pennsylvania.

56. John N. Hughes to Alexander R. Boteler, March 22, 1860, Alexander R. Boteler Papers.

57. Egerton, *Year of Meteors,* 16.

58. Everett, *Orations and Speeches,* 3:635.

59. Basler, *Collected Works,* 4:195, 235–36, 239–44, 266, 269, 271.

60. James M. McPherson, *For Cause and Comrades: Why Men Fought in the Civil War* (New York: Oxford University Press, 1997), quotation on 13.

61. Gary W. Gallagher, *The Union War* (Cambridge: Harvard University Press, 2011), esp. 39, 57–61, 67.

62. *Tribute to the Memory of Edward Everett, by the New-England Historic-Genealogical Society . . .* (Boston: New-England Historic-Genealogical Society, 1865), 3–6, 66, 72–74, 82–83, 93–95, quotations on 95.

McClellan in the Hub
Boston's Financiers and the War for Emancipation

CAROL BUNDY

> Coasting on the Common or Beacon Hill had been going on since colonial days.... my mother told me how she had a sled named "General McClellan" (all sleds were named in those days) which was much admired, but the time came when other children pointed at it and hooted, so she ran home crying and had a piece of carpet tacked over the then disreputable name.
>
> Samuel Eliot Morison, *One Boy's Boston* (1962)

Boston's brief romance with General George McClellan, formerly the commander of the Army of the Potomac and Lincoln's prospective Democratic challenger in the 1864 election, illuminates the complexity of embracing emancipation, even in a city known for its abolitionist governor, John A. Andrew, and its rabidly radical senator, Charles Sumner. For despite its history of antislavery protests in the 1850s and Radical Republicanism in the first two years of the Civil War, Boston was also home to some of the most conservative politics in the North. The wealth of much of New England was associated, indeed inextricably entangled, with the cotton economy of the Deep South, and the elite of the region was unlikely to turn against its own self-interests. Nor was a working class reliant on the jobs provided by that elite; the large immigrant population among this group felt no sympathy for the slave and might certainly also resent compulsory military service. Yet Boston's Copperhead movement never gained significant traction, in sharp contrast with that of New York and other leading commercial cities in the Union.

An understanding of McClellan's ten-day visit to Boston from January 28 to February 7, 1863, offers insight into how and why Boston's elite, despite considerable ambivalence, successfully switched from supporting a conservative war to preserve the Union (which had met with almost universal instinctual support) to a war of emancipation (which had not), or at least chose not to oppose such a radical aim.

In order to ensure the success of Boston's role in the war for emancipation, Governor Andrew forged an alliance with the city's conservative but highly pragmatic businessmen, harnessing their financial wherewithal and hands-on logistical expertise.[1] He also succeeded in neutralizing his opposition so that no significant Copperhead movement developed. Why did a large number of conservative men throw their weight behind a radical prosecution of the war? What happened to the ideals of abolition and emancipation as they went mainstream? Did a massive shift in the moral virtue of the city occur, or was something else at work? Did the elite and the working class join forces? And why did an even larger number of them fail to jump on the McClellan bandwagon?

But first, some context. Shortly after the victory of Antietam on September 17, when President Lincoln announced his intention to enact the Emancipation Proclamation, the Union reacted with a prolonged ambivalence. McClellan's reluctant and late support for the document, which he did not endorse until October 7, as well as his failure to follow up the Antietam victory with decisive military action, exacerbated this public sentiment. The general's behavior thus increased the unpopularity of Lincoln and his policies and culminated in the Republicans' "shellacking" in the midterm elections on November 5. The next day, when Lincoln dismissed the general, his conservative skeptics were outraged. To them, McClellan was the nation's only competent and trustworthy leader, the most legitimate face of northern opposition to the war policies of President Lincoln. They held high hopes for a McClellan Democratic candidacy. William Howard Gardiner, a future member of Boston's McClellan Committee, wrote, "If his enemies wished to make him President of the United States they could not have taken a better course." G. Howland Shaw, another future committee member, wrote to his brother-in-law, Theodore Lyman, who was in Paris, urging him to be sure to come "home in time to vote for him."[2]

Exactly one month later, on December 5, 1862, Dr. J. Mason Warren, one of Boston's leading surgeons, joined a citizens' committee of twelve gentlemen in writing a letter to General McClellan "to testify their appreciation of his services" and invite him "to pass a week in Boston at the [Tremont] House [hotel]."[3] The idea for a Boston visit had originated with Edward Eldredge, a wealthy merchant whose younger sister had married McClellan's older brother. Eldredge was a supporter of the general and remained so through the 1864 election, but as November turned to December he feared McClellan would spoil his chances of gaining the nomination. In his view, the general maintained too cavalier an association with New York City businessmen such as August Belmont and Samuel Barlow, men believed to be so economically entangled with the South that they were seen as virtual Confederates. Belmont and Barlow had invited McClellan to visit New York.[4]

As an alternative, Eldredge proposed a trip to Boston. To arrange the visit he contacted James Lawrence, the principal partner in A. & A. Lawrence & Co., the city's leading cotton concern. Lawrence quickly assembled a committee of twelve men, including himself and Eldredge. He enlisted Edward Everett to serve as chairman, explaining that he wanted to "prevent [McClellan's] falling into the hands of those who would be disposed to make political capital out of this visit."[5] Everett, formerly Daniel Webster's protégé, a Whig diplomat and statesman and, more recently, the 1860 Constitutional Union Party vice-presidential candidate, was also Boston's most cosmopolitan and nationally recognized political leader. Already a correspondent of McClellan, Everett sent out the invitation on the day of the municipal elections in Boston, but before the polls revealed that the city had turned out its Democratic mayor for the Republican Levi Lincoln, thus eliminating a conservative toehold at the heart of an otherwise Republican state.[6]

Three members of the McClellan Committee were self-made men who played pivotal roles in businesses connected with cotton manufacturing and the sale of cotton goods in both Boston and New York. Of course the commonwealth's association with slavery went back to the eighteenth century, but it had always been primarily a matter of business and calculation and only minimally of culture.[7] Slavery in Massachusetts was certainly nothing like the plantation system that the South had developed, and much less did it serve as the economic foundation for the larger culture; in the late eighteenth century, blacks represented less than 1 percent of the state's population, most of them servants to its wealthiest merchants. Thus when Massachusetts abolished slavery in 1783, it appeared easily to cast off any attachment to the institution. And that might have been the circumstance at the beginning of the nineteenth century, but for the overwhelming economic trend of industrialization in New England between 1820 and 1860. In these decades, New England's manufacturers and Boston's textile merchants, along with their counterparts in England and France, created a bottomless demand for cotton, and southern growers had a virtual monopoly on its production, using a plantation system that was synonymous with slavery. Thus by 1860 a significant sector of New England's economy relied on the raw material that slaves produced.

But the relationship went deeper as well as wider. Selling agents such as committee member John Lovell Little worked on a commission basis and never actually "owned" cotton goods themselves. They functioned as middlemen between the mills and their consumers and in so doing often gained tremendous influence with the manufacturers, including the power to dictate production. Ironically, southern planters represented the largest market for manufactured cotton products even though they produced the bulk of the world's raw cotton; they also relied on credit for most of the year, until they sold their crop and received their single annual payout. With this money the southern planter-purchaser cleared debts he had accumulated with the selling agent who, over the course of the year, functioned as his banker or credit broker. At the start of the Civil War these selling agents held considerable Confederate debt, and this explains their role in the ill-fated and last-minute Peace Conference of February 1861.[8]

The McClellan Committee did not solely comprise those with cotton interests. James Lawrence also reached out to seven men who represented different branches of the Boston business and social elite (see the appendix to this essay). These were the sons and grandsons of a previous generation of money makers—merchants and ships' captains who had traveled the world and brought back to Boston fortunes based on sugar, tea, and cotton or, more aggressively, on rum, opium, and slaves. These were not the proprietors of "white-shoe" firms of a later generation but opportunistic men with a working knowledge of the grittier side of capitalism. And yet most of their sons prided themselves on their ultra-exclusive social status as descendants of colonial families. The Amorys had been loyalist sympathizers with a fortune based on the sugar trade; others were the descendants of yeomen Revolutionary generals—J. Mason Warren's ancestor General Joseph Warren had been martyred at Bunker Hill—or, in the case of Thomas Jefferson Coolidge, a great-grandson of the third president.

But social exclusivity, even with its attendant conservatism, did not prevent them from practicing a financial dynamism in diversifying their wealth. Virtually all of them owned shares in a variety of cotton mills. Most either currently or formerly held a leadership position in some kind of textile concern. This diversification also included extensive investments in railroads, insurance firms, iron foundries, and countless other manufacturing operations. Thus a stake in a cotton factory was only one element of most family fortunes, even among those whose original wealth had come from textiles.

Cotton production involving mill owners, employees, and stockholders was not the only sector of New England industry to be dependent on the South as a market, however. Mills, foundries, and factories across the region turned out both the bare necessities and the desiderata of life—everything from shoes in Lynn and wire hoops in Worcester to salt cod in Gloucester, for which Southerners, including planters and slaves, were a ready, stable, and growing market. Southerners also paid Northerners to provide them with significant services, including transportation, banking, insurance, and brokerage. Over the course of the antebellum period this economic interdependence only deepened. At least 40 percent of all cotton revenues ended up in New York City, and by 1860 the South bought an estimated $150 million worth of northern goods. Of that slightly over 33 percent, or $60 million, was Boston merchandise—$20 million in shoes alone.

Here was the fruit born of the tree of Yankee ingenuity, that aspect of the New England character on which the region's mercantile wealth and culture were based.[9] It was personified in the stereotype of the shrewd Yankee trader known for a steely, taciturn, plainspoken style, a man who had learned to keep his mouth shut, to recognize his self-interest, and to exploit an opportunity when it appeared. Whether trading sugar in Demarara, cotton in Mississippi, or tea in China, this capacity to lay morality aside and focus instead on the profit motive had stood New England merchants in good stead. It was a distinctly different New England heritage than the Puritan tradition, whose moral rigor, exacting standards, and rectitude were often interpreted as self-righteous arrogance or, more quixotically, a sense of superiority that too often saw moral victory as an end in itself. It was out of the Puritan tradition that the abolitionist movement had grown, and it was this dual heritage that lay behind the rupture of the Whig party into "Cotton" and "Conscience" factions. Thus, at the same time that Boston became increasingly entwined economically in the slave system, its politics became increasingly radical.[10] By 1860 Massachusetts had elected an abolitionist governor personally pledged to lead the fight for emancipation. Of course, without the financial and practical support of leading businessmen, Governor Andrew had slender means of putting into effect his idealistic policies.[11] This reality may have permitted the anomalous political situation.

At the start of the war Andrew's working relationship with this powerful elite was so poor that he recruited two of its members, Henry Lee and Charles Amory, to serve on his staff as liaisons and gave them the specific task of bridging the gulf that separated the duly elected governor from Boston's powers-that-be. Small but indispensable inroads were made. With the assistance of the Forbes brothers, John Murray and Robert Bennet, Massachusetts regiments could proudly claim to be the first to take the field and the best supplied. The brothers had diversified their China fortune—partly made by supplying the opium trade in Canton—into iron foundries in the Appalachian backwaters and building on the edge of the frontier. Supplying troops in Washington was something they could do in their sleep. Their lines of supply were so efficient that regiments belonging to less well-organized states purchased the surplus, and within a week of the conflict's start Massachusetts was in the war business.

Nonetheless, by the end of the Peninsula Campaign, that effort was in danger of collapse; Governor Andrew was sufficiently distrustful of General McClellan's leadership that he was threatening to refuse to send more Massachusetts men to be slaughtered under an officer whom he feared was not only incompetent but also unwilling to gain the advantage. And this distrust of McClellan represented the position of Radical Republicans across the North in August and early September.

The day after Lincoln announced the Preliminary Emancipation Proclamation, Governor Andrew began to swing back into line. The promise of the executive order counterweighted his discouragement over the Peninsula Campaign and the even greater failure to end the war at Antietam. A majority of war governors met at Altoona, Pennsylvania, expressly to reestablish a united military effort. Some radicals, such as Andrew, had had their patience tested by a conservative war policy, while conservatives were alarmed by the sharp turn that the proposed Emancipation Proclamation represented. Ultimately all but six of the twenty-four Union war governors backed the president and renewed their pledges "to continue in the most vigorous exercise of all our lawful powers, contending against treason, rebellion, and the public enemies until final victory and unconditional submission."[12]

With this goal, Andrew returned to Boston knowing that such action demanded a renewed administrative effort, a fresh source of funding, and a two-pronged public relations campaign to win support from Boston's elite to underwrite new regiments, and from the city's working class to man them. He needed to establish greater cooperation than heretofore with Boston's upper class, whose longstanding ambivalence on the matter of slavery was now compounded, as 1862 drew to an end, by the deteriorated national situation: the discouraging state of the Union army, the crisis of leadership in both the army and the government, and the challenge of shifting to the radical and unpopular war aim of ending slavery. The consolidation of support for General McClellan threatened to stymie any hope of the cooperation Governor Andrew sought and needed. Worse, active opposition from the elite would snuff out any chance he might have of winning a public relations victory with the working and immigrant classes in these early days of emancipation. Recruitment could not move forward otherwise.

Meanwhile the Massachusetts People's Party held a state convention on October 6. The party's membership consisted largely of Constitutional Union Party members and conservative Republicans fed up with Lincoln but most particularly with Charles Sumner. The animus against the senator was personal as well as ideological and had an irrational intensity. Many moderate and conservative Bostonians felt that he had betrayed them. Sumner had started out as a protégé of Edward Everett and had been groomed in the 1830s to follow in his footsteps to become a cosmopolitan New Englander capable of charming the cultural elite of Europe and proving that the New England states were no longer a colonial backwater. But by the end of the 1840s they were deeply offended that the region's spokesman presented himself as a hotheaded, arrogant, emotionally extravagant, vituperative zealot. There was no sign of a prudent man, no moderation, no measured calculation. Politics aside, Sumner presented moral qualities that to conservative minds in no way embodied the character of New England.

Beyond this animus toward Sumner, the McClellan Committee's desire to bring the general to Boston was a deliberate effort to further the People's Party platform and to seek an alternative course from that of Governor Andrew. Their literature directly opposed the governor with an unequivocal statement repudiating Altoona, endorsing McClellan, supporting a war for union not emancipation, and calling for the president to retract the Emancipation Proclamation and restore habeas corpus.[13]

Everett dated his invitation December 6, and McClellan sent his reply by return post. He agreed to spend ten days in Boston but postponed twice due to ill health. (McClellan's wife had an infant child, and yet her presence was vital. The daughter of a career general, the former Ellen Marcy was a savvy political operator who had grown up in Washington, and many observers thought she was the spouse with political ambitions.) Thus a visit intended for mid-December did not take place until the end of January.

As the committee went to work planning this stay, the political and military landscape kept shifting. An astute analyst might have predicted that the winds were gaining momentum for emancipation, but many factors still hung in the balance. General Ambrose Burnside's bungling at Fredericksburg (December 12–15, 1862) encouraged many conservatives to hope for McClellan's reinstatement. For the rest of the month, cabinet machinations threw Lincoln's seeming lack of leadership into greater question and underscored the conservative conviction that the nation, poorly led, was on a path to disaster. As the wounded returned to convalesce, Boston's civilians began to appreciate the heavy price of war, and morale slumped. Differing versions of the Emancipation Proclamation and speculation as to its final form raised more questions than they answered. Ruminations on its chances of success tended to favor the skeptics: even its supporters were unsure whether slaves would fight. No one had a clear picture of what emancipation would look like, whether former slaves could be integrated into white culture, and on what terms that might occur. No businessman had a clear idea of how cotton would be grown if not by slave labor. Old soldiers were convinced the South would never surrender. French and/or British intervention on the side of the Confederacy still seemed all too possible.

Nonetheless on January 1, 1863, the Emancipation Proclamation was celebrated with great fanfare. Senator Sumner's close friend Henry Wadsworth Longfellow chaired the committee that organized a Grand Jubilee Concert at the Boston Music Hall, the proceeds intended for the relief of freed men. In fact, at the time of the concert the bill had not yet been signed. Thus while the fundraising extravaganza went forward, some three thousand Bostonians waited anxiously at the Tremont Temple for confirmation from Washington that no last-minute impediment had intervened. Not until evening did the final wording of the proclamation arrive. As it was read out loud, an eyewitness noted, "a thrill shot through the crowd; the enthusiasm was intense. The people seemed almost wild with delight.

It is the dawning of a New Day!"[14] Emancipation was no longer a concept, an idea, a future option, but the law of the land.

Almost four weeks later, on January 26, 1863, General Burnside, McClellan's successor, was relieved of his command. Although McClellan still coveted the appointment, General "Fighting Joe" Hooker, a well-known abolitionist, took charge of the Army of the Potomac. Just two days after this last disappointment, McClellan and his retinue set off for Boston. The city embraced its visitor as a military hero. "I have never known any stranger receive such marked and general attention from all classes since the old Marquis [de Lafayette] in 1825," reported the most conservative committee member.[15] Boston newspapers echoed this adulation. Of course, 1825 was an entire generation earlier, and few visitors could hope to have the stature of American's first and most vital ally. In 1842 Charles Dickens had arrived in Boston to tremendous fanfare, and for an entire month he had been shown the city's marvels. Recognized equally by the intelligentsia and the common man as a literary giant, he had been wined, dined, and treated as the international celebrity that he was. In 1852 Louis Kossuth, the former president of Hungary, had come to Boston and been feted as a symbol of the great but failed European revolutions of 1848. And in October 1860 the young Prince of Wales, traveling under the pseudonym Baron Renfrew, had visited just two weeks before the national election. An entire generation of debutantes had ever after measured their social success by their dance with the prince at the Renfrew Ball.

Many of the men who had organized Boston's entertainment of the prince in 1860 were also on the McClellan Committee in 1863. One cannot discount the degree to which McClellan's appeal rested on his celebrity status, nor the extent to which prominent or ambitious Bostonians would wish to play host to him for reasons more social than political. That McClellan's popularity more resembled Lafayette's than Prince Albert's does him credit. His celebrity had the heft and weight of some real, if controversial, accomplishment. The partisan *Springfield Republican* grudgingly acknowledged his popularity, which it sought to undercut by setting it in as cynical a light as possible: "No stranger ever goes to Boston unless he wants something and no one is invited unless the city wants something of him."[16]

Boston's infatuation with General McClellan peaked even before he left town. Several factors contributed to its decline: the ease with which a fickle public, once its celebrity mania is sated, can abandon its former favorite;

the momentum gathering around the emancipation movement; the failure of the general's strongest supporters to solidify public acclaim into a political following. But first, let us take a closer look at the details of his tour of Boston.

At 2:15 on the afternoon of January 28, the McClellan Committee boarded the express train for Worcester. There they battled their way through a large crowd mobbing the concourse, to enter a rail car freshly arrived from New Haven, which held General McClellan, his wife, and staff. After prolonged bowing and waving to the assembled throng from the rear platform, McClellan reentered the carriage. With a great whistle and puff of smoke, the train set off for Boston. A crowd massed at the Framingham station, as did yet another huge gathering in Boston at 5:30 p.m. They gave McClellan "an ovation such as equaled his reported reception by his army[,] . . . a hearty and spontaneous offering of the people to a man beloved for his public and private worth."[17]

During the following days Boston feted McClellan in its usual manner. There was the obligatory tour of Harvard and its various buildings. The students were on vacation, but "a bevy of the Cambridge women" gathered.[18] With a significant number of men away in the army, the crowds were consistently disproportionately female despite the presence of some soldiers home on leave or for convalescence. McClellan particularly spoke to one "discharged soldier who had been in nine battles under him & had been four times wounded" and "parted with him affectionately."[19] The Charlestown Navy Yard gave the general a thirteen-gun salute, the army and navy brass turned out to greet him, the Navy Yard's own band serenaded him, and he was taken around to see the machine shops, ropewalks, and foundries. Cheered by about three thousand workmen just let off for their dinner, the general once again reached out to greet veterans.[20]

McClellan was taken on inspections of various public institutions, including the public schools, the hospital for wounded soldiers, the Warren Museum with its complete mastodon skeleton, and the Boston Public Library, each considered a model of civic innovation. Then came a trip by rail to the factory town of Lynn, where "shoemaking abolitionists" mobbed him and, for good luck, threw old shoes at his departing train. An overcrowded reception at the Essex House awaited him in Salem. More orderly was a visit to the largest mill in the country, the Pacific Cotton Mills in Lawrence. At the mill's central hall, the entire population of Lawrence's school-aged children, some two to three thousand of them, serenaded Mrs. McClellan and the general and also presented them with bouquets. Then the children sang "The Star-Spangled Banner" as the party left to catch the return train to Boston.[21]

On Saturday afternoon, January 31, McClellan paid a visit to old Josiah Quincy, former mayor of Boston and president of Harvard, at his home on lower Park Street. From there he walked to the Somerset Club on the corner of Somerset and Beacon Streets, "followed by an immense crowd who gave occasional cheers." A local newspaper described how "intelligence of his whereabouts was quickly disseminated in the neighborhood, and a dense crowd was soon collected who gave enthusiastic cheers for the gallant soldier [and forced] the General [to] appear on the steps of the [Somerset] Club building."[22] Although the throng called for a speech, McClellan declined the opportunity and reentered the establishment. Nonetheless, when he left the crowd was still there, cheering him as he entered his carriage.

This constant presence of large assemblies had not been anticipated and persuaded both McClellan and the committee to arrange a public reception. Rejecting the first suggestion of Faneuil Hall, the members settled on the public rooms of the Tremont House between 1:00 and 3:00 p.m. on the following day, February 2, making sure that a large police force would be in attendance. Boston's businesses closed at noon and a crowd of four to five thousand people lined Tremont Place, forming "a continual stream in single file for between two to three hours." The Republican mayor, the city council, and other officials first greeted the general. Then came the "hoi polloi." They were all eager to shake McClellan's hand, which became "blackened, swollen, and in places blistered."[23] As might be expected from such a crowd, the full range of human expression was in evidence—a woman kissed his hand, one soldier dropped to his knees.

When the time came to end the reception, McClellan went out on a balcony to show himself to those who had not even entered the building. A committee member recalled, "This was one of the grandest spectacles I ever saw. Such a sea of faces! Tremont Street & the heads of the adjoining streets as far as could be seen, was a dense mass of human beings, men and women, and such a shout as they sent up when the General appeared! He walked back and forth on the balcony during several minutes, in full dress of course, but bareheaded, bowing occasionally in response to cheers which were incessant," and his supporters scheduled a second reception two days later. Although the McClellan Committee had not anticipated such popularity, they quickly recognized that it sent a message to President Lincoln: McClellan's mass appeal proved he was "as much the favorite of the people, at least in this part of the country, as he is of the Army."[24]

Newspapers across the political spectrum interpreted McClellan's visit as an expression of the most conservative, pro-Southern elements in Boston. Historians have generally regarded it as the high-water mark for Copperhead sympathy in the city and recognized it as an attempt to gauge whether a campaign for the presidency in 1864 made sense. That said, considerable nuance needs to be brought to the discussion. The committee did nothing to capitalize on McClellan's popular success. Nor did he once speak out publicly, not even before his largest crowd on February 2. Although the committee members certainly wanted to send a message to the president and the radical cabal surrounding him, they shied away from anything too overtly political. Their original idea had been to "prevent [McClellan's] falling into the hands of those who would be disposed to make political capital out of this visit."[25] Oddly enough, this meant not only thumbing their noses at the Republican establishment in Boston, but also denying the Democrats access to McClellan. "Leading Democrats too," Gardiner reported, "are much put out not with the General, but with the conservative gentlemen who took charge of him, did not allow him to be made common and unclean, as they would have liked. Politicians of every party were not allowed to get much hold of him."[26] To many conservatives, the rough-and-tumble of popular politics was distasteful. They subscribed to an older system of selection in which the candidate, a patrician leader, must be coerced into public office. But the days of Cincinnatian humility were long gone from American politics.[27] Without a leader, and without an advocate, popular support soon dissipated. Thus the fastidiousness of Boston's political right wing, as well as McClellan's own advisers (even after he became the Democratic presidential candidate, he did not campaign) meant they failed to capitalize on the general's appeal.

While McClellan's daytime movements stirred up Boston's masses, his evenings were reserved for a mix of the city's upper crust and its intelligentsia. The lavish dinners and parties they gave each night to entertain the general became the social events of the season. For one of these, a grand levée at the home of committee member William Gray on Mt. Vernon Street, some fifteen hundred invitations were sent out. An estimated eight to nine hundred people came, but the crowd kept moving and no more than six hundred people were present at any one time. Nonetheless, the

Gray family took all the doors off their hinges, cleared all the furniture from the rooms, and entirely removed the long windows from the rear of their house to permit entrance into a temporary room they had constructed in their garden. One family member recalled, "Everybody turned out," and added that "expecting such a jam no one wore their most elegant dress" for fear that it would be ruined in the crush of the crowd, but among the women "heads were splendidly dressed, and nothing was seen but head and shoulders."[28] So it went, night after night. A "masquerade" at James Lawrence's was followed the next evening by a smallish but more refined dinner at G. Howland Shaw's and then a formal party given by J. Huntington Wolcott. Then came dinner for twenty-eight at Charles Amory's, where the guests much admired a portrait of Lord Lyndhurst, Mrs. Amory's uncle, by her grandfather (and the sitter's father), John Singleton Copley.[29]

Perhaps the most exclusive evening was a dinner given by Dr. J. Mason Warren, who specially commissioned an enormous table and installed it in his largest room along with a mirror that filled the French windows, thus enlarging the appearance of the room and reflecting the table. To further the effect, Warren removed the gaslight fixtures and instead used seven hundred candles. The table took up so much space that the eight waiters had to serve each half of the table from different points of entry. Ornaments arrived, at vast expense, from New York, but locally made spun-sugar confections and ices also graced the table. Music accompanied a meal of some fifteen courses, including quails, chicken quenelles, jellied meats, duck, and sweetbreads cooked in pastry barques and tied with colored ribbons, which "the gentlemen placed in their buttonholes." As one newspaper reported, "the courtesies remembered" were very clearly planned and orchestrated by men who "represent the wealth, intelligence and respectability of Boston." The extravagance should be seen as "a most flattering approval of General McClellan and an open avowal of their regard, never lightly or carelessly bestowed."[30]

The most conservative committee members wrote detailed, overreaching descriptions of the general. His photograph began to circulate among households high and low. Professor Louis Agassiz spoke of his powerful brow and large head as phrenological evidence of a superior being. The buzz about McClellan was positive even among the charming daughters of Republicans such as Colonel Henry Lee of Governor Andrew's staff and John L. Motley, Lincoln's ambassador to Austria; while awaiting their session at the Brookline Riding School, the girls were "vehement in extravagant admiration of McClellan" and "pronounced him 'lovely, nice, splendid, &c.'"[31]

Perhaps because his celebrity turned the heads of those young ladies whose family's politics were firmly liberal, the excitement over McClellan infuriated Boston Republicans. "They look very glum, keep aloof, and call the whole movement an attack upon the government," Gardiner noted. Governor Andrew was in Washington, but his acolytes wrote him sniping letters, claiming that the committee intended to exhibit McClellan "à la Tom Thumb," the country's first celebrity midget and circus performer.[32] Following the Gray levée on January 30, letters speedily circulated between Boston Republicans regarding who had and had not attended. One spinster, who had not, explained that "these manifestations of honor to McClellan" were disrespectful "to the president who has removed him from command and expressed disapprobation of his conduct." Charles Eliot Norton refused all invitations and snorted about "the Hero of one thousand ungained victories."[33] But anti-McClellan peevishness almost seemed to add to his stature.

Quite evidently, Boston's high society extended to McClellan a level of celebrity similar to his success with the people. Curiosity about him, the need to see him, to shake his hand, to be one of the lucky few to exchange words—all this possessed both high and low. But how to evaluate its enduring effect? Almost everyone remarked on McClellan's "simple quiet manner" and lack of pretension.[34] He said almost nothing. This silence worked well with the public at large and further excited interest in him, but it was less effective in private. Many of the high and mighty who dined with him and were predisposed to support him came away feeling some disappointment. Edward Everett's brother-in-law Francis Brooks noted, "He is a short, thick, big headed, red, oily, stuffed looking man who does not look people in the face and in a smock frock would pass for a burly butcher."[35] Women as well as men were given exposure to the general and they voiced their reaction. Hannah Gray, a sister-in-law of William Gray and the hostess of the magnificent levée, commented that "unaware of who and what he is one would not instinctively select him as the greatest general of our time." His failure to impress, either by his person or by his personality, left conservatives standing on the sidelines growing indifferent. Brooks complained, "It is an ill judged thing, this having him on and will do him no good." Brooks was equally clear that "he is the best man we have yet and I wish he were at the head of things and our present boobys passed off."[36] And yet many insisted they had gone only to "shake hands with" the general and to please their wives.[37] They claimed, and it seems were correct, that attendance did not indicate real support.

"As a general rule I would let a furore have its run," Dr. Oliver Wendell Holmes assured his friend John Murray Forbes, adding, "It is not by attacking them that we shall gain most, but by aggressive movements from another quarter." He then offered Forbes this prediction: "I think the new 'union club' is going to be the thing."[38] Holmes was referring to a plan that appears to have originated over the previous month from conversations among several prominent gentlemen, including William Gray.[39] One of the principal forces behind the People's Party in October 1862, Gray, as we have seen, was the McClellan Committee member who gave the enormous evening levée. And now, at the home of Samuel G. Ward, the Boston representative of Baring Brothers, on the evening of February 4, two days after the general's public reception, Gray attended the founding meeting of the Union Club.[40]

Edward Everett, who in December 1862 had accepted the leadership of the McClellan Committee, not only attended this Union Club meeting but also agreed to be its president.[41] Although he was a corresponding friend of General McClellan and the Constitutional Union Party vice-presidential candidate in 1860, as early as the end of November, a full two weeks before the invitation to McClellan was sent, he wrote to his son explaining the futility of a brokered peace. Even if North and South could "patch up a compromise on the basis of separation, it will only be a temporary truce. It will be impossible to agree to a permanent boundary line of separation, and even if this could be done, the two confederacies would be eternally at war."[42] Everett's role on the McClellan Committee was not a sign of his political support for the general so much as it indicated his desire to play a part in building the new moderate consensus.

Charles Amory, the committee member who gave a dinner party for McClellan on February 3 after the visit to Lawrence, may have wished to play a similar role. His own family's money came from the rum and sugar trade, which, like cotton, depended on a plantation system of slave labor in the Caribbean. His wife's money—she was the daughter of Gardiner Greene—had similar origins in Demarara sugar. As the brother-in-law of William H. Prescott, Amory also belonged to the most cosmopolitan and conservative of Boston's social circles. For almost his entire adult life, Amory had held directorships at a variety of cotton mills, and he had served a twenty-year stint as the treasurer of the Stark Mills in New Hampshire. Despite these impeccable conservative credentials, he served on Governor Andrew's staff as a liaison to Boston's elite. Did he also play this role on the committee?

Of the twenty to thirty men attending the Union Club meeting, most were friends and kin of the McClellan Committee; three in addition to Gray and Everett were members, the same three previously singled out for having the most direct connections to the cotton or slave economy, with business and personal connections to the South. James Lovell Little, J. Huntington Wolcott, and J. Wiley Edmands were outsiders in the sense that they did not come from Boston's upper class; they represented "new money," all of it made in the cotton business. And yet they were confirmed Republicans (Edmands and Little were founding members of the party), and now they were among the first wave to join the Union Club, doing so even before McClellan had left town. It is hard not to suspect that their interest in the general never reached more than lukewarm temperature.

But before examining their motives more closely, let us look at another "aggressive movement from another quarter," the Negro Soldier Bill that, despite enormous skepticism among white Americans, was passed on February 2, 1863, the same day as McClellan's tremendous reception at the Tremont House. It opened the way for black soldiers to fight for their own freedom. Governor Andrew had been in Washington lobbying for this bill and within days had secured permission for Massachusetts to form two "colored" regiments, the 54th and 55th regiments of Massachusetts infantry, to be counted against the state's quota. Andrew immediately wrote to Francis George Shaw, the nation's most socially prominent abolitionist, to ask if his son would take the colonelcy. Thus within five days of McClellan's departure, Robert Gould Shaw arrived in Boston to begin recruiting the 54th Regiment.[43]

Andrew's insistence that the officers of black regiments would come from Boston's top drawer proved astute in the case of the McClellan Committee member G. Howland Shaw, the author of the letter that exerted family influence on his brother-in-law, Theodore Lyman, to come home and vote for Little Mac. Shaw found himself outmaneuvered by a greater family pressure. When on February 4 his nephew Robert Gould Shaw accepted the colonelcy of the 54th, the majority of the vast, wealthy, and influential Shaw-Sturgis clan rallied around. Instead of becoming a McClellanite,

Lyman, whose wife was the sister of Robert Shaw's best friend and cousin Henry Sturgis Russell, volunteered, gained a place on the staff of General Meade, and voted for Lincoln. Howland Shaw began writing checks for the 54th Regiment less than a month after his nephew accepted the colonelcy.[44] By the time the family crowded onto the balcony of 45 Beacon Street, the home of yet another uncle, at the end of May 1863 to watch Bob Shaw march through Boston at the head of the 54th, a large portion of the upper class had tempered its hostility. After Shaw had been martyred on the slopes of Fort Wagner in July 1863, Howland Shaw, a former McClellan Committee member, began pledging funds for the United States Colored Troops.

Shaw's swing toward underwriting emancipation represented a typical pattern among most elite families. As the price of war registered at home, it became evident that the reaction among women to the death of their menfolk tended to render political convictions moot. There is an almost perfect correlation between a war death and the appearance of the family's name on fundraising lists. Thus as one branch of a family was diminished, in some cases losing all its men, another felt obliged, if not actually to fight, then to open its purse.[45] In this way death, grief, and guilt knit back together elite families that had been split, in the 1840s and 1850s, by the political rift between "Conscience"—a high-minded and moralistic Bostonian support for emancipation—and "Cotton," the harshly pragmatic Yankee eye for a profit that continued to collaborate with the slave economy. In the case of families having a son, nephew, or cousin serving as an officer in a black regiment, the power of kinship overrode qualms about whether blacks could or should fight. Thus a combination of the perspective of wives and mothers, family loyalty or guilt, and the personal distaste and moral qualms regarding slavery even among its defenders worked to subvert any action based on Copperhead sympathies or inclinations. The undertow increased when the Confederacy announced draconian penalties for both captured black soldiers and their white officers. Perhaps more significantly, the South's militant stand caused the once plausible idea of a negotiated peace settlement to lose credibility.

By the spring of 1863 it was evident that the Emancipation Proclamation made good foreign policy. Charles Francis Adams, Edward Everett's brother-in-law and America's minister to Great Britain, wrote, "It has rallied all the sympathies of the working classes, and has produced meetings the like of which, I am told, have not been seen since the days of reform and the

Corn Laws."⁴⁶ Neither England nor France would become a formal ally of the Confederacy in a war to defend slavery. Thus a series of "aggressive movements," as Holmes had suggested, did alter public opinion, and it was under the auspices of the Union Club, as he had also predicted, that this difference became obvious.

Within two weeks of its first meeting the club had over two hundred members, and the mood of the city began to change. The Union Club's raison d'être was to bring together "true patriots" of both parties to "assist the cause of the Union in social circles."⁴⁷ This object might appear of little consequence, but it gave coherence to an emerging coalition of businessmen and public figures with whom Governor Andrew had begun to forge an alliance.⁴⁸

This group included many of the committee members for the Grand Jubilee Concert held at the Music Hall on January 1 to celebrate the Emancipation Proclamation and raise funds for freed men; largely liberal Republicans, they were the same men who, prior to the war, had financially supported the settlement of Kansas and the Underground Railroad, and arranged the legal defense of captured slaves as well as opposition to the Fugitive Slave Act. In the 1850s these radicals had had an antagonistic relationship with the federal government, at times openly defiant of national laws and often skirting the line of treason—in the case of five of the Secret Six who had funded John Brown's raid on Harpers Ferry, crossing that line. Not surprisingly, these men were regarded in conservative and even moderate circles as similar to Senator Sumner: highly controversial, provocative, unnecessarily confrontational—in short, people who, by their stridency, did their cause no good. In September, when the Emancipation Proclamation was announced, some of them still huffily complained that it was "too little, too late," but by the time it became law large numbers of them had rediscovered their patriotism, reembraced the Constitution as an evolving document, shifted to support the president, joined the Union Club, and begun to work for the war effort. By doing so they moved from the fringe left once again to rejoin that reasonable middle ground so valued by Bostonians.⁴⁹

Of course, the Union Club's main constituency was moderate businessmen like John Murray Forbes, whose logistical expertise had been so helpful in supplying troops at the start of the war. Amos Adams Lawrence, the Constitutional Union Party gubernatorial candidate who had been defeated by John A. Andrew in 1860, was also among them. Lawrence had stepped up to form an alliance with his former rival after the Altoona Conference in October 1862, at which time he underwrote first a battalion and then a regiment of cavalry. By February 1863, faced with recruiting difficulties and determined to avert a draft, Forbes and Lawrence were sufficiently committed to the war effort to have jointly developed a new system of bounty payments that streamlined the recruitment process and made it increasingly effective.

They and many other members of the Union Club contributed to the New England Loyal Publications Society, a privately funded organization that generated books, essays, and broadsides as well as some fifty-odd pro-Union and pro-emancipation pamphlets in a massive effort to reinforce Lincoln's war policy and to make the case for freeing the slaves. This publicity campaign ignored the moral and societal arguments that had been commonplaces of the more radical abolitionist movement of the 1850s and instead targeted the economic implications of emancipation with reasoning that appealed less to morality and more to pragmatism. In particular, it strongly pressed the argument for the production of cotton by free labor. Heretofore it had seemed that slavery and cotton production went hand in hand; to oppose one had been to oppose the other. But if experts such as Edward Atkinson in *Cheap Cotton by Free Labor* were correct, it might even be the case that the crop could be produced more efficiently by eliminating the slavery system.

The purpose was to chip away at conservative doubts and to open the larger coffers of moderate businessmen who were encouraged to stop using the Somerset Club, which in Republican circles was now referred to as the "Sambo Club." The successful social quarantining of Copperhead sympathizers played a role in their political sidelining. Instead of having a beachhead from which to work as potential agitators and naysayers, they were left to dine in splendid isolation. Seven of the McClellan Committee's twelve members remained among these solitary diners at the Somerset Club, and four (Eldredge, Gardiner, Coolidge, and Warren) continued to support McClellan up until the moment when, to their surprise, the ballot count of the 1864 election revealed his defeat. But this diehard support for McClellan from among the wealthiest and most privileged did not lead to a Copperhead movement of any significance in Boston.

Returning now to the questions asked at the beginning of this essay: What happened to the ideal of abolition as it became the reality of emancipation? What did emancipation mean to the men who made it happen?

Why, despite such financial involvement with the southern economy, were Boston's politics more radical than New York's? How is one to understand the shifting positions of certain moderate or conservative businessmen? Of particular interest: the men on the McClellan Committee who were most actively engaged in Boston's cotton economy (such as Little and Edmands) were the ones who were quickest to become members of the Union Club; indeed, they joined so rapidly that one might wonder what they were doing on the McClellan Committee at all.

Yet each was well known to James Lawrence, who put the committee together. Cousin to Amos A. Lawrence, James was the nominal head of A. & A. Lawrence & Co., the firm that their fathers had founded, and as such he represented the single largest cotton interest in New England. It can hardly be accidental that of the six members most intimately associated with the cotton interest whom Lawrence had appointed to the Committee, four were confirmed Republicans and among the first wave to join the Union Club.

To understand this seeming paradox, we must return to the business climate in New England. While New York's share of the Confederate debt was only 10 percent higher than Boston's, conservative practices required banks in the commonwealth to hold much higher reserves. This meant that no Boston bank found itself as compromised, as overextended, as beholden to cotton interests as the New York and mid-Atlantic lenders. Boston's investment strategies were also conservative, tending toward a broad diversification, with an emphasis on railroads.[50] While this investment was not without its risks, as the events of 1857 had shown, many Boston railroad investors had staked out positions that anticipated the rise of the Midwest and the promise of settlement on the vast prairie. The transcontinental railroad would bypass the Mississippi River system, eclipsing New Orleans, and instead drive all that midwestern produce to Baltimore, Philadelphia, New York, and Boston ports, while at the same time creating an alternate market of consumers for northern merchandise.

Of further consideration was the fact that of the $100 million worth of cotton cloth produced in the United States in 1860, almost 70 percent was manufactured in New England. Massachusetts mills amounted to 34.2 percent (about $33.7 million), and New Hampshire mills, largely controlled by Boston merchants, produced an additional 12.8 percent (about $12.6 million). Thus Massachusetts financiers controlled 47 percent of the domestic mills dependent on the southern cotton supply. In contrast, New York mills represented only 5.5 percent (about $5.4 million) of domestic cotton production.[51] Massachusetts and New Hampshire were nine times as invested in cotton production as New York. Even if one attempts to equalize the comparison by weighing the total of New York, the mid-Atlantic states, and Connecticut, which produced 30 percent, against that of the Boston-controlled mills of Massachusetts, Rhode Island, New Hampshire, and Maine (63 percent), New England still appears twice as invested in cotton-based industry, giving it an exceptionally dependent relationship on southern raw material rather than southern credit.

The larger issue for the region was the scarcity of cotton, the resulting closure of factories, and the attendant economic fallout. For this reason, in the autumn of 1862, as their stockpiles from a bumper year in 1860 were finally running low, its businessmen approached fighting the war with a key aim: to secure a renewed and steady supply of cotton. Understanding this sense of urgency, one can more fully appreciate Amos A. Lawrence's diary entry of October 7, 1862: "McClellan is certainly too slow."[52] While many of his conservative friends were quick to take McClellan's side and believe his excuses for not swiftly pursuing Lee after Antietam, Lawrence was looking less at politics or even the military dynamic. Instead he recognized that the crisis of the flawed victory at Antietam was that by not providing a decisive win, by not concluding the war, McClellan had been too slow to restore the easy delivery of raw cotton to northern mills. Manufacturers would now have to find a steady source of supply despite being in the midst of civil war.

From this time forward, Lawrence and others pursued almost every possible option to achieve this. Some men did a considerable business in contraband cotton, to great profit.[53] But it was a last resort: the costs involved were unsustainable. Instead northern mill owners turned to the cotton-producing communities of the Carolina and Georgia Sea Islands, which were within Yankee lines. Using their connections to the Confederacy, Northerners bought up plantations along the eastern seaboard, many of which were being auctioned for back taxes,[54] and returned them to production with freed slaves working the fields. Young Yankee teachers flocked to these communities, where they prepared the emancipated slaves for citizenship while they produced cotton that was shipped to New England mills. These activities established a model of postwar economic possibilities for cotton produced by "free labor."

Tremendous interest and funding went toward the possibility of white free settlers growing cotton in Yankee-controlled areas, in particular Texas under the military control of General Nathaniel Banks, the governor of Massachusetts from 1857 to 1861, and before that known as the "Bobbin Boy" because of his start in the Waltham cotton mills. The Texas experiment did not come off, but in the conquered Mississippi Valley, under the administration of General Banks, a cruder system of cotton production was established.[55] Although it met with the approval of more conservative Bostonians, including Samuel Hooper, who had replaced William Appleton in Congress, it represented a far more penurious approach to using former slaves, involving none of the enlightened attempts of the Sea Islands to prepare freed slaves for citizenship. Instead it established them as "serfs" on their former plantations; in effect, it was the sharecropping system that would become ubiquitous throughout the South in the following decades. Thus, even before the war ended, two versions of a free labor cotton system were in place. The Sea Islands model was intended to evolve into a system of cooperative small farmers undergoing a progressive, if paternalistic, preparation for full citizenship.

Tragically, in the years following the war these hopes were dashed, and most of the land was returned to its former white owners, while the freed slaves resorted to tenancies similar to those set up in the Mississippi Valley. By the mid-1870s, regardless of whatever alternate interpretation of Atkinson's "Cheap Cotton by Free Labor" ideal might have been possible, the reality was a sharecropping system that functioned as a de-facto form of slavery that was reinforced and broadened as political enfranchisement was reversed and the Jim Crow laws were implemented.

Given this, Amos A. Lawrence's remark in reference to the Anthony Burns fugitive slave case of 1854—"We went to bed one night old fashioned, conservative, Compromise Union Whigs & waked up stark mad Abolitionists"—must be taken with a large dose of salt.[56] Not only did ambivalence remain the dominant emotion, but there were few genuine converts to abolition or emancipation per se among Boston's elite, despite a strong antislavery bias. The business community acquiesced to, rather than embraced, emancipation, seeing it as a pragmatic attempt to solve problems created by the war itself: how to restore the steady flow of cotton from the South and how to preserve the skilled workforce in the North that was needed to keep factories operating, all with the knowledge that robbing the South of its slave labor would help bring the war to an end.

It is not possible to establish the voting potential of the mob that gathered to support McClellan, but one can be sure that the local elite regarded it with deep suspicion.[57] They were pleased to send a message to the president, but the antagonism they felt toward a resentful and oppressed Irish working class meant that a political alliance across class and cultural lines was not likely. Even so, the mood of these workers mattered. Already the governor had employed a variety of strategies to prevent civil unrest and to keep factories open while still meeting quotas. Petty criminals were allowed to enlist rather than serve their sentences. Enlistment was offered as a means to immigration and citizenship. Bounties were generous and paid in advance. Soldiers from outside Massachusetts were paid to fight under the Bay State flag. In this context Governor Andrew's success in getting two regiments of African American soldiers counted as part of the Massachusetts quota was a triple win since it not only gave the state radical kudos (a Republican win) but also cleverly preserved its skilled work force (a win for business) and protected immigrants from military service (a working-class win). Conservative businessmen might oppose emancipation, seriously doubting the capacity of African Americans to become effective soldiers, and yet see merit in supporting the 54th Regiment.

Thus out of community pride and notions of civic stewardship, as well as economic self-interest, Bostonians of various political persuasions could support emancipation for reasons that did not involve any particular interest in the slave, the morality of the plantation system, or the niceties of freedom. These considerations were beside the point, and in this sense this class of businessmen was agnostic on the subject, neither for nor against but simply considering, in a pragmatic way, how the institution served their need for cotton. Given Boston's tiny free black population, conservatives had only a minimal fear of emancipation on a personal, cultural, or practical level, and as long as their markets held and their supply of cotton was maintained, they would tolerate a free black population in the South as they had tolerated a slave population there.

To understand this agnosticism on the matter of "slave or free" better, it is worthwhile to consider more comments by Amos A. Lawrence, who saw himself as a conservative despite his financial underwriting of Kansas settlers, which even extended to the provision of weapons for their defense, including the ones used by John Brown at Harpers Ferry. After the announcement of the Emancipation Proclamation he wrote to Massachusetts congressmen Alexander Rice, one of the founders of the Republican Party but a conservative who had introduced the Crittenden

Compromise proposals in February 1861, "It has seemed to me since the war became inevitable that true conservatism consists in holding fast to the government, and in making up our minds for a long war, which would probably end by destroying slavery."[58]

Lawrence did not mean "conservatism" in the sense of a right wing on a linear spectrum of political affiliation. He was speaking from a social and business perspective that valued stability and strove to navigate the dangerously destabilizing forces of both abolitionism and secession. When he spoke of the need "to hold fast to the government," he meant the federal government. This may seem obvious, but for New Englanders this idea would have carried special meaning, given the region's historical perspective on sectionalism and the Constitution. A stronghold of Federalism through the years of the early republic, New England had been severely tested by the policies of Jefferson and Madison that resulted in America's involvement in the Napoleonic Wars. These decisions ran counter to the interests of the economy of the New England states and resulted in a severe economic depression across the region. The Hartford Convention of 1814, at which a small group of ultra-Federalists known as the Essex Junto considered secession long enough to commit political suicide but with no other effect, represented the high-water mark of New England sectionalism. Subsequently the region had more than recovered from its days of rotting ships, but the crisis had left two significant scars. One was resentment of the "three-fifths clause" in the Constitution, which gave the South extra representation based on its slave population. Seen as tantamount to incorporating the protection of slavery into the Constitution, it tipped the scales to accord disproportionate power to the southern states, thereby enshrining sectional privilege within a document intended to transcend exactly that.

This caused Yankees to characterize plantation owners as oligarchs and to speak of the Slave Power as an aggressive, war-mongering faction. The Mexican War in 1848 further cemented this attitude. In 1861, when the slave states seceded and fired on Fort Sumter, this sectional prejudice was reactivated. What the South saw as a defensive posture, protecting slavery, the North had, for twenty if not forty years, considered to be far more aggressive.

The second residual scar from "Mr. Madison's War" involved merchants who saw that Washington's admonition in his Farewell Address to rise above sectionalism had an economic application. With their entire mercantile enterprise shut down by Virginian-controlled American foreign policy—albeit offset by some highly successful privateering—the threat of a sustained chill in British–American relations made many wealthy men question the ultimate value of remaining exclusively engaged in imports. Instead of reinvesting in cargo for trading triangles that reinforced New England's position as essentially an economic extension of the British Empire, they began to invest surplus capital in what came to be called "inward development," sparking early industries that used waterpower to fuel mills producing paper, cotton cloth, lumber, and other goods. Almost immediately the quest began to find a domestic source of coal and to smelt iron successfully. In the hands of entrepreneurial types, New England wealth spread through the northern and middle states, acquiring assets and beginning to exploit natural resources. The sectional strife of the early 1800s, seemingly based on divergent economic interests, gave way to an integration of economic enterprise, creating national goals and coalitions: the heyday of the Whig Party had arrived.

Ironically, the success of this nationalism, based on an economic system in which cheap cotton fueled a nascent industrial revolution, went on to resurrect the sectional strife it had initially intended to overcome. The success of the cotton economy increased the value of the slave as well as the economic dependence of the South on the institution of slavery, making it the engine of cheap labor that fueled not only the southern agricultural economy but to a large degree other economies of the industrial North. As cotton became "king," the South began to obstruct national development, supporting economic policies that protected cotton, frustrating the growth of production and tightening the supply to markets at home. It was this irony that undercut Whig politics and eroded the centrist political middle ground, turning compromise into appeasement and propelling radicals in the North and reactionaries in the South to increasingly extreme positions.[59]

In the 1850s, holding the line against appeasing the Slave Power led to activist policies, and this may have lain behind Lawrence's claim to becoming a "stark mad Abolitionist" in 1854. Not until the magical thinking behind John Brown's insurrection and the 1860 secession of the deep South made the fragility of the Union clear did the cost of the hard line against appeasement become evident. Then the political center began to repopulate. War, and its devastating consequences, speeded this development.

With all these factors in mind, one can now better appreciate Caleb

Loring's explanation of Union Club policy at its founding meeting February 4: "loyalty to the Constitution and the Union and fidelity to the government in its efforts to suppress the rebellion. Differences of opinion upon subordinate subjects—the proclamation—General McClellan finance etc. etc. etc. are of no consideration."[60]

After a decade of dissension, of fragmentation, and a year and a half of the self-destruction unique to civil war, Boston had lost interest in "differences of opinion." The moral purity that had refreshed the antebellum period now came at too high a price. The city drew together to create the broadest coalition possible. It harnessed the wealth and ingenuity of Massachusetts businessmen to carry out an idealistic policy: a victory resulting in the freedom of America's slave population. This is the kind of expedient coalition building that is frequently seen in American politics. It could be argued that under this broad umbrella the best aspects of the New England character were brought to bear; the repair of the fractured social divides that "conscience" versus "cotton" had created in the 1850s was welcome, and to this extent a reunited New England emerged from the Civil War.

This was certainly what was hoped for, and postwar ceremonies, such as the Harvard Commemoration of July 21, 1865, which celebrated the college's Civil War heroes, attempted to express this unity.[61] But it is not what happened. For although it appeared that Governor Andrew had shown remarkable political skill in persuading Boston's business community to support his radical war aims, the pressing demand for cotton was an overriding economic necessity. It motivated businessmen to join the coalition to fight the war for emancipation, particularly as arguments proved persuasive that even cheaper cotton could be grown with free labor. In an apparent triumph for radical Boston the city reunited, with both former radicals and conservatives meeting on the newly reconstructed middle ground of a Union that embraced emancipation.

The contribution to Union victory that these "conservative" men made was not philanthropy, nor was it idealistic. It proved a highly profitable short-term investment by restoring a cotton supply to the North while the war was still being fought. As a long-term strategy, it brought an earlier end to the war, and it restored and sustained the plantation production of cotton in the South for northern mills. The Republican rationale for how cotton could be more cheaply produced by free rather than slave labor turned out to be a dark harbinger of the first seventy years of freedom. In this respect both moderate and conservative businessmen had used the emancipation of the slave to meet their need for cotton. They had used the enlistment of black soldiers to ensure their skilled work force. The compromise of such a broad coalition was a leveling out or watering down of the desired goal. For the majority of African Americans, emancipation, freedom for slaves, became a nominal freedom compromised by continued economic servitude, political disenfranchisement, and a network of repressive laws that would persist for another century before yet further federal intervention would make the sustained reforms permitting full political participation.

APPENDIX
Members of the McClellan Committee

EDWARD H. EVERETT, 69, politician. Whig, then Constitutional Union Party, then converts to Lincoln in 1863. Married daughter of Peter C. Brooks (marine insurance); 49 cousins, wife 51 cousins.

WILLIAM H. GARDINER, 66, lawyer. Whig, then Democrat. Married daughter of Thomas H. Perkins (Caribbean and China Trade); 1 sibling, wife 50 cousins.

J. HUNTINGTON WOLCOTT, 59, from Connecticut political family, self-made at A. & A. Lawrence. Whig, then Republican. Married into Frothingham family; wife 47 cousins.

CHARLES AMORY, 55, doctor, family wealth in sugar/rum trade. Married daughter of Gardiner Greene (Demerara planter); 66 cousins, wife 12 cousins.

J. WILEY EDMANDS, 54, self-made at A. & A. Lawrence. Whig, then Fremont Republican. Lived in Newton; wife from Baltimore; 8 sons.

JAMES LOVELL LITTLE, 53, self-made as agent for Pacific Mills. Whig, then Republican. Married daughter of Zebeedee Cook (New York insurance).

WILLIAM GRAY, 52, lawyer, family wealth in shipping, treasurer for Atlantic Cotton Mills. Married daughter of Caleb Loring; 17 cousins, wife 12 cousins.

J. MASON WARREN, 52, doctor/surgeon. Whig, then Democrat. Married daughter of Benjamin Crowninshield; 50 cousins, wife 27 cousins.

JAMES LAWRENCE, 51, A. & A. Lawrence. Whig. Married daughter of William H. Prescott (historian; his wife's money came from the Amory fortune); 45 cousins, wife 38 cousins.

EDWARD H. ELDREDGE, 47, merchant. Whig, then Democrat.

G. HOWLAND SHAW, 44, family wealth from China trade and Boston real estate. Married daughter of Theodore Lyman (fur trade); 48 cousins, wife 23 cousins.

T. JEFFERSON COOLIDGE, 32, family money from China trade, cotton brokering, mill management, war speculation. Whig, then Democrat. Married daughter of William Appleton.

NOTES

1. Donald J. Ratcliffe, "Decline of Anti-slavery Politics, 1815–1840," in *Contesting Slavery: The Politics of Bondage and Freedom in the New American Nation,* ed. John Craig Hammond and Matthew Mason (Charlottesville: University of Virginia Press, 2011), 286.
2. William Howard Gardiner to Mary Davis, November 16, 1862, William Howard Gardiner Letters, 1852–1863 (Ms. N-1270), Massachusetts Historical Society, Boston (MHS); Gardiner Howland Shaw to Theodore Lyman, November 9, 1862, Lyman Family Papers, 1785–1956 (Ms. N-1609), MHS.
3. J. Mason Warren, December 6, 1862, Jonathan Mason Warren Journals, 1844–1867, in John Collins Warren Papers, 1738–1926 (Ms. N-1731), MHS.
4. William Starr Myers, *A Study in Personality: General George Brinton McClellan* (New York: D. Appleton-Century, 1934), 423.
5. Edward Everett, December 8, 1862, Edward Everett Diaries, 1815–1865, in Edward Everett Papers, 1675–1910 (Ms. N-1201), MHS.
6. The election represented an overwhelmingly Democratic victory in virtually all other states.
7. New Englanders had competed with the British as suppliers to the sugar plantations of the Caribbean islands in the Atlantic slave trade. See Eric Williams, *Capitalism and Slavery* (Chapel Hill: University of North Carolina Press, 1944).
8. See Philip Foner, *Business and Slavery: The New York Merchants and the Irrepressible Conflict* (Chapel Hill: University of North Carolina Press, 1941); Hammond and Mason, *Contesting Slavery*; Sven Beckert and Seth Rockman, eds., *Slavery's Capitalism: A New History of American Economic Development* (Philadelphia: University of Pennsylvania Press, forthcoming); Ronald Bailey, "The Slave(ry) Trade and the Development of Capitalism in the United States: The Textile Industry in New England," *Social Science History* 14 (Autumn 1990): 373–414.
9. In the early nineteenth century, when, scholars have argued, continental slavery had the potential to die out, Yankee ingenuity invented the cotton gin and then developed the all-in-one cotton factory, two technologies that paved the way for cotton to become the new economic "king."

10. This included the split between Conscience and Cotton Whigs that led to the death of Whiggish Boston by the late 1840s and the rise of the Republican Party in the mid-1850s, the relentless growth of the antislavery movement including opposition to the Fugitive Slave Act, the sending of funds to free-settlers in Kansas, and the provisioning of funds to underwrite John Brown's raid on Harpers Ferry. Among more recent scholarship on the early phases, see Donald J. Ratcliffe, "Decline of Anti-slavery Politics, 1815–1840," Rachel Hope Cleves, "Hurtful to the State: The Political Morality of Federal Antislavery," and Matthew Mason, "Necessary but Not Sufficient: Revolutionary Ideology and Antislavery Action in the Early Republic," all in Hammond and Mason, *Contesting Slavery*. For the later period, see Richard H. Abbott, *Cotton and Capital: Boston Businessmen and Antislavery Reform, 1854–1858* (Amherst: University of Massachusetts Press, 1991).
11. The irony is that in the 1830s Charles Sumner and Samuel Gridley Howe had been the darlings of these very men or their parents. William Howard Gardiner was the son-in-law of Thomas Handasyd Perkins, benefactor of the Perkins School for the Blind. As its inspiration and director, Dr. Howe earned his reputation as an internationally revered humanitarian and established Boston as a beacon for the world in the treatment of the blind and deaf. But the increasing radicalization and the extreme abolitionism of Sumner and Howe ended this partnership.
12. Leonard N. Ray and the Blair County Historical Society, War Governors' Centennial Issue of *Past and Present* (Altoona, Pa.: Blair County Historical Society, 1962), 37. The dissenters were New York, New Jersey, and the four slave states: Maryland, Delaware, Kentucky, and Missouri.
13. "Massachusetts Democratic State Convention," *New York Times*, October 9, 1862.
14. James M. McPherson, *The Struggle for Equality: Abolitionists and the Negro in the Civil War and Reconstruction* (Princeton: Princeton University Press, 1964), 121.
15. William Howard Gardiner to Mary Davis, February 8, 1863, William Howard Gardiner Letters, MHS.
16. *Springfield (Mass.) Republican*, February 9, 1863, quoted in Edith E. Ware, *Political Opinion in Massachusetts during Civil War and Reconstruction* (New York: Columbia University, 1916), 121.
17. Newspaper clippings, J. Mason Warren, February 7, 1863, Jonathan Mason Warren Journals, MHS.
18. William Howard Gardiner to Mary Davis, February 1, 1863, William Howard Gardiner Letters, MHS.
19. John Langdon Sibley, January 29, 1863, Sibley's private journal (HUG 1791.72.10), Harvard University Archives (transcription at http://hul.harvard.edu/lib/archives/refshelf/Sibley.htm).
20. William Howard Gardiner to Mary Davis, February 8, 1863, William Howard Gardiner Letters, MHS.
21. Ibid.
22. J. Mason Warren, January 31, 1863, Jonathan Mason Warren Journals, MHS. Warren pasted newspaper clippings into his diary without citing their source.
23. William Howard Gardiner to Mary Davis, February 1, 1863, William Howard Gardiner Letters, MHS. Gardiner added to this letter on February 2.
24. Ibid.
25. Edward Everett, December 8, 1862, Edward Everett Diaries, MHS.

26. William Howard Gardiner to Mary Davis, February 8, 1863, William Howard Gardiner Letters, MHS.
27. Lucius Quinctius Cincinnatus, the Roman farmer who ran the republic as a benevolent dictator and then returned that power to the senate and resumed farming, was an example of political humility devoid of personal ambitions followed by George Washington and admired, particularly among Federalist circles, as the ideal of leadership.
28. Hannah Gray, February 2, 1863, Hannah Shober Gray Diary, New England Historic Genealogical Society, Boston (NEHGS).
29. Edward Everett, February 3, 1863, Edward Everett Diaries, MHS.
30. J. Mason Warren, February 7, 1863, and newspaper clippings in the same, Jonathan Mason Warren Journals, MHS.
31. Anna C. Lowell, February 2, 1863, Anna Cabot Lowell Diaries, 1818–1894 (Ms. N-1512), MHS.
32. William Howard Gardiner to Mary Davis, February 8, 1863, William Howard Gardiner Letters, MHS; Albert Gallatin Browne to John Albion Andrew, January 23, 1863, John A. Andrew Papers, 1772–1895 (Ms. N-728), MHS.
33. Anna C. Lowell, January 28, 1863, Anna Cabot Lowell Diaries, MHS; Charles Eliot Norton to George William Curtis, January 30, 1863, *Letters of Charles Eliot Norton,* ed. Sara Norton and M. A. DeWolfe Howe, 2 vols. (Boston: Houghton Mifflin, 1913), 1:259.
34. Hannah Gray, February 1, 1863, Hannah Shober Gray Diary, NEHGS.
35. Francis Brooks, February 3, 1863, Francis Brooks Journals, 1850–1891 (Ms. N-1943), MHS.
36. Hannah Gray, February 1, 1863, Hannah Shober Gray Diary, NEHGS; Francis Brooks, February 3, 1863, Francis Brooks Journals, MHS.
37. The quotation is from Robert Bennet Forbes, January 30, 1863, Robert Bennet Forbes Papers, 1817–1967 (Ms. N-49.70), MHS.
38. Oliver Wendell Holmes to John Murray Forbes, February 5, 1863, Forbes Family Papers, 1732–1931 (Ms. N-49), MHS.
39. See Martin Brimmer, "Memoranda for Mr. George S. Hale," n.d., and Caleb William Loring to Samuel Lothrop Thorndike, October 19, 1892, both in Samuel Lothrop Thorndike Papers, 1892–1893 (Ms. S-101), MHS.
40. Baring Brothers & Co., a British institution with German origins, was the preferred bank for China traders, with longstanding interests in the United States, having financed the Louisiana Purchase. By the 1850s it had two American partners, both Bostonians.
41. Edward Everett, February 5, 1863, Edward Everett Diaries, MHS.
42. Edward Everett to "Siddy," November 24, 1862, Edward Everett Letters, 1816–1863 (Ms. N-1205), MHS.
43. The colonel of the 2nd Massachusetts Cavalry steered many young men who wished to join his regiment to the nascent 54th Massachusetts Infantry, and this helped to swell its ranks and to combat the initial prejudice against it.
44. This was not an isolated situation. Shaw's parents each had some forty cousins, and as the case of Theodore Lyman shows, the tug of association—that mix of kinship and friendship so peculiarly potent in Boston—worked on everyone in multiple ways. The appeal of the Shaw family—four charming daughters, a well-liked son, and highly social parents—is captured well by the reaction of Thomas Jefferson Coolidge, who ran into them in 1861 on a trip to Cuba: "They were violent abolitionists and believed that war was necessary to cleanse us of the sin of slavery. They added much to the pleasure of our

trip." Thomas Jefferson Coolidge, *The Autobiography of T. Jefferson Coolidge, 1831–1920* (Boston: Houghton Mifflin, 1923), 24.
45. This was true of the Shaws as of the Lowells. The death of Charles Russell Lowell in October 1864 resulted in substantial donations by the John Amory Lowell family.
46. Charles Francis Adams to Edward Everett, February 27, 1863, Edward Everett Papers, MHS.
47. Caleb William Loring to Samuel Lothrop Thorndike, October 19, 1892, Samuel Lothrop Thorndike Papers, MHS. The membership figure is taken from Union Club papers in the Samuel Lothrop Thorndike Papers.
48. An example of the possible effectiveness of this kind of public–private effort was the United States Sanitary Commission, which functioned as a precursor to the Red Cross but also worked in tandem with the army, urging improvements to the rudimentary ambulances, redesigning rail cars to transport the wounded, improving medical procedures in field hospitals, and promoting the use of the "French knapsack," an early first-aid kit. Boston's medical community was deeply engaged in these efforts. To be successful, conservative and liberal doctors put aside politics and held themselves to the higher values of patriotism and humanitarianism.
49. See Peter Wirzbicki, "'Today Abolitionist Is Merged in Citizen': Radical Abolitionists and the Union War," in this volume.
50. Following the panic of 1857, William Appleton had insisted that his son-in-law, Thomas Jefferson Coolidge, give up his cotton-brokering business and instead take up the position as treasurer of one of the Lawrence cotton mills. Coolidge, *Autobiography*, 11–12.
51. Gene Dattel, *Cotton and Race in the Making of America: The Human Costs of Economic Power* (Chicago: Ivan R. Dee, 2009), 89, 85; David Meyer, "The Roots of American Industrialization, 1790–1860," *EH.Net Encyclopedia*, ed. Robert Whaples, March 16, 2008, http://eh.net/encyclopedia-2.
52. Amos Adams Lawrence, October 7, 1862, Amos A. Lawrence Diaries and Account Books, 1816–1886 (Ms. N-1558), MHS. Following this judgment, Lawrence made overtures to Governor Andrew through Henry Lee—who, as we have seen, had been appointed specifically to liaise with the elite, and whom Lawrence knew socially—offering to fund a battalion of cavalry. This was parlayed into Lawrence's underwriting an entire cavalry regiment. In addition, and in partnership with John Murray Forbes (who held no elective or appointed office), Lawrence put his name to state bonds intended to fund new infantry troops, including the 54th, to finish the war. Extremely active in recruiting volunteers, he introduced a variety of dynamic ways of using the bounty system to reach quotas without disturbing the skilled workmen needed in the factories and mills. All this work he carried out with next to no contact with the governor himself.
53. The documentation is slim, however, and one can only guess the scale of this illegal business and the degree to which Yankee mill treasurers resorted to a clandestine economy.
54. 1863 folder, Amos A. Lawrence Papers, 1817–1886 (Ms. N-1559), MHS.
55. By 1863 the war had created a highly inflated price for cotton, up to $1.90 a bale from an 1860 low of 10 cents a bale. Cotton reserves were at their lowest, since the South's embargo had finally begun to bite deep. See Dattel, *Cotton and Race in the Making of America,* esp. "Part Four: King Cotton Buys a War," 163–209. Britain and France, determined to destroy the monopoly the American South had on the production of cotton, had taken advantage of these high prices to begin growing the crop in other parts of the world, including India, Egypt, and Brazil. American entrepreneurs were anxious to

end the war quickly so that they too could benefit from the high prices and transition to the new "free labor" system that the Boston-based cotton entrepreneur Edward Atkinson advocated in his pamphlet *Cheap Cotton by Free Labor* (Boston: A. Williams, 1861), which argued, contrary to conventional thinking, that slave labor was not the most efficient means of growing cotton. Instead he promoted a more entrepreneurial free labor system, claiming that it offered substantial economies. See Richard H. Abbott, *Cotton and Capital: Boston Businessmen and Antislavery Reform, 1854–1858* (Amherst: University of Massachusetts Press, 1991), 72–94; and Eva Sheppard Wolf, "Early Free-Labor Thought and the Contest over Slavery in the Early Republic," in Hammond and Mason, *Contesting Slavery*.

56. Quoted in James M. McPherson, *Battle Cry of Freedom: The Civil War Era* (New York Oxford University Press, 1988), 120.
57. Even if we had a more exact knowledge of the voting status of the four to five thousand people in the crowd that February day, how useful would it be, given that the next election was a good year and a half away? The potential cultivation and manipulation of that vote will be addressed later in this essay.
58. Amos Adams Lawrence to Hon. G. H. Rice, October 27, 1862, Amos A. Lawrence Diaries and Account Books, MHS.
59. Daniel Webster's speech on March 7, 1850, was the litmus test. Widely admired for his ability to forge consensus in the Senate, Webster's defense of the Compromise of 1850, in which he claimed to speak "as an American" rather than as a Northerner or a "Massachusetts man," proved toxic.
60. Caleb William Loring to Samuel Lothrop Thorndike, October 19, 1892, Samuel Lothrop Thorndike Papers, MHS.
61. See Hamilton Vaughan Bail, "Harvard's Commemoration Day, July 21, 1865," *New England Quarterly* 15 (June 1942): 256–79.

The Bonds of Print

*Reading on Home Front
and Battlefield*

RONALD J. ZBORAY AND MARY SARACINO ZBORAY

Sergeant Henry Tisdale was lost for words upon departing for service in the 35th Massachusetts Infantry on the morning of August 20, 1862. The tongue-tied twenty-five-year-old grocery clerk from West Dedham visited his uncle William and sister Carrie one last time before heading for Lynnfield, an assembly point for the commonwealth's soldiers going to the front. Regretting the missed chance to unburden his feelings, he wrote in his diary that evening:

> At 11 AM left for camp bidding adieu to the folks perhaps forever. My heart was too full to speak as I bid them goodbye. There were many, many things I wished to say to them and which I fully intended to, but kept putting them off through the morning and when the hour for departure came, I could not control myself to do it. Now perhaps I may never speak to them again. . . . Cried near half the way to camp.

He continued to think of his folks long into the night.[1]

Within a month Henry saw action at the Battle of South Mountain in Maryland, where he was injured in the leg on September 14. The rifle-ball wound was bad enough to keep him laid up into the new year, but not serious enough to send him back to Dedham. Recuperating "in a tent with no fire," he found "it difficult to keep warm." But he nonetheless felt comforted by his connection through print culture to distant loved ones. "Reading newspapers and other matter sent from home and letter writing my main employment," he revealed on November 18.[2] Family members, friends, and even his former employer continued to supply him with reading materials as his days played out in the war-torn South.[3]

Like Henry, many Massachusetts soldiers—and the civilians they left behind—who were daunted by the moment of saying goodbye and who feared the chasm of loneliness that lay ahead, turned to print to fill the emptiness. Flowing back and forth between camp and home, printed books, magazines, and newspapers sometimes articulated for common people sentiments that could not otherwise be easily expressed. At other times print did not need to change hands to serve social purposes. Items read by correspondents separated by thousands of miles could provide the basis for discussions of reading experiences in letters. Traversing theaters of war and domestic scenes, print became a social medium of emotional sustenance.

It did so in other parts of the Union and Confederacy, but in Massachusetts using print for social ends was probably more pervasive and intensive. After all, since the early nineteenth century people there and elsewhere in New England had fused the social and literary dimensions of life such that engagement with the printed word was for them an integrated "socioliterary experience."[4] In other words, throughout the antebellum period, reading, disseminating books and periodicals through gift-giving and lending, and even producing amateur verse and prose were done primarily to foster social connections. Many of the practices surrounding reading and writing were thus social by nature. Arguably, half of the time, literature—including history, religious texts, poetry, fiction, and biography—was read out loud, not silently, in the home circle, at church, in Sunday schools, during social calls, or at society meetings before groups that often included adults and children of both sexes. Most "readers" were actually listeners. But solitary reading, too, usually conjured up social networks in that the books people read had frequently been given as gifts or loaned by friends and family (social and public libraries were still relatively rare), or were reminiscent in some way, through characters, plot, information, or sentiment, of a familiar face. Consequently, regardless of their genre—for antebellum New Englanders sampled an astoundingly diverse range of titles—texts were open to multiple interpretations, and diaries and letters brim with these socially circumscribed reflections on what was read.

Because of the notable geographical mobility of New Englanders, sending print matter, especially newspapers, to sojourning or relocated loved ones through the mail or express companies took a great deal of time and energy. Although New Englanders considered newspaper reading "desultory," or purposeless for self-improvement, the mailed newspaper, especially when marked with brief marginalia, played a special role in strengthening social ties. It served both as a token of the sender's remembrance of the distant relation and as a sign that all was well when constant letter writing was impossible or too time consuming. Overall, throughout the region, reading for the maintenance of social ties took precedence over solitary, atomized reading for self-edification.[5]

Socioliterary experience was fostered to a greater degree in the Bay State because the region's advanced publishing industry was centered in Boston.[6] Extensive transportation networks emanating from the metropolitan hub saturated the state's hinterland with its printed products.[7] These materials reached a wide and eager market made up of highly literate consumers,[8] who had been educated in the nation's earliest and most extensive state-sponsored common school system and immersed in an array of literacy-reinforcing para-educational institutions, including Sunday schools, lyceums, social libraries, and even professional and artisanal workplaces.[9] Crucial to "socioliterary experience" were informal means of disseminating print matter beyond the point of sale, as gifts or loans to kin and friend, in person, through the mail or express companies (initially founded in Boston in 1839), by courier, and by ship from Massachusetts ports.[10] Materials were delivered orally as well, since reading aloud was as common as reading silently in antebellum Massachusetts.[11] The practice included even newspapers, which men and women alike devoured, though they might have been loath to admit it.[12] At least two generations of Massachusetts women had followed party politics through reading newspapers such as the *Boston Post* or the *Boston Advertiser*, one of the first long-lived dailies.[13] Their facility in reading about and discussing public affairs would serve them well on the eve of the Civil War.

The war posed challenges to these longstanding patterns of socioliterary experience. Oral reading in the presence of the "empty chair" lost its appeal among civilians, and solitary reading became more common. Soldiers had less need for elegant gift books than for practical tactics manuals. For all concerned, newspapers no longer seemed a distraction from more worthy texts. Indeed, the Civil War could be called a "reading war," because its immense geographic totality could only be perceived through devoted attention to the dailies, whose dense columns covered the entire scope of the conflict.

At the same time, however, the war intensified the need for connecting through print—especially newspapers, which became, in Massachusetts, the dominant text through which social ties were maintained. This new formulation was still social but much less "literary" in the strictest sense of the word. Fewer volumes of poetry and fiction provided the basis for social transactions during the war than before it. After all, the war impinged on virtually every facet of the social world, so reading the news became essential to everyday converse and vital to epistolary discussion. Moreover, for those with kin at the front, newspapers became tracking mechanisms for their soldiers' movements. Although tracing sojourning loved ones through ships' news and other columns had always wracked New Englanders' nerves, the unrelenting, daily trial of intensively scrutinizing casualty lists or reports of regimental deployment into Confederate strongholds became unbearable. The odds of reading bad news had increased tremendously. But for those in the heat of battle, papers mailed from home became, more than ever before, emblems of domestic longing. Through bonds of print, social cohesion emerged in a time of tremendous dislocation.

In what follows we examine these bonds as evinced in 1,094 letters and 97 diaries authored between 1860 and 1865 by 123 individuals from 46 Massachusetts towns and cities.[14] Of the 66 men in this group, 37 served in the military or navy; most were privates or noncommissioned officers.[15] The remaining 29 men and 57 women wrote mostly from home, but a few of these civilians worked as noncombatants associated with federal forces in occupied zones.[16] As we read through their personal papers, we transcribed every passage pertaining to print culture, even those that seemed insignificant, and entered the information into a database for keeping the material organized, generating reports, and making queries. Here we deploy the material qualitatively, based on a close reading of the entire corpus for significant themes and recurring patterns. This kind of qualitative approach best allows us to reconstruct the thoughts, emotions, and lived experience of civilians and soldiers as they improvised their way through the changing social environment of print media.

In this, we share with some recent Civil War historians an interest in experiential history typically constructed from family letters and personal diaries,[17] though few of these scholars have focused on Massachusetts or the home front, a characteristic they share with other Civil War historians.[18] While some deductively seek answers to specific research questions involving individuals' thoughts and beliefs about the war, such as what motivated soldiers to fight, our method is largely inductive and aimed at on-the-ground transpersonal processes of engaging print. Our categories of inquiry were not predetermined but were formulated while reading the collected transcriptions. For example, we found an enormous concentration of writing on simply sending print between battlefield and home front; the prevalence of references to the act prompted questions about its significance. Other categories that filtered up through the transcriptions, such as commentary on reading, especially tracing soldiers through news columns, invited inquiries into shared spaces circumscribed by print. Surprisingly few print culture historians have asked similar questions about reading during the Civil War, whether in Massachusetts or elsewhere.[19] Even journalism historians neglect reading to focus on heroic reporters, newspapers' ideology and impact on the war, censorship and freedom of speech issues, and press coverage of specific events.[20]

The discussion is divided into two parts, dissemination and reception. Thus we first turn to avenues for sending and delivering reading materials between home front and battlefield. Getting printed volumes back and forth was more difficult and expensive than circulating periodicals, so we treat books separately from what the postal service called "transient papers," news sheets that individuals mailed at special rates. We then consider people's emotional investment in papers from home, whose clippings, enclosed in correspondence, allowed senders to focus recipients' attention on specific pieces and thus to heighten emotional bonding. Turning next to reception, we first examine the meaning of newsprint for those who attempted to trace loved ones' movements throughout the theaters of war. Because this effort might involve pooling often unreliable information from multiple sources, it could become an obsession. Yet for all their absorption in newspapers, Massachusetts readers had an antipathy for the New York press, a topic we will then explore. When they were not tracing soldiers, readers attempted to forge virtual reading circles through their correspondence, by stimulating discussion about certain texts, directing addressees to specific titles, and synchronizing reading sessions. We conclude by assaying how these patterns of dissemination and reception secured the bonds of print.

Dissemination

To keep connections between battlefield and home, Massachusetts soldiers and civilians availed themselves of a wide variety of avenues for disseminating print. The most convenient was the postal system, which delivered newspapers, magazines, and books.[21] Periodicals traveled at a more favorable rate than letters and books, even when sent by private citizens rather than publishers. These "transient papers" had to bear no marks other than the recipient's name and address, or they would be subject to a higher rate.[22]

Newspapers or magazines were often pilfered in transit, however; thus people instead stuffed clippings from them into envelopes with correspondence and paid letter rates. Books were more expensive to send by mail, but one might sometimes be tossed into a box containing other materials such as clothing or food, which were not classified by the postal service as "mailable,"[23] and sent through private express companies. The contents of these boxes sometimes resembled the inventory of a general store. One of them, sent from Massachusetts to a soldier in New Bern, North Carolina, for New Year's 1863, included "newspapers, pictorials, [and] letters," but also "tea, coffee, sugar, butter, pepper, salt, capsicum, cheese, gingerbread, confectioner's cakes, bologna sausage, condensed milk, smoked halibut, pepper-box, camp knife, matches, ink, mince pies, candy, tomato ketchup, apples, horse radish, emery paper, sardines, cigars, smoking tobacco, candles, soap . . . , pickles, and cholera mixture."[24]

When all else failed or when the opportunity arose, couriers traveling to and from the front transported letters and packages. "We have received no mail since we left camp at Brandy Station," Frank C. Morse, a Methodist army chaplain near Spotsylvania, Virginia, explained to his mother and sister in Charlemont in 1864, "and have had no opportunity of sending only by private individuals who were going to Fredericksburg," then in the hands of Union forces.[25]

The war made these avenues of delivery unpredictable, since it sent soldiers beyond the reach of mails and expressmen or disrupted carrier routes on river, road, and rail. Such tenuous circumstances made people at home fret even more than they usually did about getting things to their soldiers, for it took an enormous amount of energy just to figure out how to send material to the front. This meant scanning papers to spot emerging opportunities. One notice raised the hopes of Clara Wood, a former millworker, of getting things to her husband, Amos, a private in the 46th Massachusetts in New Bern, when in January 1863 express companies were "forbidden [from] taking things to Burnsides army."[26] She wrote to him from South Hadley Falls, "I see by the paper that Mr Ball of Chicapee is going to Newbern on the Express Steamer of Adams & Co from New York next Wednesday he cannot get a pass on the Government Steamer & he will see to the delivering articles sent by express."[27] With passes, civilians evidently could break through lines that were closed to delivery companies. In this case, Clara's plans fell through, but a few weeks later she learned "in yesterdays paper that the Express is to be slated between here & Newbern for the present."[28]

Even when conditions were optimal, packages still could go astray or be stolen,[29] probably one reason why Massachusetts soldiers seldom asked folks at home to mail or express expensive books. Chaplain Frank Morse in Virginia was confounded when a hefty tome that a former parishioner in Blandford, Massachusetts, posted in April 1864 lost its way.[30] "She sent me my 'Hopkins Evidences' a long time ago," he told his wife, Ellen, "and the book never reached me. I dont know what became of it."[31] Cost value, rather than the intangible personal, educational, or spiritual valuation invested in books, was probably uppermost in soldiers' minds in such cases. This marked a change from the antebellum period, in which New Englanders' written expressions of books' value usually centered on the personal rather than the monetary, but then there were rarely such extreme conditions as the war to imperil books in transit or on the ground. After 1861 books were still luxury items worthy of attentive care,[32] and soldiers never forgot this.

The circumstances were different for cheap papers, traditionally scorned as ephemera for desultory reading. Most soldiers merely shrugged their shoulders when newspapers went astray, even though they were valued mementos from home. After all, an issue sent as a replacement was almost as good as another that had vanished, as long as it came from loved ones. Conversely, worse than a lost book was one wastefully discarded because it would weigh down the knapsack of a soldier on the march—another discouragement from sending books southward. "There are some good books here which will be thrown away when we move and I think of sending some of them to you by mail," Morse told Ellen that same month as his regiment was leaving camp prior to the Battle of the Wilderness.[33] Fearing the literary carnage that had disgusted Henry Tisdale, who saw abandoned "camp spots . . . literally covered with extra clothing, overcoats, old shoes, knapsacks, books, magazines, hair brushes" when his regiment was on the Baltimore–Washington Pike to join the Army of the Potomac,[34] Morse, just days before his own departure, wrapped up the chapel bible along with a letter in which he instructed Ellen, "If you know of any poor family in need of a family bible you can make a present of it."[35] In relaying books destined for the refuse pile back to the civilian sphere, soldiers not only furthered print dissemination but fostered social networking over these items that would enter the community from the scenes of battle.

The more stationary the southern sojourners were, the more likely it was that books would flow from home to the battlefield. When Morse's war-weary regiment went on provost's duty in Winchester in September 1864, he once again began to solicit books from home, but very selectively—he asked Ellen for a Methodist manual he could use in his ministerial duties—with an eye to a possible future move. Rather than stockpile books, he turned to local resources, as he reported, "I can borrow quite a number of the books here so you will not have so many to send."[36]

Of course, prisoners of war were forcibly detained in one location, so it is not surprising that they would request reading matter to kill time. In September 1864, Stephen Minot Weld Jr., a captain in the 18th Massachusetts Volunteer Infantry held in Columbia, South Carolina, asked his mother in West Roxbury to "send cards (6 packs at least) and clothing and books."[37] Stationary government bureaucrats in the occupied South received volumes from loved ones, too. In October 1863, Albert Gallatin Browne, a supervising U.S. Treasury agent stationed in Beaufort, South Carolina, benefited from an "extravagant Cook Book" his wife back in Salem packed for his contraband servants.[38] Teachers of the freed people in the nearby Sea Islands, ever in need of instructional texts, also solicited books, which traveled securely southward under the protective umbrella of the U.S. Navy blockade. An African American schoolteacher from Salem, Charlotte Forten, faced this problem. "I must write home and ask somebody to send me picture-books and toys to amuse them with," she wrote in November 1862 of her charges who were "too young even for the alphabet." She was able to find a correspondent from home who "offer[ed] to send me some books for our children."[39] Thus social bonds were activated long distance over the need for print.

Forten and her fellow teachers were not the only ones who extended patterns of socioliterary experience by furthering literacy among African Americans. Soldiers and chaplains, too, undertook the project. Morse, for example, attempted to instruct his "servant" Johnny, a free African American from Warrenton, Virginia. "I intend to take pains with him and teach him to read and write," Frank wrote to his wife in July 1863.[40] Ellen took an interest in Johnny's welfare, inquired about his progress, and evidently knit socks for him. Although Frank abandoned literacy instruction, he continued training Johnny and delegated to him responsibility for the piles of tracts, documents, and papers in his tent.[41] Other soldiers confronting black illiteracy were ever ready to help make family connections through the written word. On a levee in Bonnet Carré, Louisiana, Sergeant Charles F. Read of the 3rd Massachusetts Cavalry read aloud a letter from a soldier stationed on Ship Island to his illiterate father-in-law, at his request. "It was a very good letter . . . partly poetry," perhaps an extract from published verse or an original production, Read noted, adding that "the little favor did him a great deal of good."[42] In navigating the chaotic conditions of the South, some Massachusetts soldiers relished opportunities to unite comrades in arms with their families through oral reading.

Sometimes Union scavengers and confiscators forged bonds with the home front at the expense of Confederate book owners. The penchant for war relics was notable in Massachusetts; the elaborate volumes that occupying troops lifted from private dwellings and sent home were especially prized. Edward L. Pierce, a Boston attorney appointed to supervise the Sea Island contrabands, for example, purloined "from a rebel's house—in Florida" the two-volume, lavishly illustrated *Sacred and Legendary Art* by Anna Jameson, which he deposited in a Boston abolitionist family's home to lend to Charlotte Forten when she returned North in September 1863 for health reasons. "I expect to luxuriate in it," she remarked upon receiving it.[43] As Union forces occupied Baton Rouge after the Confederate state government abandoned it in April 1862, a quartermaster sergeant and former carpenter informed his sister in Lowell of the bounty coming her way: "I sent a box home which contained the histories of Rome, England, lives of the British poets, some music and china ware, which I obtained from a deserted house."[44]

Soldiers seldom imagined how the books' owners and their families had once used or valued the items they seized, for plundering was but an extension of battlefield violence. Somehow these scavengers, too, were able to erase the Confederate lineage from the books they foraged, assigning to them a new purpose and, over time, a new genealogy of associations. "I desire my son Eddie to keep this as a memento," Browne said of a volume of Julius Caesar's *Commentaries* he found in a Savannah custom house in February 1865, "to 'read, mark, and inwardly digest' its contents gaining wisdom and knowledge thereby; and to be what was denied to his father to be, a wise and accomplished scholar."[45] In this way, literary war relics entered the family line.

Transient papers were much more common than books as mediums of social exchange, however. The flow mostly went from home to battlefield, and the items sent tended to be of local origin. Unlike books, they were cheap to buy and send, disposable, and more portable for soldiers constantly on the move. It little mattered if they were smudged by dirty hands as they made the rounds in camp. With small type and large sheets, they packed in more print per page. And, of course, unlike books, by definition they carried current news (local, regimental, and national), which was vital to a soldier's welfare. Most important of all, because these papers were mainly published in Massachusetts, they depicted the contemporary social life there and, in less tangible ways, they symbolized home.

Small wonder, then, that diaries and correspondence of Massachusetts servicemen brim with references to transient papers. "I am very much obliged to you for the [Boston] Herald which you sent me as it is something I do not often receive," wrote a black sergeant in the 55th Massachusetts Volunteers in thanking his editor-friend for a hometown newspaper.[46] Soldiers were always anxious to get papers and so took pains to give explicit instructions for how to address them. "Please write to me at Newberne and send me papers," a Needham private on his way South urged his parents in November 1862, instructing them to "direct to 43 Reg. Co. C. Newberne," so they would be there shortly after he arrived.[47]

When conditions permitted, transient papers flowed from home in a steady rhythm. Clara Wood, for example, sent her husband, Amos, in North Carolina the local *Springfield Republican* weekly, but her cousin Norris offered to relieve her of the burden of doing so, as Amos explained to her in January 1863: "As for the Paper you can send one if you would like to[.] Norris wrote me that he would send it to me every week if I wanted it." Amos added, "if he does it will save you the trouble."[48] Any breaks in the stream of transient papers caused such a feeling of deprivation that the resumption of delivery seemed all the sweeter. "Our first mail for three weeks today," Henry Tisdale, on the march near Rutledge, Tennessee, recorded in January 1863. "Most gladly was it welcomed and far into the evening we were grouped about our log fires eagerly devouring our letters and papers from home."[49]

Soldiers had a deep emotional investment in transient papers that went beyond simply having news to read or something to fill their time. In the fall of 1864, a young army engineer stationed in Alexandria, Virginia, within easy reach of Washington, Baltimore, and New York papers across the river in the nation's capital, still cherished a transient paper from his native Boston:

> My dear Father, —I have to-day received another letter from you, for which accept my thanks; also a copy of the "Boston Journal," the first Boston paper that I have seen for a long time; it looks like home almost, that old familiar page. Nothing in the world will quicken the thoughts of a wanderer sooner than the old home paper, one that we were in the habit of seeing there daily; it is next to a letter, and yet so different.[50]

Just the sight of these papers could instantly transport the recipient over time and space to home, infusing the moment of reunion with an immediacy of recalling old familiar faces and routines. The on-the-ground news was important, too, of course. "I would like to see local news of Roxbury," an Irish American captain in Arlington Heights, Virginia, beseeched his wife in August 1861. "The Norfolk Co. Journal will do for one. The Boston Journal is quite a treat." He could get national news by purchasing "New York papers here once in a while," but the hometown papers provided something unique.[51] Those on the receiving end of transient papers sometimes reciprocated with artifacts from Confederate presses to give people back home an idea of their lives in the South. These papers could also seem like novelty items to those who were unfamiliar with them. "I will send you a Richmond paper, though it is rather old, perhaps you have not seen one before," a private promised his parents in February 1864.[52] Beyond providing reading matter with which to fill time, locally produced newspapers reflected contexts of lived experience and social relations.

Sometimes the transient paper was too general a medium of social communication. Senders often wanted to use them to convey specific information, but that could not be easily done because once they inscribed papers, even with an X to mark a significant column, they were charged letter rates. Of course, some people chanced scribbling, hoping postmasters would overlook it.[53] Enclosing clippings and other printed scraps in envelopes with letters was a more efficient and precise way to say, "Read this."[54]

Clippings functioned in several ways, but virtually all of them going between battlefield and home dealt with Massachusetts-related war news. A South Acton farmwife whose son was serving as a private in New Orleans in February 1863 sent him bits "that have been cut out of paper" and in her cover letter directed his attention to their contents: "you will See that Bill Wood is wounded in the head slightly a scalp wound. [T]here was one hurt in Acton company that was Bill Whitcomb of Stow."[55] Both men were hit at Deserted House, near Suffolk, Virginia, on January 30, 1863; Wood was a lieutenant and Whitcomb a private in her son's former regiment.

When timely or abundant reports eluded soldiers in camp, they solicited clippings from newsreaders at home. Trying to piece together the ordeal of his regiment at the Battle of Cedar Mountain on August 9, 1862, Wilder Dwight had a commission for his mother: "Write me, and send me every scrap about the regiment and our lost brave men."[56] Even poetry enclosed in a letter often dealt with specific news of import for the recipient. On New Year's Eve 1864, Second Lieutenant Henry Warren Howe received from his parents in Lowell a clipping of "Sheridan's Ride" by Thomas Buchanan Read, which had appeared in early December in Boston's *Living Age*. Howe was in the 30th Massachusetts Regiment, which had participated in the Battle of Cedar Creek in Virginia, which the poem commemorated. He opened the letter in nearby Opequan Crossing and brought the clipping with him to an officers' dinner held in the home of a local family that was unsympathetic to Yankees, yet obliged to serve its enemies. He devilishly recorded the reaction when he read the poem celebrating the Union's victorious commanding general, Philip Sheridan: "The family was very much excited and provoked over it."[57]

Since they had the advantage of being easily transported, clippings could be whipped out at a moment's notice and deployed aggressively. More commonly, they had a benign purpose. Soldiers sent clippings that helped loved ones visualize their surroundings, and the new proliferation of engraved maps in newspapers afforded opportunities for pinpointing locations in actual space.[58] "I have cut out a map from the Philadelphia Inquirer, which gives a fair view of the battlefield of September 17 [at Antietam]," First Lieutenant Stephen Minot Weld from West Roxbury told his sister Hannah in the letter enclosing the diagram. "With the aid of this map and what I have marked upon it, I think, aided by this letter, that you will be able to form a good idea of the battle." He placed himself in the scene: "Except when carrying messages, I was on the hill marked 'Gen. McClellan's Headquarters,' and had a fine view of the whole affair."[59] Such details transported distant kin to theaters of battle.

Reception

So far we have described the enormous efforts Massachusetts soldiers and civilians made to get print back and forth between battlefield and home. But what happened when they got the print matter in hand? How did they read and receive these materials and the wider universe of print that would help them make sense of the war and those involved in it? As we will see, Massachusetts Civil War readers were hardly passive consumers of texts, especially newspapers. They read these with an intensity and attention to detail that can only be described as obsessive. Given the notorious unreliability of reports, they developed skills that helped them gauge veracity, through cross-referencing, consulting multiple sources, piecing together scattered bits of information, and corroborating with epistolary intelligence. Such "forensic reading" characterizes much of the reception of print in the period. But more leisurely, even escapist reading took place at times and became the basis for conversations in letters. Coordinating the reading of the same printed text established common ground for discussion among civilians and their embattled loved ones; this kind of reading is implied in clippings. But a few people who owned the same text as their distant correspondents synchronized their mutual reading sessions to take place at an exact time, across hundreds or thousands of miles. For lives pulled in different directions by the war, such arrangements united separated kin and friend within a shared virtual space of print.

One of the most common reading practices was simply tracing soldiers through the press. After all, papers were often the only means of learning about someone on the front when he was marching, fighting, or otherwise without access to mail outlets. This tracing of soldiers was no parlor game; in a war with appallingly high casualty rates, it was a desperate quest. One frantic father in Amherst wrote to his son, a lieutenant in the 37th Massachusetts Infantry whom he feared had perished in the Third Battle of Winchester on September 19, 1864, a fight in which one third of the regiment had been lost:[60]

> I had hoped to learn whether you are yet in the land of the living or have fallen among the hundreds of dead and thousands of wounded in the late glorious battle—before writing you again. But we hear nothing from you since the battle—your last date received being Sunday, the 18th, and we get as yet very meagre reports of the casualties. From the correspondent of the Herald of to-day, however, I glean enough to show that the Thirty-seventh has not escaped without serious losses—the names of Captain Loomis, Captain Pierce, Lieutenant

> Harris, Lieutenant Cozens, Lieutenant Bardwell, the last to our great sorrow reported "dangerous." We derive some encouragement from the fact that your name does not appear in a list which gives so many casualties in your regiment.[61]

As it turns out, the son sent a letter home the same day saying he only received a scratch. Soldiers were painfully aware that their townsfolk were closely interrogating the papers for information about casualties. The death lists, like the one that this father examined, were often inaccurate and so they caused needless grief. "Received a letter today from my old friend, Frank Owen, of Lowell, who says my friends there all thought I was dead and it was so reported in the Lowell papers," a clerk serving as a lieutenant in the 29th Massachusetts Regiment wrote after he was involved in the bloody Battle of the Crater near Petersburg, Virginia, on July 30, 1864.[62] One did not have to be in the direct line of fire to induce anxiety at home. In May 1862 a Boston army surgeon's wife wrote to her husband in Virginia after hearing about the Battle of Eltham's Landing, "No letter from you & I am much disappointed. The papers report a thousand killed & wounded at West Point & no names are given[.] We are longing to hear[.] We are all well & think only of you & the army."[63] Inflated figures such as these, which overestimated casualties by a factor of five, rattled civilian nerves.[64]

Clara Wood shows the degree to which civilians obsessed about conflicting reports in an effort to manage the uncertainty surrounding loved ones' well-being. She even went so far as to personify the source, granting it a sinister agency: "The paper makes me feel bad today for it says you have gone out with that expedition that had startid to reinforce Foster," she wrote to her husband on April 15, 1863, of the effort to help lift the siege of Washington, North Carolina, where General John G. Foster's troops were outnumbered by superior forces. (The same day, Amos would reassure her in a letter from New Bern, which would not arrive until sometime later, that he had not been part of this mission.) "The paper is blue enough about NC," she continued. "It has been reported that Foster had surrendered & that there was 7000 started from Newbern to go there & they were repulsed & 50 of our men killed. [B]ut it[']s been contradicted since but I do so fear the result." Overwhelmed, she moaned, "Oh the anxiety it seems sometimes beyond endurance." Even Amos's earlier letters failed to calm her ragged nerves. "I dont believe you write me as bad as it is do you?" she accused him; "I know you write the bright side so as to cheer me up but I want you to write just as it is whether good or bad."[65]

Letters from a more skeptical correspondent in her husband's regiment told her that "everybody had left Newbern," leaving Amos's company "to Guard the place" and thus making him vulnerable to attack. But she insisted, based on the news story she read, that her husband had left New Bern. Still, she was confused: "I did not credit that [report] realy it did not look reasonable I did not think." Her only recourse for clarifying the situation was to obtain yet more newsprint: "I did go up to the Office to get the paper this morning for I was so anxious to get it to see if there was anything from Newbern but there was nothing new."[66] The newspaper industry thrived upon the doleful business of tracing soldiers.

Clara's daily occupation of following her husband through the papers extended to deciphering shipping news in order to predict when a letter or transient paper from Amos would arrive.[67] She also interpreted reports of epidemics to set the odds of whether they would affect her husband and weighed stories about his regiment's intemperate habits to issue a timely admonishment to him (he defended himself against the charge).[68] After reading a report that the 46th Regiment "had orders to take three days rations & march," she told him, "I dreamed of seeing you the night I saw that in the paper & I thought you was shaking with the cold & you said you [were] blind."[69] Newsprint-based anxieties even invaded her dream life.

In their search for reliable information Massachusetts readers cast an unusually skeptical eye on the New York press, especially the *Herald* and the *Tribune,* which were becoming "papers of record" elsewhere.[70] Boston and Springfield dailies were more highly regarded, even though their pages printed copy from the New York press and reproduced the same telegraphic reports. Chaplain Frank Morse dismissed the *Herald,* saying, "it is not a paper of much character."[71] An academy student in Lenox asked her mother, "Aren't you disgusted with the Tribune? I am."[72] The names of New York papers became code words for exaggeration: "Do not, for a moment, look for the 'annihilation,' the 'hiving,' or the 'total rout' of Lee," aide-de-camp Theodore Lyman in Virginia warned his wife in May 1864; "Such things exist only in the New York Herald."[73] With "the N. Y. *Tribune* . . . abusing McClellan abominably," Lieutenant Stephen Weld told his father, "I hope you never take the paper."[74]

Of course, readers attributed journalistic shortfalls to the professional agency of editors and reporters who were becoming fixtures in theaters of war. On one occasion Weld was present when L. A. Hendrick, a *Herald* reporter, confessed to sugarcoating assessments of soldier morale and discipline. "It was amusing to hear him 'get off' the usual stereotyped phrases about the enthusiasm, alacrity, etc. of the soldiers, and then hear him say 'big lie,' etc., to each phrase" of the *Herald* copy he was writing for the next day's release.[75] Fibbing was not the only problem with journalists, for they could be too revealing. Horrified that "a full statement of number and strength" of his division appeared in issues of the *New York Times*, which "go South freely," Major Wilder Dwight complained that their "reporters cannot be checked!"[76] It is no wonder that most of these critics were soldiers. Nationally prominent papers could make or break an officer's reputation—one more reason why readers critically scanned columns for information about loved ones, themselves, and their regiments. Furthermore, Massachusetts soldiers were highly aware of journalistic practice because they themselves often sent pieces to the newspapers that folks at home would read, or acted as embedded correspondents, an extension of the amateur production for social ends that had occurred during the antebellum years. For example, Zenas T. Haines contributed to the *Boston Herald*, Patrick Robert Guiney to the *Boston Post*, and Frank C. Morse to *Zion's Herald*.[77] In this way soldiers took matters into their own hands instead of leaving reportage only to professionals.

Massachusetts readers' animus against New York newspapers was a species of selectivity they practiced with regard to other reading matter. There was only so much one could digest out of the vast ocean of print, so readers helped one another navigate it by directing their correspondents' attention to specific titles and eliminating others. The phrase "have you read . . . ?," so common in antebellum letters, continued, in various iterations, into the war.[78] "Have you read an article . . . in *Littell's*, called 'Concord Transcendentalists?'" Theodore Lyman inquired of his wife in Brookline, adding, "It is a singular production, rather entertaining some of it." What differed from the prewar pattern was that the question was frequently asked of hardcore news. "Have you read Colonel Harvey Brown's clear, manly, sensible despatch from Fort Pickens?" Wilder Dwight asked his parents, before applying an analysis of the piece's style and the character of its author: "There is a modesty, directness, absence of cant about it that stamp the man a soldier fit for command."[79] The query about reading, which could resemble more of an imperative, was often meant as an opening gesture to further literary sociabilities. "Francena, you must read 'Frank Warrington' and tell me how you like it," Henry Howe advised his sister in Lowell of a recently published novel set in the Civil War.[80] Most of this kind of directed reading, even of fiction and poetry, concerned the conflict.

To call one's attention to a particular piece of print was to invite a shared epistolary experience, one that simulated face-to-face literary conversation and group reading sessions of happier, prewar days. When one could not actually talk about books, read side-by-side with kin or friend, or listen to them read aloud, the next best thing was to use correspondence to construct and maintain a virtual reading circle. Being deprived of something that was once habitual, even self-defining, made the need all that more pressing.

The case of Frank and Ellen Morse is illustrative. Newly wed just after the war began, the couple settled into a parsonage in Blandford, Massachusetts. Frank enlisted in the 47th Massachusetts Volunteer Infantry on August 8, 1862, and became its chaplain shortly thereafter. On his way to the front in September he was already attempting to create a shared space with Ellen through print. "You will see an account of [our] removal from camp in Pittsfield in the papers," he wrote from one stopping place, and, at the next stop along the way, he asked her to "please send me all the papers you receive as soon as you conveniently can after you read them."[81] A month later, while in camp in Berlin, Maryland, he imagined a scenario of literary discussion with Ellen: "O if I could only sit down in a good quiet 'study' alone and have nothing to disturb me how I should delight to read, sing and pray and then transcribe my thoughts to you." Short of doing this, he went out into the woods and meditated, picking leaves as mementoes for her. "I have those leaves you sent pressed in my new Bible[;] shall keep them as long as I live," she replied.[82] They would remind her of him whenever she read her holy book.

Ellen obliged her husband by frequently sending the papers as he requested, but she also selected reading matter of particular interest to her, and directed his attention to specific pieces.[83] "There is a letter from a dying officer to his wife in the [Zion's] Herald this week. please read it," she enjoined him.[84] Meanwhile, they both painted pictures in their letters of social reading scenes in their respective worlds. "I wish you could take a trip with me," Frank ventured; "You would find some reading their bibles, some singing, some sleeping, some bathing, some mending clothes." Ellen had given him a vignette of her own: "If you could just step into the parsonage you would find" the family reading and sewing.[85]

By 1864 war had intensified Frank's interest in coordinating reading with Ellen. He wanted her to develop a more diversified diet of books and laid down a few examples that represented his own turn toward belles lettres and the classics, such as "Knickerbocker's" *History of New York* by Washington Irving and Milton's *Samson Agonistes*.[86] "Are you devoting much time to reading?" he inquired from his camp at Brandy Station, Virginia, in January 1864. "You better make a selection of some choice books for a winter evening pastime," he wrote, and then got her started by sending her "an interesting little book 'The Sergeant[']s Memorial,'" a biography of the author's son, a 106th New York Infantry soldier who had died of fever in March 1863.[87]

Apparently she replied that she was mostly reading the Bible "in course," as it was called—chapter-by-chapter in sequence from beginning to end—and he hit on the idea that they synchronize their reading of a block of three chapters on the exact same day. He set the starting point at Genesis 28:30 and assumed that they would begin the next day. "Then you can easily reckon from that after this reaches you," he told her, anticipating that the letter might not get to her in one day. Desperate to launch such coordinated reading in whatever way possible, he offered, "If you would prefer any other plan just mention it." With each chapter they inched forward together, step by step, toward a future of peacetime reading and prayer when the couple would be reunited: "O that we may read it together again and bow together at the family altar."[88] But there were moments along this pathway when they could hold hands. Shortly after they started their long-distance course, she visited his camp and read the Bible with him. When she returned home, she received a reassuring letter: "I have continued the reading of the Scriptures in the same course we pursued when you was here."[89]

As might be expected, Frank and Ellen lost their way along the path and could not keep up their simultaneous trek toward the Bible's end. By January 1865, they were going their separate ways, as he announced, "I have to-day been reading the books of Esther and Ruth, I think they are most exceedingly interesting and beautiful. I am also reading the Bible in course and am at the present time in Exodus."[90] In the meantime, they had experimented with secular material. "I have just read the article you referred to in the Gleaner. You ask if I think it applies to us," he wrote to her on April 27, 1864, about a short comic play, "The Smuggler of Calvados," which featured the impecunious family of "Dr. Herbal Emberic." "Part of it does," he conceded, evidently referring to their constant money troubles. "I think we get along about like the Dr's family, don't you?"[91] Although the venture in simultaneous reading had failed, Frank still imagined Ellen beside him as he perused books on his own schedule. "Now if you will promise to keep quiet and not disturb me while I am reading," he wrote to her in November 1864 as if she were in the room, "I will lay aside my pen and read Mr. [Hugh] Blair's lecture on '*Style.— Perspicuity and Precision*' Good night love!"[92] The two would continue their epistolary discussions about reading until the end of the war, when he would come home to resume his ministerial duties with a new congregation in Leyden, Massachusetts.[93]

We have seen how Massachusetts civilians and soldiers recruited print to maintain social bonds in a time of turmoil. Print somehow had a power to invite such bonding, even across enemy lines, as soldiers from the Bay State were quick to point out in letters home that described Yankees and Confederates swapping newspapers. Some officers tolerated a practice that suggested inappropriate fraternization.[94] "Their pickets and ours are on perfectly good terms," a lieutenant colonel in Georgia wrote home. "The men off duty meet each other between the lines, exchange papers, and barter sugar and coffee for tobacco."[95] Others who frowned upon the transfer nonetheless marveled at it. "To-day has been entirely quiet, our pickets deliberately exchanging papers, despite orders to the contrary," a bemused and baffled Theodore Lyman wrote to his wife. "These men are incomprehensible," he observed, "—now standing from daylight to dark killing and wounding each other by thousands, and now making jokes and exchanging newspapers!"[96] On a later occasion he complained, "Their liberties go too far sometimes," and recounted for the amusement of his wife how two rebels blithely "walked up to our breastwork to exchange papers" and were summarily captured by the irritated commanding officer.[97]

By contrast, privates welcomed the sociabilities surrounding such interactions and the chance to get news they would not otherwise have seen. Exchanges that were undetected by higher-ups could persist for days. "Did not go over to se[e] the Rebs this morning but think I shal[l] tomorrow[;] they come over to our side yesterday & exchanged Papers with our Boys," Amos Wood in New Bern confessed to his wife in May 1863. The barter that day yielded a relatively recent Richmond paper that "did not talk verry encouraging for thair side[.] [D]o not think thares a verry brite side for them to look at[,] do you[?]"[98] Thus, information that originated in the Confederate capital had worked its way into North Carolina, crossed enemy lines, and ended up in a humble parlor in South Hadley Falls, Massachusetts. The bonds between home front and battlefield were often forged in such circuitous ways.

If print could cast a benevolent spell over embittered enemies, what kind of magic did it perform with those Massachusetts family members who were being pulled apart by the maelstrom of war? To be sure, for them print could become an elixir of emotional sustenance, a crystal ball into battlefield fates, a talisman against desolation and loneliness, a prestidigitator that made troubles vanish into thin air—at least for a moment. But it could also conjure up unfounded worries, induce horrible nightmares, enchant malicious scavengers, and cast a veil of confusion over the unsuspecting. So were the bonds of print created by sleight of hand? Virtual reading communities were after all, only virtual—illusions abetting a larger cultural move from face-to-face encounters over the printed word to more distant, abstract human relations only mediated by it.[99] Already during the war, oral, group reading was receding while silent, solitary reading was on the rise. Literary gifts were declining as other luxury items took their place. Institutions were superseding home libraries as lending sources.[100] Arguably, however, print's greatest illusory effect was to prop up morale for the cause. By restoring a simulacrum of wholeness to bonds that had shattered through dislocation and death,[101] print enabled civilians and soldiers to endure a seemingly endless war.

NOTES

1. Henry William Tisdale, Lynnfield, Mass., August 20, 1862, Civil War Diary of Sergeant Henry W. Tisdale, Boston Public Library, transcription (courtesy of Mark F. Farrell) available at http://civilwardiary.net (hereafter cited as Tisdale Diary).
2. Henry William Tisdale, Convalescent Camp near Alexandria, Va., October 29 and November 18, 1862, Tisdale Diary.
3. Henry William Tisdale, Falmouth, Va., November 25 and December 8 and 17, 1862, Tisdale Diary.
4. Ronald J. Zboray and Mary Saracino Zboray, *Everyday Ideas: Socioliterary Experience among Antebellum New Englanders* (Knoxville: University of Tennessee Press, 2006).
5. Ronald J. Zboray and Mary Saracino Zboray, "Cannonballs and Books: Reading and the Disruption of Social Ties on the New England Home Front," in *The War Was You and Me: Civilians in the American Civil War*, ed. Joan Cashin (Princeton: Princeton University Press, 2002), 239–43; Zboray and Zboray, *Everyday Ideas*, 79–92, 125–30.

6. Ronald J. Zboray and Mary Saracino Zboray, "The Boston Book Trades, 1789–1850: A Statistical and Geographical Analysis," in *Entrepreneurs: The Boston Business Community, 1700–1850*, ed. Conrad Edick Wright and Katheryn P. Viens (Boston: Massachusetts Historical Society, 1997), 210–67. Cf. William Charvat, *Literary Publishing in America, 1790–1850* (Amherst: University of Massachusetts Press, 1993).
7. Francis X. Blouin, *The Boston Region, 1810–1850: A Study of Urbanization* (Ann Arbor, Mich.: UMI Research Press, 1980), 24–25.
8. Ronald J. Zboray and Mary Saracino Zboray, "Books, Reading, and the World of Goods in Antebellum New England," *American Quarterly* 48 (December 1996): 587–622. Massachusetts had near-universal literacy since the late eighteenth century (Kenneth A. Lockridge, *Literacy in Colonial New England: An Enquiry into the Social Context of Literacy in the Early Modern West* [New York: Norton, 1974]). According to the 1860 census, only 6.51 percent of whites age twenty and over could not read and write; for African Americans the corresponding percentage was 11.70 (based on James Madison Edmunds, comp., *Statistics of the United States (including Mortality, Property, &c.) in 1860, Compiled from the Original Returns and Being the Final Exhibit of the Eighth Census under the Direction of the Secretary of the Interior* [Washington, D.C.: Government Printing Office, 1866], 508). Illiteracy rates in the Massachusetts African American regiments, the 54th and 55th, were somewhat higher owing to enlistments from outside of New England where black literacy was lower (Burt Green Wilder, *Practicing Medicine in a Black Regiment: The Civil War Diary of Burt G. Wilder, 55th Massachusetts*, ed. Richard M. Reid [Amherst: University of Massachusetts Press, 2010], 4). Of the 55th's 980 enlisted men, 18.78 percent could not read (Burt Green Wilder, "The Brain of the American Negro," *Proceedings of the 1st National Negro Conference, 1909* [New York: Arno Press, 1969], 49). It is well to remember, however, that 247 of these enlistees had been slaves, barred by law if not always in practice from learning to read (Charles Barnard Fox, *Record of the Service of the Fifty-Fifth Regiment of Massachusetts Volunteer Infantry* [Cambridge, Mass.: John Wilson for the Regimental Association, 1868], 110).
9. Carl F. Kaestle and Maris A. Vinovskis, *Education and Social Change in Nineteenth-Century Massachusetts* (Cambridge: Cambridge University Press, 1980); Carl F. Kaestle, *Pillars of the Republic: Common Schools and American Society, 1780–1860* (New York: Hill & Wang, 1983); Anne M. Boylan, *Sunday School: The Formation of an American Institution, 1790–1880* (New Haven: Yale University Press, 1988); Jesse Hauk Shera, *Foundations of the Public Library: The Origins of the Public Library Movement in New England, 1629–1855* (1949; repr., Hamden, Conn.: Shoe String Press, 1965); Katherine H. Porter, "The Development of the American Lyceum with Special Reference to the Mission of the Local Associations in New England" (Ph.D. diss., University of Chicago, 1914); Ronald J. Zboray and Mary Saracino Zboray, "Women Thinking: The International Popular Lecture and Its Audience in Antebellum New England," in *The Cosmopolitan Lyceum: Lecture Culture and the Globe in Nineteenth-Century America*, ed. Tom F. Wright (Amherst: University of Massachusetts Press, 2013), 42–66; Joseph F. Kett, *The Pursuit of Knowledge under Difficulties: From Self-Improvement to Adult Education in America, 1750–1990* (Stanford: Stanford University Press, 1994).
10. David Nevin, *The Expressmen* (Alexandria, Va.: Time-Life Books, 1974), 16; Michael J. Connolly, *Capitalism, Politics, and Railroads in Jacksonian New England* (Columbia: University of Missouri Press, 2003); Allan Pred, *Urban Growth and City Systems in the United States, 1840–1860* (Cambridge: Harvard University Press, 1980).

11. Ronald J. Zboray and Mary Saracino Zboray, "Reading and Everyday Life in Antebellum Boston: The Diary of Daniel F. and Mary D. Child," *Libraries and Culture* 32 (Summer 1997): 285–323; Zboray and Zboray, *Everyday Ideas*, 128–29.
12. Ronald J. Zboray and Mary Saracino Zboray, "Political News and Female Readership in Antebellum Boston and Its Region," *Journalism History* 22 (Spring 1996): 2–14.
13. Ronald J. Zboray and Mary Saracino Zboray, *Voices without Votes: Women and Politics in Antebellum New England* (Lebanon, N.H.: University Press of New England, 2010).
14. The research presented here is part of our larger book-length study, tentatively titled "Life, Death, and Reading during the Civil War." That project's study group includes 1,106 "informants" (at least ten from each state) who wrote 5,583 letters and diaries showing evidence of reading. In 2012 Ronald J. Zboray received a twelve-month National Endowment for the Humanities Fellowship for the purpose of working on the larger project. We also received the Joseph McKerns Research Grant Award of the American Journalism Historians Association, for research at the South Carolina Historical Society for this project. We delivered "The Bullet in the Book: Reading Cultures during the Civil War," the Edward G. Holley Memorial Lecture at the plenary session of the Library History Round Table, American Library Association annual convention in Washington, D.C., June 28, 2010.
15. Military ranks/roles upon service entry for these 37 men were private (12), corporal (6), sergeant (2), lieutenant (8), captain (1), major (1), and aide-de-camp (1), plus steward (1), surgeon (3), engineer (1), and chaplain (1). Adjutant General, comp., *Massachusetts Soldiers, Sailors, and Marines in the Civil War*, 8 vols. (Norwood, Mass.: Norwood Press, 1931).
16. Prewar occupations, drawn mostly from the manuscript schedules of the 1860 U.S. census, include bookman (9), clergyman (7), clerk (8), farmer (10), banker (4), officeholder (1), laborer (31), lawyer (5), manufacturer (3), merchant (12), military (1, in service before April 1, 1861), other professional (8), physician (7), servant (3), shopkeeper (1), student (6), teacher (7). If occupations for women and younger men could not be located, the household head's occupation was assigned. *1860 U.S. Census, Population Schedule* (NARA Microfilm Publication M653, 1,438 rolls; Washington, D.C.: National Archives and Records Administration, n.d.), accessed via Ancestry.com.
17. Aaron Sheehan-Dean, "Introduction" and "The Blue and the Gray in Black and White: Assessing the Scholarship on Civil War Soldiers," in *The View from the Ground: Experiences of Civil War Soldiers*, ed. Aaron Sheehan-Dean (Lexington: University Press of Kentucky, 2007), 1–2, 9–30. Diaries and letters have long been drawn upon by Civil War historians; see, for example, Bell Irvin Wiley, *The Life of Johnny Reb: The Common Soldier of the Confederacy* (Garden City, N.Y.: Doubleday, 1943); Randall C. Jimerson, *The Private Civil War: Popular Thought during the Sectional Conflict* (Baton Rouge: Louisiana State University Press, 1988); Anne C. Rose, *Victorian America and the Civil War* (New York: Cambridge University Press, 1992); and James M. McPherson, *For Cause and Comrades: Why Men Fought in the Civil War* (New York: Oxford University Press, 1997).
18. Stephen M. Frank, "'Rendering Aid and Comfort': Images of Fatherhood in the Letters of Civil War Soldiers from Massachusetts and Michigan," *Journal of Social History* 26 (Fall 1992): 5–32. On home-front studies, see Cashin, *The War Was You and Me,* and our essay in that volume, "Cannonballs and Books," 237–61. See also Thomas H. O'Connor, *Civil War Boston: Home Front and Battlefield* (Boston: Northeastern University Press,

1997); Earl F. Mulderink, *New Bedford's Civil War* (New York: Fordham University Press, 2012); Paul A. Cimbala and Randall M. Miller, eds., *An Uncommon Time: The Civil War and the Northern Home Front* (New York: Fordham University Press, 2002); Paul A. Cimbala and Randall M. Miller, eds., *Union Soldiers and the Northern Home Front: Wartime Experiences, Postwar Adjustments* (New York: Fordham University Press, 2002).

19. David Kaser, *Books and Libraries in Camp and Battle: The Civil War Experience* (Westport Conn.: Greenwood Press, 1984). There are scattered references to soldiers' reading in Bell Irvin Wiley, *The Life of Billy Yank: The Common Soldier of the Union* (Indianapolis: Bobbs-Merrill, 1952), 153–57. Alice Fahs's *Imagined Civil War*, insofar as it acknowledges the important cultural work that the popular literary products of the war performed, complements our own investigations of literary consumption. Like us, Fahs emphasizes literary experience on the personal plane. For her, it was in tension with the demands of the nation state. Her localized readers are implied in the popular texts she recovers, but her main interest is in the published texts themselves. Alice Fahs, *The Imagined Civil War: Popular Literature of the North and South, 1861–1865* (Chapel Hill: University of North Carolina Press, 2001). She revises the work of literary scholars such as Daniel Aaron, *The Unwritten War: American Writers and the Civil War* (New York: Knopf, 1973), and Edmund Wilson, *Patriotic Gore: Studies in the Literature of the American Civil War* (New York: Oxford University Press, 1966). Fahs also briefly but tellingly introduces and comments on a series of documents highlighting North–South comparisons in print culture use in her essay "Northern and Southern Worlds of Print," in *Perspectives on American Book History: Artifacts and Commentary*, ed. Scott E. Casper, Joanne D. Chaison, and Jeffrey D. Groves (Amherst: University of Massachusetts Press, 2002), 195–222. The passages dealing with reading in Louise Stevenson, *The Victorian Home Front: American Thought and Culture, 1860–1880* (New York: Twayne, 1991), 22–45, portray reading as virtually unaffected by the war.

20. See, for example, J. Cutler Andrews, *The North Reports the Civil War* (Pittsburgh: University of Pittsburgh Press, 1955); J. Cutler Andrew, *The South Reports the Civil War* (Princeton: Princeton University Press, 1970); Andrew S. Coopersmith, *Fighting Words: An Illustrated History of Newspaper Accounts of the Civil War* (New York: New Press, 2004); Brayton Harris, *Blue and Gray in Black and White: Newspapers in the Civil War* (Washington, D.C.: Brassey's, 1999); Hazel Dicken-Garcia and Giovanna Dell'Orto, *Hated Ideas and the American Civil War Press* (Spokane, Wash.: Marquette Books, 2008); Debra Reddin van Tuyll, "Gray Ladies of the Confederacy: Newspaper Culture in the Old South, 1860–1865" (Ph.D. diss., University of South Carolina, 2000). Other journalism history sources on the war include David W. Bulla and Gregory A. Borchard, *Journalism in the Civil War Era* (New York: Peter Lang, 2010); David B. Sachsman, S. Kittrell Rushing, and Roy Morris, eds., *Words at War: The Civil War and American Journalism* (West Lafayette, Ind.: Purdue University Press, 2008); David B. Sachsman, S. Kittrell Rushing, and Debra Reddin Van Tuyll, eds., *The Civil War and the Press* (New Brunswick, N.J.: Transaction, 2000); Debra Reddin Van Tuyll, ed., *The Southern Press in the Civil War: American Wars and the Media in Primary Documents* (Westport, Conn.: Greenwood Press, 2005); Ford Risley, "The Confederate Press Association: Cooperative News Reporting of the War," *Civil War History* 47 (2001): 222–39; Joshua Brown, *Beyond the Lines: Pictorial Reporting, Everyday Life and the Crisis of Gilded Age America* (Berkeley: University of California Press, 2002); W. Fletcher Thompson Jr., *The Image of War: The Pictorial Reporting of the American Civil War* (New York: Yoseloff, 1961); and Andie Tucher, "Reporting for Duty:

The Bohemian Brigade, the Civil War, and the Social Construction of the Reporter," *Book History* 9 (2006): 131–57. One of the few sources dealing with newspaper readers is James M. McPherson, "'Spend Much Time in Reading the Daily Papers': The Press and Army Morale in the Civil War," *Atlanta History* 42.1–2 (1998): 7–18. See also Ford Risley, *Civil War Journalism* (Santa Barbara, Calif.: Praeger, 2012).

21. On postal policy, see Richard R. John, *The American Postal Network, 1792–1914*, 4 vols. (London: Pickering & Chatto, 2012); Gerald Cullinan, *The Post Office Department* (New York: Frederick A. Praeger, 1968); Arthur Henry Bissell and George H. Kirby, comps., *The Postal Laws and Regulations of the United States of America* (Washington, D.C.: Government Printing Office, 1879); Confederate States of America, Post Office Department, *Instructions to Postmasters* (Richmond: Ritchie & Dunnavant, 1861); and Richard B. Kielbowicz, *News in the Mail: The Press, Post Office, and Public Information, 1700–1860s* (Westport, Conn.: Greenwood Press, 1989).

22. *An Act to Amend the Laws Relating to the Post-Office Department, Approved March 3, 1863, Together with Instructions Predicated Thereon by the Postmaster General for the Government of Postmasters* (Washington, D.C.: Government Printing Office, 1863), 705. On transient papers see Ronald J. Zboray, *A Fictive People: Antebellum Economic Development and the American Reading Public* (New York: Oxford University Press, 1993), 119–21; and David M. Henkin, *The Postal Age: The Emergence of Modern Communications in Nineteenth-Century America* (Chicago: University of Chicago Press, 2006), 43–50.

23. *An Act to Amend the Laws Relating to the Post-Office Department, Approved March 3, 1863*, 705.

24. Zenas T. Haines, New Bern, N.C., to *Boston Herald*, January 2, 1863, in *Letters from the Forty-fourth Regiment M.V.M.: A Record of the Experience of a Nine Months' Regiment in the Department of North Carolina in 1862–3* (Boston: Herald Job Office, 1863), 61.

25. Franklin Currier Morse, Spotsylvania, Va., to Elizabeth Adams Morse and Leila Merton Morse, May 16, 1864, Frank C. Morse Papers, 1825–1941 (Ms. N-25), Massachusetts Historical Society, Boston (hereafter cited as Morse Papers).

26. Clara Pierce Wood, South Hadley Falls, Mass., to Amos Wood, January 25, 1863, in *Wood Family Letters: Unpublished Manuscripts from the South Hadley Historical Society* (Alexandria, Va.: Alexander Street Press, 2002), 2 (recto); Adams Express Company, "Burnside's Army" (advertisement), *New York Herald*, January 11, 1863.

27. Clara Pierce Wood, South Hadley Falls, Mass., to Amos Wood, February 1, 1863, ibid., 2 (recto).

28. Clara Pierce Wood, South Hadley Falls, Mass., to Amos Wood, February 15, [1863], ibid., 2 (recto).

29. Amos B. Wood, New Bern, N.C., to Clara Pierce Wood, February 16, 1863, and Clara Pierce Wood to Amos B. Wood, February 19, 1863, in *Wood Family Letters*; Zenas T. Haines, New Bern, N.C., to *Boston Herald*, January 18, 1863, in Haines, *Letters from the Forty-fourth Regiment M.V.M*, 66.

30. For background on the chaplaincy, see Bell Irvin Wiley, "'Holy Joes' of the Sixties: A Study of Civil War Chaplains," *Huntington Library Quarterly* 16 (May 1953): 287–304; Warren Bruce Armstrong, "The Organization, Function, and Contribution of the Chaplaincy in the United States Army, 1861–1865" (Ph.D. diss., University of Michigan, 1964).

31. Franklin Currier Morse, Brandy Station, Va., to Ellen J. Tuttle Morse, April 29, 1864,

Morse Papers. The book he mentions is Mark Hopkins, *Evidences of Christianity: Lectures before the Lowell Institute, January 1844* (Boston: T. R. Marvin, 1863).
32. On the "meanings of literary value" in antebellum New England, see Zboray and Zboray, *Everyday Ideas*, 223–34.
33. Franklin Currier Morse, Brandy Station, Va., to Ellen J. Tuttle Morse, April 23, 1864, Morse Papers.
34. Henry William Tisdale, Baltimore–Washington Pike, Md., April 24, 1864, Tisdale Diary.
35. Franklin Currier Morse, Brandy Station, Va., to Ellen J. Tuttle Morse, May 2, 1864, Morse Papers.
36. Franklin Currier Morse, Port Winchester, Va., to Ellen J. Tuttle Morse, October 15, 1864, Morse Papers; Thomas A. Morris, *The Doctrines and Discipline of the Methodist Episcopal Church* (New York: Carlton & Porter, 1864).
37. Stephen Minot Weld Jr., Richland Jail, Columbia, S.C., to Hannah Weld, September 4, 1864, in *War Diary and Letters of Stephen Minot Weld, 1861–1865* (Cambridge, Mass.: Riverside Press, 1912), 369. See also Joseph Emery Fiske, Columbia, S.C., to Emery Fiske and Eunice (Morse) Fiske, December 1, 1864, in *War Letters of Capt. Joseph E. Fiske, Harvard, '61: Written to His Parents during the War of the Rebellion . . .* (Wellesley, Mass.: Maugus Press, n.d. [c. 1900]), 58–59.
38. Sarah Smith (Cox) Browne, Salem, Mass., to Albert Gallatin Browne Sr., October 13, 1863, Browne Family Papers, 1802–1962 (MC 298), Schlesinger Library, Radcliffe Institute, Harvard University (hereafter cited as Browne Papers).
39. Charlotte Forten, St. Helena, S.C., November 5, 1862, and January 4, 1863, in *The Journals of Charlotte Forten Grimké*, ed. Brenda Stevenson (New York: Oxford University Press, 1988), 394, 435. On the Sea Islands teachers' need for instructional books see Nina Silber, "A Compound of Wonderful Potency: Women Teachers of the North in the Civil War South," in Cashin, *The War Was You and Me*, 39.
40. Franklin Currier Morse, Warrenton, Va., to Ellen J. Tuttle Morse, July 30, 1863, and Franklin Currier Morse, Fort Hamilton, N.Y. Harbor, to Ellen J. Tuttle Morse, August 11, 1863, Morse Papers.
41. Franklin Currier Morse, Warrenton, Va., to Ellen J. Tuttle Morse, October 29, 1863, and Franklin Currier Morse, Stone House Mountain, Va., to Ellen J. Tuttle Morse, November 17, 1863, Morse Papers.
42. Charles F. Read, August 27, 1863, Diary, Historic New Orleans Collection, New Orleans.
43. Charlotte Forten, Boston, Mass., September 16, 1863, in *Journals of Charlotte Forten Grimké*, 507; Anna Jameson, *Sacred and Legendary Art*, 2 vols. (London: Longman, Brown, Green, Longmans, and Roberts, 1857).
44. Henry Warren Howe, Carrollton, La., to Harriet Francena Howe, September 19, 1862, in *Passages from the Life of Henry Warren Howe, Consisting of Diary and Letters Written During the Civil War, 1816–1865* (Lowell, Mass.: Courier-Citizen Co., 1899), 126.
45. Albert Gallatin Browne Sr., Savannah, Ga., to Edward Cox Browne, February 14, 1865, and Albert Gallatin Browne Sr., Savannah, Ga., to Sarah Smith (Cox) Browne, February 17, 1865, Browne Papers. See also Albert Gallatin Browne Sr., Savannah, Ga., to Sarah Smith (Cox) Browne, May 4, 1865, Browne Papers.
46. William L. Logan, Folly Island, S.C., to Edward Wilkinson Kinsley, August 25, 1864, in *Voices of the 55th: Letters from the 55th Massachusetts Volunteers, 1861–1865*, ed. Noah Andre Trudeau (Dayton, Ohio: Morningside, 1996), 145.

47. Joseph Emery Fiske, New Bern, N.C., to Emery Fiske and Eunice (Morse) Fiske, November 1862, in *War Letters*, 13–14.
48. Amos Wood, Newport Barracks, N.C., to Clara Pierce Wood, January 4, 1863, in *Wood Family Papers*, 2 (recto).
49. Henry William Tisdale, Rutledge, Tenn., December 14, 1863, Tisdale Diary.
50. Eugene Harrison Freeman to John Doane Freeman, October 12, 1864, in Warren Hapgood Freeman, *Letters from Two Brothers Serving in the War for the Union to Their Family at Home in West Cambridge, Mass.* (Cambridge, Mass: H. O. Houghton, 1871), 152.
51. Patrick Robert Guiney, Arlington Heights, Va., to Jeannette Margaret Doyle Guiney, August 20, 1861, in *Commanding Boston's Irish Ninth: The Civil War Letters of Colonel Patrick R. Guiney, Ninth Massachusetts Volunteer Infantry*, ed. Christian G. Samito (New York: Fordham University Press, 1998), 42.
52. Joseph Emery Fiske, Fort Gray, N.C., to Emery Fiske and Eunice (Morse) Fiske, February 25, 1864, in *War Letters*, 49.
53. See, for example, Patrick Robert Guiney to Jeannette Margaret Doyle Guiney, c. September 1861 and May 20, 1862, in Samito, *Commanding Boston's Irish Ninth*, 52, 102.
54. Amos Wood, New Bern, N.C., to Clara Pierce Wood, April 3, 1863, *Wood Family Letters*, 1 (recto).
55. Lydia Lucinda Fletcher, South Acton, Mass., to Aaron Jones Fletcher, February 8, 1863, Civil War Letters of Aaron Jones Fletcher, Acton Memorial Library Archives, Acton, Mass.
56. Wilder Dwight, Culpeper County, Va., to William Dwight and Elizabeth Amelia Dwight, August 17, 1862, in *Life and Letters of Wilder Dwight: Lieut.-Col. Second Mass. Inf. Vols.* (Boston: Ticknor, 1891), 284.
57. Henry Warren Howe, December 31, 1864, Diary, in *Passages from the Life of Henry Warren Howe*, 82; Thomas Buchanan Read, "Sheridan's Ride," *Littell's Living Age* 83 (December 3, 1864): 482; "Sheridan's Campaign: The Situation in the Valley," *New York Times*, November 13, 1864. For another instance of sending this clipping, see Franklin Currier Morse, front of Petersburg, Va., to Ellen J. Tuttle Morse, January 6, 1865, Morse Papers.
58. David Bosse, *Civil War Newspaper Maps: A Historical Atlas* (Baltimore: Johns Hopkins University Press, 1993).
59. Stephen Minot Weld, Camp near Shepherdstown, Va., to Hannah Weld, September 23, 1862, in *War Diary and Letters of Stephen Minot Weld*, 140.
60. For the casualty figure see Mason Whiting Tyler, Winchester, Va., to William Seymour Tyler, September 23, 1864, in *Recollections of the Civil War, with Many Original Diary Entries and Letters Written from the Seat of War . . .* , ed. William S. Tyler (New York: G. P. Putnam's Sons, 1912), 287.
61. William Seymour Tyler Sr., Amherst, Mass., to Mason Whiting Tyler, September 23, 1864, in Tyler, *Recollections of the Civil War*, 286–87.
62. Augustus Davis Ayling, Concord, N.H., August 31, 1862, Diary, in *A Yankee at Arms: The Diary of Lieutenant Augustus D. Ayling, 29th Massachusetts Volunteers*, ed. Charles F. Herberger (Knoxville: University of Tennessee Press, 1999), 61.
63. Hannah Lowell Jackson Cabot, Boston, to Samuel Cabot, May 9, 1862, Almy Family Papers, 1649–1967 (MC 235), Schlesinger Library, Radcliffe Institute, Harvard University.
64. John S. Salmon, *The Official Virginia Civil War Battlefield Guide* (Mechanicsburg, Penn.: Stackpole Books, 2001), 85. There were only 194 Union casualties.
65. Clara Pierce Wood, South Hadley Falls, Mass., to Amos Wood, April 15, 1863, in *Wood Family Letters*, 1 (recto and verso), 2 (verso).

66. Ibid.
67. Clara Pierce Wood, South Hadley Falls, Mass., to Amos Wood, April 9, 1863[?], ibid., 1 (recto).
68. Clara Pierce Wood, South Hadley Falls, Mass., to Amos Wood, two letters, 1862[?], ibid., 1 (verso) and 2 (verso); Amos Wood, New Bern, N.C., to Clara Pierce Wood, 1862[?], ibid., 1 (recto and verso).
69. Clara Pierce Wood, South Hadley Falls, Mass. to Amos Wood, March 11, 1863, ibid., 1 (recto).
70. Harold Holzer and Craig Symonds, introduction to *The New York Times: The Complete Civil War, 1861–1865*, ed. Holzer and Symonds (New York: Black Dog & Leventhal, 2010), 8.
71. Franklin Currier Morse, Wilson's Station, Va., to Ellen J. Tuttle Morse, May 7, 1865, Morse Papers.
72. Ellen Wright Garrison, Lenox, Mass., to Martha Coffin Wright, July 17, 1861, Garrison Family Papers, 1694–2005 (MS 60), Sophia Smith Collection, Smith College, Northampton, Mass.
73. Theodore Lyman, near Mount Carmel Church, Va., to Elizabeth Russell Lyman, May 24, 1864, in *Meade's Headquarters, 1863–1865: Letters of Colonel Theodore Lyman from the Wilderness to Appomattox*, ed. George R. Agassiz (Boston: Atlantic Monthly Press, 1922), 124.
74. Stephen Minot Weld Jr., Cloud's Mills, Va., to Stephen Minot Weld Sr., March 20, 1862, *War Diary and Letters of Stephen Minot Weld*, 89.
75. Stephen Minot Weld Jr., Fairfax Court House, to Stephen Minot Weld Sr., March 10, 1862, ibid., 71.
76. Wilder Dwight, Department Shenandoah, Maryland Heights, W.Va., to William Dwight and Elizabeth Amelia Dwight, August 15, 1861, in *Life and Letters of Wilder Dwight*, 74.
77. William C. Harris, ed., *In the Country of the Enemy: The Civil War Reports of a Massachusetts Corporal* (Gainesville: University Press of Florida, 1999), ix; Patrick Robert Guiney, Falmouth, Va., to Jeannette Margaret Doyle Guiney, April 22, 1863, in *Commanding Boston's Ninth*, 183; Ellen J. Tuttle Morse, Blandford, Mass., to Franklin Currier Morse, October 1, 1862; see also Franklin Currier Morse, Arlington Heights, Va., to Ellen J. Tuttle Morse, September 21, 1862; Morse, Stone House Mountain, Va., to Ellen, December 5, 1863; and Morse, Brandy Station, Va., to Ellen, December 10, 1863, and May 3, 1864, Morse Papers.
78. Ronald J. Zboray and Mary Saracino Zboray, "'Have You Read . . . ?': Real Readers and Their Responses in Antebellum Boston and Its Region," *Nineteenth-Century Literature* 52 (September 1997): 139–70.
79. Theodore Lyman, Headquarters Army of the Potomac, to Elizabeth Russell Lyman, November 10, 1864, in Agassiz, *Meade's Headquarters*, 260; Wilder Dwight, Camp Hicks near Frederick, Md., to William Dwight and Elizabeth Amelia Dwight, December 15, 1861, in *Life and Letters of Wilder Dwight*, 174; Harvey Brown, Headquarters, Department of Florida, Fort Pickens, Fla., to the Editor, November 26, 1861, in "The Late Fight at Fort Pickens: The Official Report of Colonel Harvey Brown," *New York Herald*, December 14, 1861.
80. Henry Warren Howe, New Orleans, La., to James Madison Howe, Sarah Kilburn Fowler Howe, and Harriet Francena Howe, May 16, 1864, in *Passages from the Life of Henry Warren Howe*, 156; Miriam Coles Harris, *Frank Warrington* (New York: Carlton, 1863).

81. Franklin Currier Morse, Jersey City, N.J., to Ellen J. Tuttle Morse, September 8, 1862, and Franklin Currier Morse, Arlington Heights, Va., to Ellen J. Tuttle Morse, September 12, 1862, Morse Papers.
82. Franklin Currier Morse, Berlin, Md., to Ellen J. Tuttle Morse, October 2, 1862, and Ellen J. Tuttle Morse, Blandford, Mass., to Franklin Currier Morse, October 3, 1862, Morse Papers.
83. Ellen J. Tuttle Morse, Blandford, Mass., to Franklin Currier Morse, October 9, 1862, and Franklin Currier Morse, New Baltimore, Va., to Ellen J. Tuttle Morse, November 13, 1862, Morse Papers.
84. Ellen J. Tuttle Morse, Blandford, Mass., to Franklin Currier Morse, October 28, 1862, Morse Papers.
85. Franklin Currier Morse, Camp Dodge, Downsville, Md., to Ellen J. Tuttle Morse, October 12, 1862, and Ellen J. Tuttle Morse, Blandford, Mass., to Franklin Currier Morse, October 7, 1862, Morse Papers.
86. Franklin Currier Morse, Brandy Station, Va., to Ellen J. Tuttle Morse, January 6, 1864, Morse Papers. Washington Irving, [pseud. Dietrich Knickerbocker], *A History of New York: From the Beginning of the World to the End of the Dutch Dynasty* (New York: Putnam, 1864); "Samson Agonistes" was included in vol. 3 of John Milton, *The Poetical Works of John Milton*, 3 vols. (Boston: Little, Brown, 1854).
87. Franklin Currier Morse, Brandy Station, Va., to Ellen J. Tuttle Morse, January 6, 1864, Morse Papers; Joseph P. Thompson, *The Sergeant's Memorial by His Father* (New York: Anson D. F. Randolph, 1863).
88. Franklin Currier Morse, Brandy Station, Va., to Ellen J. Tuttle Morse, January 9, 1864, Morse Papers.
89. Franklin Currier Morse, Brandy Station, Va., to Ellen J. Tuttle Morse, April 2, 1864, Morse Papers.
90. Franklin Currier Morse, Petersburg, Va., to Ellen J. Tuttle Morse, January 1, 1865, Morse Papers.
91. Franklin Currier Morse, Brandy Station, Va., to Ellen J. Tuttle Morse, April 27, 1864, Morse Papers; "The Smuggler of Calvados: An Original Drama in Three Acts," *Gleaner* 1 (January–March 1864): 7, 14, 22.
92. Franklin Currier Morse, Port Winchester, Va., to Ellen J. Tuttle Morse, November 7, 1864, Morse Papers; Hugh Blair, *Lectures on Rhetoric and Belles Lettres, with a Memoir of the Author's Life* (Philadelphia: Hayes, 1858).
93. See, for example, Franklin Currier Morse, Wilson's Station, Va., to Ellen J. Tuttle Morse, May 7 and 15, 1865, Morse Papers. On the move to Leyden, see Franklin Currier Morse, Leyden, Mass., to Elizabeth Adams Morse and Maria M. Morse, September 22, 1865, Morse Papers.
94. One soldier was court-martialed for exchanging papers; see "Capt. Albert S. Cloke" (obituary), *New York Times*, March 6, 1890.
95. Charles Fessenden Morse, Near Ackworth's Station, Ga., to unidentified recipient, June 9, 1864, in *Letters Written during the Civil War, 1861–1865* (Boston: T. R. Marvin, 1898), 169.
96. Theodore Lyman, Headquarters Army of Potomac, near Spotsylvania, Va., to Elizabeth Russell Lyman, May 20, 1864, in Agassiz, *Meade's Headquarters*, 106.
97. Theodore Lyman, City Point, Va., to Elizabeth Russell Lyman, July 4, 1864, ibid., 182. Officers themselves exchanged papers with their Confederate counterparts; see Theodore Lyman, City Point, Va., to Elizabeth Russell Lyman, June 19, 1864, ibid., 172.

98. Amos Wood, Camp Lee, New Bern, N.C., to Clara Pierce Wood, May 19, 1863, *Wood Family Letters*, 1 (recto).
99. Some of these changes are traced in Ronald J. Zboray and Mary Saracino Zboray, *Literary Dollars and Social Sense: A People's History of the Mass Market Book* (New York: Routledge, 2005).
100. Ronald J. Zboray and Mary Saracino Zboray, "Home Libraries and the Institutionalization of Everyday Practices among Antebellum New Englanders," *American Studies* 42 (Fall 2001): 63–86.
101. Drew Gilpin Faust, *This Republic of Suffering: Death and the American Civil War* (New York: Knopf, 2008).

III RECONCILIATION

Mourning Charles Sumner

The Flag Resolution and the Complications of Civil War Memory

SARAH PURCELL

On December 2, 1872, the first day of the third session of the forty-second Congress, Massachusetts senator Charles Sumner introduced two of his last bills on the floor of the U.S. Senate. He expected the most important act he introduced that day to be the supplement to the Civil Rights Bill, which he had advocated since 1865 and which the Senate would pass, partly to honor his death, just two years later, in March 1874. Although he anticipated little notice for his other bill, it caused a firestorm. Just after the session opened, Sumner introduced legislation that sought to influence the memory of the Civil War by regulating the Army Register, the official records of conflicts and casualties, and the regimental flags of the United States. The very brief bill read in full:

> Whereas the national unity and good will among fellow-citizens can be assured only through oblivion of past differences, and it is contrary to the usage of civilized nations to perpetuate the memory of civil war: Therefore *Be it enacted, &c.* That the names of battles with fellow-citizens shall not be continued in the Army Register or placed on the regimental colors of the United States.[1]

On its face, Sumner's bill seemed concerned with national unity and recognized that Civil War memory—or the suppression thereof—would play an important role in the future "civilization" of the United States alongside the politics of African American equality that his Civil Rights Bill would seek to ensure. Sumner's move against military memory, however, turned out to be one of the worst political blunders of his entire career.

The controversy over the politics of Civil War memory that Sumner's resolution unleashed in turn affected how he would be remembered upon his death two years later. Perhaps because he had long put his faith in politics rather than armed force, he underestimated the importance and durability of military memory. His bid to erase Civil War battles from the Army Register and from regimental flags, which veterans saw as deeply meaningful symbols of their national service, flipped his own political reputation on its head. Republicans censured Sumner, and Democrats praised him for striking a note of reconciliation. In the process, his own utility as a symbol of the fight against slavery was compromised, as commemorations of his death in 1874 showed.

Sumner was born in Boston in 1811, and following his graduation from Harvard in 1833, his devotion to humanitarian philosophy was transformed into antislavery politics as he practiced law and traveled in Europe. He believed that law was the basis of social order, and unlike many Garrisonian abolitionists he saw politics and law as the best ways to fight the evils of slavery.[2] Sumner broke with the Whigs in the 1840s and became one of the founders of the Free Soil Party, under whose banner he was first elected to the U.S. Senate in 1851. His strong antislavery politics and fiery oratory earned him hatred in the South, where he was considered "a rank abolitionist."[3] He decried the Fugitive Slave Act, and he embraced the Republican Party upon its founding in 1856, becoming one of its most outspoken antislavery members. In that same year, Preston Brooks caned Sumner on the floor of the Senate for denouncing "The Crime Against Kansas"—just one measure of how dangerous proslavery forces considered his oratorical and legislative powers to be. His promotion of the Freedman's Bureau during the Civil War, his opposition to Andrew Johnson and other forces of moderate Reconstruction, and his continual insistence on black rights, including the franchise, ensured that Democrats continued to view him as an enemy, while radical Republicans hailed him as a champion of freedom.

Yet Sumner underestimated the importance of the military conflict itself as the center of Reconstruction-era memory. Even though during the war he had twice proposed similar restrictions on regimental flags, his 1872 bill was considered a disavowal of Union heroism.[4] Sumner, a bitter enemy of President Ulysses S. Grant, had been effectively ejected from the Senate Republican caucus following his support of the Liberal Republican Horace Greeley in the 1872 presidential election. Sumner claimed that he had never abandoned the fight for African American freedom when he opposed Grant and supported the Liberal Republicans, but the break further opened him to charges of disloyalty. His biographer David Herbert Donald explains the flag bill as part of his anti-Grant maneuvering, pointing out that Sumner had told a campaign-season crowd in Massachusetts that the president could never "promote true reconciliation" because Grant himself was "a regimental color with the forbidden inscription" that would "flaunt in the face of the vanquished" their defeat in the war.[5] Sumner's flag bill made little progress in Congress; it was defeated by a joint resolution introduced in the House, which argued that "the national unity cannot fail to be strengthened by the remembrance of the services of those who fought the battles of Union in the late war of the rebellion."[6]

Even before Sumner's bill died in Congress, however, he faced stiff opposition back in his native state. Massachusetts chapters of the Grand Army of the Republic, many of which had strong radical Republican commitments, had for years pursued political action based on the belief that "we cannot forget the past with its privations and sacrifices, nor forgive the treason which caused them." The Massachusetts GAR was gaining strength after opposing the Liberal Republican ticket, and therefore breaking with the senator, in the 1872 election.[7] Sumner's Republican opponents in the Massachusetts House hoped to gain traction in the upcoming senatorial elections and felt that they could mobilize support from outraged veterans. On December 18 they introduced a resolution of censure against Sumner, calling his bill "an insult to the loyal soldiery of the nation."[8] The Massachusetts legislature, which happened to be meeting in special session, passed the resolution quickly, in one day, after a series of parliamentary maneuvers gave Sumner's supporters little chance to object. It took a fourteen-month petition campaign, led in part by John Greenleaf Whittier, and a series of heated hearings to get Massachusetts legislators to rescind the act against Sumner, a move they accomplished in February 1874, just one month before the senator's death.[9]

Sumner worried that the memory of Civil War battles would continue sectional division and overshadow the efforts to win African American rights. He thought that to guarantee the passage of the Civil Rights Bill and finally protect blacks would require sectional reconciliation that sidestepped the memory of southern military defeat, which could stir up bitter hatred. Sumner correctly anticipated what would in fact happen over the next several decades, as dominant strains of Civil War memory that privileged battles inspired continued southern hatred of the North (enshrined in the Lost Cause) and created an image of sectional reconciliation based on the shared sacrifices of Union and Confederate soldiers in battle.[10]

Sumner was wrong, however, to believe that legislation could suppress military memory, let alone to think that Congress would be willing to address the matter. He was shocked at the public outcry against his bill and against him, writing to Willard P. Phillips, "I cannot comprehend this tempest."[11] The press excoriated him; one paper called his resolution "an insult to every soldier and patriot who fought to save this Government."[12] Thomas Nast caricatured Sumner in the December 28, 1872, *Harper's Weekly* as haughtily ignoring an amputee veteran, a soldier's widow, and a war orphan who are begging for Congressional relief. The cartoon portrays Sumner as manipulating Civil War memory: a paper in front of him reads "The only record of the rebellion shall be Charles Sumner and his speeches," even as plans for "monuments and burying grounds for Union dead" and "U.S. History" lie in the wastebasket at his feet.[13] Ironically, Sumner's own reputation was the main thing threatened by his move to forget the war.

Issues of African American rights and equality, the great causes of Sumner's political career, were already waning as Reconstruction showed signs of expiring in 1873 and 1874. In fact, many felt that Sumner's Civil Rights Bill passed in the Senate less than a year after his death mainly out of deference to the dead senator. In the following years the House of Representatives gutted the legislation, which it had never fully supported, and the Supreme Court declared it unconstitutional in 1883.[14] African American leaders worried that with Sumner's death, their last strong legislative advocate had expired.

By taking on the politics of Civil War memory, whether out of opposition to Grant or not, Charles Sumner threatened his own legacy and actually hurt his prospects of being useful to the cause as an object of public memory after his death. Sumner was well accustomed to being cast as a political symbol, having been considered a martyr to the cause of liberty ever since his 1856 caning.[15] The caning had done much to tie Sumner symbolically to the cause of emancipation and African American equality, both of which he continued to pursue with an aggressive fervor that united him to African Americans and sometimes alienated other white politicians.[16] When he died, a great outpouring of public mourning issued forth—stretching from congressional obsequies in Washington, D.C., to his burial in Massachusetts. But the memorials for Sumner were imbued with some of the same controversy that the senator himself had sought to prevent, in particular concerning what Americans should remember about the great issues of the Civil War. On a national scale and in Massachusetts, mourning Sumner was an occasion to celebrate the success of the antislavery movement and black freedom, but the long shadow of the flag bill controversy also dramatized the ongoing conflict about the legacy of the Civil War and the lifespan of Reconstruction. Sumner was certainly hailed as a national hero and a revered son of Massachusetts, but he was not a strong enough symbol to suppress political conflict over race and Civil War memory.

Charles Sumner died early on the morning on March 11, 1874. He had endured poor health since his 1856 beating at the hands of Preston Brooks on the U.S. Senate floor, and his death was preceded by severe bouts of chest pain, which doctors later testified bore no relationship to his previous injuries.[17] Congress, already preparing to adjourn because of the death a few days earlier of former president Millard Fillmore, took immediate notice of Sumner's passing. As national newspapers filled with announcements of the senator's death, Congress prepared a grand funeral in Washington. On March 13, Sumner's remains were brought from his D.C. home to the U.S. Capitol in a procession led by prominent African American men, including Frederick Douglass and P. B. S. Pinchback, who had defended Sumner when other Republicans had excoriated him for opposing Grant in 1872.[18] Sumner's body lay in state in the Capitol rotunda, attended by thousands of mourners, and spectators packed the Senate chamber—draped in black crepe for the occasion—to witness his funeral there. Congressional representatives, the president and vice president, members of the diplomatic corps, and other government dignitaries also attended the rites. After the ceremony, Congress adjourned; a Massachusetts committee accompanied Sumner's remains on a special train to New York and then on to Boston.[19]

There, "universal sorrow" descended on the inhabitants, and many homes and store windows were decorated in Sumner's honor.[20] Both the state legislature and city government adjourned to prepare for the senator's funeral and burial, and several newspapers mentioned that any lingering animus toward the senator had been pushed aside as the commonwealth prepared to inter one of her most illustrious statesmen.[21] One paper in the western part of the state wrote, "Charles Sumner was never so much to Massachusetts as on this day of his funeral. For the moment, at least, his death has broadened and deepened his power over her people."[22]

Before Sumner's remains had even arrived in Boston, a huge public meeting in his honor had convened at Faneuil Hall, where Mayor Samuel C. Cobb, Richard Henry Dana, and other city luminaries eulogized him.[23] After the funeral train arrived on March 14, Sumner's remains lay in state in the Doric Hall of the Massachusetts State House, where tens of thousands of disorderly and sometimes rowdy men and women paid their last respects.[24]

Sumner's service and burial on Monday, March 16, became one of the largest civic funerals in Boston's history. In the afternoon his body was moved from the state capitol to King's Chapel, on Tremont Street, and Beacon Street was so packed with onlookers for the procession that "vigilant exertions of a large police force" were necessary to keep the funeral route open.[25] So many mourners wanted to enter King's Chapel that only those issued tickets by the state legislature were allowed inside, and one paper claimed that even part of the choir was barred from participating.[26] After the Reverend Henry C. Foote conducted the service, Sumner's procession continued from the chapel on to Cambridge, where his body was interred in Mount Auburn Cemetery, the picturesque parklike resting place that Sumner himself had often used as a city retreat.[27] The graveside service was concluded with prayers and hymns sung by the men of the Apollo Club.[28] The Boston City Council organized an additional memorial service held at the Music Hall on April 29, where Senator Carl Schurz of Missouri, who brought oratorical star-power and a reputation for political controversy, delivered a lengthy eulogy.[29] It became the best-known speech in honor of Sumner, among dozens delivered at churches, clubs, and memorial meetings, as well as on the floor of Congress, where official tributes were presented on April 27.[30]

Even in the midst of all the mourning that celebrated Sumner's long political career, the flag bill controversy and the Massachusetts censure occupied a prominent place in the public memory of the senator. The Democratic *New York World* cast doubt on the sincerity of many of the accolades, noting that Sumner had died with a shattered reputation: "The generous American instinct which forgets all political differences on the brink of the grave, insures to Mr. SUMNER the usual pomp of eulogy, but the encomiums which will come from the lips rather than the heart, cannot disguise the fact that, like poor Mr. GREELEY, he died a broken-hearted man."[31]

Sumner's battles on behalf of African American rights and his caning by Preston Brooks occupied important space in his obituaries, but his more recent break with the Republican Party and the controversy over war memory clouded an unalloyed heroic picture of him in both Republican and Democratic papers.[32] The *New York World* raged that public eulogies of Sumner were an "empty mockery" because he "was isolated and estranged from the party which owed him a great debt of gratitude." The editors sought to use Sumner's partial disgrace to score points against the Republican Party, even though party leaders denounced Sumner for the flag bill, on the basis that "a party which thus casts aside its honored leaders has outlived its original principles."[33] One of the traditional purposes of public mourning for political figures in the United States was to reinforce unity that could seem to bind up partisan or sectional differences, but the last chapter of Sumner's career did not allow him entirely to fill that purpose.[34] Even as senators honored his dying words—"You must take care of the civil rights bill . . . don't let it fail!"—Sumner himself seemed to symbolize something of the disarray and growing partisanship of Reconstruction.[35]

Reports of his death kept the flag controversy in the public eye, even as many tried to downplay the effect on Sumner's reputation. John Greenleaf Whittier, who believed that the General Court "never did anything more unjust, uncalled for, foolish and wicked than that resolution of censure of her great senator," hoped that rescinding it would allow Massachusetts to keep alive "the memory of his tireless devotion to duty, his courage . . . , stainless honor and tender regard for the rights of all" rather than the "stigma of ingratitude" the censure implied.[36] Whittier hoped that "the folly of the Extra Session of 1872" would be superseded by the power of public mourning for Sumner to suppress "all enemities [sic], jealousies and party hatreds."[37]

The timing of the censure's removal, however, meant that newspaper reports of Sumner's death were not able to heap panegyrics upon him without recalling his flag resolution and giving their readers an opportunity to debate anew what his attitude toward the Civil War's legacy had really been. The *Chicago Tribune* wrote, "It is a rather singular fact that, on this last day in the Senate, and the last day that he was alive on earth and in the discharge of his duties, the resolution[s] expunging the censure voted by the Massachusetts Legislature on account of his battle-flag resolutions were presented by his colleague, Mr. Boutwell, and read in his presence."[38] With varying degrees of dramatic flourish, many other newspapers recounted the same scene.

Sumner told several associates that he had not been feeling well, but, as the *New York Times* reported, "After the presentation in the Senate of the resolutions of the Legislature of Massachusetts expunging from its records the resolutions of censure . . . the Senator was feeling much better."[39] The Chicago-based *Inter-Ocean* noted that the excitement of the day perhaps proved too much for Sumner; after the announcement, he "was greatly affected by this event, and talked about it to his friends in quite a cheerful mood. For some time before the session closed, however, the excitement seemed to have wearied and depressed him."[40] Sumner had indicated that he intended to speak after the announcement on the Senate floor, but he reconsidered and engaged only in private conversation "after consulting with some of his personal friends."[41] Several papers noted that Sumner left the Senate "in unusually cheerful spirits" because of the announcement, after which he went home to dine with friends.[42] He became ill after dinner and never recovered.

In the days following Sumner's death, many of his supporters expressed thanks that the censure had been lifted while he was still alive. When he heard that the senator had passed away, Kenneth Allen, a student in Worcester, Massachusetts, rehearsed Sumner's biography in his diary as he prepared to travel to Boston for the funeral exercises. Allen too noted that "the unjust resolution of censure" had been repealed just before he died.[43] Thomas Russell eulogized Sumner at the Commercial Club in Boston on March 21 and remarked that "those who voted for the censure join us in rejoicing that it was removed in time to cheer the last days of our great senator with the thought that his heart and the heart of Massachusetts beat in harmony."[44] When Samuel Johnson eulogized Sumner at the Parker Memorial Meeting House in Boston on March 15, he tried to emphasize the senator's Republican principles and his work for African American freedom, even if the "pressure of infirmities" might have weakened his support for the Republican Party. Johnson told his audience that Sumner's political vision must have been restored by the ability of Massachusetts fully to "atone for her one harsh and hasty censure on his motives and aims." Another noted Boston preacher, Caleb Bradlee, praised Massachusetts legislators in a sermon for "wiping clean the former mistake" of censuring Sumner and thanked God that the senator had lived to hear the news.[45]

Some of Sumner's most important Massachusetts critics had, indeed, had a change of heart about him during his last months and in the period just following his death. The *New York Times* reported that when the state legislature met to arrange for Sumner's funeral solemnities, "the fact the resolutions rescinding the censure of the dead statesman had been so recently passed, was the subject of congratulation among the members."[46] The president of the Massachusetts Historical Society, Robert C. Winthrop, who had been a bitter enemy of Sumner's since the 1840s, had reconciled with the senator in the last months of his life and had finally supported his election as a member of the organization in September 1873. Winthrop, who was a conservative political independent, announced Sumner's death at a meeting of the society and acknowledged that few leaders were so much "on the lips of the people in all parts of the country,—sometimes for criticism and even censure," but that he ought to be remembered well now.[47] Prominent members of the society "all made complimentary remarks," and Winthrop served as a pallbearer at the senator's funeral.[48] Sumner's former critics, whether in the General Court or in the halls of the Massachusetts Historical Society, could easily realize that continuing the enmity over Sumner's support of the Liberal Republicans or over his flag resolution would work at cross purposes with their desire to hold him up as a posthumous hero for any number of causes: black rights, Republicanism, or the glory of the commonwealth of Massachusetts.

Some Democrats and Southerners tried to use Sumner's death to continue pushing his idea that Civil War memory must be put to rest in the interest of national reconciliation. Just the sight of a Democratic newspaper supporting Sumner emphasized forgetting the past, since they all had bitterly opposed him for over twenty years. In 1851 one leading Boston Democratic paper had written, "For a Democrat to support Mr. Sumner is to place himself in direct hostility to the Democracy of the Land."[49] Now the Democratic *Boston Statesman and Weekly Post* argued that Sumner had "closed his career with an effort to restore fraternity among the . . . sad memories of a destructive civil war" and called his efforts to wipe out battle commemoration "the noblest act in all his public career," one that would actually ensure his own long public memory.[50]

One Connecticut newspaper obituary exaggerated Sumner's emphasis on southern forgiveness, noting his achievements as a legislator and abolitionist and erroneously reporting "among his later efforts . . . his proposition to remove from public buildings the war flags captured from the confederate states during the rebellion."[51] The *New Orleans Picayune* pleaded, "Let the grave cover all that was inimical to Southern ideas and sentiments in the deceased senator, and let us only remember that he would have put away from the federal archives all show and sign of the triumph of countrymen over countrymen."[52] The *Louisville Courier Journal* wrote: "Fifteen years ago the news that Charles Sumner was dead would have been received with something like rejoicing by the people of the South. . . . Today they will read it regretfully, and their comment will be: 'He was a great man. He was an honest man. As he has forgiven us, so have we long ago forgiven him.'"[53] Democrats and Southerners exaggerated Sumner's political transformation by the end of his life; he opposed Grant, but he was still a strong advocate of black rights and wished to be affiliated with the Republican Party. But his flag resolution had created a rhetorical opening to paint him as an advocate of total southern forgiveness: it was framed as similar to Horace Greeley's 1872 plea that the North and South should "clasp hands across the bloody chasm"—an expression of unconditional absolution.[54]

Not all Southerners were so convinced that Sumner had been a friend or that his memory was an appropriate subject of praise. When Mississippi congressman Lucius Q. Lamar delivered a eulogy for Sumner on the floor of the Senate during the official day of mourning on April 27, he was attacked by fellow southern Democrats for lauding their former bitter enemy. Lamar explained in a letter to Alabama senator Clement Claiborne Clay that he had spoken up because he believed Sumner's political change of heart was real: "The most advanced & offensive assailant of our institutions . . . had become an advocate of amnesty & peace & fraternity with our people. His own legislature had censured him." Lamar felt that the occasion of Sumner's death would be an excellent chance to explain the southern point of view on Reconstruction to Northerners because "every word said about him, on the occasion of his funeral, would be read all over the North."[55] Lamar's eulogy used Sumner's death to make what newspapers called "an earnest appeal for the drawing together in brotherly love of the North and the South," something that would not have been possible without Sumner's own spin on Civil War memory.[56] The flag resolution, and its place in the public mind around the time of Sumner's death, paved the way for making wider arguments that Americans should put the war behind them.

Republicans were not willing to let the memory of the flag resolution be used only to create reconciliationist memory, however. Some commentators fought back against the idea that Sumner wanted to forget the war, arguing that his flag resolution was simply misunderstood. The senator himself was mystified that the Massachusetts legislature had considered his resolution to be anti-veteran. He wrote to Willard P. Phillips just after the censure that he was "at a loss after all my work through the war" to explain how "any body can charge me with insulting the soldier."[57] Sumner did not understand that it would be impossible to forget the war, or even to remove the names of battles from regimental flags, without many veterans taking that as a mark against their service. For veterans, flags "captured the main themes of love, courage, honor, and duty" that could not be separated from the memory of the war.[58] The war itself overshadowed the political accomplishments of men such as Sumner, especially since his flirtation with the Liberal Republicans showed cracks in the political legacy of the conflict.

After his death, Republicans who wanted to use Sumner's memory to continue their political battles had either to apologize for his straying from the course or to agree that his resolution had been grossly misconstrued by the legislature and by the public. In a widely reprinted Sumner eulogy, the staunch Massachusetts Republican George William Curtis claimed, for example, that the state had "censured him for the resolutions which the people of the State did not understand, and which they believed, most unjustly to him, to be somehow a wrong to the precious dead."[59] It was not politically advantageous to leave the public thinking that Sumner had devalued military sacrifice—even though that was a hard presumption to overcome.

The *Chicago Tribune*, the city's main Republican newspaper, reexamined the flag resolution in a series of articles appearing just after Sumner's death, and it too argued that the public had severely misunderstood the senator's intent. At first, the *Tribune* editors said that the "row" that erupted after the battle flag resolution had been proposed had been unwarranted because his critics had blown Sumner's intentions out of proportion. The paper's first editorial on the subject complained that "the average party organ informed its readers that the Senator was craftily plotting to destroy the flags of all the volunteer regiments of the country. Their colors were to be torn down from public hall and State-Houses and defaced, lest the feelings of 'Rebels' should be hurt." The *Tribune* pointed out that simply removing the names of Civil War battles could hardly be an insult to "the loyal soldiery of the nation" since many volunteer regiments flew flags bearing the names of battles in which they had not even fought.[60]

The *Tribune* editors went even further in a second article, proposing that "the most fitting mark of respect to the great Senator would be the passage of his famous battle-flag resolution, word for word as it came from the brain which has now done with earthly thinking." Although the *Tribune* editors shared no political interest with men such as Lucius Q. Lamar, their rhetoric prefigured Lamar's congressional obituary of Sumner when they argued that after nine years "the one thing needful now is to heal the wounds made by the long struggle." They asked the public to "dispense" with "flaunting the memorials of fratricidal strife in the faces of our enemies and present friends."[61] Republicans who sympathized with Sumner's flag resolution showed signs of fatigue with Reconstruction. Ultimately, the Republicans who were most willing to promote southern forgiveness were the ones who could most forthrightly deal with Sumner's flag resolution in the context of mourning his death.

It should not be surprising, then, that Carl Schurz agreed with the *Chicago Tribune* and that his eulogy of Sumner became the most prominent and widely disseminated effort to rehabilitate the senator's posthumous reputation in regard to the flag resolution. Like Sumner, Schurz was a Republican operative who had lost faith in Grant by the time of the 1872 presidential election. He was an even stronger supporter of the Liberal Republican movement than Sumner had been, but, perhaps because he lived longer, he was able to integrate back into Republican power circles more successfully after the dissolution of the Liberal Republican movement and as Reconstruction came to an end. Boston city officials invited Schurz to deliver the main eulogy for Sumner at their celebration in his honor, which took place at the Music Hall on April 29, 1874, three weeks after the senator's death. Of all the speakers who mourned Sumner in the months after his passing, Schurz, the former Union general and Missouri senator, took on Sumner's flag resolution and what it meant for Civil War memory in the most forthright terms.

Schurz flatly refused the notion that the flag resolution had sullied Civil War memory or Sumner himself, a man who had left "a legacy to the American people and to mankind." After rehearsing the senator's political achievements through the war years and immediately afterward, Schurz argued that Sumner had broken with Grant out of pure motives: disgust for corruption and true opposition to the annexation of Santo Domingo. He assured the audience that Sumner had been fully willing to forgive the South, since although he had despised the oppression of slavery, he had harbored no ill will toward the "former oppressor." Moreover, Sumner's flag resolution was in no way an insult to "the soldiers who had spilled their blood in a war for human rights," but rather a genuine attempt to recreate a sense of unbroken American nationalism. Every "civilized nation" that had survived a civil conflict had had the good sense to downplay its victories, Schurz maintained, and he gave examples from Irish, Scotch, Hungarian, French, and German history. Imagining a reunited American military, he asked, "Should the Son of South Carolina, when at some future day defending the Republic against some foreign foe, be reminded, by an inscription on the colors floating over him, that under this flag the gun was fired that killed his father at Gettysburg?"[62]

Speaking rather frankly to his Boston audience, Schurz claimed that the Massachusetts censure of Sumner had been a wrongful and "bitter arrow in his heart." He counted it as fortunate that Sumner had lived to see the censure lifted, and he tried to turn the senator's death into a lesson about political integrity and independence, claiming that Sumner had used his "battle-axe" for righteous causes, though he had often been misunderstood.[63] Schurz surely sought to vindicate himself along with Sumner by emphasizing that it had been possible to oppose Grant and to advocate southern forgiveness while still maintaining true Republican principles.

Indeed, Schurz made a connection between the senator's flag resolution and his work for African American freedom, one that even Sumner himself had not made on the day he introduced both the Civil Rights Bill supplement and the resolution. Schurz argued that contention over names on army regimental battle flags was trivial, in the end, when real questions of African American rights were so much more important to public memory of the Civil War. Bostonians, indeed all Northerners, ought to be willing to obliterate the memories of their military gains as long as they could remember the progress made on behalf of black men and women and that the union was preserved. "Do you want shining mementos of your victories?" Schurz asked. "They are written upon the dusky brow of every freeman who was once a slave; they are written on the gate-posts of a restored Union; and the most shining of all will be written on the faces of a contented people, re-united in common national pride."[64] Schurz claimed that the accomplishments of the war should be enough to make its legacy meaningful; flags and relics were not useful. In this way, Sumner's memory could stand for reconciliation *and* for racial justice, but it required verbal acrobatics from Schurz.

Certainly most of Sumner's African American mourners—and there were many—did not agree. Because of his tireless legislative efforts on their behalf, blacks all over the country felt the loss and worried about what it meant for the continuation of Reconstruction. African Americans convened special church and civic services to commemorate Sumner in Boston, Savannah, Little Rock, Pittsburgh, Davenport, Louisville, New York, Richmond, Wilmington, Chicago, Philadelphia, Portsmouth (Virginia), Toronto, and elsewhere.[65] While African American mourners might have agreed with Schurz's attempt to rehabilitate Sumner as a symbol of the fight for equality and freedom, they were not willing to use him as a symbol of pardon. Blacks were willing to forgive the flag resolution, but they were not willing to endorse it as a way to forget southern misdeeds.

Though Sumner was a hero to many black orators, they were quite willing to address his faults, including his 1872 support of Greeley and his flag resolution. Many African American leaders seemed to calculate that moving forward with the politics of racial reform would mean using Sumner as a symbol while also maintaining memories of the difficult past. In a tribute delivered at a memorial service held by the "colored citizens of Boston" in Faneuil Hall on April 14, U.S. Representative Robert Elliott of South Carolina claimed that there was no need for silence about Sumner's faults. Elliot declared outright that he had differed from Sumner in the 1872 presidential race, but he did not believe that the senator's actions during and after the election had clouded his support for African American rights: "As his life was wholly consecrated to Duty, so his death was wanting in no element of moral grandeur. He fell with armor on, with face still inflexibly turned towards present duties, fronting eternity with the simple trust which God gives to his faithful servant."[66] The Reverend Henry McNeal Turner told the huge audience of Sumner mourners at Savannah's St. Philip's African Methodist Episcopal Church that he had assured Sumner at their last meeting in 1873 "that I, like thousands of other colored men in the country, loved him, but could not endorse his rabid fight on the President." Despite this disagreement, Turner also praised Sumner as "Christlike."[67] African American orators saw the senator's faults, but they could not afford to forget his advocacy and sacrifice on their behalf.

In this vein, Joshua B. Smith, a former abolitionist who was by the 1870s an accomplished Cambridge caterer and a state legislator, stood out as one of the leading men of Boston who sought to preserve Sumner's memory.[68] Smith understood the power of interracial commemorative efforts; in 1865 he was the first to conceive of and begin fundraising for the Robert Gould Shaw memorial on the Boston Common. Smith had engaged Sumner to help lead the effort for a monument, and the two were longtime friends.[69] After the senator's death, Smith became what one newspaper called "one of the most thorough and reverential mourners" of Sumner.[70] Smith knew all too well how controversial the senator had become in his final years of life, since he had introduced the resolution that had cleared Sumner's censure in the Massachusetts legislature and had hand-delivered news of its passage to Washington, D.C., on the eve of Sumner's death. Smith had constantly attended to the senator during his last years of disfavor in Massachusetts, when Sumner felt that "little regard was paid to [his] public services."[71] Smith was unwilling to let the man whom he regarded as a great hero and leader of the black race fade in the public's mind.

Smith's purpose in holding on to Sumner as a strong symbol became clear in the eulogy he delivered at the city memorial in Faneuil Hall on the day Sumner's body arrived in Boston for his funeral. One newspaper reported that Smith "spoke with a genuine earnest feeling that captivated all hearts."[72] He worried that without Sumner, the fight for African American equality would be lost: "Our ship . . . which he has commanded is still adrift: we are standing out now in the open sea, with a great storm." Smith hoped for "a good man to take hold where he left off" to lead "those five millions of people of the United States" who were still too weak to lead themselves. He expressed a lack of confidence that any black man could lead the cause as effectively as Sumner had: "We are not educated up to that point. We cannot speak for ourselves: we must depend on others. . . . We can weep; but we must beg of you to give us a man who will still lead us forward."[73] While Sumner had sometimes seen his own relationship with African American leaders in paternalistic terms, Joshua Smith was the only black orator who fully adopted that vocabulary when he argued that "We stand to-day like so many children, whose parents have passed away. We can weep; but we don't understand it."[74]

Other African American leaders, although less enamored of Sumner's paternalism, also recognized the enormity of his lost leadership. The distinguished committee that had planned the celebration for Boston's "colored" population noted that "Mr. Sumner had been the life-long friend of the colored race, and had, more than any other man, helped to raise them, socially and politically, and to his memory they owed a debt of gratitude which could never be repaid." In Savannah, Henry McNeal Turner wondered, "On whom shall Sumner's mantle fall?" Frederick Douglass, who eulogized Sumner in Washington, D.C., on the day of his burial, was alone among African American orators when he expressed confidence that Sumner's political leadership for black rights would not disappear. Douglass told his audience at the Sumner Memorial Hall: "The man is now living who will seize the banner laid down by Charles Sumner and lead us to higher plains of privilege." Douglass implied that either Wendell Phillips or someone else would be able to complete the senator's work.[75]

Black orators who eulogized Sumner differed with Carl Schurz on the meaning of Civil War memory. Schurz claimed that racial justice was the greatest legacy of the war, and that as long as "the faces of a contented people" showed happiness at a Union restored and slavery ended, the North could afford to forgive the Confederacy. Black orators disagreed that the work of the Civil War was over, however. Douglass certainly did not think the time had come for forgiving former slaveholders and Confederates.[76] Whether they had a new political leader in mind, as did Frederick Douglass, or they worried that no new white political leader would emerge, as did Joshua B. Smith, they knew that the fight for equal rights was not over.

Sumner himself had pleaded that his colleagues continue the work of equal rights on the very day he introduced the flag resolution into Congress. Although he wanted to obliterate northern victories from the Army Register and from regimental flags, he was resolute that the battle for black equality must continue. When Sumner introduced the supplementary Civil Rights Bill into the Senate on that day, he said: "I, Sir, am anxious to see universal amnesty; but with it must be asserted also universal justice. Our colored fellow-citizens must be admitted to complete equality before the law. In other words, everywhere, in everything regulated by law, they must be equal with all their fellow-citizens."[77] Sumner believed that war memory was separable from the continuing political battle for equal human rights: forgiveness and amnesty for the Confederate past, even forgetting the war, would be possible as long as the future fight on behalf of African Americans continued. In some sense, black leaders were wise to worry, since it would be many decades before any white senator would take up the call for African American rights so vociferously. Sumner's Civil Rights Bill did not last long, and instead of full equality Americans faced many more decades of legal segregation and racial injustice. After Sumner was gone, it was not the war that was forgotten in mainstream American culture, but rather much of the struggle against slavery and racial oppression.

The mourning for Charles Sumner in 1874 showed just how inseparable the two issues of war memory and equal rights were. It was not easy to celebrate Sumner as a martyr to liberty or as a symbol of the fight for African American freedom without acknowledging the political difficulties his flag resolution had caused. Sumner had strayed from the Republican fold in 1872, and he had misunderstood the extent to which the memory of Civil War battles *could* be forgotten. By the time voices for reconciliation between North and South became louder in the 1880s, they tended to tout the common sacrifices of white Civil War soldiers as the very thing worth remembering.[78] It was that very potent social image that made it so hard for African American sacrifices and struggles to gain attention. Charles Sumner's own public memory—as the white freedom fighter or the opponent of Grant or the advocate of black rights who was willing to forgive the South—was important but unstable.[79] Mourning for Sumner could not rise above the contradictions that would bring about the unraveling of Reconstruction within just a few more years.

NOTES

1. *Congressional Globe*, 42nd Cong., 3d Sess., December 2, 1872, 2.
2. Anne-Marie Taylor, *Young Charles Sumner and the Legacy of the American Enlightenment, 1811–1851* (Amherst: University of Massachusetts Press, 2001), 81. Taylor's is the best work on Sumner's early life and the formation of his antislavery philosophy and politics.
3. "Infamous Coalition," *The Floridian and Journal* (Tallahassee, Fla.), January 25, 1851.
4. On the previous resolutions, see Edward L. Pierce, *Memoir and Letters of Charles Sumner*, vol. 4 (Boston: Roberts Brothers, 1893), 550.
5. Sumner quoted in David Herbert Donald, *Charles Sumner and the Rights of Man* (New York: Knopf, 1970), 564; on Sumner's opposition to Grant see Joan Waugh, *U.S. Grant: American Hero, American Myth* (Chapel Hill: University of North Carolina Press, 2009), 143.
6. *Congressional Globe*, 42nd Cong., 3d Sess. December 16, 1872, 221, 235.
7. Mary R. Dearing, *Veterans in Politics: The Story of the G.A.R.* (1952; repr., Westport, Conn.: Greenwood Press, 1974), 175–76 (quotation), 207–8.
8. Frederick J. Blue, *Charles Sumner and the Conscience of the North* (Arlington Heights, Ill.: Harlan Davidson, 1994), 205; Pierce, *Memoir and Letters*, 4:551–52, quotation on 551; *Hartford Daily Courant*, December 19, 1872.
9. Pierce, *Memoir and Letters*, 4:589; *Trenton (N.J.) State Gazette*, February 13, 1874; "Senator Sumner Vindicated," *San Francisco Bulletin,* February 20, 1874; J. Wilfred Holmes,

"Whittier and Sumner: A Political Friendship," *New England Quarterly* 30 (March 1957): 71.

10. See David W. Blight, *Race and Reunion: The Civil War in American Memory* (Cambridge: Harvard University Press, 2001); Charles Reagan Wilson, *Baptized in Blood: The Religion of the Lost Cause, 1865–1920* (1980; repr., Athens: University of Georgia Press, 2009); Matthew J. Grow, "The Shadow of the Civil War: A Historiography of Civil War Memory," *American Nineteenth Century History* 4 (Summer 2003): 77–103; Frances M. Clarke, *War Stories: Suffering and Sacrifice in the Civil War North* (Chicago: University of Chicago Press, 2011). Several scholars now stress that war memory did not always emphasize reconciliation, and even when it did the memory of racial strife did not necessarily subside. See Barbara Gannon, *The Won Cause: Black and White Comradeship in the Grand Army of the Republic* (Chapel Hill: University of North Carolina Press, 2011); Caroline E. Janney, *Remembering the Civil War: Reunion and the Limits of Reconciliation* (Chapel Hill: University of North Carolina Press, 2013).

11. Charles Sumner to Willard P. Phillips, December 21, 1872, in *The Selected Letters of Charles Sumner*, vol. 2, ed. Beverly Wilson Palmer (Boston: Northeastern University Press, 1990), 614; see also Papers Concerning the 1872 Resolution of Condemnation against Charles Sumner (MS Am 1225), Houghton Library, Harvard University. On reactions to war memory during the election of 1872, see Blight, *Race and Reunion*, 128; J. Mathew Gallman, "Is the War Ended? Anna Dickinson and the Election of 1872," in *The Memory of the Civil War in American Culture*, ed. Alice Fahs and Joan Waugh (Chapel Hill: University of North Carolina Press, 2004), 154–79.

12. "Charles Sumner Belly-Aching about a Vote of Censure," *Idaho Statesman*, April 3, 1873. The *Baltimore Sun* noted that Sumner was "very unpopular" in Massachusetts just after the censure, November 17, 1873.

13. Thomas Nast, "Let Us Have Complete Restoration, While You Are About It," *Harper's Weekly*, December 28, 1872, 1021.

14. Bertram Wyatt-Brown, "The Civil Rights Act of 1875," *Western Political Quarterly* 18 (December 1965): 769–70.

15. Williamjames Hull Hoffer, *The Caning of Charles Sumner: Honor, Idealism, and the Origins of the Civil War* (Baltimore: Johns Hopkins University Press, 2010); David Herbert Donald, *Charles Sumner and the Coming of the Civil War* (New York: Knopf, 1960), 290–301; T. Lloyd Benson, *The Caning of Senator Sumner* (Belmont, Calif.: Thomson/Wadsworth, 2004).

16. Manisha Sinha, "The Caning of Charles Sumner: Slavery, Race, and Ideology in the Age of the Civil War," *Journal of the Early Republic* 23 (Summer 2003): 233–62.

17. Both doctors and newspapers described Sumner as suffering from angina pectoris. C. E. Brown-Séquard to John Collins Warren, March 21, 1874, John Collins Warren Papers, 1738–1926 (Ms. N-1731), Massachusetts Historical Society, Boston (MHS); for newspaper coverage see, for example, *Chicago Daily Tribune*, March 12, 1874.

18. "By Telegraph, Charles Sumner," *Sioux City Daily Journal*, March 14, 1874. A large folio scrapbook held by the Newberry Library contains hundreds of newspaper articles about Sumner's illness and death; no record exists of who assembled the book or donated it to the Newberry, but the collector obviously followed news of his death extremely closely. "Sumner. Newspaper Articles," General Collection, Newberry Library, Chicago (hereafter cited as Newberry Scrapbook). The other U.S. senator from Massachusetts, George Frisbie Hoar, also assembled a file of article clippings about Sumner's death and

funerals: George Frisbie Hoar (1826–1904), Scrapbooks (1850–1876), American Antiquarian Society, Worcester, Mass. (hereafter cited as Hoar Scrapbooks, AAS). A good range of newspaper quotations is reproduced in C. Edwards Lester, *The Life and Public Service of Charles Sumner* (New York: United States Publishing Company, 1874), 517–59. On Pinchback's defense of Sumner see Stephen W. Angell, "A Black Minister Befriends the 'Unquestioned Father of Civil Rights': Henry McNeal Turner, Charles Sumner, and the African-American Quest for Freedom," *Georgia Historical Quarterly* 85 (Spring 2001): 44.

19. See "The Dead Statesman," *San Francisco Bulletin,* March 14, 1874; "Our Honored Dead," *Chicago Daily Tribune,* March 13, 1874; "The Memory of Mr. Sumner" and "The Late Senator Sumner," *New York Times,* March 13, 1874; "Obsequies of Mr. Sumner," *New York Times,* March 14, 1874; "Congressional Tributes to the Dead," *Baltimore Sun,* March 13, 1874; "The DEATH of SENATOR SUMNER," *Boston Daily Evening Traveller,* March 12, 1874, Newberry Scrapbook; "The Sumner Obsequies," *Philadelphia Inquirer,* March 14, 1874; *A Memorial of Charles Sumner from the City of Boston* (Boston: Printed by Order of the City Council, 1874), 67.

20. "General Grief at Boston," *Springfield (Mass.) Daily Republican,* March 12, 1874; "Boston's Tributes to the Distinguished Dead," *Springfield Daily Republican,* March 13, 1874; "Sorrow for Sumner in Boston," *Macon (Ga.) Weekly Telegraph,* March 17, 1874.

21. Elias Nason, *The Life and Times of Charles Sumner* (Boston: B. B. Russell, 1874), 339–40.

22. "The Dead Senator," *Springfield Daily Republican,* March 16, 1874.

23. Nason, *Life and Times,* 340.

24. "The Dead Statesman," *Springfield Daily Republican,* March 16, 1874.

25. "The Dead Statesman," *Little Rock Daily Republican,* March 17, 1874; *A Memorial of Charles Sumner,* 69; "Lying in State," *Boston Daily Advertiser,* March 16, 1874, Hoar Scrapbooks, AAS.

26. See the ticket "Funeral Services over the Remains of Charles Sumner" (Boston: Committee of the Legislature, 1874), manuscript collections, box 1874, MHS; "Scenes and Incidents," *Springfield Daily Republican,* March 17, 1874, Hoar Scrapbooks, AAS.

27. "The Dead Statesman," *Little Rock Daily Republican,* March 17, 1874; "Funeral of Charles Sumner," *Baltimore Sun,* March 17, 1874; Blanche M. G. Linden, *Silent City on a Hill: Picturesque Landscapes of Memory and Boston's Mount Auburn Cemetery,* rev. ed. (Amherst: University of Massachusetts Press in association with Library of American Landscape History, 2007), 238–39.

28. Pierce, *Memoir and Letters,* 4:604–5.

29. *A Memorial of Charles Sumner,* 73–79.

30. Carl Schurz, *Eulogy on Charles Sumner, Delivered by Carl Schurz before the City Government and Citizens of Boston . . .* (Boston: Rockwell & Churchill, 1874); "Extracts from the Eulogy Pronounced by Carl Schurz on Charles Sumner," *Advocate of Peace* 5 (June 1874): 47–48; *Memorial Addresses on the Life and Character of Charles Sumner . . . Delivered in the Senate and the House of Representatives . . .* (Washington, D.C.: Government Printing Office, 1874). Eulogies delivered in New Orleans, Kalamazoo, Savannah, Little Rock, Washington, D.C., Chicago, New York, and many other cities were published in pamphlet form and in newspapers for months after Sumner's death.

31. "Death of Charles Sumner," *New York World,* March 12, 1874, Newberry Scrapbook.

32. Heroic obituaries, which especially focus on his caning, include "Charles Sumner," *New York Times,* March 12, 1874.

33. "Death of Charles Sumner," *New York World,* March 12, 1874, Newberry Scrapbook.
34. On the tradition of political mourning, see Andrew Burstein, "Immortalizing the Founding Fathers: The Excesses of Public Eulogy," in *Mortal Remains: Death in Early America,* ed. Nancy Isenberg and Andrew Burstein (Philadelphia: University of Pennsylvania Press, 2003), 91–107; Sarah J. Purcell, *Sealed with Blood: War, Sacrifice, and Memory in Revolutionary America* (Philadelphia: University of Pennsylvania Press, 2002); Sarah J. Purcell, "All That Remains of Henry Clay: Political Funerals and the Tour of Henry Clay's Corpse," *Common-Place* 12 (April 2012), www.common-place.org.
35. Sumner quoted in Blue, *Charles Sumner,* 208.
36. John Greenleaf Whittier to Willard Peele Phillips, February 10, 1873, in *The Letters of John Greenleaf Whittier,* ed. John B. Pickard, vol. 3 (Cambridge: Harvard University Press, 1975), 288 (first quotation); John Greenleaf Whittier to Henry Wilson, March 11, 1874, ibid., 3:315 (second and third quotations).
37. John Greenleaf Whittier to Charles Sumner, February 17, 1874, in *Letters of John Greenleaf Whittier,* 3:314 (first quotation); John Greenleaf Whittier to Henry Wilson, March 11, 1874, ibid., 3:315 (second quotation).
38. "Charles Sumner; Sudden Death of the Distinguished Statesman," *Chicago Daily Tribune,* March 12, 1874.
39. "Death of Senator Sumner," *New York Times,* March 12, 1874.
40. "Dead. Hon. Charles Sumner Expired . . . ," *Chicago Inter-Ocean,* March 12, 1874.
41. "Incidents in the Senate and at the Death Bed," *Baltimore Sun,* March 12, 1874.
42. "Death of Charles Sumner," *New Hampshire Sentinel,* March 19, 1874.
43. Kenneth Allen Diary, March 12, 1874, Mss. Octavo Vols. A, AAS. Allen incorrectly noted that the censure was lifted "a month or two ago."
44. Thomas Russell, *Remarks of Hon. Thomas Russell in Memory of Charles Sumner Made at the Commercial Club, Boston, March 21, 1874* (Boston: Printed for the Club, 1874), 7.
45. Samuel Johnson, *A Memorial of Charles Sumner* (Boston: A. Williams, 1874), 4; Caleb D. Bradlee, *Death and the Resurrection, A Sermon . . .* (Boston: John Wilson and Son, 1874), 13.
46. "The Late Senator Sumner," *New York Times,* March 13, 1874.
47. Anne Bentley, "Celebrating Charles Sumner: Abolitionist, Orator, Reformer, and Statesman," Object of the Month, Massachusetts Historical Society website, www.masshist.org; "March Meeting," *Proceedings of the Massachusetts Historical Society,* vol. 13 (1873–75), 261–62, quotation on 261; "The Massachusetts Historical Society," *Chicago Daily Tribune,* March 13, 1874; on Winthrop's reconciliation with Sumner see Donald, *Charles Sumner and the Rights of Man,* 573.
48. "Massachusetts Historical Society," *Boston Evening Journal,* March 12, 1874, Newberry Scrapbook.
49. "Mr. Sumner's Faneuil Hall Speech, Boston Times," *Richmond (Va.) Enquirer,* January 17, 1851.
50. "Charles Sumner," *Boston Statesman and Weekly Post,* March 13, 1874, Newberry Scrapbook.
51. "Obituary. Charles Sumner," *Daily Constitution* (Middletown, Conn.), March 13, 1874.
52. *New Orleans Picayune* quoted in Jeremiah Chaplin and Jane Dunbar Chaplin, *The Life of Charles Sumner* (Boston: D. Lothrop, 1874), 445.
53. "Mr. Sumner and the South," *New York Times,* March 13, 1874.
54. See the Thomas Nast cartoon "Let Us Clasp Hands over the Bloody Chasm," which

lampooned Greeley's statement and also became fodder for his critics, *Harper's Weekly,* September 21, 1872, 732.

55. Lamar to Clay, September 5, 1874, quoted in "Why Lamar Eulogized Sumner," ed. Mattie Russell, *Journal of Southern History* 21 (August 1955): 377, 376. On other uses of similar imagery by Lamar, see Thomas J. Brown, "The Monumental Legacy of Calhoun," in Fahs and Waugh, *Memory of the Civil War in American Culture,* 147.
56. *Chicago Daily Tribune,* April 28, 1874. Georgian Robert Toombs bitterly criticized Lamar for his eulogy of Sumner and reportedly threatened to fight Lamar; "Personal," *Harper's Weekly,* June 13, 1874, 495.
57. Charles Sumner to Willard P. Phillips, March 16, 1873, in *Selected Letters of Charles Sumner,* 2:618.
58. Robert E. Bonner, *Colors and Blood: Flag Passions of the Confederate South* (Princeton: Princeton University Press, 2002), 76. Bonner was speaking of Confederate soldiers' attachment to their regimental flags, but the same can be said of Union veterans; GAR posts revered both regimental flags and the U.S. flag as symbols of their Civil War service. See Stuart McConnell, *Glorious Contentment: The Grand Army of the Republic, 1865–1900* (Chapel Hill: University of North Carolina Press, 1992), 224–31; see also Howard Michael Madaus and Richard H. Zeitlin, *The Flags of the Iron Brigade* (Madison: Wisconsin Veterans Museum, 1997).
59. George William Curtis, "Charles Sumner: A Eulogy," *Harper's Weekly Supplement,* June 20, 1874, 531.
60. "The Sumner Battle Flag Resolution," *Chicago Daily Tribune,* March 13, 1874.
61. "The Homage Due Sumner," *Chicago Daily Tribune,* March 14, 1874.
62. Carl Schurz, "The Oration," in *Charles Sumner: Memoir and Eulogies,* ed. William M. Cornell (Boston: James H. Earle, 1874), 105, 140–41, 149–51.
63. Ibid., 152–55, 159.
64. Ibid., 152. On Schurz's opinion about the limits of the fight for African American rights, see Eric Foner, *Reconstruction: America's Unfinished Revolution, 1863–1877* (New York: Harper & Row, 1988), 498.
65. "Colored People's Wishes," *Iowa State Register,* March 12, 1874; "Meeting of Our Colored Citizens," *Little Rock Daily Republican,* March 13, 1874; "Pittsburgh," *Sioux City Journal,* March 14, 1874; "The Colored People at Davenport," *Chicago Daily Tribune,* March 15, 1874; "Memorial Services and Meetings in Other Places," *New York Times,* March 17, 1874; "Eulogy on Sumner," *New York Times,* May 18, 1874.
66. *Oration of Hon. Robert B. Elliott, M.C. of South Carolina, Delivered in Faneuil Hall, April 14, 1874, under the Auspices of the Colored Citizens of Boston* . . . (Boston: Published for the Committee of Arrangements by Charles L. Mitchell, 1874), 18.
67. Turner quoted in Angell, "A Black Minister," 49, 51.
68. See "A Colored Man's Veneration for Charles Sumner," *San Francisco Bulletin,* January 22, 1875; "Boston. The Legislature and Senator Sumner," *Hartford Daily Courant,* March 1, 1873.
69. Interestingly, Smith thought the memorial should take the form of a traditional statue of the heroic commander. Kirk Savage, *Standing Soldiers, Kneeling Slaves: Race, War, and Monument in Nineteenth-Century America* (Princeton: Princeton University Press, 1997), 196–97; "Robert Gould Shaw and the 54th Regiment Memorial," Museum of African American History, Boston and Nantucket, www.afroammuseum.org.
70. "A Colored Man's Veneration."

71. Sumner made the remark to George Washington Warren, who also noted that Smith was consoling Sumner with gifts of fruit during his distress. Warren praised "the bountiful caterer" for "tendering his homage and aid to the one to whom he reverently looked up as the special friend and elevator of his race." "Sumner, Chase, and Agassiz," *San Francisco Bulletin,* April 15, 1874, reprinted from Warren's reminiscence of Sumner published in the *Bunker Hill Times.*
72. "Boston Correspondence . . . The Sumner Obsequies," *Hartford Daily Courant,* March 21, 1874.
73. Smith's eulogy quoted in Nason, *Life and Times,* 341.
74. Smith quoted ibid. On Sumner's paternalism see Angell, "A Black Minister," 32.
75. *Oration of Hon. Robert B. Elliott,* 3; Henry McNeal Turner, "The Conflict for Civil Rights," quoted in Angell, "A Black Minister," 54; Frederick Douglass, "Eulogy for Charles Sumner: An Address Delivered in Washington, D.C., on March 16, 1874," in *The Frederick Douglass Papers,* ed. John W. Blassingame, ser. 1, vol. 4 (New Haven: Yale University Press, 1974), 398.
76. See David W. Blight, "For Something beyond the Battlefield: Frederick Douglass and the Struggle for the Memory of the Civil War," in *Beyond the Battlefield: Race, Memory, and the American Civil War* (Amherst: University of Massachusetts Press, 2002), 93–119.
77. "The Supplementary Civil Rights Bill Again . . . Remarks in the Senate," in *The Works of Charles Sumner,* vol. 15 (Boston: Lee & Shepard, 1883), 290.
78. See Nina Silber, *The Romance of Reunion: Northerners and the South, 1865–1900* (Chapel Hill: University of North Carolina Press, 1993), 96–123.
79. Sumner's memory continued to be most potent in Massachusetts. The most significant and lasting public tribute to him was the statue in his honor in Boston sculpted by Thomas Ball; see Thomas Ball Letters, 1869–1882 (Ms. S-275), MHS.

Reporting from the South

Massachusetts Teachers and Freedmen's Education

AMY F. MORSMAN

On January 4, 1865, residents of the island community of Nantucket, Massachusetts, opened their local paper to learn the latest news of the war. On this day, however, they found something more, a letter from one of their own who was hundreds of miles to the south. Miss Anna Gardner had written straightaway to the *Nantucket Inquirer* in order to inform her northern neighbors of the progress that the Union was making within the Confederacy. She wrote not of battlefield exploits, but of the changing conditions of the freed slaves who were safe behind Union lines in eastern North Carolina. Gardner described this coastal area as "studded with schools for colored people." She proudly explained that "thousands of both children and adults" attended them, "manifest[ing] the greatest eagerness to pluck the hitherto 'forbidden fruit' of knowledge—and greedily devour[ing] every item of information which is communicated to them."[1] Anna Gardner was a teacher of the freed people. Her work, like that of many other Massachusetts civilians who descended on the South during the war and postwar years, focused on uplifting and reconstructing the lives of those who were most vulnerable in this conflict. Gardner's January 1865 letter reminded Bay Staters that the war effort and their potential involvement in it extended well beyond the battlefield to include issues of lasting social importance.

While by that time most Americans were optimistic about the Union's ultimate victory over the Confederacy, Gardner and other northern reformers were concerned about the problems that would persist or even intensify once the fighting was over. They knew that the consequences of massive slave liberation would be complicated and would create difficult circumstances for those who were trying to make new lives for themselves outside of slavery. These reformers sought to keep the northern public engaged in the struggles of the freed people and committed to helping them through the uncertainty of the postwar period. An examination of the letters of Anna Gardner and other Massachusetts freedmen's teachers helps to shed light on the lesser-known civilians from the state who experienced the war and its aftermath in the South firsthand in several ways. It provides a vivid sense of how Southerners—both black and white—reacted to the changes that the Confederate defeat engendered, exposes the priorities and prejudices of the northern aid agencies that sent these teachers to the war-torn region, and reveals the challenges the teachers faced in achieving their goals with the freed people. Scholars have made good use of sources such as these, demonstrating how, without ever bearing arms for the Union, these "soldiers of light and love" had a direct impact on a significant segment of southern society.[2]

In this essay I build on that scholarship but also pursue a somewhat different path. I shift the focus to the teachers' letters themselves, not only examining what they say about the long, complicated process of emancipation, but also asking, What did Northerners learn from this correspondence? How did the teachers, acting as conduits between the two regions, try to influence northern attitudes about the war and the important reform efforts being debated in Reconstruction? Americans had never experienced anything like this massive, costly civil war, and most Northerners had not fully anticipated the revolutionary consequences that it would bring to the institution of slavery. It is likely, then, that the critical issues developing hundreds of miles away in the war zone were quite unfamiliar to readers in places such as Nantucket, Boston, Springfield, and Pittsfield. Keeping track of loved ones in the military and cheering on armies made sense to those on the northern home front, but understanding the conditions in the war-torn South was more difficult. Just as, elsewhere in this volume, Ronald and Mary Zboray examine the powerful connections that Massachusetts soldiers maintained with their families through print, I explore how letters like the one Anna Gardner wrote in January 1865 might have enlightened northern readers about many aspects of the southern situation, and how the teachers' desire to connect their work to their home region contributes to a more complex understanding of postwar northern society.

Gardner's prose was not merely descriptive; it was also persuasive. She made a point of telling the readers of the *Nantucket Inquirer* what she thought was important for them to remember and to value in her letter. About the freedmen's schools she wrote, "Unique as every thing is in this city to the New Englander, he will find nothing of more startling and absorbing interest than these institutions of learning and the surrounding camps." "What a commentary they are on the past," she exclaimed, "and what a prophecy of the future!"[3] These were the elements of the war that now required Northerners' attention, and Gardner was not shy about saying so. Thus it is useful to view Gardner and other northern aid workers not just as teachers, but also as foreign correspondents. They devoted a tremendous amount of energy and time to bringing literacy and other basic competencies to masses of ignorant people in the South, but they also worked hard to convey the details of their mission to the people at home who were in a position to help. Their letters provided insight and commentary on what seemed like an alien culture in need of reform, and were intended to help make the distant South and its most pressing challenges more familiar to those at home.

Exploring the origins and evolution of the larger freedmen's aid movement in the North and the role that teachers played within it is essential to understanding how these men and women might have influenced other Northerners. Though the focus here is on Massachusetts, the humanitarian efforts that developed during the war were not solely based in the commonwealth; freedmen's aid societies cropped up in hundreds of communities across the North soon after the war began. Members of these organizations raised funds to send material support and teachers to Union-occupied areas where freed people were in need. Many of these societies had a strong religious identity and agenda. They used their connections to church congregations all across the country, not just in New England, to convince Americans to give generously to this cause during the war and its immediate aftermath. It was long thought that Northerners were solely responsible for this initiative, but more recent scholarship has revealed that Southerners, especially the freed people themselves, were substantially involved in their own uplift, much more so than historians had earlier believed. Former slaves pooled their meager funds and contributed their own labor and materials to build schools for their communities and hire teachers, a good number of whom came from the North. At the same time, however, southern blacks also depended on many of their own to lead the education effort.[4]

Massachusetts, and New England more generally, received the most credit early on for bolstering freedmen's education and the larger aid effort.[5] Perhaps that is because Bay Staters were among the first groups of aid workers heading into the South. They helped launch the Port Royal Experiment, a cooperative effort between Union military personnel and northern civilians to rehabilitate the communities of slaves abandoned by their masters on the Sea Islands after Union naval forces defeated the Confederates at Port Royal, South Carolina, in November 1861.[6]

It may also be because the secretary of the U.S. Treasury had tapped a Boston attorney named Edward Pierce to lead the Port Royal aid campaign. Northern readers almost certainly learned about his appointment and his work to organize a significant humanitarian response in New England. They also could read his observations on the situation firsthand in an article he wrote for the *Atlantic Monthly* in 1863. "They are learning that the world is not bounded north by Charleston, south by Savannah, west by Columbia, and east by the sea," Pierce wrote of the freed people he observed. "They are acquiring the knowledge of figures with which to do the business of life. They are singing the songs of freemen." Highlighting the remarkable strides the former slaves had made, Pierce instructed his northern audience to "remember that a little more than a twelvemonth ago they knew not a letter, and that for generations it has been a crime to teach their race; then contemplate what is now transpiring, and you have a scene which prophets and sages would have delighted to witness." Clearly Bay Staters were heavily involved in this aid work from the start, and they did not hesitate to emphasize its value in important sources of public commentary.[7]

Once the Union armies began making serious inroads into Confederate country, Northerners realized that the reforms they had initiated with the abandoned slaves at Port Royal would need to be expanded across the growing occupied territory. At this point, numerous freedmen's aid societies were established in northern cities, towns, and villages, following a long tradition of organized charity that had addressed a multitude of social needs across the region.[8] The New England Freedmen's Aid Society was one such group. Founded in 1862, it became one of the more prominent of these organizations and was certainly the most active in galvanizing interest for the freedmen's cause within Massachusetts. Based in Boston and involving well-established professionals, politicians, and reformers, this nonsectarian group channeled most of its energies into sustaining the teachers it sponsored in the field.[9]

Education was, of course, only one aspect of the lives of the freed people, and it was not the only concern the early aid societies had sought to address. But by 1863, when Northerners began discussing the burning question of the day—"What shall be done with the negro?"—they could not agree on the answer.[10] Many of them came to realize that helping slaves deal with the opportunities and challenges of freedom was a worthy undertaking, but they were not of one mind about the future of the freed people and their status within the nation.[11] Some argued that former slaves deserved special assistance to make the most of their liberation, while others believed that the country owed them nothing and should refrain from giving them votes, land, and protection. Though this debate lasted for years and took many forms, the one element of freedmen's aid around which most Northerners could rally was education.[12]

Several of the larger organizations published their own newspapers or periodicals, and these publications made their highest priority clear: to capture the northern public's attention and keep it focused on education in particular.[13] In the first issue of the *Freedmen's Record*, the organ of the New England Freedmen's Aid Society, its editors explained that their chief aim was the material, logistical, and emotional support of every teacher in the field, and they emphasized that this work could not go forward without the help of generous civilians on the home front.[14]

This kind of fundraising plea appeared in every issue of the *Freedmen's Record*, but that is not all that filled its pages. The society also explained their careful process for finding suitable teachers: screening candidates based on high standards for health, maturity, experience, and moral and religious grounding and requiring that every candidate come to Boston to be interviewed by the society's teachers' committee.[15] They did not hesitate to lay the responsibility for educating the freed people squarely on the backs of New Englanders, but they did so in a confident and celebratory fashion. Building on Northerners' pride in their school system, the *Record* declared that "New England can furnish teachers enough—men and women with minds trained in her own common schools, and hearts glowing with enthusiasm to repair the wrongs done to the colored race for a century." Their region, the editors proclaimed in January 1865, could "make another New England of the whole South; and, God helping, we will not pause in our work until the free-school system . . . has been established from Maryland to Florida, and all along the shores of the Gulf,— once black with slavery and ignorance, now flaming with war."[16]

The editors' confidence was not unwarranted; New Englanders—scores of them from Massachusetts—did come forward for this mission. In December 1865 the New England Society reported having 140 teachers in the field, touching the lives of ten thousand students, young and old. Its army of teachers numbered more than a hundred for every subsequent year until 1871, when it placed 71 teachers in the South to educate approximately three thousand pupils.[17]

Once it found eager volunteers, the New England Society had an organizational infrastructure in place to maximize their usefulness in both the South and the North. It sent these teachers where they were most needed among the freed people and also arranged for each one of its smaller branch societies, mainly within Massachusetts, essentially to adopt a teacher, developing a closer relationship with that educator and doing what it could to ensure his or her success. Teachers were encouraged to correspond with the society's teachers' committee in Boston as well as with the members of the auxiliary that was sponsoring them, thus establishing strong, useful channels of communication between the regions.

As a result, the society received abundant mail from all over the South. Instead of filing these teachers' reports away, the society incorporated the most interesting parts of them into every issue of the *Freedmen's Record*, anticipating that the more New Englanders knew about the conditions in the South and the work of the organization, the more they would want to get involved. In the first issue, the editors wrote that for the first three years of the New England Society's existence the organization had done little to advertise its purpose and goals, but confessed, "We now see reason to regret that we did not long ago give them the largest publicity."[18] Eleven issues later, the editors were gratified to see that the *Record* had "done its work in thus diffusing knowledge and interest throughout the community." Whereas at the beginning of 1865 twenty-two branch societies were affiliated with the larger New England organization, by December there were more than seventy.[19]

In that same issue, the society shared the thoughts of an officer in one of its largest and most active branches, who recognized the value of the *Record* but wished that it could do even more. Miss Anna Lowell, secretary of the Roxbury auxiliary, commented that the paper had "done much good in enlightening the public mind, with regard to the great work which is going on for the benefit of the freedmen, and the need of increased zeal in its behalf," but she noted that it was circulating "not so widely as it should" and hoped that subscriptions would increase so that the society could reach more people and therefore have a greater impact.[20] Members of this prominent aid organization recognized that the freedmen's teachers were important beyond the scope of their work in the South. They were absolutely vital in keeping this humanitarian movement going, but only if they communicated the salient details of their missions, the "facts of public interest," to the people of the North.[21]

The members of the society's teachers' committee and the editors of the *Freedmen's Record* did an admirable job of relaying meaningful and moving stories about the teachers and their students to the reading public. For example, the society often highlighted the correspondence it received from Harriet Jacobs, the famous author and runaway slave. After finishing her memoir, *Incidents in the Life of a Slave Girl*, in 1861, Jacobs had traveled to Washington, D.C., to assist the thousands of black refugees who were languishing near the capital; she soon opened the Jacobs Free School and wrote to the New England Society expressing gratitude for its help with that process. As soon as the *Freedmen's Record* was up and running in early 1865, its editors used the space to show off this now notable woman's contribution to their cause. They reminded northern readers of Jacobs's harrowing tale of slavery and escape and then brought her story full circle by describing her triumph as a leader to her people near the nation's capital. "Was any dream of the night dearer and sweeter to her than the present reality," the editors asked, "—her people freed, and the school-house, built mainly by her own exertions, named in her honor, and presided over by black and white teachers, working harmoniously together?"[22]

The editors did not stop there, however. They used other aspects of Jacobs's current circumstances to shame Bay Staters into further action. "This woman, this lady, —who for years has been treated as a friend in the family of one of our celebrated literary men, and who has won the respect and love of all who have associated with her,—cannot ride in the streetcars at Washington, and is insulted even in a concert-room in Boston, on account of the slight tinge of color in her skin." "We have made great progress," they concluded, "but much yet remains to be done." Indeed, "much yet" in both the Confederacy *and* the Union.[23]

Harriet Jacobs was not the typical freedmen's teacher, however. By 1865 she was a celebrity in certain circles in New England, whereas the vast majority of educators had never made a name for themselves beyond or even within their home communities and would dwell in obscurity their whole lives. These were ordinary people, but they were well qualified for an extraordinary task. The New England Society's screening standards suggest that they were likely educated, experienced, and equipped to handle the particular challenges of working with former slaves. In fact, the society made it clear that those whom they sent to the South would need to be prepared for much more than they might ever have encountered in schoolrooms in the North. The editors of the *Record* explained that their definition of "teacher" did not mean "those solely who are expected to teach the ordinary branches of school education." Rather, "all are expected to give instruction in those arts of civilized life which the negro needs quite as much as book-learning," including "lessons of industry, of domestic management and thrift, lessons of truth and honesty, lessons which may help their pupils (children and adults) to unlearn the teachings of slavery."[24]

The individuals selected for this purpose may have shared these qualifications, but they were actually a diverse group. Though many Americans at the time referred to the teachers as "Yankee schoolmarms," those from the North did not all come from New England, nor were they all women. Research also suggests that even the New Englanders included blacks as well as whites, males as well as females, mature as well as young people.[25]

The teachers also came from a variety of backgrounds and approached the work with different motivations. Many felt a sense of religious purpose and answered the call that came from their churches and missionary associations, while others viewed a stint in the South as an opportunity for adventure or a practical way to earn a little money. A smaller subset believed that Confederate defeat and emancipation had created the best conditions for establishing true racial equality, and they saw teaching among the freed people as a way to bring that about. What drove the Northerners to the work also affected how long they remained committed to it. Though plenty were motivated by some feeling of duty, the vast majority of these teachers lacked a radical, or even very strong, interest in reform, and so it is not surprising that most of them remained at their posts for only two to three years. Some, though, did not have a choice in the matter; they returned home when funds dwindled and their teaching positions were not renewed. And a rather startling number of Northerners were unable to continue their work because disease and fatigue, the two primary hazards of the job, cut short their lives.[26]

Regardless of who the teachers were or how long they served, the New England Freedmen's Aid Society eagerly received their reports and sought to share their stories with the larger public through the *Freedmen's Record*. As time passed and the situation in the South evolved, the teachers' experiences changed, and consequently so did what they wrote about for northern audiences. The war established one set of conditions in which they labored; Reconstruction created another. Wartime teachers were responding to a new humanitarian crisis in the midst of a great national emergency; they therefore felt supported by the Union military and their communities back home and were buoyed by a sense of patriotism. Those who served the freed people after the war faced different issues and different attitudes among Americans in both the South and the North.

The editors of the *Freedmen's Record* captured this important shift. "How changed is the prospect within the last twelve months!" they wrote in the September 1865 issue. "Then, we were trembling, though in hope, at the approaching election, on whose issue depended the questions of national life or death. Now, the nationality is saved; but the great questions of reconstruction and universal justice are not yet answered." Though postwar policies were still in flux, it was clear that the job of the aid societies was not over; in fact, it became more important than ever once the conflict had officially ended and all slaves had been freed. "Our special work is immensely enlarged by this progress," the *Record* noted in September 1865. "Instead of a few islands or border towns, where we could plant straggling schools, the whole broad field is now thrown open to us: from every quarter comes the call for help."[27]

The society was also keenly aware of how central its concerns were to the discussion everywhere about the future place of the freed people in American society. The *Record* maintained that education was entwined in all the public debates about extending suffrage to black men: "Every negro who can read is an argument for the ballot for him. . . . If it is denied him, he will need all the civilizing power of education, all the influence of judicious friends, to show him that his rights may yet be gained without violence or ruin."[28] These arguments made good sense and underscored the importance of maintaining or even increasing the number of teachers in the South at war's end.

This was, however, precisely the point when the freedmen's aid movement began to lose its momentum. Abolition societies were disbanding, and their successors, the aid organizations, began to feel the pinch of waning interest and declining resources. This process was gradual, but even within a year after the Confederate defeat, some groups were experiencing financial trouble, and by 1870 many had ceased to exist for want of funds.[29] The New England Society was the longest lasting regional organization, but by 1872 it too struggled with raising money and had to cut drastically the number of teachers it could employ in the South.[30]

Of course, Northerners never expected these organizations to last forever. Indeed, they had been created to address a specific problem, and the members themselves looked forward to the joyous day when they could disband, for that would mean southern communities were successfully educating the freed people on their own. The New England Society, like other northern groups, intended to withdraw its aid gradually as the former slaves "became able to stand on their own two feet." In their minds, this "was the way to make [them] manly and self-reliant." Many members of the society were pleased that they could send fewer teachers, supplies, and money to the region because southern states and the families of students were embracing those educational responsibilities themselves. Others from the North worried that it was too early to begin withdrawing the teaching corps and that the institutions they had created would suffer under the supervision of Southerners. As their schools were consolidated or were folded into new public educational systems, supporters of freedman's aid felt both a sense of accomplishment about the work they had done and uncertainty about the legacy of their investment.[31]

As the number of teachers diminished, so did the financial donations that Northerners gave to the freedman's aid movement. There is no easy explanation for why this decline in philanthropy happened when it did. Perhaps after enduring a bloody four-year war along with the assassination of their president, Northerners wanted to focus on peace and turn their attention to other issues. With abolition accomplished, freed people may not have seemed such a burning concern to a growing number of them. While Union victory in April 1865 brought a welcome relief to the northern public, for southern whites the outcome of the war was devastating. They did not allow defeat and emancipation to keep them down for long, however. By 1866 they were taking steps to reassert their economic, social, and political dominance in the region, while at the same time the freed people were asserting their autonomy. Conflicts, big and small, developed as a result.[32] These postwar circumstances made freedmen's teachers' jobs even more challenging and their outreach to the northern public all the more important.

Anna Gardner was present in the South as a freedmen's teacher during the war as well as Reconstruction, and her correspondence reflects the changing circumstances of this period. Raised a Quaker on Nantucket, Gardner became a staunch abolitionist in her young adult years. She was involved in the island's antislavery organization and played a central role in organizing the 1841 antislavery convention at which Frederick Douglass was invited to give his first public speech. Gardner also taught black students on Nantucket for many years in the antebellum period and succeeded in integrating the local high school despite considerable opposition. By the time she shifted her focus to educating freed people, she was middle-aged, an experienced teacher and reformer, and no stranger to racial controversy. During the war, she worked in eastern North Carolina. After the war, the New England Freedmen's Aid Society sent her to Charlottesville, Virginia, where she labored until 1871, when conflicts with local whites led to her transfer to communities further south.[33]

Throughout these years, Gardner was a steadfast correspondent with Ednah Dow Cheney, the head of the New England Society's teachers' committee, and she was a regular participant in the teachers' receptions the society hosted in Boston every summer. She was also a favorite of the editors of the *Freedmen's Record,* who frequently published all or part of her reports in their publication. She took many opportunities to share her perspective on the former slaves' situation with Northerners, either in person when she was home for vacation, or in print through the *Freedmen's Record* or her hometown paper, the *Nantucket Inquirer.*[34]

In the letters she wrote during the war, Gardner celebrated the freed people she had come to know in New Bern, North Carolina. She marveled at their ambition, their creativity, and the remarkable strides they had achieved in such a short time in school. For example, she made the Emancipation Day celebration put on by local blacks on January 1, 1865, the focus of her report to the teachers' committee that month. She described the magnificent parade of freed people representing each school and every Union League chapter in the New Bern area. The day was one of "thrilling emotions and sympathetic rejoicing" as once ignorant slaves displayed through orations and exhibitions the knowledge they had gained since emancipation. Gardner claimed that these people were fast approaching the levels of competency held by their white oppressors, and she wished that "the eyes of sceptical Northerners who think the negro incapable of receiving our civilization" could have seen this sight. She also emphasized that "this grand celebration, in design and execution, was wholly the work of colored people; they having completed all their arrangements without need of aid (except pecuniarily) from their white friends." Then she asked, "What more convincing evidence do we need of their ability 'to help themselves'?"[35]

Gardner's vivid description of the parade and her final question seem designed to inform as well as provoke readers in the North. By using the collective "we," she may have intended to make her countrymen feel a part of her cause, while also calling on them to invest even more in the efforts to reconstruct the South. Gardner's comments were just what the *Freedmen's Record* was looking for, and northern readers would find her entire letter published in the paper's very next issue.

In the years that followed, Gardner continued to praise her hardworking, creative pupils, but her focus fell more on the mounting difficulties developing for freedmen's aid workers in the postwar South. When she was transferred to Charlottesville, local whites refused to give her lodging, so Gardner made a home in the military barracks. She was, at least initially, the lone white northern woman amid hundreds of Union soldiers and black government dependents. The freed people quickly came to comfort and support Gardner, but the white community remained hostile to her throughout her years in Virginia because of her mission among their former slaves, and perhaps also because her work challenged Southerners' sense of appropriate gender roles. She could tolerate the personal snubs, but she grew angry when residents of Charlottesville tried to prevent her students from attending school or made it difficult for the former slaves to earn a living wage or exercise their political and social rights.

For instance, at the end of Gardner's first academic year in Charlottesville, she and her students prepared a School Examination, a culminating event that was open to the local public and allowed the freed people to demonstrate what they had learned. Gardner sent word of the event to the *Charlottesville Chronicle,* asking the newspaper to advertise the program and send someone to attend and report on the event favorably. According to the *Chronicle*'s editor, James C. Southall, Gardner had blamed the paper for exacerbating "the prejudices existing in this community" toward educating the freed people and toward the teachers who instructed them, and she had suggested that the editor could help to "modify" those prejudices by reporting on the School Examination. Southall took issue with Gardner's characterization of the paper's attitude toward freedman's education: "We expressed a 'prejudice' against persons, who came on here to teach the negroes, going on to Washington and petitioning for the sending back here of the military who had just been ordered away. And we also exhibited a prejudice against white people associating on equal terms with negroes." Southall pointed out that "these things are distinct from instructing negroes, which we warmly approve of." For Gardner, relating to the freed people as equals was an essential part of her educational mission. Her vision of "instructing negroes" was clearly not the same as Southall's, and she thought it wise to let northern readers see in black and white the views of vocal southern whites on this issue. She sent all her correspondence with Southall to Boston, where the *Freedmen's Record* happily published it under an appropriate title, "The World Moves, but Moves Slowly."[36]

Less than a year later, Gardner asked the *Record* to publish even more debate between herself and Southall on the purpose of the freedmen's aid movement and the proper kind of education for Charlottesville blacks. In February 1867, in anticipation of her students' graduation, Gardner wrote to Southall requesting that he donate paper certificates or diplomas acknowledging the graduates' readiness to teach others "the rudiments of an English education." Taken aback by the temerity of this northern woman, in his reply Southall claimed "a deep . . . interest in the welfare of the negro race" but expressed concern over the kind of education that local freed people were actually getting at Gardner's Jefferson School. "The impression among the white residents of C-ville is, that your instruction of the colored people . . . contemplates something more than the communication of the ordinary knowledge implied in teaching them to read, write, cipher, &c.," Southall wrote. He accused Gardner of presenting "politics and sociology" and of coming into the Charlottesville community "not merely as an ordinary school teacher, but as a political missionary; [and] that you communicate to the colored people ideas of social equality with the whites." This he regarded as "mischievous, and as only tending to disturb the good feeling between the two races." To be fair, Southall acknowledged the possibility that he was mistaken about what Gardner did in the classroom, but he declared that if he was right about her intentions as a teacher, he would not supply the requested diplomas, for he could not "subject myself to the implication of countenancing your conduct."[37]

Gardner's brief reply quoted the Golden Rule: "I teach fundamental principles of 'politics' and 'sociology,' viz.:—'Whatsoever ye would that men should do to you, do ye even so unto them.'" She signed her letter

"Yours in behalf of truth and justice."[38] She likely hoped that the northern readers of the *Freedmen's Record* would see things more her way.

Gardner's clashes with Southall were not the worst of it in Charlottesville. Powerful whites sought to keep freed blacks down at every turn. This was particularly troubling for Gardner, who as their teacher watched ambitious, responsible freed people devote themselves to learning only to have their employers punish them for it by firing them or withholding their pay. She had anticipated that education and suffrage would increase the "self-respect and manliness" of the former slaves, and she had hoped that the "industry and perseverance" they exhibited in their jobs would make them self-sufficient during the winter of 1867–68. But at this point, only a few years after the war, most of her students and their families remained vulnerable and oppressed. She blamed both the resilient "secessionist element of the South" and northern politicians who failed to make good on their bold plans for reforming the former Confederate states. Her home region had let them all down. "But, alas for our country!" Gardner exclaimed. The results she expected from Reconstruction would have come if "the chosen representatives of the people [had] been true to their trusts; had they clutched the golden opportunity which God vouchsafed them, to bless mankind, of every shade of complexion, and every condition of society."[39] Gardner was wise to share her disappointment with society members in the North and with the readers of the *Freedmen's Record*, for it seemed that outrage was increasingly required to get them to move.

Anna Gardner remained in the South for another decade, and though she helped countless freed people gain an education and become teachers themselves, conditions there were never conducive to the kind of changes she hoped Reconstruction would bring.[40] In fact, the friction between her and ascendant whites of Charlottesville continued and ultimately caused her to lose her position as head teacher of the Jefferson School for freed people in 1871.[41] Her colleague Philena Carkin, a native of Lowell, Massachusetts, characterized her as too antagonistic toward the local whites. In her memoir, she described Gardner as "uncompromisingly radical" and "too outspoken," and she wondered if Gardner might have had an easier time in Charlottesville had she been more diplomatic with white Southerners.[42] But that was not Anna Gardner's way. The New England Freedmen's Aid Society ultimately found a place for Gardner in a freedmen's school in Elizabeth City, North Carolina, and later sent her to Camden, South Carolina. She finally returned to the North in 1878.

Well before that time, one of Gardner's main channels of communication, the *Freedmen's Record,* had ceased publication. As the New England Freedmen's Aid Society struggled to stay alive, it had to cut expenses. It shut the *Record* down in the late 1860s and closed its own doors in 1874 for financial reasons. Some teachers whom the society had placed in rural areas of the South pleaded for the organization to stay in operation, while others in urban centers assured its officers that their schools would survive if relinquished to the state-run systems of public education developing in the southern states. Society members rationalized that their eleven years of work in the freedmen's aid movement had created lasting institutions that had enhanced countless lives, even if there was more work to be done.[43] They believed that their endeavors would live on in the South through these schools and the small number of northern teachers who remained in the field, yet they failed to consider how the society's closing would affect the northern public's connection to the movement, the freed people, and the larger project of Reconstruction. Who would continue to inform northern readers about the ongoing educational efforts or the obstacles that freed people were still navigating in the tricky social, economic, and political terrain of the postwar South? The burden of that task would fall to a much smaller group of teachers and aid workers who remained there permanently.

While Anna Gardner served considerably longer and was a more vocal advocate for the freed people than most northern teachers, another Massachusetts native, Caroline F. Putnam, fulfilled the role of foreign correspondent for decades more. A reformer who moved south after the war, she enjoyed a long life among the freed people in northern Virginia and maintained a vibrant correspondence on this topic with Northerners for many years. Unlike Gardner and most other teachers, she was not sponsored by any official freedmen's aid organization, and though she was a Christian woman her decision to teach in the South was influenced far more by her egalitarian racial convictions than by any sense of religious mission. Putnam also embraced the role of teacher somewhat late; as she was arriving in the fall of 1868, many other northern educators, who had begun their service during the war, were headed home too tired or poor to continue the effort. Putnam made Lottsburg, Virginia, a rural community in the state's Northern Neck, her residence for forty-nine years. She died there in 1917 and was buried across the road from the Holley School, which she had founded and named in honor of her companion, Sallie Holley.[44]

In all that time, Putnam frequently sent long letters to her northern friends and important organizational contacts, who helped support her school in a variety of ways. Like Anna Gardner, she intended these letters to be tools of persuasion, and not just for her most intimate circle. This was a practice she had begun years before the war. Putnam had been born in Massachusetts, reached maturity in New York, attended Oberlin College, and traveled throughout the Northeast during the antebellum period promoting the antislavery lectures of Sallie Holley. She published reports about their travels and the public's reception of Holley's lectures in the *National Anti-Slavery Standard,* the weekly newspaper of William Lloyd Garrison's American Anti-Slavery Society. When Putnam became a teacher, she turned again to that newspaper as a platform to express her opinions about the freed people with whom she worked, their progress, and their proper place in postwar society.[45]

It was essential for Putnam to keep her supporters informed because through their donations they were her school's lifeline. She did not come to Virginia through the sponsorship of a large relief organization; in fact, it is not quite clear how she was able to finance her school year after year, except that her extant letters include continual attempts to tap into her connections with abolitionists for fundraising purposes. Thus it made sense for Putnam to highlight the successes of her pupils in her private and public letters to the North, but it was equally important to make her benefactors aware of the difficulties her students faced. At first glance, the stories she shared with northern readers seem similar to those written by Anna Gardner, but most of them included a greater level of detail and displayed an even stronger tone and intensity. Putnam, like Gardner, was deeply disturbed by the racial oppression her students and their families suffered. She argued that these people, along with her northern donors, were what made her school a long-lasting success, and she openly marveled at the strength and ingenuity they exhibited while enduring great poverty and discrimination.

After living in Lottsburg for only a few months, Putnam sent a long, powerful letter to the *National Anti-Slavery Standard* that highlighted for Northerners some conditions that were unique to the postwar South.[46] She wrote the letter in December 1868, after making a holiday visit to the Thompsons, a family of freed people whom she knew through her school. Putnam reported that with the New Year fast approaching, they were quite anxious, for at this time every year freed people had to negotiate new labor contracts with their employers. While Americans in other parts of the country were looking forward to a festive day of new beginnings on January 1, former slaves wondered about the work conditions they might face with their next employer and the conflicts that could develop in the contract negotiation process. In this particular year, they had even greater reason for concern, because less than two months before the black men of Lottsburg had voted in their first election, and they had overwhelmingly supported Ulysses S. Grant. Henry Thompson was one of these, and he was going to pay a price for his vote. He told Putnam that he was going to lose his job and the house his family had been renting on account of his employer-landlord's distaste for his political activity.[47] Thompson defended his right to vote and even asked his landlord if he valued his ability to do the same.

In her letter to the *Standard*, Putnam expressed pride in Thompson for asserting himself with his spiteful employer, but she emphasized the concern and the fury she felt over his vulnerable situation. Here was a hardworking freedman, a politically engaged citizen, a trustee of her school, and a father with "rows and rows of children, big and little" who were about to lose their home. Putnam hoped to make northern readers appreciate Henry Thompson's crisis and understand that becoming truly free was a long, dangerous process that required everyone's vigilance and support.

Putnam may have decided to give this family a central place in her letter after seeing firsthand how another Northerner reacted to the situation. When she visited the Thompson home, she brought her friend and benefactor Colonel Charles W. Folsom, a former Union army officer and civil engineer who had recently arrived from Massachusetts. According to Putnam, Folsom became highly distressed after meeting the Thompson family. He worried about "all those humble children" being turned out of their home—"for the sake of choosing Grant President!" He wished aloud to be able to "show that sight" to some of his conservative friends in the North who were uninformed and ambivalent about the process of reconstructing the South: "Think of that family of twelve children, liable to be turned out shelterless, . . . because their father must vote as he thought best for their good!" Imagining how his friends back in Massachusetts might respond if they had the chance to meet Henry Thompson, Folsom told Putnam, "I think they would be converted, hear his sensible talk and put themselves in his place." Putnam shared this exchange with Folsom in her letter to the *Standard*. She wanted readers to see that he was clearly affected by his encounter with the Thompsons and, more important, that he was moved to action. Before returning to New England, Folsom provided the finances and materials necessary to help Henry Thompson establish himself as a shoemaker, an occupation for which Henry already demonstrated great ability. Caroline Putnam knew that most other Northerners would not have the benefit of witnessing what Folsom had seen in Lottsburg that December. His response, though, likely shaped her expectations for how other Northerners might react, if only she could effectively relay to them the Thompsons' and other former slaves' complicated emancipation story.

Putnam aimed to do that by keeping the spotlight on "these loyal people" in the correspondence she sent north for publication. Just one month later, another letter appeared in the *Standard*. In this one, Putnam reminded her readers of African Americans' wartime service and sacrifice, and she argued that Northerners were obligated to respond in kind during this struggle in Reconstruction. "Who is going to stand by [the freed people] and help them bear it?" she asked. "Now let Republicans see to it their devoted allies suffer no further persecution by this cruel deprivation of a free-hold. Let every officer and soldier who was gladdened by the sight of a black face, in *his* need during the struggle of war, now eagerly put forth his might to relieve his faithful friend and brother!"[48] Putnam failed to realize, though, that many northern men may have never looked upon African Americans as their "faithful friend and brother," at least not outside the context of war. Her public appeals did not elicit the response she desired. Not only was the larger northern public unmoved by her calls for action, but the Republican politicians driving Reconstruction policy in Washington seemed content with only half measures that fell short of really enforcing the important legacies of emancipation. It seems that eventually Putnam abandoned the press as part of her reform strategy and focused instead on the relationships she could cultivate with individual Northerners through private letters.

This more direct form of correspondence lasted for decades, and it required that Putnam strike a better balance between the good news and the bad coming out of the South. The people who remained long-term supporters of the Holley School came primarily from the social networks that Putnam and Holley had built within the antebellum antislavery movement; these were networks that also included supporters of woman's rights and temperance reform. They donated not just money, but also an amazing variety of materials—books, magazines, clothes, shoes, paintings, plants, and more—that might be useful for the school, the students, and their families.

Though most of these supporters were ideologically in sync with Putnam and her radical reform agenda, like donors today they still needed assurances that their aid was fulfilling its intended purpose. Putnam was therefore careful to express her tremendous gratitude for their generosity and to relay anecdotes showing how strong they were making her school community.[49]

Her letters to the May family of Leicester, Massachusetts, provide the most useful and abundant examples of how the charity of some Northerners and the welfare of Putnam's school fed off of one another. From the late 1870s through the 1890s, she maintained a frequent correspondence with Samuel May Jr., along with his wife, Sarah, and their two grown daughters. Samuel May, a former Unitarian minister and general agent of the Massachusetts Anti-Slavery Society, most likely knew Putnam from their shared antislavery work before she moved to Virginia.[50] He was also active in the New England Freedmen's Aid Society, serving as the president of its Leicester branch,[51] but it seems that over the years he and his family channeled the lion's share of their charity to Putnam and the freed people of Lottsburg. It may also be that the Mays, longtime supporters of woman's rights, were fond of Putnam, because as a strong, independent woman and freedmen's teacher she embodied much of their reform agenda. They regularly sent large boxes of goods and warm notes of moral support to the Holley School while periodically making monetary contributions.

As a way of expressing her appreciation for the Mays' assistance, Putnam wrote letters detailing not only how their aid physically nourished the teachers and students and strengthened the school's academic mission, but also how their charity helped foster greater independence among the freed people. The contents of their packages became a kind of currency at the Holley School, which Putnam used to trade with blacks for their goods and services. When her pupils' parents came looking for coats, hats, dresses, shoes, and quilts that Northerners such as the Mays had donated, they paid for them with chickens and eggs for the teachers' table and guano for their garden, or by offering to gather kindling for the schoolhouse fires, do the laundry, or plant potatoes in Putnam's garden.[52] Relaying this information to the Mays and perhaps others like them sent a clear message that the freed people associated with the Holley School were not dependents looking for a handout. They were responsible adults who had skills and energy all their own to contribute to the school community. They were also caring parents who took their children's education seriously.

Given the longevity of the May family's relationship with Putnam's school, it seems likely that her rich letters kept them invested for quite a while in the freedmen's aid movement. No one can know for sure, though, since only Putnam's side of their correspondence has survived. Fortunately, a few letters from other Massachusetts residents remain, and they offer at least some sense of the direct effect that the outreach of a freedmen's teacher could have.

Abigail Alcott, mother of the famous author Louisa May Alcott and a cousin of Samuel May Jr., came to support the freedmen's aid movement because of her previous involvement in antislavery reform.[53] Like the Mays, Alcott was also involved in the postwar woman's rights movement and in charitable organizations in her community of Concord, Massachusetts. As a member of the Union Bible Society, a female sewing group that donated its proceeds to charitable causes, Alcott alerted the rest of the women to the needs of Putnam's school. In the 1870s she encouraged them to clean out their cupboards and help fill a barrel with their donated household items and clothing.[54] When it arrived in Lottsburg, Putnam wrote a very gracious letter of thanks to the Concord society, with a level of detail similar to that of her letters to the Mays. Abigail Alcott was an elderly woman and may have anticipated garnering only enough interest among her society members to make a one-time contribution to the freed people of Lottsburg. What developed, however, was a long-distance relationship between their school and this charitable organization that lasted for at least fifteen years, and it is quite likely that the messages Putnam sent from the South kept these northern women interested in a cause that had for the most part already petered out.

Abigail Alcott died in 1877, but Louisa May encouraged the Concord bible society to continue donating to the freedmen's aid movement. A few months later the members sent another barrel full of helpful items for Putnam's school. It included a note from the secretary of the society, Miss Ellen Emerson, explaining that she had also enclosed an autograph by her father, Ralph Waldo Emerson, which she thought could be sold for the benefit of the school. According to her, the society had been moved by Putnam's generous descriptions of the institution, the sustained commitment to it by the local freed people, and how the charitable efforts of Northerners like themselves were helping to complete the process of emancipation. "The society has often heard your letters and feels a most affectionate interest in your work and in those individuals whose stories you have from time to time written," she wrote.[55]

The real people of Lottsburg—students as well as parents—captivated these women. They appreciated Putnam's perspective as a Northerner in the South, but they were especially gratified to hear directly from some of her students, whom she encouraged to write their own letters of thanks to the society. "The letters you have sent . . . have been just the right thing," Emerson wrote to Putnam in 1879, adding "Will you please tell the children that their pretty little notes were a most agreeable surprise to us, and every one of the ladies wanted to read every one of the notes with their own eyes."[56] It is easy to imagine these middle- and upper-class white women in Concord eagerly putting aside their knitting to pass the letters from Lottsburg around at their monthly meetings. At least this small group had been touched by Putnam's efforts to keep the campaign for freedmen's aid and education going. At least it was aware that the former slaves were not only appreciative of northern support but also anxious to make the most of their lives through hard work and self-improvement.

But how many other Northerners ever came in epistolary contact with devoted teachers such as Caroline Putnam or paid attention to their reports in the newspapers? It is worth asking: How far, both literally and figuratively, did the messages of these freedmen's teachers go? Who were the Northerners who actually received these messages, and how did they affect them? The available sources offer no satisfactory answer to these questions. Almost all of the correspondence examined here is one-sided; it conveys what information teachers sent north but offers precious little about how Northerners responded. It is difficult to determine how many readers were aware of the evolving freedmen's aid movement. While many Northerners followed current events by regularly reading newspapers, few among the larger public followed the publications that carried freedmen's teachers' letters and reports. Given their ties to abolition and freedmen's aid organizations, it makes sense that educators such as Gardner and Putnam chose to publish most of their correspondence in the *Freedmen's Record* and the *National Anti-Slavery Standard,* but these were not the best choice for those who were trying to influence a large northern audience. By writing to these reform-oriented papers, the teachers were essentially preaching to a choir that was getting smaller by the year.[57]

When nineteenth-century photographers tried to capture the essence of the freedmen's aid movement, they often took pictures of teachers with their students crowded around a schoolhouse door, or of a teacher with a book and a small child in her lap.[58] It might be more useful to envision these men and women with pen and paper, bent over a candle at night writing to people hundreds of miles away. Caroline Putnam and Anna Gardner spent countless hours doing just that. Both were extraordinary women who went to great lengths to educate the freed people as well as keep them and their situation on the minds of Americans who had once been sympathetic to their plight. As foreign correspondents, they and other teachers informed Northerners about many things. Some of their letters contain rich descriptions of the southern countryside, including scarred battlefields, massive burial grounds, dilapidated plantations, and majestic natural scenery.[59] Others expose their frustrations with life in the South: the politics and the people, and sometimes even the freedmen. In fact, these northern teachers, even the most radical of them, were creatures of their time and were thus inclined toward some level of racism. Some of their letters reflect their own limited thinking about the freed people and the long-lasting effects of slavery upon them.

Overall, though, their letters seem to have been written with a consistent pointed message. For both Gardner and Putnam, the biggest challenges they saw in the South did not lie with the freed people, regardless of how disadvantaged they were. In their minds and in the correspondence they sent north, the freed people were not the problem in the postwar period; the problem was everyone else.

As Caroline Putnam, Anna Gardner, and the members of the New England Freedmen's Aid Society attest, the aid movement came into existence at a key point in the process of emancipation and involved hundreds of devoted people, some of whom not only had a powerful influence on the South but also tried to extend that impact to the North. They believed that the benefits of freedmen's education could have a broader transformative effect on attitudes throughout the whole country, and they felt moved to share that conviction publicly. They also wanted to emphasize that in order for the Reconstruction of the South to be a success, the freed people would need a fair chance to complete the process of emancipation.

Getting that opportunity, however, was not entirely up to them or to the teachers with whom they worked. Southerners would need to allow this process to happen, and Northerners would need to ensure that it occurred. Ultimately, neither group behaved as the teachers believed it should. When assessing the outcomes of Reconstruction, most historians agree that this attempt to remake the South failed not only because of the stubborn resistance of conservative white Southerners, but because white Northerners lost interest in the former slaves and in bringing about lasting change.⁶⁰ Massachusetts teachers such as Anna Gardner and Caroline Putnam tried to keep this from happening, but their voices were likely too small to attract much attention amid the larger transformations taking place at the time. That does not detract, of course, from the great service they did for so many freed people.

NOTES

I thank Barbara White of Nantucket, Massachusetts, for her very generous research assistance about Anna Gardner. I am also grateful to the staff of the Massachusetts Historical Society for their assistance and support through the Malcolm and Mildred Freiberg Fellowship and to Middlebury College for helping fund my research through an Undergraduate Collaborative Research Grant and a Long-Term Professional Development Grant.

1. Letter from Anna Gardner, *Nantucket Inquirer,* January 4, 1865.
2. For scholarship on the freedmen's aid movement see Jacqueline Jones, *Soldiers of Light and Love: Northern Teachers and Georgia Blacks* (Chapel Hill: University of North Carolina Press, 1980); James McPherson, *The Struggle for Equality: Abolitionists and the Negro in the Civil War and Reconstruction* (Princeton: Princeton University Press, 1964), chaps. 7 and 17; Julie Roy Jeffrey, *The Great Silent Army of Abolitionism: Ordinary Women in the Antislavery Movement* (Chapel Hill: University of North Carolina Press, 1998), chap. 6; Ronald Butchart, *Schooling the Freed People: Teaching, Learning, and the Struggle for Black Freedom, 1861–1876* (Chapel Hill: University of North Carolina Press, 2010); Carol Faulkner, *Women's Radical Reconstruction: The Freedmen's Aid Movement* (Philadelphia: University of Pennsylvania Press, 2003).
3. Letter from Anna Gardner, *Nantucket Inquirer,* January 4, 1865.
4. Butchart, *Schooling the Freed People,* 82–86. Butchart found that the number of teachers from the South, both black and white, actually dwarfed the number from New England.
5. Ibid., x–xii. Butchart determined that white residents of New England constituted only a fraction of the northern teachers who worked in freedmen's schools. But though their numbers may have been comparatively small, their influence in organizational life and public discussion of freedmen's aid was significant, and this was likely aided by the reputation of Massachusetts as a strong supporter of the abolition movement.
6. Akiko Ochiai, "The Port Royal Experiment Revisited: Northern Visions of Reconstruction and the Land Question," *New England Quarterly* 74 (March 2001): 94–95. Technically, the cause of freedmen's relief began at Fort Monroe, Virginia, where Union forces first gained a foothold, but the efforts to aid former slaves as part of the Port Royal Experiment were much more substantial.
7. Edward L. Pierce, "The Freedmen at Port Royal," *Atlantic Monthly* 12 (September 1863): 307–8. Susan Goodman shows that many influential activists used the *Atlantic* as a forum for their concerns; she describes the periodical as the "conscience of the American public" at the time. Even though it never reached above 50,000 subscribers, the *Atlantic* was still quite influential among northern readers because of the high profile of the authors who contributed to it. Susan Goodman, *Republic of Words: The Atlantic Monthly and*

Its Writers, 1857–1925 (Hanover, N.H.: University Press of New England, 2011), ix–xii.
8. On the history of charitable organizations in New England, see Conrad Edick Wright, *The Transformation of Charity in Postrevolutionary New England* (Boston: Northeastern University Press, 1992).
9. McPherson, *Struggle for Equality*, 169–70.
10. This question served as the title for a lecture given by Frederick Douglass in May 1863, but it was invoked in countless other places during the war and in the immediate postwar period. See "What Shall be Done with the Negro? A Lecture by Frederick Douglass," *New York Times*, May 16, 1863.
11. For the purposes of this essay, "Northerners" include all residents of the states that remained in the Union during the Civil War, although the audience most likely to encounter the correspondence sent by Massachusetts teachers was in New England. McPherson, *Struggle for Equality*, 81–82, 110–12, 169–73; Jeffrey, *Great Silent Army of Abolitionism*, 218–19. See also Stephen Kantrowitz, *More Than Freedom: Fighting for Black Citizenship in a White Republic, 1829–1889* (New York: Penguin, 2012), 309–53.
12. For the disagreements about freedmen's aid, see McPherson, *Struggle for Equality*, 154–69.
13. "Meeting Minutes," 1862, 22–24, New England Freedmen's Aid Society Records, 1862–1878 (Ms. N-101), Massachusetts Historical Society, Boston (hereafter cited as NEFAS Records, MHS).
14. *Freedmen's Record*, January 1865, 1. Initially, the New England Freedmen's Aid Society called the paper *The Freedmen's Journal*, but it quickly realized that there was already another publication by that title and changed the name to the *Freedmen's Record*. For the sake of simplicity, in all citations the title is given as *Freedmen's Record*.
15. *Freedmen's Record*, July 1866, 125.
16. "Branch Societies," *Freedmen's Record*, January 1865, 2.
17. Educational Commission Records [1862–1874], box 1, folder 1, NEFAS Records, MHS. Figures and reports are on the following page numbers: teachers sent by NEFAS in 1865, 76; teacher reports for 1868, 117; reports for 1869, 135; reports for 1870, 143; reports for 1871, 153; and a final set of complete numbers for 1872, 155. In that year the society supported 63 teachers in the South, mainly in South Carolina and Georgia.
18. "The New England Freedman's Aid Society," *Freedmen's Record*, January 1865, 2.
19. "Our 'Record,'" *Freedmen's Record*, December 1865, 189.
20. *Freedmen's Record*, December 1865, 200.
21. *Freedmen's Record*, February 1865, 1.
22. "Jacobs (Linda) School, Alexandria, VA," *Freedmen's Record*, February 1865, 19.
23. Ibid. The "celebrated literary man" mentioned here as a friend to Harriet Jacobs is most likely John Greenleaf Whittier or Ralph Waldo Emerson. For a similar criticism of racism in the North, see Charlotte Forten's comments in the May 1864 issue of the *Atlantic*. Forten, a member of a prominent free black family from Philadelphia, was the first African American teacher from the North to work among the former slaves at Port Royal. Her articles in the *Atlantic* provide incredible detail about the people and the challenges she encountered while teaching there. Charlotte Forten, "Life on the Sea Islands," *Atlantic Monthly* 13 (May 1864): 591.
24. "Second Annual Report of the New-England Freedman's Aid Society," *Freedmen's Record*, April 1865, 49.
25. Butchart, *Schooling the Freed People*, 79–84.
26. Ibid.

27. "The Situation," *Freedmen's Record*, September 1865, 137–38.
28. Ibid., 138.
29. Educational Commission Records [1862–1874], box 1, folder 1, NEFAS Records, MHS. See 94–95 for a discussion of financial troubles in 1866 and 109 and 130 for financial concerns in 1867–68.
30. Ibid., 155.
31. Ibid., 143; Butchart, *Schooling the Freed People*, 153–55; Katherine Lydigsen Herbig, "Friends for Freedom: The Lives and Careers of Sallie Holley and Caroline Putnam" (Ph.D. diss., Claremont Graduate School, 1977), 258–59. See also Educational Commission Records [1862–1874], box 1, folder 1, NEFAS Records, MHS, 153–55, on the transition from society-supported schools to new public schools.
32. See Eric Foner, *Reconstruction: America's Unfinished Revolution* (New York: Harper & Row, 1988); Ronald Heinemann et al., *Old Dominion, New Commonwealth: A History of Virginia, 1607–2007* (Charlottesville: University of Virginia Press, 2007), 242–60.
33. Barbara White, "Anna Gardner: Teacher of Freedmen, 'A Disturber of Tradition,'" in *Nantucket's People of Color: Essays on History, Politics, and Community*, ed. Robert Johnson Jr. (Lanham, Md.: University Press of America, Inc., 2006), 71–72, 95–96.
34. For examples of Gardner's correspondence with the NEFAS and the editors of the *Freedmen's Record*, see "The World Moves, but Moves Slowly," *Freedmen's Record*, July 1866, 128; "Second Festival for Returned Teachers," *Freedmen's Record*, August 1866, 141–42; "Correspondence between a Northern Teacher and a Southern Editor," *Freedmen's Record*, April 1867, 54; "Report of the Committee on Teachers, Presented by Mrs. E. D. Cheney," *Freedmen's Record*, May 1867, 69.
35. "Anniversary Celebration of the President's Proclamation at Newbern. By an Eye-Witness," *Freedmen's Record*, February 1865, 21.
36. "The World Moves, but Moves Slowly," *Freedmen's Record*, July 1866, 128.
37. "Correspondence between a Northern Teacher and a Southern Editor," *Freedmen's Record*, April 1867, 54.
38. Ibid.
39. "Charlottesville, Nov. 16th, 1867," *Freedmen's Record*, December 1867, 189. See also White, "Anna Gardner," 85.
40. Gardner was instrumental in establishing a normal school for blacks in Charlottesville in the late 1860s. White, "Anna Gardner," 86–91.
41. Ibid., 95–96.
42. Philena Carkin, "Chapter 17th: Friendly White Citizens," in "Reminiscences of Philena Carkin," vol. 2, manuscript, 1910 (MSS 11123-a), Special Collections, University of Virginia Library, Charlottesville, 35.
43. "Freedman's Aid Society," *Boston Globe*, March 21, 1874.
44. Ronald Butchart, "Caroline F. Putnam," in *Women Educators in the United States, 1820–1993: A Bio-bibliographical Sourcebook*, ed. Maxine Schwartz Seller (Westport, Conn.: Greenwood Press, 1994), 389–91. Holley taught in Lottsburg for a time and bought land there for the construction of a schoolhouse.
45. Herbig, "Friends for Freedom," 267–71. For example, see "From Virginia: Extract of a Letter from Miss Caroline F. Putnam," *National Anti-Slavery Standard*, January 2, 1869, 3.
46. "From Virginia: Extract of a Letter from Miss Caroline F. Putnam." All quotations in this and the next two paragraphs are from this letter.
47. As local whites emerged from the depressing circumstances of Confederate defeat, they

reengaged in state politics and sought to regain local control from Republicans. They feared how southern black men would vote, and so, as landlords and employers, they often used whatever influence they could over the political decisions of their black tenants. As the years passed, fewer safeguards existed in the South to prevent the political harassment of landless freed people by their white superiors. See Heinemann, *Old Dominion, New Commonwealth*, 242–50.

48. "Affairs in Virginia: Letter from Miss Caroline F. Putnam," *National Anti-Slavery Standard*, February 20, 1869.
49. See, for example, Caroline Putnam to Mr. May, April 25, 1894, Samuel May Papers, 1825–1903 (Ms. N-536), MHS. In this letter, Putnam noted that Colonel Folsom had procured sixty secondhand chairs and thirty double desks from Cambridge, Massachusetts, and that almost twenty years later he was still donating to the school, this time with strawberry plants and raspberry canes.
50. For more biographical information on May see "Samuel May, Jr. (1810–1899)," Worcester Women's History Project, www.wwhp.org/Resources/Biographies.
51. *Freedmen's Record*, August 1866, 170.
52. Caroline Putnam to Samuel May, November 1874–Spring 1875 (this letter was begun in November 1874 and sent in the spring of 1875), undated (but January 1894), and April 6, 1894, Samuel May Papers, MHS.
53. "Samuel May, Jr.," Worcester Women's History Project. Abigail Alcott also had a brother of the same name, the well-known abolitionist and Unitarian minister Samuel Joseph May (1797–1871) of Syracuse, New York.
54. Miss Ellen T. Emerson to Sallie Holley and Caroline Putnam, February 8, 1878, and April 5, 1879, in I. B. Holley Jr., ed., "Schooling Freedmen's Children," *New England Quarterly* 74 (September 2001): 483–85; Caroline Putnam to Mr. May, March 15, 1893, Samuel May Papers, MHS.
55. Miss Ellen T. Emerson to Sallie Holley and Caroline Putnam, February 8, 1878, in Holley, "Schooling Freedmen's Children."
56. Miss Ellen T. Emerson to Sallie Holley and Caroline Putnam, April 5, 1879, ibid. For an example of a student's letter, see Susie Blackwell to Mrs. Bradbury, March 20, 1888, Samuel May Papers, MHS.
57. According to the December 1868 edition of the *Freedmen's Record* (185), the New England Freedmen's Aid Society decided to reduce publication of the paper to four times a year, and the paper folded before the society did in 1874. The *National Anti-Slavery Standard* ceased publication in April 1870, after the National Anti-Slavery Society disbanded upon the passage of the Fifteenth Amendment. As we have seen, Anna Gardner also sent articles and letters to her hometown paper, the *Inquirer and Mirror* in Nantucket, but with the island's entire population hovering around four thousand people, that reading audience was relatively small. For population statistics on Nantucket, see Elizabeth Oldham, "Nantucket in a Nutshell," *Historic Nantucket* 49 (Winter 2000), available at www.nha.org/history.
58. See Butchart, *Schooling the Freedpeople*, ii.
59. See Anna Gardner's letters in the *Nantucket Inquirer*, December 7, 1864, and January 4, 1865, and in the *Inquirer and Mirror*, November 4, 1865.
60. Heather Cox Richardson offers a succinct overview of scholars' positions on this issue in *The Death of Reconstruction: Race, Labor, and Politics in the Post–Civil War North, 1865–1901* (Cambridge: Harvard University Press, 2001), x.

The Union of Gentlemen Restored

College-Educated Northern Veterans, Reconciliation, and Northern Honor

KANISORN WONGSRICHANALAI

On Tuesday, June 17, 1902, Charles Francis Adams Jr., direct descendent of two U.S. presidents, son of Lincoln's ambassador to the United Kingdom, and president of the Massachusetts Historical Society, posed a question in a speech before the Phi Beta Kappa Society at the University of Chicago: "Was Robert E. Lee a traitor?" Technically, Adams explained, one ought to say yes, but then he offered some mitigating circumstances: "If Robert E. Lee was a traitor, so also, and indisputably were George Washington, Oliver Cromwell, John Hampden, and William of Orange." Each of these individuals "violated his allegiance, and gave aid and comfort to the enemies of his sovereign." Focusing on Washington, Adams continued, "A Virginian like Lee, he was also a British subject; he had fought under the British flag." When the Revolution began and "Virginia seceded from the British Empire, he 'went with his State,' just as Lee went with it eighty-five years later."[1]

Considered rebels by their contemporaries, Adams observed, Washington and his men were afterward glorified "as 'the rebels of '76,' much as Lee later commanded, and at last surrendered, much larger armies, also designated 'rebels' by those they confronted." "Except in their outcome," Adams concluded, "the cases were, therefore, precisely alike: and logic is logic. It consequently appears to follow, that, if Lee was a traitor, Washington was also." In order to emphasize how his own opinion had changed over time, Adams recalled that he himself had been "face to face with some fragment of the Army of Northern Virginia, and intent to do it harm." During the war, "there was not a day when I would not have drawn a deep breath of relief and satisfaction at hearing of the death of Lee, even as I did draw it at hearing of the death of Jackson." Time had altered that perspective. Instead of wishing Lee and his men ill fortune, he admitted, "I glory in it, and in them as foes,—they were worthy of the best of steel. I am proud now to say that I was their countryman." Later in the speech Adams made it clear that Lee's personal qualities had influenced his reassessment of the Confederate commander: "Every inch a soldier, he was as an opponent not less generous and humane than formidable, a type of highest martial character;—cautious, magnanimous and bold, a very thunderbolt in war, he was self-contained in victory, but greatest in defeat."[2]

Why would Charles Francis Adams Jr., Civil War commander of African American troops and loyal Unionist, rise to the defense of Robert E. Lee, the man on whose shoulders had rested the fate of both the Confederacy and the American Union? I will argue that college-educated Northerners' ideas about honor—a specific variant of the more well-known southern honor—help illuminate why reconciliation was a logical progression of their ideology at war's end. Often referred to by contemporaries as "character," northern honor revolved around the notion of obeying one's conscience; thus its adherents could not fault southern men of honor who fought for a cause that their consciences justified.

The topic of northern honor has not received adequate historical examination. Scholars have been drawn to the study of the seemingly medieval southern code, with its arcane traditions and challenges and duels.[3] The result of this intensive study of southern society is twofold. First, it has given historians a better sense of what life was like in that region than in the North during the antebellum period. Second, it has reinforced their impression that Northerners lacked any equivalent code of conduct. Such beliefs have perpetuated a misunderstanding of northern culture and society.

Many historians of the post–Civil War era have shown how northern and southern whites celebrated each other's bravery, deemphasized controversial issues such as slavery and race, ignored African Americans' contributions in the war, and overcame their differences. Reconciliation has been presented as a celebration of white bravery in an attempt to settle old scores and bring the Union back together in a fraternal bond of camaraderie.[4] Nina Silber has argued that the romanticization of the southern plantation lifestyle grew out of Northerners' concerns about internal ethnic and class tensions as well as the rapid changes that industrialization had wrought in their own society. This aided the drive toward reconciliation, since Northerners looked to a mythologized vision of a bygone South—purposefully created by the region's writers—that Union armies had uprooted during the war. Northerners, Silber writes, "transformed their anger against the southern aristocracy into feelings of pity and respect, ultimately sentimentalizing the unhurried and leisurely lifestyles of the planter class." Focusing on "middle- and upper-class northern men," Silber contends that "these individuals and their cultural offerings increasingly set the dominant tone on the reunion question."[5]

David Blight has argued that at the heart of the postwar conflict lay the contentious issue of race, which "served as the antithesis of a culture of reconciliation. The memory of slavery, emancipation, and the Fifteenth Amendment never fit well into a culture in which the Old and New South were romanticized and welcomed back to a new nationalism." Thanks to the power of the reconciliation impulse, "the war was remembered primarily as a tragedy that led to greater unity and national cohesion, and as a soldier's call to sacrifice in order to save a troubled, but essentially good, Union, not as the crisis of a nation deeply divided over slavery, race, competing definitions of labor, liberty, political economy, and the future of the West."[6]

In his groundbreaking *Race and Reunion,* Blight identifies three strains of Civil War memory: the reconciliationist, white supremacist, and emancipationist visions. The first "took root in the process of dealing with the dead from so many battlefields, prisons, and hospitals," while the second "took many forms early, including terror and violence, locked arms with the reconciliationists of many kinds, and by the turn of the century delivered the country a segregated memory of its Civil War on Southern terms." Finally, the emancipationist vision was "embodied in African Americans' complex remembrance of their own freedom, in the politics of radical Reconstruction, and in conceptions of the war as the reinvention of the republic and the liberation of blacks to citizenship and Constitutional equality." Blight eloquently traces how "in the end . . . the forces of reconciliation overwhelmed the emancipationist vision in the national culture," and "the inexorable drive for reunion both used and trumped race."[7]

Late nineteenth-century Americans' concerns about their masculinity and gender roles also influenced the supremacy of the reconciliation impulse. Jackson Lears identifies a deep sense of anxiety in the Gilded Age (roughly the period between the end of the Civil War and the beginning of the twentieth century), noting that Victorian Americans became disillusioned with the prevailing culture of ease and moneymaking. Rekindling masculinity offered individuals hope for rejuvenation. This need to challenge oneself in new ways and places coincided with a nostalgic look back at the martial success of the Civil War generation and helped foster reconciliation. "Affluent Americans were becoming impatient with the inherent limitations of a society given over to material comfort, as well as with the anemic gentility of late-Victorian religion and culture," Lears observes. "Military heroism," he continues, "repudiated calculating gain and affirmed the inevitability of loss—including the ultimate loss, death itself. The soldier's willingness to risk all for a cause he believed noble (even if he was mistaken) seemed a powerful antidote to the self-seeking calculus governing commerce." Reconciliation required the cooperation of both Northerners and Southerners. As Peter S. Carmichael demonstrates in his study of young college-educated Virginia soldiers—the counterparts to the men who are the focus of this essay—the former Confederates who survived the war embraced Reconstruction as an opportunity to modernize their region and assume their own societal leadership roles.[8]

Although convincing, this consensus remains incomplete. Could mere exhaustion after the ordeal of Reconstruction and a disregard for the rights of freed people have been sufficient to bring Northerners and Southerners together? Could fear of a changing society and anxiety about the alteration of the very fabric of America have been enough to send Northerners running to visions of an idyllic plantation life? Seeking explanations for this behavior in the postwar period is logical, but it can yield only a partial answer. The seeds of gentlemanly reconciliation lay in the antebellum period, and a more thorough interpretation must take into account long-standing class-based codes of honor. Charles F. Adams's speech suggests that he applied a sophisticated and unspoken paradigm to evaluate Lee. To explain Adams's behavior, which was, in turn, representative of many of the men of his educational and wartime background, one must go farther back in time. College-educated New England veterans' attempts to reconcile with the South were the logical outcome of their intellectual trajectory, which can be traced to the antebellum and wartime periods, when ideas about proper behavior strengthened other established beliefs. In order to explain how and why elite New Englanders embraced reconciliation, scholars must take into account the social context of their intellectual worldview, which developed before the first shots signaled the beginning of the Confederate rebellion. Students of history must also understand how college-educated New Englanders viewed secession. Their impressions of who led the rebellion are important to understanding how they responded at the time of the conflict and after it ended.

Rather than place all Southerners into the same category, elite Northerners made clear distinctions between the strongest supporters of rebellion—whom they referred to as secessionists—and those who felt bound by duty to fight on behalf of the Confederacy, perhaps men like themselves who had not yet assumed political leadership roles in the South. Although they blamed their southern counterparts for failing to set good examples for their less fortunate neighbors, they nevertheless sympathized with them as fellow gentlemen. Educated Northerners' experiences in the Confederacy during the war confirmed for them that the southern leadership class had been corrupted by slavery but remained similar enough to their northern peers. More important, they continued to view southern gentlemen as honorable. Northern elites, rather than blame all Southerners for secession, accused radical agitators in both sections of starting the conflict. Meanwhile, their interactions with enslaved African Americans in the South led to uneasiness and uncertainty about the freed people's postwar role. Concerned about the biracial society the war created, northern gentlemen deferred to their southern counterparts on that issue.

In the first part of this essay I draw on the writings of antebellum college students to examine the tenets and dictates of northern honor. College men's writings reveal the extent to which honor pervaded the worldview of a professional class whom nineteenth-century schools had trained to become society's leaders. Focusing on college men helps to identify a ready sample of the gentleman class. Institutions of higher learning attracted men from all walks of life, but regardless of one's social standing prior to entrance, graduates would emerge as professionals, many becoming attorneys, businessmen, physicians, clergymen, or teachers. The sentiments in college compositions illustrate how these young men understood the traits of the gentleman class. Their service during the war demonstrated their embrace of those values. College education may also help explain why these young men, who could have observed the war from the safety of their law or business offices, chose to volunteer. All students at antebellum colleges had to complete a capstone moral philosophy course in their senior year. Generally taught by the institution's president, it exhorted them to use their education for good, reiterating the point that these young men would become society's leaders.⁹ In wartime, many college-educated gentlemen took the charge literally.

As budding shepherds of American society, these young men identified with moderate political forces. Although some of them supported abolition, most evinced a more conservative outlook and preferred gradual societal changes to more dramatic ones. The manner in which they discussed social reformers and secession reveals their reservations about both. Their wartime and postwar diaries, correspondence, and public addresses help show how college-educated northern soldiers' encounters with southern life strengthened their ideas about the region's corrupt leaders and fortified their trust in southern gentlemen. These sources reveal a consistent theme based on ideas about northern honor that helps to explain how reconciliation between sectional enemies could occur so seamlessly after the end of a bloody and horrific civil war.

Northern Honor

College-educated New Englanders viewed the world through a lens of honor and, as a result of their similar education and occupations, identified with their counterparts in southern society. Although Confederates failed to win independence, their willingness to die for the cause demonstrated their commitment, proved their bravery, and validated the traits of courage and honor that northern gentlemen cherished themselves.

Northern honor, or character, influenced how nineteenth-century men led their lives. In its broadest form, character can be defined as an idealized internal standard of behavior that emphasizes independent thought and selfless action. Whereas southern honor revolved around reputation, northern character focused on internal beliefs, including the conviction to follow one's conscience regardless of public acceptance. Northern gentlemen could claim that their actions were nobler than those of Southerners because they did not defer to the demands of others.

Examining popular, contemporary writings as well as the college essays of young northern gentlemen groomed to lead society presents a good opportunity to explore how they defined character for themselves. The popular nineteenth-century intellectual and author Ralph Waldo Emerson deemed it "a reserved force, which acts directly by presence and without means." A man who uses character as his guide does not feel intimidated by others and has an unshakeable self-confidence. "The conscience of the society," he always knows the righteous course "as the magnet arranges itself with the pole." The analogy of the compass illustrates the most crucial point: the man of character remains true no matter the circumstances. In another contemporary work on the subject, John Foster urged men of character to act with decisiveness and confidence lest they be known as "the sport of . . . casual impulses." Thus they would pursue their course without fear of "contempt and ridicule."[10] Contemporary discussions, therefore, emphasized self-confidence and the courage of one's convictions. Young men training to become gentlemen hoped that they could emulate these lofty ideals and develop character for themselves.

In their college writings, young northern men demonstrated their adoption of contemporary definitions of character. Robert Pitman, a student at Wesleyan University, thought it was "above success" and reminded his audience "that it is of more consequence what a man *is* than what he *has*." Dartmouth College student Levi Little argued that the world "wants men of character: men whose minds are their own—who think for themselves & call no man master." Wilder Dwight, a student at Harvard, argued that all objects one interacts with in life, "in short every influence to which we are subjected has its own part in our education and a greater or less effect upon the character." Thomas B. Fox Jr., another Harvard student, discussed the difficulties of maintaining the ideal. "Men," he wrote, "are enticed by their fellows, and because they are *cowardly* they give themselves up to pleasure, and deviate from the path which they *know* is the path [of] duty." Remaining true to one's character required discipline and courage to stand independent of the crowd. Fox also cautioned against slavishly refusing to think for oneself out of sentimentality. He criticized "the men who do not seek to make all the advancement they can, . . . [and] are afraid to think freely as their ancestors did, from mere reverence for their ancestors." One might even question such individuals' patriotism, he added.[11]

College men argued that they, above all others, cultivated this ideal through their education. Wilder Dwight observed that one seldom encountered "a person, whose character has such just and fair proportions." "Youth," he maintained, "is the season when we are most susceptible" to positive and negative behaviors and, thus, the most important period to cultivate good ones. The process required constant vigilance. Either vice or virtue, Dwight later wrote, "must give a tone to the character, and the more strongly we are guarded against vice the more secure we are in virtue." A man needs to know himself before he can control his behavior. "Each can see for himself how far conscience has ruled his motives hitherto, and then, knowing the strength of his conscience, he can be his own prophet of the issue of the conflict between them," Francis V. Balch, a Harvard student in the class of 1859, explained. "This conflict," he continued, "is the great fact of life, but its object is not the destruction of any other part of our nature, but the ruling of it; not the destruction of the stock, but the forcing of its sap to the uses of the graft."[12]

Colleges prepared their graduates to become leaders in society and, as a result, emphasized the importance of self-sacrifice for the common good. Moral philosophy courses marked the culmination of the antebellum college curriculum. These classes encouraged young gentlemen to use their education to serve less fortunate members of society. A man, Wilder Dwight contended, "is not merely a piece of machinery. He is, it is true, a part of society, and, as such has certain duties and responsibilities, but he is also an individual, and, as such, responsible for the just and fair proportions of his whole character, and for the full and faithful discharge of the various and difficult duties of life." One Wesleyan student noted, "Each member of society is more or less responsible for the common good." William Potter, a Harvard law student, wrote in his diary that all men had been "created to serve some particular purpose" and ought to conduct themselves so that, at the end of their lives, they could "have the proud consciousness of knowing that the 'World is better because *he* has lived in it.'"[13]

Men of character acted in accordance with their consciences no matter how unpopular that course of action might be. This inner quality assumed that the educated elites knew what was "right" according to their circumstances. Honorable northern men also needed to take society's benefit into consideration. Those who pursued actions deemed detrimental to the greater good—promoting sectional tension or secession, for example—revealed their selfish interests and opened their character to question.

A Theory of Secession

Being selfless men of character was only one aspect of elite New Englanders' identities. They were also Americans and, as such, they viewed any threat to the progress and posterity of the nation as dangerous. They criticized radicals, whom they considered social agitators, from both sections. Whether abolitionists in the North or slaveholders advocating expansion in the South, northern gentlemen rejected all individuals and groups who increased sectional tension and threatened peaceful relations in the Union.

Trained to accept a moderate and conservative view of affairs, college-educated men criticized antebellum reformers for advocating unnatural changes. Edwin Grover of the Harvard class of 1857 feared that "the tendency of men is to outrun progress itself, and to leap higher than the necessities of circumstances require or their proprieties admit." Unless "checked by some restraining and regulating influence," Grover cautioned, "agitators and reformers will defeat their own ends by outdoing their tasks." In 1851 George Clary, educated at both Dartmouth and the Yale School of Medicine, criticized reformers for being "impulsive in their nature" rather than accepting "that cautious, conservative spirit which renders men loth to relinquish the old & well trodden paths." He described the "whole armies of independent reformers" that had arisen "with religious toleration, right of suffrage, trial by Jury, Emancipation, chartism, socialism, congress of nations emblazoned on their shields." Acknowledging the benefit of some reforms, Clary nonetheless urged caution, reasoning that activists' zeal might lead to "no result but revolution & counter revolution threatening to leave society at last dissolved into its natural & barbaric elements." Dartmouth student Osgood Johnson, a native of Massachusetts, criticized "reformers of the present day." The "roaring of fanatics & crazy women has not relieved the condition of the slave" he noted, but had actually strengthened slavery. Revolutions could not "advance farther than the intelligence of the people" and reformers appealed to "the worst passions of the multitude—not their sober & better feelings."[14]

Wilder Dwight warned of "an acrid and bitter philanthropy," which sought to secure "to women the full enjoyment of those 'inalienable rights' to which she is said to have a claim." Criticizing women's rights reformers of the era, he urged patience: "The social relations will improve and as man rises higher in his sphere so will woman in hers. Assisting each other both may make great improvement, but let neither attempt to occupy the other's place." Claiming that both sexes had their strengths—"It is manifestly absurd that man should ever equal woman in gentleness, refinement, affection or curiosity, or that woman should equal man in strength, wisdom, manliness or sternness"—Dwight concluded, "Woman is not to improve her condition by changing her sphere, but to employ all the aids which can support her as a wife, sister and mother; for here her influence is unbounded enough to satisfy the highest ambition."[15]

Growing up in an era of peace between the United States and European nations, young men feared that internal and domestic conflicts would tear their country apart. Harvard student Charles Gregory, studying the results of the 1850 census, marveled at the fact that in "the period of the last half century, the United States have attained to a population of over twenty-three millions, having more than quadrupled their numbers in fifty years." At the same time, the nation had expanded its territory, which now encompassed "nearly three millions of square miles." Accommodations for "religious worship far exceed those of England," while "asylums for the destitute, the unfortunate, or the vicious are of such marked excellence as to serve as models for other nations to imitate," and the "system of public schools has attracted the admiring gaze of the civilized world." Gregory also pointed to the erection of telegraph lines and the construction of canals and aqueducts as signs of American progress. The world, he mused, had "never seen the splendid spectacle of a hundred millions of free people united into a democratic republic." There was, however, "one cause of alarm; one institution yet remains which renders us obnoxious to keen reproach and the charge of inconsistency": slavery. William Potter called the institution "a blot upon the escutcheon of some of our states" and hoped for its demise.[16]

New England college students recognized the problem of slavery but accepted the fact that the Constitution protected Southerners' rights to their property in human beings. As a result, they advocated moderate and gradual reform. Charles Gregory hoped that "the moral conflict which has commenced, and the gentle but powerful influence of Christianity will render the institutions of Slavery obsolete before the opening of the twentieth century." William Potter declared, "I am opposed to the extension of slavery, because I do not wish to see another foot of soil, cursed by an institution, which now cripples the national progress of so many states." Yet because of his reverence for the Constitution, he "would protect it, by every available means, where by the Providence of God it at present exists." Like many free labor advocates at the time, Potter believed that "we can constitutionally prevent its extension." Once "no slave shall breathe the air of our free land," he thought, "then shall we truly live a happy, free and united people." Slavery could "be deplored, but not now remedied"; he feared that unless someone devised a lasting solution, the topic would continue to "distract our nation."[17]

College-educated men expressed common contemporary racist views, arguing, for example, that even as free persons African Americans could not fully assume the same roles as whites in society. Such concerns also influenced their opposition to immediate emancipation. Many Northerners also thought Southerners better qualified to manage the issue of race relations, partly out of fear that freed people would move North. Henry Lyman Patten of the Harvard class of 1858, for example, worked as a tutor in Georgia after his graduation and referred to slavery as a "necessary evil," citing the "insurmountable difficulties at present" that would attend its removal. Although he acknowledged the injustice of the system, he could not imagine a suitable solution. These young men's racial prejudices influenced their beliefs and heightened their fear about emancipation. Osgood Johnson argued that an individual's inner capabilities needed time for proper development. "If today every slave at [the] South were set free, there would be undeniably no more real liberty than before," he argued. Even though southern society "would be changed," the "mass of slaves would be the same in internal character as now." He predicted that it would "take years to effect those changes necessary to advance them [the enslaved] in liberty." Reformers who wished immediately to elevate enslaved laborers out of bondage, therefore, were trying "to accomplish at once what cannot be done in a generation."[18] Thus even before the war began, elite New Englanders expressed doubts about African Americans' capacity for freedom and deferred to Southerners on the issue.

College men even criticized the character of social reformers, viewing them as unpatriotic agitators. At an abolitionist and women's rights gathering, William Potter expressed his admiration for Wendell Phillips's style but regretted that he used his "splendid talents . . . only to revile his country, to overturn and trample under foot the religion of the gospel, and to destroy the present well ordered relation of woman to man." He described William Lloyd Garrison as "a smooth, oily looking, bald headed fanatic with nothing attractive in his manner or in the substance of his remarks, and decidedly lacking in gentlemanly politeness." Potter was stunned when Garrison stated, "I hate this accursed Union," and appalled by the crowd's lack of outrage at the radical sentiment. The convention itself drew up a resolution, which "denounced the Constitution as a compact with the devil, and an agent with hell." "Gracious Heaven," Potter commented, "can it be that men born in America, and fostered under the influence of our own institutions, can hold such sentiments as these[?]" Where, Potter wondered, had such thoughts arisen? "Is it the full development of a New

England education, has it been imbibed from the writings of French philosophers, or is it like the origin of Evil, involved in an obscurity which cannot be fathomed?" Potter warned that, in America, "our modern Athens, there are advocates of . . . a religion of hate, of a government which would be worse than anarchy itself, and of a society, which would be destitute of everything which renders society dear." He concluded that the presence of such social agitators was "one of the evils of a Republic like our own, which follows from its very form and constitution that even Treason may be preached, so long as such preaching results in no overt acts."[19]

Ultimately, college men tolerated differences of opinion but condemned direct action, which interrupted social peace and threatened to unleash greater violence. After John Brown's raid on Harpers Ferry, Virginia, Thomas B. Fox Jr. argued that the authorities had every right to punish the radical abolitionist: "The man who conscientiously believes the government of his country to be in a measure wicked, and then resorts to violence, is not punished for his opinions but for his deeds. He is held responsible for the way in which he works, not for the belief which impels him." Not judging Brown's ideals but rather his actions, Fox declared, "The public security demands that such men should serve as warnings, and not as inducements to rebellion."[20]

Long before the Harpers Ferry raid, college men identified secession as the ultimate threat to the Union. Writing in 1855, Dartmouth student David Quigg warned that it would be "most base & shameful if we prove incapable to discharge the duties necessary to fulfill this trust" of securing the "precious inheritance" from the founders. Speaking to his audience about contemporary issues—the violence in the Kansas Territory—Quigg cautioned that "anarchy & civil war, that destroyed the ancient republics & which is the destruction of all nations without God & conscience," might yet reach America. Sectional tension and conflict threatened "to destroy, the fairest structure of government, that human prudence & human foresight ever reared," but he would not attempt to describe the "consequences of disunion" for they were too terrible and too many.[21]

In the Land of Southern Gentlemen

Secession became a reality and ruptured the Union after the election of 1860. College-educated men whose professional-class status and financial resources would have shielded them from risking their lives in the war nevertheless volunteered to serve in the Union cause. As they visited the South, these men also passed judgment on the region's leadership class. Influenced by selfish slaveholding politicians, this group had neglected the Union and the common good. College-educated soldiers marching through the South also commented on the poor condition of the region and the ignorance of the populace. As a result of what they witnessed, they concluded that southern gentlemen had lost their way, become corrupted by their interests in slavery, and neglected their duties as society's leaders. As they examined the homes of wealthy Southerners, some men noted the aristocratic architecture, which they considered out of place in a republic. The criticism, in essence, employed the language of character. Despite their condemnation of southern life, elite Northerners expressed some sympathy for their counterparts—men of their generation who had not yet assumed political roles—and this helped support reconciliation after the war.

Marching through the South, college-educated New Englanders commented on the hierarchical and aristocratic nature of southern architecture and the landscape. Traveling along the Mississippi River, George Clary described a plantation with its "little village of negro huts, many of them neatly painted," clustered around "the large sugar houses." The master's mansion fronted "the river, with its broad acres of sugar cane extending for a mile or two in the rear." The setting reminded him that the "race of proud princes—the Feudal System of the Rebellion" controlled the region. A few days later, Clary described another plantation, which boasted "huge sugar houses with their village of negro huts, often neatly painted white," and the "mansion of the Nabob fronting close upon the river." Clary admitted the richness of the region, seeing magnolias in bloom and the "vast fields of sugar cane." The scene, he commented, was "unsurpassed for its luxuriance by anything that I have seen."[22]

Some elite New Englanders took pleasure in mocking the southern aristocracy's sense of superiority. After landing at Hilton Head, South Carolina, William T. Lusk, who had spent a year at Yale before the war, commented, "And now we vile Yankee hordes are overrunning the pleasant islands about Beaufort, rioting upon sweet potatoes and Southern sunshine." He mused that he had come ashore where "lived the Pinckneys, the Draytons, and other high-blooded Hidalgos, whose effervescing exuberance of gentlemanly spirit have done so much to cause our present troubles." Mocking antebellum claims of southern superiority and invincibility, he crowed,

"Yankee hordes, ruthless invaders—the vile Hessians—infest their splendid plantations." Caspar Crowninshield, a Harvard graduate, declared the ruin of slaveholders a "just retribution for their insolent pride and arrogant spirit." After describing the "luxuriant" scenery and wealth of southern plantations, George Clary concluded, "No wonder the lords of the manor fancied themselves the lords of creation. But how are the mighty fallen!" On another occasion Clary wrote, "I love to hear them wail over their departed blacks." He felt "a satisfaction, after so many years of enduring their haughty overbearing manner, in seeing them at length obliged to own up to their weakness and to be compelled to ask favor from Yankees."[23]

Reveling in their own wealth, southern leaders had neglected their responsibilities as society's leaders. "It is one of the painful facts of the rebellion that nearly all the most cultivated and enlightened people in this country, at least, are on the side of the rebellion," James Garfield, an Ohio native who had attended Williams College, observed. Anti-Union sentiments probably grew "out of the fact that leaders of the rebellion were the aristocrats of the South, and they have led off that element with them." William Wheeler, a graduate of Harvard's law school, wondered what "the dominant class" had ever "done for the poor white in their midst." The powerful men of the South had "closed the doors of industry upon him, their own brother, thus keeping him poor; they have refused him education, thus keeping him ignorant; and they have encouraged him in all the vices that spring from idleness, thus ruining body, mind, and soul." All this was done intentionally, "in order to keep him as a tool for their political and, now, for their military purposes." Campaigning in Virginia, James C. Rice, a Massachusetts native educated at Yale, "had an interview with a delegation of citizens representing Gloucester [County]" who sought "protection as to the lives and property of the people of the County." The delegation "represented the wealthiest part—the slaveholders of the County," and Rice commented, "I am sorry to say, that this entire class of people are violent secessionists," even though "this entire county is strongly Union in sentiment. Aged men and women with tears streaming down their wrinkled cheeks looked upon the old Union flag again and thanked God."[24]

As much as they criticized southern aristocrats, northern gentlemen paused to reflect that these individuals were in many ways their own counterparts. With that realization also came pity. Southern homes sometimes resembled the ones these northern soldiers had left to come south. Stationed near Beaufort, South Carolina, Charles Francis Adams Jr. visited "a new house on a beautiful island . . . surrounded with magnificent cotton fields, built evidently by a gentleman of refinement." As a "result of war," the garden had become a trash pile. Inside the house, Adams found "broken furniture, scraps of books and letters, and all the little tokens of a refined family." Scattered over the floors and piled in the corners were "the remains of a fine library of books of many languages, and panels and glasses were broken wherever so doing was thought an easier course than to unlock or open." He added, "I wandered round and looked out at the view and wondered why this people had brought all this upon themselves; and yet I couldn't but pity them." "For," he explained, "I thought how I should feel to see such sights at Quincy."[25]

Caspar Crowninshield, who accompanied Adams, expressed similar sentiments. He remembered passing "Island after Island, plantations of some wealthy Southerner, with the dark low houses of the planter, & the whitewashed huts of the slave, now desolate and abandoned." He admitted to feeling "a greater pity for the misguided gentlemen of the South than I should care to acknowledge," and could not "shake off a feeling of sympathy for the poor secesshers, as I look round and see their fine houses, and old family furniture, clocks, glasses, & everything else destroyed." He imagined the owner as "a fine fellow, with a pleasant family of, girls, lovely, and well educated, boys manly, frank, and hospitable." The similarities between southern and northern homes haunted him. "What the devil am I doing here in their house?" he asked. "What am I fighting for? Is it in order that dirty illiterate New York politicians may rule the country, or Massachusetts abolitionists?" Less than a year into the conflict, Crowninshield found himself wishing that "the *gentlemen* of the North & the *gentlemen* of the South" might "unite to take the government of the country into their own hands."[26]

Sympathy for southern gentlemen also extended to others who suffered as a result of the war. Thomas H. Hubbard, a Bowdoin College graduate, wrote to his father about encountering the Bartons, family friends they had met before the war at Moosehead Lake in Maine. Mrs. Barton looked "very old and, though very ladylike, is a bitter rebel." He conceded that she had "good cause . . . for it now at least," because she had lost two sons in the war and two others had been wounded. Meanwhile, their "farm of 1100 acres is rapidly being stripped of fences[,] buildings, wood and forage." Hubbard wrote that despite all this, "Mrs. B sends her regards to you, Father." After a correspondent observed that he seemed to spend a lot of time "visiting

... the families of the natives of this region," William Wheeler responded, "In spite of your thorough patriotism and hatred of all that is hostile to our cause, you would yet be the first to help the wounded and destitute, even though rebels, and to feel sorry for families desolated and ruined, even in Virginia." Encountering wounded men or a "lonely distressed" woman sparked his sense of "common humanity." He maintained that although he may have pitied their plight, he did not "sympathize with these people in any of their ideas." Empathizing with those who suffered did not mean that he would not fight them to the end.[27]

A Gentlemen's Reconciliation

College-educated Northerners expressed magnanimity as the war turned in their favor. Although they never accepted the Confederacy's claim to legitimacy, because Southerners had poured their hearts and lives into it they attained honor as Northerners understood it: southern men had remained true to the cause they believed just. This recognition opened the door for reconciliation between gentlemen.

As the war drew to a close, college-educated men feared that radical politicians would again endanger the Union. No longer concerned about secessionists, these men worried that radical abolitionists might scuttle peace to achieve their own ends. Two months before the end of the fighting, while on leave in New England, Charles Francis Adams Jr. feared that the cry of vengeance would harm any hope for a lasting peace. "Reconstruction is looming rapidly up here and public opinion in New England stands in great need of guidance," he wrote to his father, noting that the "old Puritan vindictiveness is beginning to stick out strongly." He had expected this among radical abolitionists and "[Senator Charles] Sumner's friends ... but I find it among those not his friends." He regretted to report that his "doctrines, of yielding any terms involving simply property and life but not principle, for the sake of good feeling after Peace, in a sad minority." His fellow New Englanders seemed "as ugly and vindictive as possible. They really don't want peace, unless with it comes the hangman. They will insist upon it that this mighty revolution was, after all, only a murderous riot and that the police court and the constable are just about what it needs to quiet it."[28]

The South had lost the war, the argument about secession, and slavery. To some, this satisfied the cause of justice and served as sufficient punishment.

John C. Gray, a Harvard graduate who had disapproved of Lincoln's use of executive power to emancipate the enslaved, expressed relief that emancipation had come as a result of a constitutional amendment. "That is the right way of going to work and better than a thousand of your juggling emancipation proclamations," he declared at the close of the war. Looking ahead to Reconstruction, he doubted that future generations of Southerners would automatically become loyal Unionists. "That depends entirely on the treatment they receive," he told his mother. "If they are kept under military government or reduced to the state even that Ireland was in at the beginning of the century, I see no reason to suppose that the children will grow up with any less hatred of the North than their fathers have, such at least has not been the case in Italy, Hungary, Ireland or any countries which have been subdued and kept under despotic rule." Gray proposed to leave the defeated rebels in peace after they had formed new pro-Union governments.[29]

Unconvinced that newly freed people could assume roles of citizenship, some educated Northerners proposed to leave the issue in the hands of Southerners. John C. Gray could see "no advantage" to granting freedmen civil rights, arguing that "it would embitter the white men as much as if all negroes were allowed to vote, while the number who could vote would be so few that it would not materially strengthen the loyal vote for the state." He proposed instead to allow southern whites who had taken the loyalty oath to "choose their legislature, make the members of the legislature take the same oath, and let them work away without interference." As a result, he said, "personal liberty would be secured to the negroes and their families, and more it would not seem to me wise to demand for them."[30]

Some northern gentlemen adopted a southern perspective on Reconstruction because they settled in the region. Luther C. Howell, who had attended Amherst College, sensed good investment opportunities in the South and remained in Selma, Alabama, after the war. He planned to buy into a cotton farm. "We have already shown their class [southern planters] how to fight now we will show them how to farm it," he bragged. Living in the region, Howell adopted parts of the planters' worldview. He rejected the "bosh . . . talk" of Radical Republicans such as Charles Sumner and Thaddeus Stevens, who claimed that freedmen faced oppression under the new state governments. White Southerners, Howell argued, had no reason to subjugate blacks. An African American's "value as a laborer is his protection & it is proving to be a very sure one hereabouts," he wrote, adding, "I don't take any stock in the idea that they are being oppressed every negro who desires to work can get plenty of it to do and their employer uses them well in order to keep them as there is nothing else to keep them from breaking the contracts." After spending over a year on his cotton plantation, Howell admitted, "Politically I am more in sympathy with this people than I should be if I lived north for there are so many lies told about them that I get indignant at the northern papers." He promised not to become "a good southern Rebel" but declared, "In my opinion it is not a good thing to keep sticking pins into your enemy when you have already knocked [him] down with your club."[31]

Not all college-educated men opposed civil rights for African Americans. Indeed, some dedicated part or all of their postwar careers to helping the freed people. But even those individuals approached the subject of civil rights from a patronizing position and doubted that formerly enslaved African Americans could immediately take on the responsibilities of citizenship. Samuel Chapman Armstrong, a graduate of Williams College and a former commander of African American soldiers, worked for the Freedmen's Bureau after the war. He fully believed that white officers and agents knew what was best for the former slaves. Armstrong became a champion of black education, helping to found the Hampton Institute (now Hampton University). He called for an agricultural and industrial education as opposed to a more civic-minded approach to training future citizens. Armstrong's belief in delaying the attainment of equal rights found many adherents. A young man named Booker T. Washington became Armstrong's protégé at Hampton and helped promote his philosophy to future generations of African Americans.[32]

Back in the northern states, support for a lenient Reconstruction policy drew on the emerging idea of reconciliation. In 1872, for example, William F. Bartlett's dissatisfaction with Ulysses Grant led him to support the Liberal Republicans, who opposed the president's reelection. Bartlett, who had attended Harvard before entering the army, had sympathized with the South's grievances before the war but still fought for the Union. After the Confederacy's demise, he wished for a return to antebellum relations. In a speech to commemorate the centennial of the Battle of Lexington in 1875, he spoke his mind to the ceremony's guest of honor, President Grant:

> I have a prejudice, which is shared by all soldiers, in favor of peace. And I think I may safely say, that, between the *soldiers* of the two great sections of our country, fraternal relations were established long ago. I have a strong prejudice against any man or men who would divide or destroy or retard the prosperity and progress of the nation, whose

corner-stone was laid in the blood of our fathers one hundred years ago to-day. Moved by this prejudice, I to-day despise the men who would, for the sake of self or party, stand in the way of reconciliation and a united country. . . . And, sir, the only really belligerent people in the country to-day, north and south, are those who, while the war lasted, followed carefully the paths of peace. . . . Look to their heroes, their leaders,—their Gordons, their Lees, their Johnstons, Lamar, Ransom, and Ripley,—and tell me if you find in their utterances anything but renewed loyalty and devotion to a reunited country. These are the men . . . by whom and through whom you must restore the South, instead of the meaner men for whom power is only a synonym for plunder. . . . [D]o not repel the returning love of these men by suspicion or indifference.

Bartlett praised South Carolina's return of a wartime African American unit's flag to Massachusetts and called the soldier who returned the banner his "brother," adding, "And I am proud that he was an American soldier. As an American, I am as proud of the men who charged so bravely with Pickett's Division on our lines at Gettysburg, as I am of the men who so bravely met and repulsed them there." He explained the South's decision to secede by claiming that men could not always "choose the right cause; but when, having chosen that which conscience dictates, they are ready to die for it, if they justify not their cause, they at least ennoble themselves." Referring to the setting of his speech, Bartlett declared, "And the men who, for conscience' sake, fought against their government at Gettysburg, ought easily to be forgiven by the sons of men who, for conscience' sake, fought against the government at Lexington and Bunker Hill."[33] Here again the theme of character emerged as a way to forgive former enemies who had demonstrated honor on the field of battle.

In the years and decades that followed, the college-educated men who had fought so desperately to crush the Confederacy's hopes of independence embraced their former counterparts as equally brave soldiers fighting in a terrible war. Charles Francis Adams Jr., who had condemned the instigators of the conflict in 1861, revealed his fascination with Confederate bravery as early as 1863. After rebel general Thomas J. "Stonewall" Jackson died, Adams declared: "I am sure, as Americans, this army takes a pride in 'Stonewall' second only to that of the Virginians and confederates. To have fought against him is next to having fought under him." The culmination of Adams's postwar reconciliation attempts was his address in 1907 at Lee Chapel in Lexington, Virginia, to honor the centennial of Robert E. Lee's birth. Adams declared the general to be "essentially a Man of Character." He also told the crowd, "Admitting the facts, I add as the result of much patient study and most mature reflection, that under similar conditions I would myself have done exactly what Lee did. In fact, I do not see how I, placed as he was placed, could have done otherwise." Again confirming the main tenet of character, Adams maintained that, whichever side a man chose to fight on in 1861, "if only he decided honestly, putting self-interest behind him, he decided right."³⁴

Adams's praise of Lee mirrored the reaction of many men of his educational class and military background. The men who had fought against the Confederacy rallied around their former enemies in the postwar world. Historians have correctly pointed out that reconciliation was a potent and powerful force in the closing decades of the nineteenth century, but such a reunion of white males should not come as a surprise if one also considers the worldview they embraced in the years before and during the Civil War. Professional gentlemen viewed their society through a lens of northern honor, and the tenets of that creed guaranteed that their onetime enemies who fought with such distinction would be embraced again as brothers who had demonstrated their convictions on many a bloody field.

NOTES

1. Charles Francis Adams, *"Shall Cromwell Have a Statue?"* (Boston: Charles E. Lauriat, 1902), 7–8.
2. Ibid., 8, 34–35.
3. For a sampling of the literature on southern honor, see, among others, Bertram Wyatt-Brown, *Southern Honor: Ethics and Behavior in the Old South* (New York: Oxford University Press, 1983); Kenneth S. Greenberg, *Honor and Slavery: Lies, Duels, Noses, Masks, Dressing as a Woman, Gifts, Strangers, Humanitarianism, Death, Slave Rebellions, the Proslavery Argument, Baseball, Hunting, and Gambling in the Old South* (Princeton: Princeton University Press, 1996); and Bertram Wyatt-Brown, *The Shaping of Southern Culture: Honor, Grace, and War, 1760s–1890s* (Chapel Hill: University of North Carolina Press, 2001). For an excellent study of masculinity in the antebellum era, see Amy S. Greenberg, *Manifest Manhood and the Antebellum American Empire* (New York: Cambridge University Press, 2005).
4. Gary W. Gallagher, in his study of memory, art, and film, has succinctly summarized how America's Civil War generation interpreted the conflict, breaking their ideas down into four distinct themes. Gary W. Gallagher, *Causes Won, Lost, and Forgotten: How Hollywood and Popular Art Shape What We Know about the Civil War* (Chapel Hill: University of North Carolina Press, 2008), chap. 1.
5. Nina Silber, *The Romance of Reunion: Northerners and the South, 1865–1900* (Chapel

Hill: University of North Carolina Press, 1997), 2–11. See also Gallagher, *Causes Won, Lost, and Forgotten*, chap. 1.
6. David W. Blight, "Quarrel Forgotten or a Revolution Remembered? Reunion and Race in the Memory of the Civil War, 1875–1913," in *Union and Emancipation: Essays on Politics and Race in the Civil War Era*, ed. David W. Blight and Brooks D. Simpson (Kent, Ohio: Kent State University Press, 1997), 157, 171.
7. David W. Blight, *Race and Reunion: The Civil War in American Memory* (Cambridge: Belknap Press of Harvard University Press, 2002), 2.
8. Jackson Lears, *Rebirth of a Nation: The Making of Modern America, 1877–1920* (2009; repr., New York: Harper Perennial Edition, 2010), 21–30; Peter S. Carmichael, *The Last Generation: Young Virginians in Peace, War, and Reunion* (Chapel Hill: University of North Carolina Press, 2005), chap. 8. Elliott Gorn, in his study of prizefighting, distinguishes between working-class and middle- and upper-class ideals of masculinity during much of the nineteenth century. By the end of the century, however, middle- and upper-class men felt drawn to the working-class ideal in reaction to "the artificiality and stuffiness of modern life" and thus became more interested in boxing. According to Gorn, "boxers seemed autonomous" in a world where so much of professional men's lives were controlled by their institutions. Elliott J. Gorn, *The Manly Art: Bare-Knuckle Prize Fighting in America* (1986; Ithaca, N.Y.: Cornell University Press, 2010), 252–53.
9. On moral philosophy education see Wilson Smith, *Professors and Public Ethics: Studies of Northern Moral Philosophers before the Civil War* (Ithaca, N.Y.: Cornell University Press, 1956); and D. H. Meyer, *The Instructed Conscience: The Shaping of the American National Ethic* (Philadelphia: University of Pennsylvania Press, 1972).
10. Ralph Waldo Emerson, "Character," in *Essays: Second Series*, vol. 2 (1844; repr., Boston: Houghton Mifflin, 1883), 90–91, 96, 103; Joseph F. Kett, *Rites of Passage: Adolescence in America, 1790 to the Present* (New York: Basic Books, 1977), 105; John Foster, *Essay on Decision of Character* (repr., Burlington, Vt.: Chauncey Goodrich, 1830), 11, 32, 57, 60–61, quotations on 11 and 60.
11. Robert Carter Pitman, "Portraiture of Character . . . ," August 4, 1845, Commencement Orations, 1833–55 (1000-131), Special Collections and Archives, Wesleyan University, Middletown, Conn. (hereafter cited as Commencement Orations, WU); Levi Little, "Men of the right sort," July 27, 1854, Commencement Parts Records, 1771–, Rauner Special Collections Library, Dartmouth College, Hanover, N.H. (hereafter cited as Commencement Parts, DCL); Wilder Dwight, "Whether Education should aim to develop all the faculties equally . . . ," March 11, 1852, Dwight Family Papers, 1815–1942 (Ms. N-13), Massachusetts Historical Society, Boston (MHS); Thomas B. Fox Jr., "Few Men have Courage enough to appear as good as they really are," January 9, 1858, and "Memorials of Patriotism in America," undated, Fox Family Papers, 1795–1936 (Ms. N-209), MHS.
12. Wilder Dwight, "We were young, full of the ardor which science in its first freshness inspires . . . ," April 12, 1851, and Wilder Dwight, "Burke at the close of his eloquent description of the queen . . . ," November 6, 1851, Dwight Family Papers, MHS; Francis V. Balch, *An Oration, Delivered before the Class of 1859, June 24, 1859* (Boston: Alfred Mudge & Son, 1860), 22.
13. Dwight, "Whether Education should aim to develop all the faculties equally . . ."; Francis Asbury Loomis, "Oration—Influence," August 4, 1852, Commencement Orations, WU; William E. Potter Diary (AC323), June 13, 1860, Princeton University Archives, Department of Rare Books and Special Collections, Princeton University Library (PUL).

14. Edwin Grover, "The influence of science and learning on the popular opinions of their day," July 15, 1857, General Information about Harvard Commencement, Class Day, and Exhibitions in Academic year 1856/1857 (HUC 6857), Harvard University Archives (HUA); George Clary, "Reformers," August 1851, George Clary Papers, 1843–1881, Connecticut Historical Society, Hartford (CHS); Osgood Johnson, "The slow progress of useful Revolutions," July 29, 1852, Commencement Parts, DCL.
15. Wilder Dwight, "Iphigenia in Tauris complains that the condition of women is lamentable. . . .," March 18, 1852, Dwight Family Papers, MHS. These college students' fears about women's rights campaigners may have been a result of the movement's close affiliation with radical abolitionists. Dwight may have also misunderstood what the women's rights supporters demanded. According to Sara M. Evans, "In making a claim on public rights . . . [women's rights supporters] never, despite the fears of their opponents, seriously questioned women's primary responsibility for the home and for children." Sara M. Evans, *Born For Liberty: A History of Women in America* (1989; repr., New York: Free Press, 1997), 101–2.
16. Charles Augustus Gregory, "The Last Census," October 17, 1854, General information about Harvard commencement, Class Day, and exhibitions in academic year 1854/1855 (HUC 6855), HUA; William E. Potter Diary, July 4, 1860, PUL.
17. Gregory, "The Last Census"; William E. Potter Diary, December 21, 1859, and July 4, 1860, PUL.
18. George E. Pond, "Henry Lyman Patten," in *Harvard Memorial Biographies*, ed. Thomas Wentworth Higginson, vol. 1 (Cambridge, Mass.: Sever & Francis, 1867), 417–18; Johnson, "The slow progress of useful Revolutions."
19. William E. Potter Diary, May 31, 1860, and June 1, 1860, PUL. In another instance, Potter tried to attend a memorial for John Brown. His purpose was not to honor the abolitionist martyr but rather to observe the "miserable fanatics holding the meeting," for they presented a "phase of human nature we wished to study." Ibid., December 3, 1860.
20. Thomas B. Fox Jr., "Ought John Brown to be put to death?," Fox Family Papers, MHS.
21. David Quigg, "The relation of the new States to the old," July 26, 1855, Commencement Parts, DCL.
22. George Clary to Sarah Clary, May 12, 1862, and George Clary to Eliza Clary, May 14, 1862, Clary Papers, CHS.
23. William Thompson Lusk to Elizabeth Freeman Lusk, November 9, 1861, in *War Letters of William Thompson Lusk, Captain, Assistant Adjutant-General, United States Volunteers 1861–1863, Afterward M.D., LL.D.* (New York: privately printed, 1911), 97; Caspar Crowninshield to unnamed recipient, May 18, 1862, Crowninshield-Magnus Papers, 1834–1965 (Ms. N-1056), MHS; George Clary to Eliza Clary, May 14, 1862, and George Clary to Eliza Clary, February 16, 1864, Clary Papers, CHS.
24. James Abram Garfield to Lucretia Garfield, February 23, 1862, in *Crete and James: Personal Letters of Lucretia and James Garfield*, ed. John Shaw (East Lansing: Michigan State University Press, 1994), 127; William Wheeler to unnamed recipient, November 12, 1863, in *Letters of William Wheeler of the Class of 1855, Y.C.* (Cambridge, Mass.: H. O. Houghton, 1875), 432; John M. Pellicano, *"Well Prepared To Die": The Life of Brigadier General James Clay Rice* (Fredericksburg, Va.: John M. Pellicano, 2007), 67–68.
25. Charles Francis Adams Jr. to Abigail Brooks Adams, February 2, 1862, in *A Cycle of Adams Letters, 1861–1865*, ed. Worthington Chauncey Ford, 2 vols. (Boston: Houghton Mifflin, 1920), 1:111–12.
26. Caspar Crowninshield to his mother, January 16, 1862, Crowninshield-Magnus Papers,

MHS. Although they did not explicitly say so, perhaps Adams and Crowninshield also felt a sense of guilt at their violation of private homes, usually viewed in Victorian society as the dominions of women. Northern gentlemen might have felt uncomfortable behaving in such an unchivalrous manner. In her study of soldier–civilian interaction during Sherman's March to the Sea, Lisa Tendrich Frank argues that "elite white Confederate women often asserted their femininity, as well as their regional identities, to respond to the campaign, playing upon the assumptions about their gender and class." Frank contends that "femininity, in these interactions, became both a weapon for women to draw upon and a weakness for soldiers to prey upon." The Union army, she argues, waged "a gendered form of warfare." Lisa Tendrich Frank, "Bedrooms as Battlefields: The Role of Gender Politics in Sherman's March," in *Occupied Women: Gender, Military Occupation, and the American Civil War*, ed. LeeAnn Whites and Alecia P. Long (Baton Rouge: Louisiana State University Press, 2009), 33–36.

27. Thomas Hubbard to John Hubbard, November 13, 1864, Hubbard Family Papers, 1789–1934 (M 95), George J. Mitchell Department of Special Collections and Archives, Bowdoin College Library, Brunswick, Maine; William Wheeler to unnamed recipient, September 25, 1863, *Letters of William Wheeler*, 421–22. As Joseph T. Glatthaar has noted, "Soldiers may have developed personal relationships with individual southerners," but they also "stripped away the component characteristics of each individual southerner, ignored all positive qualities, and concentrated on one overriding feature—that southerners, at least from a Federal perspective, had caused this war and were fully culpable for all the sacrifices and sufferings Union soldiers had endured throughout the war. The result was that soldiers could feel genuine affection for individual southerners, yet possess such a deep-seated hostility for the Southern people that they could seek vengeance through the destruction of military and nonmilitary property on an unprecedented scale." Joseph T. Glatthaar, *The March to the Sea and Beyond: Sherman's Troops in the Savannah and Carolinas Campaigns* (New York: New York University Press, 1985), 76.
28. Charles Francis Adams Jr. to Charles Francis Adams Sr., February 7, 1865, in *A Cycle of Adams Letters*, 2:252–53.
29. John C. Gray Jr. to John C. Ropes, February 8, 1865, and John C. Gray Jr. to Horace Gray, May 14, 1865, in *War Letters, 1862–1865, of John Chipman Gray and John Codman Ropes* (Boston: Houghton Mifflin, 1927), 452, 484–86.
30. John C. Gray Jr. to his father, May 14, 1865, ibid., 486–87.
31. Luther Clark Howell to Sidney Howell, July 25, 1865, Luther Clark Howell to his sister Clara, March 6, 1866, and Luther Clark Howell to "Friend Day," September 7, 1866, Luther Clark Howell Papers, 1855–1874, College Archives and Special Collections, Amherst College Library, Amherst, Mass.
32. Robert F. Engs, *Freedom's First Generation: Black Hampton, Virginia, 1861–1890* (1979; repr., New York: Fordham University Press, 2004), 83, 87–89, 158.
33. Quoted in Richard A. Sauers and Martin H. Sable, *William Francis Bartlett: Biography of a Union General in the Civil War* (Jefferson, N.C.: McFarland, 2009), 156–59, 163–65.
34. Charles Francis Adams Jr. to Charles Francis Adams Sr., July 23, 1863, in *A Cycle of Adams Letters*, 2:56–57; Charles Francis Adams Jr., *Lee's Centennial: An Address by Charles Francis Adams, Delivered at Lexington, Virginia, Saturday, January 19, 1907* . . . (Boston: Houghton, Mifflin, 1907), 2, 7–8.

About the Contributors

CAROL BUNDY is the author of *The Nature of Sacrifice: A Biography of Charles Russell Lowell, Jr., 1835–64.*

DEAN GRODZINS is a research associate at Harvard Business School and visiting scholar at the Massachusetts Historical Society. His publications include *American Heretic: Theodore Parker and Transcendentalism.*

MATTHEW MASON is an associate professor of history at Brigham Young University. His publications include *Slavery and Politics in the Early American Republic.*

AMY F. MORSMAN is an associate professor of history at Middlebury College. She is the author of *The Big House after Slavery: Virginia Plantation Families and Their Postbellum Domestic Experiment.*

RICHARD S. NEWMAN, director of the Library Company of Philadelphia, writes on African American history and the history of the abolitionist movement. His publications include *Freedom's Prophet: Bishop Richard Allen, the AME Church, and the Black Founding Fathers.*

SARAH PURCELL is a professor of history at Grinnell College, where she is also the director of the Rosenfield Program in Public Affairs, International Relations, and Human Rights. She is the author of *Sealed with Blood: War, Sacrifice, and Memory in Revolutionary America.*

JOHN STAUFFER is a professor of English and American literature and African American studies at Harvard University. His eight books include *Giants: The Parallel Lives of Frederick Douglass and Abraham Lincoln.*

KATHERYN P. VIENS is the research coordinator at the Massachusetts Historical Society. Among her publications she is the coeditor of three collections of essays, including *Entrepreneurs: The Boston Business Community, 1700–1850* and *Margaret Fuller and Her Circles.*

ABOUT THE CONTRIBUTORS

PETER WIRZBICKI is Collegiate Assistant Professor in the Social Sciences at the University of Chicago. His New York University dissertation, which he is revising for publication, is titled "Black Intellectuals, White Abolitionists, and Revolutionary Transcendentalists: Creating the Radical Intellectual Tradition in Antebellum Boston."

KANISORN WONGSRICHANALAI is an assistant professor of history at Angelo State University. He is the coeditor (with Lorien Foote) of *So Conceived and So Dedicated: Northern Intellectuals in the Civil War Era* and the author of the forthcoming *Northern Character: College-Educated New Englanders, Honor, Nationalism, and Leadership in the Civil War Era*.

CONRAD EDICK WRIGHT is the Worthington C. Ford Editor and director of research at the Massachusetts Historical Society. His works include *Revolutionary Generation: Harvard Men and the Consequences of Independence* (University of Massachusetts Press, 2005).

MARY SARACINO ZBORAY is a visiting scholar in the Department of Communication at the University of Pittsburgh. She is a coauthor of many books and articles on the history of reading, including *Everyday Ideas: Socioliterary Experience among Antebellum New Englanders*.

RONALD J. ZBORAY is a professor of communication and director of cultural studies at the University of Pittsburgh. He is the author or coauthor of five books, including *Voices without Votes: Women and Politics in Antebellum New England*.

INDEX

*Page numbers in **boldface** refer to illustrations.*

Abbott, Lyman, 107
abolitionist movement, 2–3, 9–37, 41n24, 58, 74–99; Boston's elite and, 184–85, 285, 290; changing attitudes at outbreak of Civil War, 74, 90–99; defined, 10, 13–14, 15–16; democratic principles, 63, 75–76, 88, 105; film portrayals, 14–15; idealism, 88, 98, 105–6, 110, 181, 188; internal discord, 2, 53, 62–63, 68, 103–5; mob attacks on, 10, 76, 83, 86–87; in other states and countries, 5n2, 13, 86, 92–93, 106–7, 111; pacifist views, 123; postbellum concerns, 103–30; racism, 81, 82–84, 97, 111–12; regional pride, 78–84, 90, 96, 185; twentieth-century views of, 13–15, 16; twenty-first century views of, 15–16; utopian streak, 90; violence debates, 110, 120–23; women's rights, 76, 82, 296n15
Abolitionists, The (PBS), 15
Adams, Charles Francis, 28, 56, 57, 66, 85; on Emancipation Proclamation, 179–80
Adams, Charles Francis, Jr., 275–76, 278, 288–89, 290, 293–94, 297n26
Adams, John, 17
Adams, John Quincy, 57, 60, 94
African Colonization Society, 84
Agassiz, Louis, 175
Albert, Prince of Wales, 171
Alcott, Abigail, 268

Alcott, Louisa May, 268
Allen, Kenneth, 234
Allen, Richard, 117
Altoona Conference, 168, 169, 181
American Anti-Slavery Society, 130, 264
American Colonization Society, 84–85
American Freedmen's Aid Society, 125
American Peace Society, 123, 127–28
American Society for Promoting National Unity, 87
Amory, Charles, 166, 168, 175, 177–78, 189
Anderson, Robert, 9
Andrew, John A., 2, 28, 34, 63, 121, 163, 193n52; and Boston's business community, 164, 167–69, 180, 185, 188; on cultural reconstruction, 126–27; Cushing and, 3–4; defense of John Brown, 26; and Negro Soldier Bill, 178; vigilance committee work, 58, 67
Anthony, Susan B., 129
Antietam, Battle of, 164, 168, 183, 206
Appleton, William, 184, 193n50
Archer, William, 1
Armstrong, Samuel Chapman, 292
Arnold, Benedict, 79
Ashworth, John, 100n24
Atkinson, Edward, 115–16, 181, 194n55
Atlantic Monthly, 96, 114, 118, 252, 271n7
Attucks, Crispus, 82, 83
August First celebrations, 106

{301}

Balch, Francis V., 282
Ball, Thomas, 248n79
Banks, Nathaniel P., 28, 118–19, 184
Baring Brothers & Co., 177, 192n40
Barlow, Samuel, 165
Bartlett, William F., 292–93
Bates, Edward, 33, 151
Batchelder, James, 19
"Battle Hymn of the Republic, The," 36
Bearse, Austin, 73n57
Beecher, Henry Ward, 89
Bell, John, 139, 145, 148–49, 154, 155–56
Belmont, August, 165
Bender, Thomas, 93
Benfey, Christopher, 16
Bergeson-Lockwood, Millington, 15
Birth of a Nation (Griffith), 14
black activists, 83–86, 89, 97–98, 104, 112, 120, 128; attacks on, 95
black cultural reconstruction, 123–27, 130
black education, 202–3, 215n8, 249–71
black soldiers, 9, 30, 32, 34, 46n73, 46n81, 91, 95, 101n66, 119–23, 179, 185, 189; Lincoln on, 11. *See also* "Bucks of America"; Massachusetts 54th and 55th Regiments; Negro Soldier Bill
Blair, Hugh, 213
Blight, David, 277
Bonner, Robert, 142
Booth, John Wilkes, 11–12
Booth, Mary, 106
Boston Advertiser, 197
Boston Herald, 204, 210
Boston Journal, 205
Boston Post, 78, 87, 197, 210
Boston Statesman and Weekly Post, 235
Boston Times, 235
Boutwell, George, 107, 233
Bradlee, Caleb, 234
Bramhall, Cornelius, 71n30
Breckinridge, John C., 3, 151, 152, 154
Brodie, Fawn, 40n23
Brooks, Cleanth, 14
Brooks, Francis, 176–77
Brooks, Preston, **21**, 22–23, 228, 231, 233
Brown, Harvey, 210
Brown, John, 3, 13, 21, 23, 69, 80, 84–85, 116; in Boston, 23–24; Emerson and Thoreau on, 25–26; Harpers Ferry raid, 24–28, 143–44, 185, 187, 191n10, 286; in Kansas, 24; reactions to death, 24–27, 28, 83, 87, 296n19; Secret Six fundraisers, 23, 180
Brown, John, Jr., 85
Brown, William Wells, 85, 89
Browne, Albert Gallatin, 202, 203–4
Browne, John W., 59–60, 61, 73n57
"Bucks of America," 31, **32**, 34
Burlingame, Anson, 22–23, 28, 79
Burns, Anthony, 19–20, **20**, 68, 77, 184
Burnside, Ambrose, 170, 171
Butchart, Ronald, 271nn4–5
Butler, Andrew, 22
Butler, Benjamin, 28

Calhoun, John C., 75, 78
Cameron, Ben, 14
Carkin, Philena, 262
Carmichael, Peter S., 278
Cedar Creek, Battle of, 206
Cedar Mountain, Battle of, 206
Chamberlain, Daniel H., 11, 38n9
Channing, William F., 73n57
Chapman, Maria Weston, 109–10
Charleston Mercury, 24
Charlottesville Chronicle, 260
Chase, Salmon P., 113, 114
Cheney, Ednah Dow, 259
Chesnut, Mary, 22
Chicago Tribune, 233, 237–38
Child, Lydia Maria, 23, 25, 90, 107, 110, 118–19; support of black soldiers, 122–23; on women's suffrage, 129
Christian Recorder, 117, 119, 122, 123
Cicero, Marcus Tullius, 83
Cincinnatus, Lucius Quinctius, 174, 192n27
Civil Rights Bill, 12–13, 227, 229, 230, 233, 239, 242
Clarke, James Freeman, 88, 90, 96
Clary, George, 283, 287–88
Clay, Clement Claiborne, 236
Clay, Henry, 150, 154
Clifton House, 23, 43n44
Cobb, Samuel C., 232
Cochin, Augustin, 106
colonization and emigration, 10, 11, 18, 84–85
Colver, Nathaniel, 53, 66–67

Commonwealth, 94–95, 96
Compromise of 1850, 18, 194n59
Connecticut, 50, 183
Constitutional Union Party (CUP), 139–40, 145–57, 169, 180
Cook, Orrin, 113–14
Coolidge, Thomas Jefferson, 166, 181, 190, 192n44, 193n50
Coombs, Leslie, 145
Copeland, Morris, 30
Copley, John Singleton, 175
Copperhead movement, 4, 28, 163, 164, 174, 179, 181; peace of 1864, 123
cotton and textile industry, 19, 78, 79, 87, 165–66, 177, 182–84, 187–88, 190n9, 193n55
Craft, Ellen, 63
Crater, Battle of the, 208
Crittenden, John Jordon, 146, 153
Crittenden Compromise, 85, 89, 185–86
Crowninshield, Caspar, 288, 289, 297n26
Crummell, Alexander, 84
"cultural reconstruction." *See* black cultural reconstruction
Curtis, George William, 237
Cushing, Caleb, 3

Dana, Richard Henry, 19, 65–66, 67, 68, 87, 232
Davis, Jefferson, 26, 89, 154
Delany, Martin, 18, 84
Delbanco, Andrew, 16, 101n53
Dickens, Charles, 171
disunionism, 25, 76–79, 87, 89–90; Garrison and, 29, 74–75, 89; vs. nationalism and Unionism, 77–78, 143, 150
Donald, David Herbert, 229
Douglas, H. Ford, 85
Douglas, Stephen A., 27–28, 151–52, 155
Douglass, Frederick, 11, 15, 26, 29, 87, 111–12, 119, 259; on the Constitution, 76–77; on the Constitutional Union Party, 151; on cultural reconstruction, 127, 128; on disunionism, 76; *Douglass' Monthly*, 117–18; on emigration, 85; 54th Infantry and, 34; on Lincoln, 86; on New Englandism, 83; postwar concerns, 104, 128, 130, 242, 272n10; Sumner and, 231, 242; on *Uncle Tom's Cabin*, 18;

Underground Railroad and, 48; on use of force, 120
Douglass, Lewis, 122
Downing, George T., 85, 86
Dowse Library, 29, **30**
Dred Scott decision, 82, 84, 108, 128
Du Bois, W. E. B., 13
Dwight, Wilder, 206, 210, 281–82

economic issues: freed blacks, 112–19, 124, 126, 181, 183–84, 188–89, 194n55, 291–92; interdependence between the North and South, 165–67, 170, 182, 184, 187, 188; "inward development," 187; New England business practices, 113, 115–17, 119, 124, 167, 182–87
Edmands, J. Wiley, 178, 182, 189
Egerton, Douglas, 146, 150–51, 156
Eldredge, Edward H., 164–65, 181, 190
Elliott, Robert, 240
Eltham's Landing, Battle of, 208
emancipationist movement, 3, 10–16, 28–32, 164, 172; defined, 10, 13–14
Emancipation League, 2, 29
Emancipation Proclamation, 12, 29, 32–34 **(33)**, 110, 126–27, 164, 170–71, 179–80, 185, 191; Preliminary, 32, 46n73, 168, 169
Emberton, Carole, 121
Emerson, Ellen, 268
Emerson, Ralph Waldo, 24, 25–26, 78, 106, 268, 272n23; on character, 280–81; on civilization, 96–97, 98; on the "true Boston," 79
Emmons, Halmer, 60
Everett, Edward, 3, 139–57, 169; abolitionism and, 152–54; background, 141, 189; "The Character of Washington" speech, 139–40, 142–43, 157; Constitutional Union Party candidacy, 139–40, 145–57, 165, 177; McClellan and, 165, 170, 177–78

Fahs, Alice, 217n19
Fifteenth Amendment, 129, 130
Fillmore, Millard, 141, 155, 231
First Confiscation Act, 28
Fisher, Sidney George, 155
flag resolution controversy, 4, 227–33, 235–43
Folsom, Charles W., 265–66, 274n49

Foner, Eric, 150
Foote, Henry C., 232
Forbes, John Murray, 168, 177, 180–81, 193n52
Forbes, Robert Bennet, 168
Forten, Charlotte, 82–83, 84, 118, 202, 203, 272n23
Fort Sumter attack, 3, 4, 9, 29, 90–92, 186; 1865 commemoration, 9–10
Fort Wagner attack, 34–36 (**35**), 120, 122, 179
Foster, John, 281
Foster, John G., 208
Foster, Stephen, 14
Fox, Thomas B., Jr., 281, 286
Frank, Lisa Tendrich, 297n26
Frank Leslie's Illustrated Newspaper, 34
Franklin, John Hope, 13
Frank Warrington (Harris), 210
freedman's aid movement, 117, 124–26, 251–53, 257, 261, 263, 268–69
Freedman's Bureau, 228, 292
Freedmen's Record, 117, 124–26, 253–57, 259–63, 269, 274n57; title, 272n14
Free Soil Party, 58, 61, 63–64, 69, 72n31, 228
Frothingham, O. B., 94
Fugitive Slave Act, 1, 18–20, 50–52, 54, 59–60, 77; 1850 revision, 61–62, 63–66, 77, 79, 88, 108, 120, 180, 191n10
"fugitive slave clause," 49–50, 55

Gallagher, Gary, 157, 294n4
Gannon, Barbara, 15
Gardiner, William Howard, 164, 174, 176, 181, 189, 191n11
Gardner, Anna, 249–51, 258–64, 269–71, 274n57
Garfield, James, 288
Garnet, Henry Highland, 84–85, 120
Garrison, George Thompson, 9, 36, 122
Garrison, William Lloyd, 21, 53, 62–63, 86, 87–89, 101n66, 103, 107, 112, 114, 122; on Banks's Louisiana project, 119; on Brown, 26; changing attitudes, 74, 75, 91–92, 104, 108, 110, 124–25; at Charleston commemoration, 9–10, 12, 36–37, 104; collegiate opinion of, 285; on cultural reconstruction, 130; on the Constitution, 29, 53, 75, 76–77, 99n2, 285;

Emancipation League and, 29; on end of abolition cause, 129–30; on Haitian emigration, 85, 100n38; Lincoln and, 10–12, 38n9; McClellan and, 164; vigilance committee work, 67, 69
gender politics, 81–82, 100n24, 116, 277, 297n26
Gettysburg, Battle of, 3, 141, 239, 293
Glatthaar, Joseph T., 297n27
Gleaner, 212–13
Goldfield, David, 16
Goodman, Susan, 271n7
Gorn, Elliott, 295n8
Graham, William, 1
Grant, Ulysses S., 20, 46n73, 265, 292; Sumner's opposition to, 228–29, 231, 236, 238–39, 243
Gray, Hannah, 176
Gray, James, 54–55
Gray, John C., 291
Gray, William, 174–75, 176, 177–78, 189
Greeley, Horace, 228, 232, 236, 240
Greenberg, Amy, 121
Greene, Gardiner, 177
Gregory, Charles, 284
Griffith, Camillus, 51
Griffith, Martha ("Mattie"), 26
Grimes, Leonard, 121
Grover, Edwin, 283
Guiney, Robert, 210

Haines, Zenas T., 210
Haitian Emigration Bureau, 85
Hale, Sarah Everett, 155
Hall, C. S., 29
Hamlin, Hannibal, 152
Hannum, James, 56–57, 61
Harper, Frances Ellen Watkins, 122
Harpers Ferry raid, 24–28, 143
Harper's Weekly, **8, 10,** 13, 26, **27,** 34–36 (**35**), 123; on black soldiers and suffrage, 46n81; Sumner caricature, 230
Hartford Convention, 186
Harvard Commemoration of 1865, 188
Hayden, Lewis, 19, 22, 24, 67–68
Hegel, Georg Wilhelm Friedrich, 92–93
Heinzen, Karl, 92–94
Higgins case, 51–52, 65
Higginson, Thomas Wentworth, 19, 23,

76–77, 81; joins First South Carolina Volunteers, 122; on vigilance committee, 69
Hillard, George S., 146
Hinton, Richard, 85
Hoar, George Frisbie, 244n18
Holley, Sallie, 263–64, 266, 273n44
Holmes, Oliver Wendell, Jr., 87
Holmes, Oliver Wendell, Sr., 177, 180
Holst, Hermann Eduard von, 12
honor: conservative nature of, 283–84; defined, 276, 280; Northern, 276, 279–82, 290, 294; Southern, 276, 278–79, 280, 288–90, 293–94
Hooker, Joseph ("Fighting Joe"), 171
Hooper, Samuel, 184
Horton, James, 13
Houston, Sam, 145
Howe, Henry Warren, 206, 210
Howe, Julia Ward, 36
Howe, Samuel Gridley, 23, 36, 58–61, 63, 67, 191n11; "Address to the People of the Northern States," 59, 71n30
Howell, Luther C., 291–92
Hubbard, Thomas H., 289
Huggins, Nathan, 13
Hunkers, 79, 80

Inter-Ocean, 234
Irish immigrants, 16, 81, 100n20, 185
Irving, Washington, 212

Jackson, Francis, 52, 58, 63, 67, 71n30
Jackson, Thomas J. ("Stonewall"), 276, 293
Jacobs, Harriet, 18, 36, 118; *Incidents in the Life of a Slave Girl*, 118, 255
James, Henry, 13
Jefferson, Thomas, 14, 17, 186
Jim Crow laws, 184, 189
John, Richard R., 5n6
"John Brown's Body," **8,** 9, 28–29, 36
Johnson, Andrew, 228
Johnson, Osgood, 283, 285
Johnson, Samuel, 234
Jones v. Van Zandt, 72n35

Kansas, 20–24, 77, 180, 185, 191n10, 286; admitted to Union, 109; Lawrence attack, 21, 23, 24; Pottawatomie attack, 24

Kansas-Nebraska Act, 19, 108; Everett and, 141, 154; Sumner and, 22
Kantrowitz, Stephen, 15, 128–29
King, Martin Luther, 105
Kirk, George, 60
Kirkpatrick, Jennet, 69n2
Know-Nothing Party, 16, 22
Kossuth, Louis, 171
Kraditor, Aileen, 131
Ku Klux Klan, 14

Lafayette, Marquis de, 171
Lamar, Lucius Q., 236, 238
Latimer, George, 54–56, 57
Latimer Journal and North Star, 54–55
Latimer Law, 56, 57, 66
Lawrence, Abbott, 78
Lawrence, Amos A., 19–21, 180–81, 183, 184, 185–86, 187, 193n52
Lawrence, James, 165–66, 175, 182, 190
Lears, Jackson, 277–78
Lee, Henry, 168, 175, 193n52
Lee, Robert E., 9, 183, 275–76, 278, 293–94
Lewis, R. W. B., 14
Liberator, 21, 53, 69, 73n53, 88, 89, 91–93, 95, 115, 119, 122–23; last issue, 128
Liberty Party, 53
Lincoln (Spielberg), 14–15
Lincoln, Abraham, 3, 26, 29, 88; abolitionism and, 10–12, 14; assassination, 11–12; black abolitionists on, 86; on black soldiers, 11; 1860 election and aftermath, 83, 86–89, 150–52, 155–56; First Inaugural Address, 156–57; Garrison and, 10–12, 38n9; Gettysburg Address, 141; pressure to free slaves, 29–30, 32; Second Inaugural Address, 122; Stowe meeting, 18; on Unionists, 150; wartime unpopularity, 164, 169. *See also* Emancipation Proclamation
Lincoln, Levi, Sr., 17, 165
List, Charles, 73n57
Littell's Living Age, 206, 210
Little, John Lovell, 166, 178, 182, 189
Little, Levi, 281
Livermore, George, 29–34
Longfellow, Henry Wadsworth, 170
Loring, Caleb, 187–88
Loring, George, 105

Louisville Courier, 236
L'Ouverture, Toussaint, 25, 80, 83
Louisiana, 118, 125, 203
Lowell, Anna, 254–55
Lowell, Charles Russell, 193n45
Lundy, Benjamin, 43n44
Lusk, William T., 287–88
Lyman, Theodore, 164, 178–79, 192n44, 209, 210

Madison, James, 186
Mann, Horace, 23
Martin, J. Sella, 89; *The Hero and the Slave*, 97–98
Martin, Waldo, 13
Marx, Karl, 92–93
Mason, Eliza, 25
Mason, James, 25
Massachusetts: constitution, 17, 49–50; kidnapping laws, 50, 52; political conservatism, 163–64, 174, 185–86, 283–84; progressive tendencies, 16–17, 89; racial equality measures, 16–18, 34, 41n26, 49, 56, 78, 108, 165; racism, 111–14, 255; role in Civil War, 28, 34, 98, 107; role in Reconstruction, 105, 107, 249–50, 254
Massachusetts Abolition Society, 51, 53
Massachusetts Anti-Slavery Society, 53, 58, 70n13, 103, 127, 129, 130, 267
Massachusetts Historical Society, 29, 32, 33, 235, 275
Massachusetts Kansas Committee, 23
Massachusetts People's Party, 169, 177
Massachusetts regiments, 168–69; 2nd, 192n43; 3rd, 203; 18th, 202; 22nd, 113; 29th, 208; 30th, 206; 37th, 207; 43rd, 204; 46th, 200, 209; 47th, 211; 54th, 34–36 **(35)**, 95, 119–20, 121–22, 178–79, 185, 192n43, 193n52, 215n8; 55th, **8, 9**, 36, 122, 178, 185, 204, 215n8
Masur, Kate, 121
May, Samuel J., and family, 105, 107, 108, 267–68
Mazzini, Giuseppe, 76
McClellan, Ellen, 170, 172–73
McClellan, George B., 163–65, 181, 183, 188; Boston visit, 168–78; in newspaper war reports, 206, 209

McClellan Committee, 164–66, 169–73, 177–79, 181–82; member list, 189–90
McDaniel, W. Caleb, 5n2, 75–76
Meade, Geroge, 179
Melish, Joanne, 114
Melville, Herman, 14
Merriam, John, 24
Mexican-American War, 186
Mill, John Stuart, 76
Milton, John, 212
Minardi, Margot, 112
Minkins, Shadrach, 68
Mirror of Liberty, 52
Missouri Compromise, 19
Morison, Samuel Eliot, 163
Morris, Robert, 23, 58, 67–68, 89
Morse, Frank C. and Ellen, 200, 201–3, 209, 210, 211–13
Morse, Samuel, 87
Motley, John L., 28, 175
Mount Vernon Ladies Association of the Union, 141–42

Nantucket Inquirer, 249, 251, 259, 274n57
Nast, Thomas, 230
National Anti-Slavery Standard, 82, 89, 90, 264–66, 269, 274n57
Nebraska, 88
Negro Soldier Bill, 178
Nell, William Cooper: *Colored Patriots of the Revolution*, 18, 22, 30–32 **(31)**, 34, 82–83; on emigration, 85; vigilance committee work, 53, 58, 59, 62, 64–65, 67, 71n30
Nevins, Allan, 27
New England Educational Commission for Freedmen, 115
New England Emigrant Aid Society, 20–21
New England Freedmen's Aid Society, 117, 124, 126, 252, 253–59, 262–63, 267, 270, 274n57
New-England Freedom Association, 49, 59
New England Loyal Publications Society, 181
New England Women's Suffrage Association, 129
New Jersey, 155
New Hampshire, 182–83
New Orleans Picayune, 235–36

INDEX {307}

New York, 1, 50, 143, 155
New York Committee of Vigilance, 48, 52
New York Herald, 209–10
New York Ledger, 142
New York Times, 210, 234, 235
New York Tribune, 209
New York World, 232–33
North American Review, 141
North Carolina, 208, 249, 259
Northup, Solomon, 108
Norton, Charles Eliot, 176
Novick, Peter, 13

Oakes, James, 32
Owsley, Frank, 13–14

Parker, Theodore, 23, 62–67, 72n50, 73n53, 79–80, 83, 93, 109; racial views, 81; "A Sermon of Conscience," 63, 64
Parker, William, 120
Patten, Henry Lyman, 285
Peace Conference of 1861, 89, 166
Pearson, Jonathan, 56
Peninsula Campaign, 168
Pennsylvania, 1, 55, 143, 155
Perkins, Thomas Handasyd, 191n11
Phelps, A. B., 71
Philbrick, Edward, 115
Phillips, Wendell, 3, 14, 21, 26, 29, 32, 87, 87, 89, 110, 119, 125, 242; changing attitude, 90–91, 107; on the Civil War, 94; collegiate opinion of, 285; on the Constitution, 57–58, 63, 66–67, 75, 76; on Lincoln, 30, 86, 110; on "nationality," 77; postwar concerns, 130; regional pride, 79–81
Phillips, Willard P., 230, 237
Pierce, Edward L., 113–15, 203, 252
Pierce, Franklin, 19, 21
Pillsbury, Parker, 103, 110
Pinchback, P. B. S., 231
Pine and Palm, 85
Pionier, Der, 92
Pitman, Robert, 281
Port Royal Experiment, 113, 114–16, 252, 271n6, 272n23
Potter, William, 282, 284, 285–86, 296n19
Prescott, William H., 177
Prigg v. Pennsylvania, 55, 59, 60

printed matter during war, 195–214; black instruction, 202–3, 215n8; dissemination, 199–206; looting of books, 203; newspaper unreliability, 209–10; reception, 207–13
Puritan heritage, 17, 78, 79, 80–81, 167; fanatic tendency, 80
Putnam, Caroline F., 263–71

Quaker support of Civil War, 29
Quarles, Benjamin, 13
Quigg, David, 286
Quincy, Josiah, 173

Ramold, Steven, 4
Read, Charles F., 203
Read, Thomas Buchanan, 206
reconciliation motives, 276–77, 287, 290, 292, 294
Redpath, James, 84–85, 100n38
Reynolds, David, 25
Rhodes, James Ford, 12
Rice, Alexander, 185–86
Rice, James C., 288
Richmond Enquirer, 24–25
Richmond Whig, 24
Robertson, Stacey M., 5n2
Rock, John, 22, 83–84
Rosenstone, Robert, 14
Ruggles, David, 48, 52
Russell, Henry Sturgis, 179
Russell, Thomas, 234

Sanborn, Franklin, 23, 26, **27**
Saxton, Rufus, 125–26
Schurz, Carl, 232, 238–40, 242
secession, Northern elite view of, 279, 283, 286, 293
Second Confiscation Act, 30
Seward, William Henry, 85, 88, 149–50
Shaw, Francis George, 178
Shaw, G. Howland, 164, 175, 178–79, 190, 192n44
Shaw, Robert Gould, 30, 122, 178–79; memorial, 241, 247n69
Sheridan, Philip, 206
Sherman, William Tecumseh, 46n73
Silber, Nina, 276–77
Sims, Thomas, 68, 69, 77

Sinha, Manisha, 15, 23
"Slave Power," 20, 69, 73n50, 76, 103, 108–9, 186, 187
slavery: "contraband" designation, 28, 36–37; free press and, 109; polygamy and, 22; Northern collegiate view of, 284–86; religious arguments against, 17–18, "slave code," 27. *See also* abolitionist movement; emancipationist movement; Fugitive Slave Act; United States Constitution
Smalls, Robert, 9, **10**
Smith, Gerrit, 23, 76
Smith, John, 22
Smith, Joshua B., 22, 58, 59, 61–62, 67, 89, 240–41, 248n71
Smith, Lydia Hamilton, 40n23
Somerset Club, 181
Sozialistischer Turnerbund, 87
Southall, James C., 260–62
South Carolina, 78, 88, 89, 91; First South Carolina Volunteers, 122, 126; Union occupation, 113–15, 125–26, 183, 202, 287
South Mountain, Battle of, 195
Southern Rights Democrats, 3
Sprague, Pelleg, 54
Springfield Republican, 171, 204
Stanton, Edwin, 30
Stanton, Elizabeth Cady, 129
Stauffer, John, 104
Stearns, George, 23, 34
Stevens, Thaddeus, 14–15, 40n23, 291
Stewart, James Brewer, 26
Stone, Lucy, 129
Story, Joseph, 54–55
Stout, Harry, 16
Stowe, Harriet Beecher, 18
suffrage: black, 11, 16, 75, 111, 121–22, 125, 127, 129, 189, 228, 291; female, 75, 76, 129, 140; voter intimidation, 265, 274n47
Sumner, Charles, 12–13, 14, 19, 21–22, 34, 108, 163, 227–43, 291; background, 228; death and reactions, 13, 230–43, 244n18, 248n79; Foreign Relations chairmanship, 28; Livermore and, 30, 32–34; postwar Senate career, 4, 227–31, 234–36, 241–42; Senate caning, **21**, 21–24, 228, 229–30, 232–33; in Spielberg's *Lincoln*, 15; vigilance committee membership, 58; wartime unpopularity, 169, 191n11

Taney, Roger B., 128
Taylor, Anne-Marie, 243n2
teachers, 4, 116–17, 125, 249–71; backgrounds and motivations, 256, 263; textbooks, 202
Texas, 57, 184
textiles. *See* cotton and textile industry
Thirteenth Amendment, 15, 37n1, 128, 291
Thompson, Henry, and family, 264–66
Thoreau, Henry David, 24, 25–26, 80
Tisdale, Henry, 195–96, 201, 204
Tocqueville, Alexis de, 76
Torrence, John, 51–52, 57
Torrey, Charles T., 51–54, 58, 65
Transcendentalists, 80, 88, 94, 98, 210
Tulloch, Hugh, 13–14
Turner, Henry McNeal, 240, 241–42

Underground Railroad, 38, 53–54, 61–62, 180
Union Bible Society, 268
Union Club, 2–3, 177–78, 180–82, 188
Unionism, 139–57, 169
Unitarianism, 17
United States Constitution: slavery and, 29, 47, 49, 53, 57–58, 63, 66–67, 75–77, 81, 87, 92, 99n2, 132n21, 284; as evolving document, 180; "three-fifths clause," 50, 186; Unionists's reverence for, 143–45
United States Sanitary Commission, 193n48
United States Supreme Court rulings, 54–56, 72n35, 82, 230

Van Evrie, John, 106
Varon, Elizabeth, 143
Vermont, 1, 41n26
vigilance committees, 47–48, 64, 69nn1–2, 70n13, 72n50; first Boston Vigilance Committee, 51–54, 58; second Vigilance Committee, 49, 58–61, 66, 71n30; third Vigilance Committee, 19, 62–69, 73n57
Virginia, 25, 26, 78, 113, 260–63, 271n6, 275–76, 288

Walker, David, 41n24, 111

Walker, Quok, 17
Ward, Samuel G., 177
Ward, Samuel Ringgold, 112
War of 1812, 186
Warren, George Washington, 248n71
Warren, J. Mason, 164, 166, 175, 181, 189
Warren, Joseph, 166
Warren, Robert Penn, 13–14
Washington, Booker T., 292
Washington, George, 139, 141–44, 145–46, 148–50, 192n27, 275; Farewell Address and sectionalism, 142–43, 144, 148, 150, 186; as slaveholder, 154
Watkins, William J., 120
Webster, Daniel, 79, 86, 194n59; Everett and, 141, 154, 165
Weeden, Benjamin, 58, 59
Weekly Anglo-African, 86, 95
Weld, Stephen Minot, Jr., 202, 206, 209–10
Weston, Anne, 68
Wheeler, William, 288, 289–90
Whig Party, 155–56, 167, 179, 184, 187, 188, 191n10; "Conscience" faction, 58, 60–61; "Cotton" faction, 19, 79

Whitcomb, Bill, 206
Whittier, John Greenleaf, 29, 229, 233, 272n23
Wide Awakes, 139–41
Wilderness, Battle of the, 201
Williams, George Washington, 13
Wilson, Henry, 9, 12, 28
Winchester, Third Battle of, 207
Winthrop, Robert C., 28, 235
Wise, Henry, 25
Wolcott, J. Huntington, 175, 178, 189
women's rights, 75–76, 82, 129, 140, 283–84, 296n15
Wood, Bill, 206
Wood, Clara and Amos, 200–201, 204, 208–9, 213
Wood, Robert, 49
Woodward, C. Vann, 13
Wright, Elizur, 68
Wright, Henry C., 110, 123

Yancey, William, 18, 27

Zion's Herald, 210, 211